DATE DUE

BIBLO & TANNEN PUBLICATIONS

HISTORY

OF

ROMAN PRIVATE LAW

HISTORY

OF

ROMAN PRIVATE LAW

PART II

JURISPRUDENCE

VOLUME II

BY

E. C. CLARK, LL.D.

BIBLO and TANNEN

NEW YORK

1965

First published 1914

Reprinted with the permission of the Cambridge University Press

Biblo & Tannen Booksellers and Publishers, Inc.
63 Fourth Avenue   New York, N. Y. 10003

Library of Congress Catalog Card Number: 64-13392

Printed in U.S.A. by
NOBLE OFFSET PRINTERS, INC.
NEW YORK 3, N. Y.

§ 10. PUBLIC AND PRIVATE LAW

On the division and classification of a Corpus Juris by
subject-matter generally I must refer to what has been
said above (§ 1, pp. 20, 32) as to the practical character
of such a division and the educational character of such
a classification.

It is proposed in the present sections to consider primarily
the divisions of subject referred to or employed in the Roman
Institutional system, with regard not only to their proper
meaning (upon which modern Jurists have by no means
been agreed), but also to the sense in which they have been
employed in Blackstone's Commentaries, in the modern form
(Stephen's) of Blackstone, and in other recent schemes or
systems of law, notably in the Codification of the German
Empire and the rearrangement of "English Civil Law" after

the pattern of the Bürgerrecht, under the auspices of the last editor of Stephen. As a matter of secondary but not less important consideration I shall have to notice, from the same points of view, other divisions which do not appear, or are not employed directly, in the Institutes, but have been inferred from or added to the Institutional treatment by modern writers; such as that of Rights and Wrongs, of Rights *in rem* and *in personam*, of **Public and Private Law.**

To the last named of these antitheses I fully endorse Austin's objections, if it is to be taken as a working division of Law either for practice or education. But it is noticed too often, expressly or implicitly, both in Roman and modern Jurisprudence to be passed over without remark, and I shall therefore try to dispose of it at the outset.

It would be incorrect to say that the distinction of Public and Private is not mentioned and recognised by Roman writers on Law: but I do not think it will be found to have much more than a nominal or academic existence as a main division of the Roman Corpus Juris.

So far as we can guess at the contents of the missing lines at the beginning of Gaius' Institutes, he says nothing about this division of Law. In § 8 he speaks of "*all* the law in use among us" as relating to Persons, Things or Actions. It is clear, however, that *all* the Roman Law is not considered under this well-known division, no notice being taken, in the Institutional work thus divided, either of Criminal Law except as ancillary to something else, or of what I may call, by anticipation, the Law of Public Conditions.

Justinian treats, in *his* Institutes, of the same subject-matter as Gaius, which however he *does* describe as Private Law, giving in the same section (1. 1. 4), a brief statement of the division of Law into Public and Private, which will be considered directly. It is true that he does, in his last Title

De publicis judiciis, with which there is apparently nothing
to correspond in Gaius[1], treat briefly of Criminal Law.   But
he notes, at the same time, that this title is on procedure
perfectly different from what has been treated in the preceding work, and that it is mainly added as a sort of finger-post
to the larger treatment of the same subject in the Digest[2].

In the division above referred to, which is taken by
Justinian from Ulpian's *Institutiones*, *privatum jus* is described
as relating to the interest of individuals, *publicum* to the
condition of the Roman State—Ulpian's further words, that
the latter consists *in sacris, in sacerdotibus, in magistratibus*,
being omitted[3].

Now, of the two headings, the first must be allowed to
represent, in rather a vague way, the actual subject-matter of
the Institutes—the Rights, Wrongs and Remedies of individuals in a private position or character—which might
reasonably constitute a first or Institutional Course for
Students of Law.   But as to the second, it is open to the
objection that, taken in one sense it does *not* cover the
whole remaining Corpus Juris, taken in another it *does* couple
together two very incongruous subjects.   Under its strict
or natural meaning *jus publicum* as defined by Justinian
might be called in general terms the Law of Public Conditions.   It will clearly include what we call Constitutional
Law, and the Rights and Duties of Official persons generally:
it might fairly be extended to cover " the Church," as
a National Institution: possibly *all* Public Institutions,

---

[1] Gaius, 4. 187, is generally considered to be the end of the work.   See,
inter alia, Göschen's Preface to his first edition, p. xxix of his third.

[2] Instt. 4. 18. pr, 12.

[3] Cf. Just. 1. 1. 4, and Ulpian, Dig. 1. 1. 1. 2.   The latter goes on
Privatum jus tripertitum est; collectum est enim ex naturalibus praeceptis
aut gentium aut civilibus.   The whole passage is a strong evidence for
Professor Goudy's arraignment of *triads* (see below, § 11, p. 452).   It is a
strange medley of general object, specific detail, and " source."

including such matters as are classed in Stephen's Blackstone under the head Social Economy of the Realm[4]. But
it is difficult to see how the important subject of Criminal
Law could well come in, even under the head of Ulpian's
Magistratus, much less under Justinian's *status rei Romanae*
without rather forced reasoning. Nor can I find any direct
statement by the great Roman jurists expressly classing
Criminal Law under *publicum jus* as a general head. That
it was or should have been so classed is commonly inferred
by moderns from the use of the term *publica judicia* in
Justinian's last Title on Crimes referred to above. I
cannot here go into the three or four different significations which *publicum* in this phrase successively underwent.
As to its original one, Austin's view that *publicum* first
indicated trial by or before the people may possibly be
correct[5]. But it is under the later and vaguer meanings of
publicum judicium (see below, p. 441) that Criminal Law
would probably have been classed expressly under *publicum
jus*, if the Roman Jurists had ever gone into the details of
Public and Private Law as an exhaustive division of their
Corpus Juris, which they have not done in anything preserved
to us.

This is one of the *dichotomous* divisions favoured by the
Roman Institutionalists as well as by our own—even more,
I think, by Hale than by Blackstone[6]—which are often both
perplexing and misleading, particularly when the attempt is
made to combine several of them into one system[7]. Several

---

[4] Book iv. Of Public Rights, Parts 1, 2, 3. So too in Roman Law, we
find legacies to *ecclesiae, ptochotrophia,* &c. treated by Justinian, Cod. 1. 2.
24, under *divinum publicumque jus* as distinguished from *privata commoda*.

[5] Austin[5], 44. 751; St. 371.

[6] See his "Analysis" *passim*.

[7] An instance may be found in Abdy and Walker's Justinian, p. 484. See
also Holland's remarks as to the way in which such divisions run across
one another. Jurisprudence[10], pp. 120, 121.

of them are really only proper for a comparatively limited branch of subject-matter, e.g. *stricti juris* and *bonae fidei*, perhaps *in rem* and *in personam*, &c. Where they are, or are intended to be, exhaustive—that is to apply to a whole body or system of Law—dichotomous divisions are liable to the fault that, while one branch is fairly clear and homogeneous, the other is often a group of subjects which have only a very fanciful or theoretical connexion with one another. Accordingly, in the latter case, we shall find all that perplexing variety and vagueness of views, taken by different authorities, on which Austin descants in Lecture 44, with regard to the particular division now under consideration. The passages in question are mostly from the later Jurists of the classical period such as Papinian, Modestinus and Ulpian. I give some of the *references*, which Austin or his editors often omit.

Tutela, which certainly seems to be treated as matter of private relation in Gaius' Institutes, and which according to one of the latest Jurists, Modestinus, is no *reipublicae munus*[8], has become, as well as *cura*, a *publicum munus* with Justinian[9]. The same act in law may be in one point of view public, in another private. *Testamenti factio* is actually stated by Papinian to be *non privati sed publici juris*[10]. Godefroi and other old commentators took this rather enigmatical passage to refer to the *formalities* required, Savigny in particular to the supposed representation of the five classes[11]. More probably the words are to be taken in the close technical sense of *testamenti factio*, i.e. power or right of testation depending mainly upon *commercium*, which *was* a matter of *state* allowance or denial[12].

In certain passages, again, of the Digest, *publicum jus*

---

[8] Dig. 27. 1. 6. 15.   [9] Just. 1. 25. pr.   [10] Dig. 28. 1. 3.
[11] Godefroi's Corpus Juris (ed. 1720), l.c.; Savigny, Syst. ii. § 67, p. 51.
[12] See Moyle on Just. 2. 10. 6.

can only be translated by some such expression as our Common Law (or Right), "the Law of the land," "a rule of Law," or even Public Policy. This remark applies principally to certain wise saws and maxims which have been passed on from hand to hand, like some phrases of Scripture, with more solemnity than significance, e.g. *Jus publicum privatorum pactis mutari non potest: Privatorum conventio juri publico non derogat*[13].

Attempts have been made to give these expressions a more definite meaning. In some of them *jus publicum* has been explained to signify *law proceeding from the people*, i.e. Statute: in others, which the above explanation will not suit, law *absolute*, as distinguished from what is *presumptive* or *permissive*: but exceptions have to be admitted, in each case, which destroy the value of the explanation[14].

As if purposely to thicken the haziness of this division of Roman Law, the question has been raised, rather by modern than Roman jurists, under which head Procedure generally ought to be classed. Criminal procedure would, I think, be held without much hesitation to belong to the Public branch[15]; at least, to go with Substantive Criminal Law, wherever that is placed. But Savigny, with many modern followers, goes further, and makes out a claim, good enough on *a priori* grounds, for Civil procedure to be admitted to

[13] The above passages (Papinian, Dig. 2. 14. 38; Ulpian, 50. 17. 45. 1) are criticised by Austin[5], 44. 755; St. 272, 273. See also Dig. 26. 2. 29; 39. 2. 18. 1; 26. 1. 8; 27. 1. 36. 1; 47. 22. 4. In the speech pro Domo attributed to Cicero, 49. 128 (cf. 53. 136), *publicum* is common or general, as distinguished from Pontifical law. In pro Caecina, 26, 74, *Civilis ac publica lex* is simply law general as opposed to class privilege or even personal influence—*contra alicujus gratiam*.

[14] See particularly Mommsen, Sr. i. 3, n. 1 and Sohm[2], p. 28.

[15] See Austin[5], T. and N. p. 928; Just. 4. 18. 1; and such passages as Dig. 39. 4. 5, where Paulus contrasts triple restitution, by an extortionate tax gatherer, with an additional criminal punishment—Alterum utilitas privatorum, alterum vigor publicae disciplinae postulat.

the same compendious category. And accordingly Sohm
omits this subject, as a substantive head, from his "System
of Roman Private Law" altogether[16]. This last classification
is, of course, quite irreconcileable with the scheme of the
Roman Institutes, and its *jus quod ad actiones pertinet,* as
a treatise on Private Law. Thibaut reckons both *Tutela*
and *Patria Potestas* under Public Law[17].

Some of the above discrepancies may be accounted for
by differences of date; some by the intrinsic difficulty, in
many private relations or proceedings, of determining how
far they are or are not matters of public concern. This
latter question, arising naturally among the formative units
of the Early Roman, as of most early polities, tends to re-
appear under the paternalism, or despotism, of the Empire.
There is also, of course, to be taken into account, the author's
point of view in the particular passage, and his special
argumentative object, as e.g. in Papinian's dictum on *testamenti factio.* But, whatever the cause, it is certain that,
in the literature of later Roman Law which has come down
to us, the distinction of Law into Public and Private cannot
be considered as either clearly marked or consistently carried
out. It is obvious that this distinction does not stand,
either in the Codex or the Digest, as a working division
of Law.

For the purposes of this section it is not necessary to go
further back than the class of writers to whom reference has
been made, except so far as the distinction, which they apparently did *not* use for a practical division, may be claimed
to have been so definitely used, in earlier times, as to recom-
mend itself, on that ground, for modern adoption. I cannot,
however, find sufficient evidence alleged for any very clear

---

[16] System, i. § 9, pp. 26, 27. See Austin[5], 44. 754; St. 372 and 43. 743
on Hugo's system; Moyle[4], p. 99, &c. ; Sohm[2], p. 27.

[17] System des Pandekten Rechts, cit. Austin[5], 44. 747.

previous use of the distinction between Public and Private
Law. Passages, for instance, like those cited by Holland,
for a definite recognition by Greek writers, are scarcely wide
enough[18]. In the quotation from the speech against Timo-
crates, the "Public law" referred to is the very special
question of disabilities or penalties incurred by the proposer
of constitutional change. In that from Aristotle's Rhetoric
the distinction is merely the line drawn by Blackstone between
public and private *offences*.

Various theories as to the origin of this distinction in
the early history of Roman Law have been formulated,
mainly by German writers of a past generation, some of
which are briefly referred to by Dr Moyle in the Introduction
to his "Justinian[19]." Into them I cannot enter here. The
special developement of "Private Law" among the Plebeians
is, in my mind, open to much question; and, still more so,
the separate origination of different branches of Early Roman
Law in different Ethnic stocks. But however these questions
may be, for the nonce, decided, I can find no trace of any
primary division into Public and Private Law recognised
either in pre-decemviral records and traditions or in the
Twelve Tables. It is of little point to quote Livy and
Ausonius[20], who are merely using the looser language and
expressing the popular ideas of their own time.

The earliest occurrence of the word *public* as applied to
law at all is in the old form of testation *per aes et libram*,
where the phrase *lex publica* apparently means either the
Code generally of the Twelve Tables or a special clause
referring to this mode of testamentary disposition. My

---

[18] Jurisprudence[10], 124, n. 4.

[19] Moyle's Justinian[4], pp. 14—16.

[20] Livy, 3. 24, does not even allege an original distinction: Qui nunc
quoque...fons omnis publici privatique est juris. Ausonius (11. 61) adds
a *jus sacrum*, which would, to judge by our fragments, cover good part of
the Decemviral *Criminal* Law.

own explanation of *lex publica* is given above (§ 5, p. 308). Whether that be accepted or not, I think it is obvious that *public* here refers rather to mode of legislation than to subject-matter.

Judicium publicum may have originally meant trial by or before the actual popular assembly, though it is doubtful whether the phrase existed at all before the "people" had come to be replaced by *quaestores*. There is much to be said, in spite of Justinian's explanation[21], for the view that these criminal trials were called "public" as being "of public interest," because, to use Blackstone's words, their subject-matter affects the whole community.

Such an interpretation of the word would probably (as has been remarked above, p. 436) have led, in a detailed classification of Roman Law made under the heads of Public and Private, to an express inclusion of Criminal Law under the former. This does not appear to have been done, and it is quite possible that, with many jurists, to the end, the *publicum* of the Criminal trials really indicated nothing but difference of procedure.

In the time of Cicero the expression *publicum privatum-que jus* was no doubt established and Q. Tubero, the son of Cicero's friend Lucius, is represented as having written many books on the two several subjects[22]. But we have no means of deciding what branches of law were comprised under Tubero's *jus publicum*, or indeed whether he really used the term as having a definite signification. Of the somewhat vague use of it by Cicero himself instances have been quoted above (n. 13). It would be mere waste of time to multiply quotations from non-juristic authors, such as Terence's *publicum jus* or Persius' *publica lex hominum*,

---

[21] Just. 4. 18. 1.
[22] Pomponius, Dig. 1. 2. 2. 46.

which describe a "common right" or a "universal rule" approximating to the Law of Nature in its vaguest sense[23].

To turn to our English Jurists: Bracton, at the beginning of his book, copies the passage from Ulpian above referred to (p. 435) in full, and enlarges upon it, but makes no further use of the division[24]. Nor does it appear in Glanville, Fleta, Britton, Fortescue, Coke or Hale. Blackstone uses the distinction by way of subdivision in his "Rights of Persons" and in his "Wrongs" both of which will be considered hereafter.

Austin justly objects to the extreme ambiguity of this distinction, which lies mainly in the vague and indeterminate character of its first term[25]. After his usual fashion, however, he would retain the term Public Law, but in a sense of his own. In this "strict and definite signification," Public Law is to be confined to that portion of law which is concerned with "political conditions," that is to say with the powers, rights, capacities and incapacities which are peculiar to political superiors, supreme or subordinate[26], the "Public Rights of Persons" in Blackstone's first Book—the inclusion of which, in that Book, wins the rare approval of Austin[27].

Under this head might, one would think, be comprised not only what is ordinarily called Constitutional but also Administrative Law, in the widest sense of both terms

---

[23] Terence, Phormio, 2. 3. 64; Persius, 5. 98. The *publica lex* of Gaius, in Dig. 47. 22. 4, *may* refer, as explained above (§ 5, p. 308), to a clause of the Twelve Tables: it may, on the other hand, be the rendering of a vague Greek original.

[24] Bracton, 1. 5. 2, 3, fol. 3. See too P. and M. i. 208.

[25] Austin[5], 44. 753, 754; St. 372, 373.

[26] Ib. 745, 746; St. 366, 367. I need not here reconsider the question of rules *for the conduct of the Sovereign* one or many, which are necessarily admitted by the practical good sense of Austin into a Corpus Juris, although under the formal protest that they are *Ethical maxims* not *positive Law*, the Sovereign having no *status*, no *legal Rights* or *Duties* (see above, § 4, pp. 237, 238, &c.).

[27] Austin[5], 44. 750, 751; St. 368, 370. His praise is really due to Hale, with whom this arrangement originated.

(see § 4, p. 170), including *inter alia* the whole staff of
officers charged with the administration of Justice. The
latter would apparently have been so included by Bentham.
The account, however, of the English Courts has been
detached by Blackstone from his Public Rights of Persons,
and placed, in connexion with the subjects of redress and
prevention, partly under his heading of Private Wrongs
(Book iii. chs. 3—7), and partly under that of Public
Wrongs (Book iv. ch. 19). This separation is also approved by Austin, on the ground that the powers and
duties of Ministers of Justice may more conveniently be
connected with the Law of Procedure. It certainly appears
to me, on the other hand, that an account of the Courts
might be better treated, with the rest of the Law of Public
conditions, as a homogeneous mass, apart from Procedure,
whether we choose to regard the mass, with Blackstone, as
a subdivision of Personal Law, or, as was probably meant by
Bentham, under the first head in the only main division of
a Corpus Juris which commended itself to him—Constitutional, Civil and Penal [28].

In support of Blackstone's coupling together Political
and Private conditions in his first Book, Austin urges the
difficulty of distinguishing the two in respect of their origin
and purpose [29]. For the practical purposes of the present
section these matters are immaterial, or so at any rate in
comparison with the question whether the primary account
of the Courts should or should not be taken together with
Procedure. What little need be said on the subject of origin
will come better in the more detailed treatment of the
Rights of Persons in English Law. On the philosophical
view as to the common objects of Private and Public Law

[28] Bentham, Vue Générale, ch. 1, p. 190; ch. 21, p. 351; ch. 22, p. 357
and below, p. 447.   See, however, p. 448.

[29] Austin [5], 44. 747, 748; St. 368.

of this kind I may refer to a passage in Gierke's *Grundzüge des Deutschen Privatrechts*, where he contrasts the sharp division (?) in Imperial Roman Law between Public and Private *Recht* with the connexion or interdependence of the two, both in the developement of modern German Law itself and in the less systematised treatment of the earlier German Institutional works [30].

In his proposed use of the term Public Law, as confined to the Law of Political Conditions, Austin follows Justinian, and has the support *eo nomine* of a considerable amount of continental usage—indeed, under the style Public Rights, that of modern English Institutionalists as well (see § 15, on Modern Personal Law). It is to be remembered, however, that Public Law, in this use, is one member of a *triple* division of the Corpus Juris. In the ordinary antithesis to Private, the division is into *two* parts, and Public must be taken, as it has more frequently been taken by Jurists, in the wide and vague signification rejected by Austin, and subject to the charges which he justly brings against it.

Professor Holland, however, objecting, with reason, to this somewhat arbitrary restriction of Public Law, would retain that phrase in its wider sense to express one of two exhaustive divisions of a Corpus Juris. The connecting link which he recognises as sufficient to group together all, or nearly all, the legal relations and conditions, over which this compendious term has been extended, is that the State regularly enters into them *as a party* [31]. This distinction does not refer merely to some supposed *suit* or *cause* wherein the State is or is not engaged, which is the *differentia* suggested by Hunter [32]. It is meant to apply also to the

---

[30] Holzendorff, Encycl. des Rechtswissenschaft [6], i. 435; see, however, above, pp. 437, 439.

[31] Jurisprudence [10], p. 124.   [32] Roman Law, p. xxxvii.

primary Rights, or uninfringed rules, of Constitutional Law
or Political Condition generally. Whether this dividing
line can be clearly made out is open to question [33]. Anyhow the suggested link of connexion, in Public Law, seems
scarcely strong enough, even from a logical or academical
point of view, to group together two subjects *primâ facie* so
heterogeneous as Criminal and Constitutional Law. In the
practical study of modern Law they would not, I think, be
coupled together, though undoubtedly they often must in
early legal history.

Private Law, on the other hand, can obviously be treated
as a whole, made up of really cognate parts—the rights and
duties of private citizens, their wrongs, and the treatment of
those wrongs by private action. In point of style, there are
reasons (see below, p. 449) for preferring that of *Civil* Law,
in spite of the varying senses in which that phrase has
undoubtedly been used. And it should, in any case, be
remembered that, if the style Private Law is retained, the
division so styled, however tempting its verbal opposition to
Public, must be set against at least *two* separate heads
rather than one.

The distinction, indeed, of Public and Private appears to
me, like Austin's favourite opposition of Rights *in rem* and
in personam to be rather one which "pervades," or appears
in several departments of, a Corpus Juris, than one which is
fitted for a main division. It is intelligible, and practically
applicable for the purpose of distinguishing Wrongs which

---

[33] See Markby (Elements[3], ch. 7, 150, 151) who, while accepting
the traditional dichotomy as convenient though unscientific, criticises un-
favourably a criterion of Public Law as that in which the State is *interested*.
Planiol (Traité Élém. de droit Civil[4], i. p. 9) defines Public Law as regulating
the acts of persons "qui agissent dans un intérêt général en vertu d'une
délégation directe ou médiate du souverain." This does not seem very
specially to apply to *droit* pénal, which is, however, included in his *droit
public*.

have been considered and treated as more specially dangerous to the community from those which have been treated simply as violations of private Rights, and left accordingly to private prosecution. It is intelligible as a distinction between two classes of Rights of Persons, whether the Public class be educationally treated according to the view of Blackstone or of Bentham (above, p. 443). Nor can I see the great impropriety which some authors have found in its employment as a division of International Law. The particular expression "Private International Law" is well understood, and its subject-matter fairly well determined, though possibly, if the matter were *res integra*, the more descriptive style "Conflict of Laws" might be preferred[34].

International Law generally has been sometimes coupled, by foreign Jurists, with Constitutional Law, as Public Law *external* and *internal*. The subjects are certainly more cognate than those of Criminal and Constitutional Law, and may very well be taken *pari passu* in a course of legal study. I doubt if their connexion can be drawn much closer than this[35]. Public Law has also been said of International Law alone, mainly, I think, by writers of the 18th century; and Publicist most frequently means a writer on that subject, though the name has also been given to writers on Constitutional Law[36].

To return however to the question of a main division in

[34] See § 9, pp. 431, 432, where this particular subject has been rather anticipated.

[35] See the Droit des Gens of G. F. de Martens (ed. Vergé). t. 1, pp. 39, 40; also Woolsey's Introduction to the study of International Law[4], § 2, p. 18, n. The recent "Jahrbuch des öffentlichen Rechts" by Drs Jellinck, Laband and Piloty purports to combine the two subjects, but hitherto contains a larger proportion of Constitutional than of International Law.

[36] Preferably in France, according to Littré, s.v. Publiciste. For the more general meaning of Publicist with us, and for good English uses of Public Law = International, see Murray's English Dictionary. Of foreign usage, Bynkershoek's Quaestiones Juris Publici is a well-known instance.

a National Corpus Juris. While Private Law is intelligible
enough for this purpose, the other branch of the antithesis
would certainly seem to be better abandoned, for its general
ambiguity and coupling together of incongruous subjects,
and in particular for the irreconcileability of opinions which
it seems to involve as to the proper place of Procedure.
For practical schemes of legislation or legal study Public
Law is little used as a division, e.g. in Codes or publishers'
lists of legal works arranged under subject-matter, which
generally follow rather the triple arrangement hereafter
preferred.

Bentham's Law, Constitutional, Civil and Penal. Of all
the principal divisions of a Corpus Juris for educational purposes, the above, which is preferred, on more general grounds,
by Bentham (above, p. 443), seems, in the main, the best.
As to the particular contents, however, of the first member,
treatment and opinions vary, and some exception may be
made to the style.   That the larger sense in which this style
has been taken above (p. 442) is intelligible and convenient
has been proved by the excellent work of Sir William Anson
now in its fourth edition; which appears to me one of the best
introductions to the intelligent study of modern English
Law.   For the early history and developement of our Law,
Constitutional or otherwise, it is enough to mention the
name of Maitland.   Whether his works, for all their authority
and charm, fall quite within the capacity and appreciation
of the average law student may perhaps be questioned.
I may add that, in early Law generally, the distinction of
Bentham's main divisions, particularly the first two, is difficult if not impossible to be maintained.   This is equally
obvious when we look at the constituent elements of the
nascent English and of the nascent Roman polity.

Whether, for modern conditions, the Constitutional Law
of a country, in the wide sense in which the term is here

used, *can* be *statutorily* consolidated into a homogeneous mass, is a question not very satisfactorily answered by experience. The *Staatsrecht* of the German Empire no doubt brings together a great deal of matter scattered about, in other cases, under various heads such as Organic Laws, Preliminary Titles, &c. But, besides the general difficulty arising from the inevitable survival, in this particular branch, of a certain amount of unwritten or customary Law by the side of a Code, there is, no doubt, the particular difficulty, noted by Blackstone and Austin (above, p. 443), of separating the Offices concerned with the administration of Justice from Procedure, which, being mainly remedial, belongs naturally to the subject of Wrongs. Laband, to take a modern example, in his commentary on the *Staatsrecht*, maintains that the general Law of the Constitution of the Courts (*Gerichtsverfassungsgesetz*) is too much complicated with the Procedure part of Civil and Criminal Law to be satisfactorily taken as a separate subject under the head of Constitutional Law[37]. This is obviously the case with French Codified Law, where the structure and functions of the various Judicative bodies are to be gathered partly from special *lois constitutionelles* and partly from the various sources of the *Code de Commerce*, and the *Code d'instruction Criminelle*. Perhaps these instances may be enough to suggest that the so-called Constitutional Law of Bentham, if it is to include, as seems certainly desirable, the Law of all Public Conditions, must be rather the result of literary treatment than of statutory enactment. A special difficulty, as to the proper place, in an educational system of Law, for the subject of Corporations or Juristic Persons will be treated in later sections (§ 11, p. 462; see too § 13, p. 503).

Penal Law. The second term in Bentham's triad— Civil Law—is scarcely explicable without some previous

---

[37] Staatsrecht des Deutschen Reiches⁴, iii. § 88, pp. 399.

consideration of the third. The part of a Corpus Juris really intended by him under the style of Penal Law is that which deals with Public Wrongs. Now it will be shewn hereafter that the style itself will include also the cases where something beyond "efficient redress" may be recovered, but simply in the private interest and option of the person aggrieved (below, § 22), whereas Public Wrong is, on the whole, better marked out by a style referring to its *treatment* as Criminal, matter of public charge (*crimen*) or accusation. This distinction of the latter procedure from the *civilis actio*, or private citizen's remedy, it is, that bears upon Bentham's second head, to which I come last.

Civil Law is here taken to mean the Rights and Duties generally, together with the Wrongs and Remedies for Wrong, of the Private Citizen. It therefore includes Civil Procedure or Private Actions, and, if that subject is separated from the substantive branch, it is only so as a subdivision. Civil Procedure, and Criminal Procedure or Instruction, although possibly, for convenience, codified under separate heads, should, nevertheless be regarded together as equally ancillary to the main subjects of Civil and Criminal Law. (See further, § 22, *ad finem*.)

§ 11. PERSONAE, RES, ACTIONES. PERSONAE

Difficulties of Austin. In entering upon this time-
honoured division of Private Law, some reference is unavoidable to the peculiar difficulties which Austin has introduced
into the subject as regards the first two members of the
triad.

One of these lies in his explaining the words or notions
Person and Thing twice over, by separate methods: i.e. in his
taking them first severally, as entirely independent ideas
(Lectures 12, 13); second, at a distinct part of his work
(Lectures 40, 41, 42), together, as constituting by their antithesis or opposition to each other an important division of Law,
in respect of its "purposes and subjects." This separate treatment cannot be usefully maintained, as the meaning of the
words in question has been materially affected by their antithesis and one of their most important uses is in the division.

A second difficulty is this. When Austin speaks of the
Law of Things and the Law of Persons, he naturally means
what he conceives to have been the fundamental principle
intended by the Roman and the English Institutional writers
under their respective phrases made up of Thing and Person.

Now, while I myself believe the fundamental principle of division to have been the same in both Institutional works, but *not* to be that of Austin, others again may question the identity of principle between the Roman and the English Institutes. I have therefore been careful as far as possible throughout to call Austin's division the Law of Persons and Things, that of Hale and Blackstone the Rights of Persons and Things and that of Gaius and Justinian the *Jus Personarum* and the *Jus Rerum*[1].

History and importance of this classification. The triple division of subject-matter generally attributed to Gaius, in whose Institutes we first meet with it, has been recently represented as an old traditional arrangement, perhaps descending even from the early Pontifical Jurisprudence of Rome[2]: but I can find no decisive evidence in favour of this view. Neither can any appreciable connexion be made out of the division in question with the order of the Twelve Tables, so far as we know it. A later source of this classification has been suggested in the Edict of Hadrian, with which Gaius was of course familiar, writing as he did late in the reign of Hadrian's successor Pius[3]. This view is based upon a passage in Hermogenianus' Epitomae, from which Just. 1. 2. 12 is taken. "Since all law was made for the sake of men, we will first speak of the Status of Persons, afterwards of the rest, following the order of the *Edictum Perpetuum*," etc. It is possible, however, that the "order of the Edict" refers exclusively to the "rest," in which Hermogenianus intended to

---

[1] See Moyle's Justinian[4], p. 85. As regards the genitive construction in these phrases *jus personarum* is classical, but *jus rerum* and *jus actionum* questionable. See Savigny, Syst. i. § 59, p. 401, n. *m*. Also below, p. 460.

[2] Karlowa, Rechtsgesch. i. 725; Krüger, Sources, p. 252, n. 1. The extremely vague references to *personae* and *res* in Varro's *Indigitamenta*, as gathered from Augustine *De Civ. Dei*, § 9, *ad finem*, are far too remote to have any significance.

[3] Clark, Sources, p. 125.

follow that order[4]. Neither Rudorff nor Lenel shew ground for supposing the Edict to have had any general preliminary notice of Status. The main value indeed of the extract from Hermogenianus and the sentence of Justinian's Institutes founded on it, is that *personae* are not *status* but *homines*.

Not only the authorship but the importance of this triple division have been questioned by good authorities on Roman Law. Savigny suggested that it rests upon an individual and casual fancy of Gaius, not uniformly followed either by the Institutional writers of that author's age or even by himself[5]. This view seems to be followed by Sir Henry Maine and to some extent by Dr Moyle[6]. It is, however, at least probable that the arrangement of Gaius' *Res quotidianae was* that of the Institutes, and that the same arrangement was adopted not only by Ulpian in his *Liber singularis Regularum* but also by the earlier author, possibly Pomponius, of the *Fragmentum Dositheanum*[7].

Professor Goudy of Oxford wrote an interesting article, four years ago, on the artificiality of Roman juristic classifications. He there dwelt on the illogical coupling together of subjects into sets of *four*, in the Institutes or Digest. He has since published, under the style of Trichotomy in Roman Law, an elaborate criticism of similar sets of *three*, including naturally this famous one of *Personae, Res, Actiones*. His point is that these sets are in many cases simply the result of a fancy for certain leading numbers, that they produce unreal, and therefore misleading lines of demarcation.

I think there is a great deal of truth in this theory, and

---

[4] Dig. 1. 5. 2; Moyle[4], p. 503 (Introd. to Book iv.); Krüger, Sources, p. 304.

[5] System, i. § 59, p. 396. With regard, by the way, to Austin's citations from Savigny (e.g. 41. 696, n. 85), it must be remembered that his knowledge did not, of course, extend to the *System*. See Notes to Lecture 41, p. 708.

[6] Maine, Early Law and Custom, ch. 11, pp. 362—368; Moyle[4], pp. 91, 92.

[7] Krüger, Sources, p. 253; Mommsen in Böcking's Fragmenta Ulpiani[4], pp. 110, 111; Karlowa, i. 765.

that it furnishes the key to a good many difficulties in the
Roman arrangement both of the Institutes and the Digest.
I have myself elsewhere (§ 10, p. 436) remarked and com-
mented on a similarly misleading Dichotomy, as to Public and
Private Law, though I believe *that* to have been based rather
on supposed conveniences of education than on the symbolism
or sanctity of numbers. At the same time, with regard to
the particular triad of which I am now speaking, we cannot
ignore the fact that it was taken, with some modifications,
by Justinian's compilers, and that the scheme of *his* Institutes
has been not only accepted by a long series of modern
jurists, but to a certain extent adopted by our own Institutional writers Hale and Blackstone, as well as by the
codifiers of Law in several continental nations. We must,
therefore, unavoidably enter into some enquiry as to what
has been or can be made out of it, whether in ancient or
modern times.

I ought first, perhaps, to notice a somewhat fine point
which has been raised, or rather revived, by Dr Emerton and
is referred to in a note of Moyle's[8]. According to the strict
classical use of *vel*, as distinguished from *aut*, the words of this
division should mean, not that the whole body of law spoken
of is divided into three departments mutually exclusive of
one another, but that it may be regarded from one or other of
three points of view. That is, the distinction should be
considered as *all pervading* (to use a favourite expression of
Austin or some of his German authorities), i.e. applicable to
each one of the bundles of rights and duties in the given
body of law, rather than as a basis of classification.

Since, however, Gaius *does* use it as such a basis, it would
seem that the point taken does not come to more than this.
The *main* subject of the first division will be *personae*, of the

[8] Moyle[4], p. 93, n. 1. Dr Emerton's views were communicated to me in
a separate pamphlet published by Stevens and Sons, London, 1885.

second *res*, of the third *actiones*: but, these being, in strictness, rather points of view than exclusive divisions, the lines of demarcation cannot be very exactly drawn, and there may be a certain amount of over-lapping.   Thus understood, I think Dr Emerton's argument will fairly meet some criticisms of Austin as to the manner in which Gaius' design is carried out at least in the first two divisions (see § 12, pp. 476—478): but it cannot disprove the divisions themselves, which are a matter of observed fact.

Personae.   Coming now to the members of the triple division, we may so far follow Austin as first to look at *persona*, in its legal use, *alone*.   Two different significations are noted by him, of which one is more in accordance with the earlier meaning of the word, the other, as it seems to me, with its use by Gaius in this particular division of Law[9]. The history of the interesting word *persona* has been often told and its various meanings genealogically traced with more or less success.   The oldest, which is that of an actor's mask, is most probably derived from *per sonare*, the idea being, as stated by an etymologer of Caesar's time, rather that of strengthening the utterance by passing it through a confined aperture than simply of concealing the face of the performer or assuming some other visage[10].   The latter, however, is the idea rather conveyed by the earliest usages known to us of this word and its derivatives.   The old Oscan farces (*Atellanae fabulae*), which had established themselves at Rome towards the end of the 3rd century before Christ, and were acted by maskers representing fixed conventional characters, like those in our own pantomime, were called *personatae*[11].

[9] Corssen, *Ausspr.*[2] i. 483, attributes the juridical meaning of the word almost entirely to the antithesis with *res*. But I do not think the independent history of *persona* can be entirely left out.

[10] Gavius Bassus in Aul. Gell. 5. 7.   The word has, however, been connected with a supposed root *swen*, to shine.

[11] See Festus, f. 217, Personata fabula.

The transition of meaning from the mask to the character represented by the mask is easy enough. So we find the word *persona* in the comedies of Plautus and Terence with the meaning of stock parts or characters, such as *adulescens* the young blood, *parasitus* the hanger-on, *servus* the gyp, or butler, who is generally the wit, *meretrix, miles, ancilla*, &c.[12] *Persona* comes also naturally to be used in the sense of any familiar or well-known type in society, &c., elsewhere than on the stage, e.g. the *persona* of ladies' counsel unlearned in the law, fixed by Cicero upon Aebutius[13]; of first, second or third persons in grammar, by whom, to whom, or of whom speech is made[14]; of self, adversary or *judex* in a suit[15]. Cicero also uses the word in the sense of public position as distinguished from private character or disposition[16].

The above use of *persona*, which, in a work on Law, naturally takes the form of *legal* condition, or *status*, is claimed by Austin as the literal and proper meaning of *personae* in the distinction between *jus personarum* and *jus rerum*[17]. It is a meaning undoubtedly often occurring in Gaius, in the Institutes of Justinian, and in the Digest; but it is not, in my opinion that of *personae* in the *jus personarum*, the true conception of which is necessary, if we are to explain the obvious institutional meaning, Roman and English, of the other member of the antithesis.

[12] See Terence, Eunuchus, Prol. 25—35; Plautus, Merc. 1. 1. 17 (dependent, however, on an emendation), &c.

[13] Cic. pro Caecina, 5. 14.

[14] Varro, L. L. 8. 8. 20. Cum item personarum natura triplex esset: qui loqueretur, ad quem, de quo.

[15] Cicero de Oratore, 2. 24. 102. Tres personas unus sustineo, meam, adversarii, judices. Possibly some such Court use of the word transferred to vulgar parlance, like our *party*, is the best explanation or justification of the pun alliterative in Plautus, Persa, 5. 2. 6. Qui illum Persam atque...omnes personas Male di...perdant!

[16] Cic. ad Atticum, 9. 11. Et naturam et personam meam.

[17] Austin[5], 12. 352, 353; 13. 363, 364; St. 163, 164, 172, &c., &c.

Cicero more than once, in his letters, speaks of a man's *persona*, as his personality, or *person* almost in our sense of body—e.g. where he contrasts Caesar's tenderness towards the reputation or memory of Pompeius with his treatment of the latter's *person*, i.e. the man himself [18].

In passages of Suetonius too, *personae* are *men*, considered no doubt with regard to their rank or position, as we might say "personages [19]." But for our present purpose, the word gets its more definite meaning partly from its opposition to *res* by the Roman Institutionalists and partly from the actual contents of their first Book, on the *jus personarum*. I only claim to have established so far that *personae* can, and does, mean *human individuals*, in the Institutes of Gaius and Justinian, as it apparently means divine individuals, not characters, in the Creed of the latter.

It is submitted, then, that, in the phrase *jus personarum*, the definition, quoted by Austin from "modern civilians," of *persona* [20]—*homo cum statu suo consideratus*—is correct, if *status* be taken in its wide and proper sense, so as to include *any* condition recognised by the law, whether it comprise a greater or less amount of legal rights, or, as in the case of the

[18] So mea persona in Ep. ad Att. 8. 11 D, § 7. As to Pompeius, Ep. ad Fam. 6. 6. Nunquam nisi honorificentissime Pompeium appellat. At in ejus personam multa fecit asperius. Here, for *ejus personam*, we might clearly read *ipsum*. As to whether our meaning of *body* comes from this use, or from the *appearance presented* to the sight of others, see English Dictionary, s.v. iii.

[19] Caesar, 43 ; Tiberius, 32, &c. It is from this use of the word, as meaning "man of importance," according to Professor Skeat, that we get our "Parson." Blackstone's explanation of "representative of the Church," from *persona Ecclesiae* (which phrase occurs in Glanville, 13. 24; see too Coke, Inst. 300 [b]), is very tempting, but the designation seems to be found, in early English and French, too often independently of any word for Church, to admit this. *Persona* in such uses seems to be merely "the official"; in fact *personatus* is used in the Papal letters, e.g. iv. 343, of Calendar Papal Registers, as a dignity or office "with or without cure." See too Proc. Soc. Ant. Newcastle-upon-Tyne, 3. 2. 61.

[20] Austin [5], 12. 348; St. 162: cf. 40. 684; St. 346.

slave, none at all. This definition is, it is true, followed by an unfortunate passage of the same author[21] in which he goes on to exclude the slave from the number of *civil*, or legally recognised, persons, on the strength of two or three passages in the Digest, not connected with the Institutional division of *personae* and *res*, and of very variable degrees of authority[22].

I am afraid I must differ here from Dr Moyle, whose better knowledge seems to have been subordinated by Austin. There is no doubt that the Roman jurists of the best period *do* speak of slaves as *persons*, and in too many passages to be regarded as slips of the pen[23]. It is only in later times of much less accurate thought and expression that we read of slaves *not having* a *person*[24]: a statement not to be confused with the more intelligible one of Justinian that a slave has no *caput*[25].

Caput. On this subject and its connexion with *status* I am here obliged somewhat to digress from my main argument, as to the meaning of *personae* in the *jus personarum*, on account of the special difficulties started by Austin.

As between *status* and *caput*, the former is *generic*, the latter rather *specific* or *particular*. We could speak of two persons *ejusdem status*, not, I think, *ejusdem capitis*. *Caput* literally *head*, and so *life*, would seem to mean the individuality

---

[21] Heineccius, Elem. 1. 3. §§ 75, 76. Mr Campbell, St. l.c., cites "Recitationes," 1. 3.

[22] E.g. in particular Modestinus, Dig. 4. 5. 4, where it is said, of the slave being manumitted, *Hodie* incipit statum habere.

[23] As Moyle[4], p. 86. For instance Ga. 1. 9, 48—50; Ulpian, Dig. 50. 17. 22. In personam servilem nulla cadit obligatio.

[24] Nov. Theod. 2. 17. 2. Servos...quasi nec personam habentes. For passages quoted from Theophilus and Cassiodorus, see Moyle, l.c. n. 1.

[25] Just. 1. 16. 4. As to the apparent contradiction with Paulus, Dig. 4. 3. 1, see n. 28.

or individual existence of a free citizen. Those who were *capite censi*, on the Censor's roll, were registered simply by that individual existence with no entry of property[26]. A man *capitis* (sc. *crimine*) *accusatur* or *damnatur* on a charge which involves the loss of his civic existence whether of actual life or not. This appears to be the strict meaning of loss of *caput*, though the expression is sometimes oratorically extended to any very serious loss of reputation, e.g. by bankruptcy, as in the last two chapters of Cicero's speech pro Quinctio[27].

It is not unnatural that a man's legal individuality should be identified with the man himself, as we see in the occasional expressions *liberum* and *servile caput*, which mean respectively a free man and a slave[28]. Here *caput is* nearly equivalent to *persona*. But these are only occasional expressions, *caput* being most often spoken of separately from the man, as something which he has, or loses, or of which he suffers diminution. Individuality or personality seems to me, on the whole, the best rendering of this difficult word.

The much debated *capitis deminutio minima* is explained by our Roman authorities sometimes generally as change of *status*[29], sometimes specifically as change of

---

[26] Nullo aut perquam parvo aere. Aul. Gel. 16. 10. 10. Niebuhr's idea, adopted by Savigny (System, ii. Beil. vi. 13, pp. 485, 486), that *caput* meant the space occupied by the individual's description on the roll, seems to involve both an anachronism and an inconsistency. *Caput* = chapter is surely later than the old phrases *capitis damnare*, &c. : and, on the above view, how would the lowest class be specialised as *capite censi*?

[27] See Modestinus, Dig. 50. 16. 103. Licet capitalis Latine loquentibus omnis causa existimationis videatur, tamen appellatio capitalis mortis vel amissionis civitatis intelligenda est. *Latine* seems to mean "common parlance." See, on Cicero's exaggerations, Greenidge, Infamia, p. 27, n. 3.

[28] Ulpian, Tit. xi. 5; Ga. 1. 166; Paul. Dig. 4. 5. 3. 1. In the last passage *servile caput* is merely a somewhat loose expression for an individual who is a slave. So Savigny, ii, p. 486.

[29] Ulpian, Tit. xi. 13. The instances quoted, however—*adoptio* and *in manum conventio*—are changes of family. Gaius, Dig. 4. 5. 1 appears to be said of *Capitis minutio* generally; but, from the passages which follow,

family[30]. In the majority of cases there can be found a step downwards in legal condition, either final or temporary: but as, in some, there is merely a change in agnatic family position, I believe, with Puchta, the latter to be the true gist of the *capitis deminutio minima*: even this passing out of the former agnatic circle is truly and literally a part-loss of legal individuality[31].

If the above explanation of *caput* be accepted, it can only be apparently equivalent to *status* in occasional and not very accurate statements. A person's legal individuality might truly be said to be made up of several *status*, or recognised legal conditions, notably the principal or ordinary ones of Freedom, Citizenship and Family[32]: but to call these *tria capita*[33] is absurd, and has not the slightest real authority. *Capita* does undoubtedly sometimes mean "chief points" in good Latin: but this meaning has nothing to do with a man's legal *caput*, that being a whole from which some part can be taken away, not a part, however principal or "capital."

I believe it refers specially to the *minima*. See Ga. 1. 162, where a change *in deterius* (though it may be only formal and temporary) can be made out for all the cases cited if the emendation of *ut* for *aut*, before *manumittatur*, be adopted (see Muirhead, R. L². p. 427. n. 1, and Gaius, l.c. p. 63).

[30] Paulus, Dig. 4. 5. 11. See, however, 3. 1, where the same author relies, in emancipation, upon the intervening (imaginary) servile condition.

[31] On the attempt to get over the difficulty as to the property of the Vestal dying intestate, see Moyle[4], pp. 182, 183. The earlier *locus classicus* on the subject is the 6th Appendix to the 2nd vol. of Savigny's System. See, too, §§ 68—70, in the same volume. It is the breaking of family ties (included no doubt in the two greater *deminutiones*) on which Horace specially dwells in his lines upon the captive Regulus: Fertur pudicae conjugis osculum Parvosque natos ut capitis minor Ab se removisse, &c., Odd. 3. 5. 41—43. For a recent statement of the whole question, see Muirhead, l.c. (Professor Goudy's Appendix), pp. 422—427.

[32] See Paulus, Dig. 4. 5. 11, and Heineccius, Elem. 1. 3. §§ 65—67, which appears to be the same with Austin's (42, p. 724) citation from Recitt. 52.

[33] Austin[5], 12. 351; cf. 42. 716, 717; St. 361.

To return, however, to *personae*. In all the passages
referring to the antithesis *personae-res*, the later developed use
of the word *persona* is clearly to be recognised, and should be
sharply distinguished from that of character sustained or legal
condition, the introduction of which into that antithesis causes
endless ambiguity and misapprehension. How far soever the
subject of the first Book of the Institutes may practically
coincide with that of *status* generally, the *personae* of the *jus
personarum* are individual *men* who may be slaves or free,
sui juris or not[34]; men for whose sake law was established[35],
not *status* (plural) or characters: so that the quotation *unus
homo sustinet plures personas*[36], wherever it comes from, is, in
this application, simply misleading.

The same meaning of *persona* is clearly indicated in the
well-known phrase *actio in personam*, where, whether *in*
means *against* or *as regards*, *persona* certainly means a human
defendant: perhaps, too, in the fact that Gaius and Justinian,
while they admit a possessive genitive in the phrase *jus
personarum* do not use the modern expression *jus rerum* but
jus quod ad res pertinet.

I may here briefly notice some arguments based by Austin
upon Theophilus' Greek translation of Justinian's Institutes[37].

The Greek πρόσωπον or προσοπεῖον, in the sense of
mask, has also passed naturally into the meaning of stock
characters presented, of which there is a long list in Julius
Pollux[38]. But it should be remembered that the late Greek
rendering of the juristic *persona* by πρόσωπον is a mere
literal translation and therefore furnishes no independent explanation of the Latin term. That the πρόσωπα of Theophilus are *men* is clear throughout the whole of his paraphrase

---

[34] Ga. 1. 8, 48.   [35] Inst. 1. 2. 12, from Hermogenianus, Dig. 1. 5. 2.
[36] Austin[5], 12. 352; St. 163.
[37] Austin[5], 12. 353; 13. 363; St. 164, 172.
[38] Onomasticon, 4. 19. 3—5.

of Just. 1. 3. pr.   I may also remark that the phrase quoted
from this author by Austin as a translation of *jus personarum*
—ἡ τῶν προσώπων διαίρεσις is really a rendering of Justinian's
opening words in Tit. 3, *summa itaque divisio*, &c.: the heading
de jure personarum being translated, περὶ νόμου προσωπικοῦ.
The heading, too, in our Gaius, *De conditione hominum*, one
of the other grounds alleged by Austin for denying that *Jus
Personarum* means the Law of (individual) Persons, is not by
Gaius himself but by a "secunda manus[39]."   These points
are not of much intrinsic importance, but, if relied upon as
arguments, such slight misrepresentations have to be noticed
and set right.

Juristic Persons.   Before passing to *Res* I must add a
few words on what are called *legal, juristic* or *fictitious* Persons.
Under these headings, of which neither the style nor the
idea is really Roman, Austin[40] couples the very different
cases of (*a*) a *universitas personarum*—a *populus, curia,
collegium* or *corpus*[41] as opposed to a *singularis persona*;
(*b*) a *praedium dominans* where certain rights of the owners
of landed property, for the time being, are attributed to the
property itself; and (*c*) a *hereditas jacens* (not yet taken up)
which can, we are told, like a *municipium decuria* or *societas*
play the part of an individual person[42], i.e. the defunct[43].

Of these three so-called fictitious personalities, *b* and *c*
undoubtedly belong to the Roman *jus rerum*.   On the
universitas personarum (also a non-Roman term) which is
equivalent to the *Corporation aggregate* of English legal
phraseology, there is little to be said here.   The history of
Roman *collegia*—the term being used to denote any corporate

[39] See Gaius by Krüger and Studemund[5], p. ix, n. 7.

[40] Austin[5], 12. 354; St. 164.

[41] See Ulpian, Dig. 4. 2. 9. 1.   Note that an *act of intimidation* is here
predicated of the corporate body.

[42] Florentinus, Dig. 46. 1. 22.

[43] Just. 2. 14. 2; Gaius, Dig. 28. 5. 31. 1; Ulpian, Dig. 41. 1. 34.

or quasi corporate association—is a long and difficult one[44]. In the Institutes, Corporations are mentioned once or twice[45] as owners of property, but there is no independent treatment of them anywhere and certainly no indication of any special connexion with the *Jus Personarum*. In the Digest, the short Title on suits by or against a *universitas* comes in certain preliminary matter to Civil Procedure, relating particularly to representation in Court[46]. The Title dealing expressly with *collegia* and *corpora* (Dig. 47. 22) treats of such as are vitiated by illegality or lack of State recognition, in the part devoted to Public Wrongs.

In the Commentaries of Blackstone a concluding chapter of the Rights of Persons is devoted to Corporations, as *artificial* in distinction from *natural* Persons, i.e. human individuals. The subject would appear to be classed by him under the head of Persons in *private* relations, but he *may* really have taken what seems to have been the different view of Hale, or here followed a diagonal of his own[47]. It has also been assigned to the department of Civil (practically = Private) Law in very recent codificatory and educational systems[48]. The proper place, however, for the subject, in an educational scheme of Law, will be better considered in a later section on Modern Personal Law.

[44] See Karlowa, ii. 59—69; Sohm, §§ 37, 38; and the other authors there quoted.

[45] E.g. Ga. 3. 145; Just. 2. 1. 6.

[46] Dig. 3. 4. Quod cujuscunque universitatis nomine vel contra eam agetur. It is sandwiched between appointed and volunteer agency, Dig. 3. 3 and 3. 5.

[47] Blackstone, i. pp. 422, 467. With Hale (Analysis, § 1, p. 1), bodies corporate are persons *civil* or *politic*.

[48] E.g. the German *Bürgerliches Recht*, which is followed by Mr Jenks in the Digest of English Civil Law.

§ 12. JUS PERSONARUM

In treating of the division, or part division, of a Corpus Juris by subject-matter, whatever notice may be taken of *Personae* and *Res* as independent ideas, must after all be regarded as merely preliminary to their consideration in the arrangement of Gaius. I come now, therefore, to the first member of his triad, upon which, in particular, modern opinion has been most divided.

According to the view here adopted, the *Jus Personarum,* in the original conception of those who devised the triple division Personae, Res, Actiones, is the Law of the individual persons *themselves,* as distinguished from the Law relating to their Property (see below, § 13, p. 502). We must admit the difficulty of drawing a clear line throughout between the

legal incidents and relations which concern a man's property
and those which concern or constitute his personal condition,
though the idea is certainly not so absurd as Austin represents it[1]. It is upon the partial manner in which the first
part of the above conception is carried out, in Book 1 of
Gaius and Justinian, that the varying theories as to the
actual contents of the book are based, amongst others that
of Austin.

The English Institutionalists Hale and Blackstone correctly appreciated the distinction intended by the Roman
ones[2]; they adopted it in their own scheme, and carried it
out in some respects more logically and fully than its original
authors. But, with Hale and Blackstone, the distinction in
question was subordinated to a more fundamental one of
Rights and Wrongs. This, amongst other reasons, led to
their *wording* of the Roman distinction as Rights of Persons
and Rights of Things; expressions no doubt faulty and
ambiguous, which are justly censured by Austin[3]. The
general principle, however—the distinction of what I may
now call Personal and Property Law—is the same in the
two first Books of Gaius or Justinian and of Blackstone.
Nor is it materially affected, in the latter case, by the English
division put first, of Rights and Wrongs: for the only Wrongs
treated in the Roman Institutes come practically under the
third head, of Actiones. As to *contents*, however, the Roman
Personal Law differs considerably from that of Blackstone,

---

[1] Austin[5], 40. 687; St. 346.

[2] See the first section of Hale's Analysis of the Civil Part of the Law,
and Blackstone, Comm. i, p. 122; ii, p. 1. The latter author, however,
differs from Hale and the Romans by bringing in the idea of *person = body*
(see above, § 11, n. 18).

[3] Austin[5], 13. 363, 364; St. 172. He however, as justly, blames Bentham
(Traités[2], iii. p. 294) for condemning the Roman expressions on the score of
Blackstone's improper rendering (Austin[5], 42. 724). On the English "Rights,"
see further, § 13, pp. 501, 502.

in that it does not deal with Persons in public or official positions, which subject forms three quarters of his first Book.

The conception of the distinction of *Jus Personarum* and *Jus Rerum,* by Austin, is entirely different from that just described. With him, to put it briefly, the latter of the two is Law General, the former Law Special. His retention of the old terms in a new sense is defended by himself in a somewhat arrogant way. Most people would, I think, rather agree with Dr Moyle in blaming him for the arbitrary use of phrases, which have in general meant something distinctly different, in a very perplexing mixture of current or prevalent meanings with his own[4]. And he certainly is not justified in censuring the Roman Institutionalists for their inadequate carrying out of a scheme which we have no sufficient ground for supposing to have ever entered into their consideration[5].

A determination of the true intention and subject of the *Jus Personarum* in the Roman Institutes has been matter of much discussion among modern jurists; and is not without its bearing upon the possibility and desirability of a similar department in a modern system of Law, educational or otherwise.

I propose to consider some of the principal theories on this subject, upon which remarks are scattered through Austin's Lectures 40—43, mostly under the heading "Erroneous views." Before doing so, however, it may be as well to glance at the actual matter in question, as far as possible without any preconceived view, taking Gaius as the representative of the original design, which was no doubt somewhat modified by Justinian.

In considering the **detail of Gaius' Book 1**, we must

[4] See Austin[5], 42. 712, and Moyle[4], p. 85.

[5] See particularly Lecture 43 and Table 2, with the notes upon the latter.

first take note of the fact that he was, no doubt, actually,
as Justinian was professedly, dealing only with Private Law.
This accounts at once for the omission of all men in official
positions. The *prudentes* of § 7 are, like the *magistratus* of
§ 6, merely enumerated as sources of Law, not as classes of
personae. So too the public officers of Justinian's time do
not come in the Institutes but in the latter part of the first
Book of the Digest. This omission, of persons "in public
conditions or relations"—to use Blackstone's phrase—
constitutes one main difference between the Roman first
Book of Institutes and his.

When, leaving the subject of Sources (Ga. §§ 1—7), we
come to the triple division itself, we find that the first 47
sections of Gaius' and 7 titles of Justinian's *Jus Personarum*
deal with the obviously personal distinction of **Slave** and
Free and with the different conditions of different classes of
Freedmen. There are a few sections on the legal capacity, or
rather incapacity, of the less favoured of the latter (§§ 23—
27); but, with these exceptions, the first quarter of the
Book treats almost exclusively of the modes by which men
enter into, and pass out of, the above conditions, or into that
of full *civis.* That is, it is practically confined to Investitive
and Divestitive Facts, to use Bentham's terms, which are
adopted in Hunter's Roman Law as to considerable part of
Book 1.

Family Law strictly so called. The second main
division in the *Jus Personarum* recognised by Gaius and
Justinian is that some persons are under their own control
or authority *sui juris*, some under that of others[6]. The

----

[6] Ga. 1. 48—50; Just. 1. 8. pr. This rendering of *sui juris* is discussed
in P. J. p. 26. The meaning of *juris* will be easily admitted in the present
phrase. Greater difficulty has to be faced in Ga. 2. 2, 3 or in such passages
as Res Quotid. Dig. 41. 1. 7. 5 and Papinian, Dig. 41. 3. 45. pr. *loca juris
gentium publica.* I think, however, that generally *jus* may in these cases be
taken in a *subjective* sense of *right* approximating to power, control or

individual subjects first treated are the well-known ones of
potestas, manus and *mancipium*; these, however, only with
regard to the positions of subordination, the corresponding
positions of authority, or rather the positions generally of
independence, being left to be gathered or inferred from
the account of the former[7]. This is the beginning of the
chief subject of the *Jus Personarum*—Family Law—which
extends over half the first Book of the Institutes or, if we
include *tutela* and *cura*, three-fourths. It is here that we
have a very brief account of the personal condition of the
slave, his purely vicarious capacity for acquisition of property
being sandwiched, in some half-dozen words, between his
subjection to the master's power of life and death and the
recent modifications of that power by the humane Emperor
Antoninus (§§ 52, 53).

The connecting link, of the filial and servile condition,
is the *potestas* in which they both are. Of the actual condition of free persons in *potestas, manus* or *mancipium* no
description is given but one brief note on the last[8]. Their
peculiar proprietary relations come (like all detail in the
case of the slave) in the second and third Books; and that
personal liability to noxal surrender, which was an obvious
survival of an original power of life and death, under the
Law of Actions, in the fourth. Marriage is brought in as
a means of producing children *in potestate*, but is treated
at great length, three-quarters of the whole space (§§ 55—96)
being devoted to the case of marriage between persons, one
of Roman, one of "Latin" or Peregrine condition. Adoption
follows, also as a means of acquiring children *in potestate*
(§§ 97—107).

Next come *manus* and *mancipium* treated avowedly and

ownership. E.g. *Publicus juris gentium*, Just. 2. 1. 3 = common, of universal
(or world's) right, control or ownership.

[7] Ga. 1. 50; Just. 1. 8. pr.   [8] Ga. 1. 141.

almost exclusively with reference to the modes by which persons come into these conditions (Ga. 1. 108—123); for the note on *property* requiring mancipation, or not, is added simply on account of the variation in the *form* of this conveyance. Finally we have the modes by which persons pass out of these conditions, and *potestas*, so far as the subject has not been already anticipated (§§ 124—141).

Tutela and Cura. The remainder of Gaius' first Book purports to deal with persons who, though free and not under the general control of *potestas manus* or *mancipium*, are nevertheless, on account of tender years or sex, under the limited and special forms of control known as *tutela* and *cura* or *curatio* (Ga. 1. 142—200). He begins with the cases for which tutors can be appointed, and goes on to the different kinds of *tutores* and how they respectively take or are appointed to that position. In this part of the work, unlike the legal conditions previously considered, more space is allotted to the persons exercising control than to those placed under it. But here again the greater part is taken up not so much with the conditions themselves as with the Investitive and Divestitive Facts.

The subject of *agnatio* or relationship through males, is here introduced by Gaius (1. 155; Just. 1. 15. 1) simply as an Investitive Fact of *tutela* ; and the remarkable digression on *capitis minutio* (Ga. 1. 159—163; Just. 1. 16), because of its destruction of the privileges of *agnatio* in that regard. The more substantive treatment of *agnatio* by Gaius comes in, as concerned with inheritance, under Property Law (Ga. 3. 11—17). Yet the subject is a matter directly of family relationship, and the non-treatment, except incidentally, of "kinship[9]" in Gaius' first Book is one of the arguments against Savigny's view that the design was to deal therein with Family Law pure and simple (see below, p. 490).

[9] Moyle[4], p. 90.

In the one case of *tutela*, as distinguished from other positions of control, Gaius (1. 189—193) does bring in indirectly some account of the legal condition of the classes of persons placed under this control, of why they are so placed and what are their incapacities or, in other words, their need for tutorial interposition. But the cases are mentioned rather as illustrations or reasons for the general rule of incapacity, than as individual applications of that rule, these coming, where we should expect them to come, under Property Law. They are accordingly treated by Gaius elsewhere—partly in the second Book of his Institutes, partly in his work on the Provincial Edict. From this last book comes a good deal of the title interpolated by Justinian in the first Book of the Institutes under the heading *De Auctoritate Tutorum*[10]. I may remark that this heading does not mean the *power* but the *sanction* (literally *complementary action*) of the Tutor; the title being practically a brief statement of the cases of *incapacity*, on the part of the *pupillus*, for which that sanction was in the time of Justinian required.

Cura need not detain us here. It was an extension of the principles of *tutela* to cases for which *tutela* was not provided or was insufficient. The powers, moreover, of the Curator were rather substituted for, and exclusive of, the ward's capacity, than complementary to it. How far these two cases (*tutela* and *cura*), particularly the latter, might seem at first sight to belong more to Property than to Personal Law will be considered directly.

At what is undoubtedly the end of his first Book[11] Gaius adds a short note on the obligations of Tutors and Curators to give security, in some cases, for the faithful discharge of their trust. To this Justinian appends a considerable amount

[10] Cf. Dig. 26. 8. 9 and Just. 1. 21.
[11] See Göschen, Gaii Institt. Comm. iv³. p. xxxiii.

of fresh matter, on the prior obligation to *undertake* the office
of Tutor or Curator, the grounds of excuse from such obligation and the liability to suspension, removal, &c., on suspicion
alleged of breach of trust[12].

At first sight, as has been already suggested, *tutela* and
perhaps still more *cura*, might seem to relate to dealings
with Property alone and so to be out of place in Personal
Law. The *tutela suae rei* of the Twelve Tables[13] at once
occurs to the mind, and undoubtedly nine-tenths of the
passages relating both to *tutela* and *cura* turn on the manage-
ment of the ward's estate. But, besides the fact that the
personal training and education of the ward is proved by
several passages to have entered into the duty of the Tutor,
as into that of the English Guardian[14], it must be remembered
that the whole of the functions of both Tutor and Curator
depend upon a general personal disqualification or incapacitation of the ward.

That there are individual **notices of Property Law**
scattered through the first Book of Gaius cannot be denied,
but I think it may be shewn that they come in for the most
part incidentally to conditions of Personal control or rather
subordination to control, not as substantive contents of the
Book. The brief notice, for instance, of disqualifications as
to property among the *dediticii* and *Latini*, and the scouted
reason of female incapacity for business as a ground for the
personal tutelage of women, may be compared with the fuller
treatment of similar matters in Books 2 and 3[15].

---

[12] Ga. 1. 199; Just. 1. 24—26.

[13] Tab. V. l. 3; Muirhead[2], App. p. 436.

[14] Paulus, Dig. 26. 7. 12. 3. Cum tutor non rebus dumtaxat sed etiam
moribus praeponatur, &c.; also Dig. 27. 2 generally. See, however, below,
p. 489.

[15] Ga. 1. 23—25, 190 with 2. 63, 64, 80—85, 110, 111, 121; 3. 39—76,
107—109, 114, &c.

Besides these occasional interpolations of matter relating to Property in Book 1 of Gaius' Institutes, we have also, however, to notice very patent **omissions of Personal Law** in the same Book, which are not so easy to account for, and have accordingly led to what I am inclined to consider much misapprehension of its scope and design.

On the condition of slavery we have perhaps as much as could be expected from the crude simplicity of the old Roman view as finally, but very partially, modified by Antoninus[16]. On the normal condition of *civis*, the freeman possessed of full legal rights, we have nothing. On the incapacities of persons having a legal *status* intermediate to this condition and slavery, there is a little information, brought in apparently rather by way of explaining the difference between a particular class, and others of a similar name, than with any definite design of describing the rights and duties of classes generally[17]. The same almost incidental treatment of the conditions themselves is perceptible in the positions of control and subordination belonging to Family Law, as dealt with by Gaius : a notable addition being made, as we have seen (p. 469), to one of them, by Justinian, from the more advanced work, for everyday practice (*Res quotidianae*), of his predecessor, and from other sources. On the other hand the modes in which the various positions of dependence or authority are entered upon and quitted are very fully set out.

[16] See Gaius, 1. 52, 53. Florentinus' derivation (Dig. 1. 5. 4) of *servi* as the captives whom generals are wont to *keep* instead of *killing* (*servare nec occidere*), though etymologically impossible, preserves a popular idea of the condition and its origin. See too the severities occasionally mentioned, without remark, in Plautus' plays. The steps in the amelioration, such as it was, in the slave's personal condition, are well given in Mr Buckland's Roman Law of Slavery, pp. 36—38.

[17] Ga. 1. 22—24 on the *Latini Juniani*. The following sections 25—27, on the *dediticii*, are the nearest approach to the substantive treatment of a class or condition.

To conclude this brief sketch of the detail of Gaius' Book 1, I shall assume provisionally that his intention was to describe, from a legal point, the *personal* condition, of different classes of men in private conditions, as distinguished from their relations to "property." But, in the carrying out of this design, we have to take account of the not unnatural tendency in an early Institutional writer, on the one hand, to assume as known, and therefore to omit, normal conditions *in toto*, and even abnormal or mixed ones to a considerable extent, so far as description of the *status* or condition goes : on the other hand, to go fully into the circumstances of transition from one condition to another—the Investitive and Divestitive Facts—in an unequally graded society where the gradations were of very considerable practical importance. Nor must we forget Gaius' evidently predominating interest in the historical developement of the Law of Persons, and in the various stages by which it reached its condition in his life-time. We may compare the space almost unnecessarily given, in works on the English Law of Real Property, to early feudal tenure, which is considered to be justified by its survivals in modern practice.

Many, however, of the questions here mooted will be more fully considered when we come to compare the view above maintained with other theories of modern authors as to the true subject of the *Jus Personarum*.

Modern theories of the Jus Personarum. The chief of these, which it will be necessary to notice here, are that the subject of Gaius' first Book is : (1) Capacity for Right (*Rechtsfähigkeit*) ; (2) Family Law ; (3) The Law of Special or Particular Conditions. Hugo and Thibaut may be taken as representatives of the first : Savigny is the author of the second ; Austin, who professes a preference for the views of Thibaut, has nevertheless put them into a form peculiar to himself in the third. His theory is followed with slight variations by a considerable number of recent authorities.

The theory, however, that the *Jus Personarum* treats of Capacity for Legal Right is also still somewhat widely adopted, both amongst those who do and those who do not accept the view that the subject of Book 2 is Property Law; and, although it does not seem entirely to explain the contents of Gaius' Book 1, it has an independent value as indicating what must form an important part of the contents of any modern Personal Law. It has been in the main accepted by Böcking, Karlowa, Sohm and Moyle[18].

Hugo. My principal knowledge of the theory of Hugo is derived from its criticism in Savigny's System, to which work it probably owes in great part its vogue. There is nothing, of course, about this criticism in the notice of Hugo's work by Austin, whose lectures were completed and published long before the publication of the "System" (see below, p. 479).

By *Rechtsfähigkeit* is meant, as I take it, a general power of holding and acquiring individual rights, whether the latter be identified with material objects or not. But, as treated in the *Jus Personarum*, it was understood by Hugo to be confined to the three characters or conditions *libertas, civitas*, and *familia*, corresponding to the three *capitis minutiones*[19]. This accounts for the exclusion of *peregrini* from consideration in Book 1.

Two slight modifications of this doctrine of Capacity are deserving of consideration, partly as leading up to the view of Austin, partly as taking a somewhat closer note of the actual contents of Gaius' *Jus Personarum*.

Thibaut. In the *Versuche* of Thibaut, whom of all his

---

[18] Moyle[4], pp. 87, 91; Karlowa, i. 725; Sohm[2], p. 164.

[19] See Goudsmit, p. 89; Savigny, System, i. §§ 59, 60, especially, p. 398, n. *g*.

predecessors Austin seems most to favour, it is not quite
clear whether his words refer to the Roman subject-matter
or to an ideal[20]. I think on the whole that he has the former
in his mind and that he takes the view of Hugo, but understands Capacity in an extremely bare sense. His *Personenrecht* deals with the differences of Persons, so far as these
influence the difference of Rights and Duties, but excludes all
Rights and Duties *themselves*, which belong, under the head
of Incorporeal Things, to the Law of Things. On the comparatively small amount of subject-matter thus left to the
Jus Personarum, Austin suggests[21] that Thibaut may have
regarded it as including "properly" nothing but the "titles"
or facts by which *status* or conditions are invested and divested.
And this view might no doubt be taken of the first Book of
Gaius, from his slight notice of the conditions themselves
which he enumerates, and much fuller treatment of the
manner in which they are entered and left. The comparative exclusion of normal capacity (see above, p. 472)
from this division of Law does not seem to have been noticed
by Thibaut or Hugo. Nor do they take account of the distinction between conditions Public and Private.

Blondeau. The idea of Capacity is also employed by
Blondeau, who however takes a new or at least more specific
view of the *Jus Personarum*. This author, to whose Ana-
lytical Tables of the Roman Law a rather unintelligible
importance is given by Austin[22], divides the Corpus Juris
into the Law of Capables and Incapables. By the former

[20] Das Personenrecht *soll* von den Verschiedenheiten der Personen handeln,
&c. See Austin[5], 41. 701, 708 and citation on 709. These Personen appear
to be *men*; with Mühlenbruch (Doctrina Pandectarum, ii. 1, cited by Austin[5],
42. 714; St. 359, they are *potestates* or *facultates juris*.

[21] Austin[5], 41. 708. The words of Thibaut's objection to the idea of
Status as an "inlying quality" (Austin[5], 41. 699, n. 87) rather point in this
direction.

[22] Austin[5], 42. 718.

class he apparently means Roman citizens *sui juris* and not in *tutela*, by the latter all persons who are deficient in more or fewer of the Rights of which such citizens are capable. The Law concerning Capables is therefore, if I may anticipate, pretty nearly the "Law of Things" according to Austin, i.e. an exposition of the Rights of an ordinary freeman and citizen. By Blondeau's Law concerning Incapables is meant the *Jus Personarum*. And this, no doubt, somewhat agrees with what we have observed in Gaius' first Book, of the prominence given to positions of subordination or deficiency compared with those of authority and competence.

Austin's objections to theory of Capacity. It is worth our while to notice Austin's criticism of the theory of Capacity as the true subject of the *Jus Personarum*; because, while some of his points are mere pedantic literalism, the chief one is much better and more clearly put than in the similar argument of Savigny. One of his objections, to the division of Capables and Incapables, is that there is probably no one completely Capable or completely Incapable; another that while some persons have *less* capacity for rights and obligations than the ordinary citizen, some have, even in private conditions—*a fortiori* in public—more[23]. Again he urges, rather inconsistently with the former of these objections, that many *status* consist, according to the larger and more proper meaning of the word, mainly of *in*capacities, e.g. that of slave or infant free person; some perhaps entirely of disabilities or exemptions as to ordinary rights and duties[24].

---

[23] "E.g: tutor or guardian, magistrate, &c." Note to Lecture 42, p. 724. This, I suppose, ought to be called *supercapacity*. The note is omitted in St. As in many cases, the omission makes for perspicuity but scarcely does justice to Austin's subtle reasoning.

[24] Austin[5], 42. 715; St. 360.

A more pertinent argument is, that a Capacity may be general, or common to all persons in a Political Society, whereas the conditions or *status* (plural) treated in the Law of Persons are only those of special classes[25]. This is an indisputable difficulty in the actual treatment of their *Jus Personarum* by the Roman Institutionalists; but it is not essential to a logical treatment of *Jus Personarum* considered as Personal Law. Normal or universal Capacities *are* included by Blackstone, for instance, in his Book i.

With the exception of the last point, which I have endeavoured to meet above (pp. 471, 472), these objections of Austin appear to me of little weight, as depending upon an unnecessarily strict or literal meaning of Capacity. This term, when used as a basis of classification or division (which process must inevitably enter into *any* Law of Persons), may surely be taken to include *all degrees*, from the normal or even the supernormal down to entire negation. The strongest objection against the theory of Capacity, as the sole subject of a Law of Persons, depends not upon the *lacunae* in Gaius' treatment, nor upon questions of degree, but upon the intrinsic inadequacy of the idea to cover all that we should reasonably expect to be included in the plan of a Personal Law, or Law of the Persons themselves, as distinguished from the Law of their Property.

The word Capacity cannot, it is urged by Austin, be with propriety applied to such rights and duties, in a *status* or condition recognised by Law, as arise *immediately* from that *status*, but only to such as arise *mediately* through some subordinate fact. The distinction is certainly subtle, and it is a question whether better illustrations might not be found than that given by its author[26]. Nevertheless there is,

---

[25] Austin[5], 42. 714.
[26] Austin[5], 42. 715; St. 360. Cf. Austin[5], 40. 701, 702; St. 356. The subject is treated very well by Salmond, Jurisprudence[2], p. 212 c; from whom,

in his general statement, the undoubted truth that most of the *status* or legal conditions, which it is of any use to consider, whether general or special, are *not* Capacities or bundles of Capacity merely, but aggregates of direct or immediate rights and duties *together with* Capacities.

In strictness, then, this objection to the theory of Capacity is a strong one: though it may be questioned whether the authors who devised the somewhat ambiguous term intended that it should be confined to the strict sense of Austin and Thibaut. It may rather have been extended so as to cover the rights and duties forming part of a *status* as "arising immediately" from it, as well as Capacity properly so called. That is, Capacity may fairly have meant, as Dr Moyle puts it[27] the being invested with, as well as the being capable of acquiring, rights. But it may now be well to consider what *sort* of rights are coupled with Capacity, as constituting a legal *status* or condition.

Capacity part of Personal Law. Perhaps the most obvious application of the idea of Capacity lies in its reference to Property, and in its being conceived as a general ability to acquire or enjoy items of Property (see § 16, p. 543), apart from any particular object. The same conception may, without any moral or logical difficulty, be extended to that of incurring any *obligations* of such a character that they can come under the aggregate called a man's *bona* (ib. p. 545), that aggregate being demonstrably separable from the man, whereas the "ability" in question is something inseparable or Personal. A still more complete conception of Capacity must include the ability to acquire *any* legal right, and, on the other hand, to incur *any* legal liability, civil or criminal.

however, I venture to differ, in believing that there *is* a proper place for a statement of general or normal capacity in matter "introductory to the main body of legal doctrine."

[27] Moyle, Justinian[4], p. 86.

All this should come and does come into a more adequate treatment of Personal Law than that contained in the Roman *Jus Personarum*; such as we find in Blackstone and still more in modern codes.

The Roman *Jus Personarum* does, however, certainly include rights and duties, equally inseparable (or *personal*) with this general ability to acquire or incur, but which can scarcely, by any forcing of words, be called Capacities. To such belong, most obviously and conspicuously, the enjoyment or fulfilment of the *mutual* relations belonging to or arising out of the Family, so far as that institution has been recognised as creating any mutual relations at all[28]. The large part played by the Family in the *Jus Personarum* has not unnaturally led to Savigny's view as to the true subject of that department, which will be considered next.

It is not of course to be brought against Savigny that his theory does not take sufficient account of certain rights unconnected with the Family, which come distinctly within the conception of Personal Law, but which, though recognised as doing so by the English Institutionalists, are omitted from the *Jus Personarum* by the Roman. I refer to such *normal* rights (see above, p. 471) as those of Personal Security, Liberty and Private Property, which are described as Absolute by Blackstone, truly in respect of their apparent non-relative character (see § 13, p. 505), though fancifully in his reference of them to a state of Nature. The conclusion, however, which I wish to draw at present is that

[28] Otherwise the position of the Patriarch (or ? Matriarch) *is* simply proprietary. In the more advanced stage of Roman and modern civilisation (which Petruchio's reading of the 12th commandment scarcely represents, Taming of the Shrew, 3. 2.), it may be admitted that the husband or father may no doubt divest himself voluntarily of his particular relations as such: but they cannot be taken by his creditors, see § 16, pp. 549, 550, any more than his capacity to acquire property.

since two of these individual rights, as well as the Family relations, cannot reasonably be called Capacities, Capacity, though it is or ought to be an important part of Personal Law, does not properly describe that subject as a whole.

That the Absolute rights last referred to are matter of Personal Law would appear to be self-evident, but it may be worth while to point out how they come in, in the antithesis of Persons and their Property. These Rights are of course *bona* in the sense of being beneficial (see § 16, p. 545), but not in that of *separable assets*. A man can be deprived of them by criminal sentence, and such deprivation will constitute a diminution of his legal personality (see above, § 11, p. 458), but they cannot be taken by or for his creditors.

Savigny's objections to theory of Capacity. The conclusion at which I have myself arrived is in agreement with Austin's *pro tanto*: that while Capacity is or ought to be an important part of Personal Law, it does not adequately describe the subject of that Law as a whole. The theory of Savigny, however, can scarcely be understood, without considering *his* special objections to the view of Hugo.

In introducing Savigny's theory it must first be remarked, in justice to Austin, that only the earlier treatises of the German were known to the English Jurist, when the latter delivered his Lectures. Savigny's criticism of Hugo's theory, and his own suggested alternative, are to be found in the "System," which was not published till 1840. It is to this work that Dr Moyle refers in his valuable Introduction to Book 1 of Justinian's Institutes.

The chief objections, in the System, against the theory of Capacity, are that it does not satisfactorily account either for the omission of one of "the three leading divisions" of Capacity for right—that of *Cives, Latini* and *Peregrini*—

nor for the inclusion of *Tutela*, which has nothing to do with such Capacity[29].

As to the first objection, it must be questioned whether too much stress is not laid here, as elsewhere by modern writers on Roman Law, upon the fancy for triads and recurring numerical division generally, to which reference has been made in a previous section[30]. In the particular triad however which Gaius here employs, there *was* a real distinction to be drawn, between *liberti* who are *Cives*; *liberti* who are called by the name, and have the legal *status*, of *Latini*; and those who are called and have the *status* of *Peregrini dediticii*. All are freemen and, as such, recognised by the Roman State. They *are* treated in point of capacity by Gaius: that of the *dediticii*, however, being almost *nil*[31]. *Latini* proper and *Peregrini* are also dealt with, *à propos* of the ways in which they can become Roman citizens and have children in power[32]; on the attainment of which *status* there is what might be thought a disproportionately full treatment of Investitive facts (see § 12, p. 466). It is, we must admit, only from this Family point of view that these outsiders seem to come into the scheme of Gaius' *Jus Personarum* at all.

Dr Moyle, who takes broadly the view of Hugo as to the *Jus Personarum*, considers the omission of the *Peregrini* a grave flaw, but accounts for it on the supposition that Gaius' *Jus Personarum* was only meant to include persons who possessed a *status jure civili*[33]. For the graver difficulty, to my mind, of the inclusion of sets of rights and duties, which

---

[29] System, i. § 59, p. 398, notes *h* and *i*. The other two divisions meant are those of *liberi-servi* and *sui* or *alieni juris*.

[30] See § 11, pp. 452, 453.

[31] Ga. 1. 22—27.   [32] ib. 29, 74—78.

[33] Moyle[4], p. 88. Vague statements that the distinction of *cives* and *peregrini* is matter of Public Law, do not seem very conclusive. See, however, Savigny, System, i. § 55, p. 365; § 59, p. 399.

do certainly come in the *Jus Personarum*, but cannot well be covered with the meaning of Capacity (see above, p. 478), he would account by a rather forced extension of that meaning.

The second objection of Savigny above referred to—that the theory of Capacity for legal right does not account for the introduction of *Tutela*—is rather too subtle. It depends on the allegation that *Tutela* has nothing to do with the Capacity for enjoyment or possession of legal rights, but only with the Capacity for *dealing with them*, a deficiency in this latter (*Handlungsfähigkeit*) being the particular want which the Tutor's *auctoritas* supplies[34].

This amounts, as I understand it, to saying that the Tutor is simply and solely a trustee, of somewhat limited powers, in respect of the ward's Property. As an objection against Hugo's theory, it appears to me to be based, after the manner of some arguments by Austin (see p. 477), upon an arbitrarily narrow meaning of *Rechtsfähigkeit*, which may surely, without much stretching, include any of the three senses, to enjoy, acquire or dispose of Rights.

Whether the *modern* Trustee ought to come, on account of the peculiar obligations imposed on him in any legal dealing with his *cestui que trust's* interests generally, into Personal Law; or whether he should be left, on account of the main subject-matter with which he deals, entirely to Property Law, is matter of question. That the subject of *Tutela* comes into the *Jus Personarum* is due to the personal conditions of subservience and control, or at least of general incapacitation and supplementary *auctoritas* (above, pp. 468, 469). But these objections of Savigny, I confess, appear to me slight compared with the conclusive one mentioned above (pp. 477, 478).

---

[34] System, i. § 59, p. 398; iii. § 106, p. 22. The *slave's* dealing with rights is of course (see note *a* in the last passage) that of a mere instrument.

In his own view of the first Book of Gaius, as Family Law, **Savigny**, it must be noted, to begin with, distinctly recognises a *Jus Personarum* as a Law of individual persons i.e. Men, who are the Bearers or Subjects of legal rights or relations[35]. With regard to this use of the word Subject he applies to the *Jus Personarum* the word Subjective and speaks of it as dealing with the original Self and the Self enlarged in the Family[36]. I should not have encumbered the discussion of the *Jus Personarum* with this terminology, but for a difficulty gratuitously raised by Austin, who elects to use the words Subject and Object, in connexion with rights, in a sense peculiar to himself[37].

Now there are certainly objections to this use of the pair of words in connexion with a right at all, except in cases where the right bears directly and simply on a material item of Property[38]. But, if they are to be used, it is surely better to take them in the sense in which they are generally understood[39] than to discard that meaning with Austin, and complicate the matter by references to Kant or Locke.

[35] System, i. § 59, p. 401; ii. § 60, p. 1 (Träger oder Subject); also Beil. vi. pp. 461, 465, &c.

[36] ib. § 55, p. 344.

[37] By *subject* Austin means the material *thing* (including of course *slave* or other human being) *over* which the right exists; by *object* the *acts or forbearances* to which the right entitles its possessor. See Austin[5], 42. 713 and cf. 14. 368 (both omitted in St.).

[38] With Sohm[2], pp. 164, 165, the *subjects* are "the persons capable of having private rights": the objects are material things over which the right exists directly (Real right), or indirectly through the act of another, the debtor (Obligatory right).

[39] Besides Sohm (last note), see Girard[5], p. 7, "une personne qui en (d'un droit) est le *sujet* qui l'exerce, une chose qui en est l'*objet*, sur laquelle il porte." See too pp. 91, 239. The same phraseology is adopted, in the translation of Goudsmit's Pandects (a translation which has received the express approval of the author), for the headings of chs. 3 and 6. I note too, that Prof. Whittuck, in his edition of Poste's Gaius, while he retains, from the original work, a primary meaning of *object* = "act or

By *Jus Rerum* Savigny understands *Vermögensrecht* which Austin correctly renders, in Latin, as *jus facultatum*, but incorrectly, in English, as "the Law of rights and duties, or the Law of things incorporeal[40]." It may be questioned whether the idea of duties enters at all clearly into that of *Vermögen*, and the rights or powers expressed by it are certainly not *all* rights, but only such as are "over things" or "accrue outwards," i.e. are *not* strictly personal or *subjective*[41]. I do not indeed think that *Vermögensrecht* is quite an adequate term to describe *Jus Rerum* or Property Law. *Vermögen* itself is best translated "Means," the idea being that of Potentiality simply, as Beneficiality is in *bona*[42].

Savigny justly insists upon the effect of separation from Public Law, and the consequent confinement of the *Jus Personarum* to Private *status*; considering, however, the last named subject to coincide with Family Law. From this coincidence, and generally from the limited scope of the *Jus Personarum*, results, according to him, the frequent use of the word *status* or *conditio*, not in the general meaning of legal condition, but in the special one of the positions occupied by the individual in the several family relationships[43].

Status. In noting this and other specialisations of the general word *status* I am perforce obliged to something of a digression upon that troublesome and debated subject, with which the true conception of the Roman *Jus Personarum* seems unavoidably complicated, and which at any rate bulks large in Austin. In an Institutional work confined according to Ulpian and Justinian (above, § 10, pp. 434, 435)

forbearance," by allowing a secondary one = "material thing," so far eliminates Austin's peculiar sense of *subject* (see n. 20).

[40] Austin[5], 41. 708, notes (omitted in St.).

[41] See Savigny, System, i. § 53, pp. 339, 340, n. *b*.

[42] See Rattigan, Savigny's Jural Relations (a translation of the Second Book of the System), p. 177, n. *g*; also below, § 16, pp. 545, 546.

[43] System, i. § 59, pp. 399, 400; ii. App. vi. p. 465.

to Private Law, we naturally expect the *status*, recognised as having a legal bearing, to be confined to private conditions or relations. Hence the express distinction drawn in Justinian's Institutes[44], between *status* and *dignitas*. But as to determining *which* of such private conditions were intended to be treated in the *Jus Personarum*, it is mere circular reasoning for us to define that division of Law as being *de statu hominum*, since any approximation to definiteness in this use of the word is mainly due to the Institutional division itself, its exclusion of Public Law and its opposition to the *Jus Rerum*. I do not therefore propose to enter, except very briefly, into the wider question what is meant by *status* in the writings of "the Roman Jurists" generally, including under that phrase the compilers of Justinian's Institutes and Digest.

The employment of the word specially to designate *private* conditions is however, fairly borne out by the arrangement of Digest, Book 1. After preliminary matter on Law generally, and the sources of Roman Law in particular, we come to the 5th Title (= Chapter), bearing the Rubric (= Heading) *De statu hominum*.

If the subject of *Status* is considered to be fully represented by the contents of this Title, it is mainly taken up with the questions of slavery, freedom, and free birth. It may be remembered, however, that the Rubric of one Title does seem occasionally to cover the subject-matter of several following ones[45]. It is not improbable, therefore, that the subjects of the next two Titles, on *potestas* generally

---

[44] Just. 1. 16. 5. It also appears to me to be opposed, in Ulp. ad Sab. Dig. 1. 5. 20 to *dignitas, magistratus* and *potestas*—the last *not* meaning *patria potestas*. See, however, Savigny's note (System, ii. Beil. vi. p. 455, n. *b*) on this somewhat vaguely expressed passage.

[45] E.g. Dig. 12. 1. De rebus creditis. See Roby's Introduction to the Study of Justinian's Digests, pp. xxxvii, xliii.

and the modes in which it comes to an end[46], were regarded as falling under the *Status hominum* by the authors of these Rubrics. The authority of Rubrics is not first-rate, as they are sometimes later than the text. But those of the Digest have as good a standing as any[47]. Arguments on the other hand such as that of Austin[48] founded upon the Rubric prefixed to Gaius, 1. 9 are worth little, these Rubrics being only the work of a "corrector," or "secunda manus."

To return to Digest, Book 1. We may remark the omission, from Title 5, of the whole subject of *Latini* and *Dediticii*, who play a considerable part in Gaius' first Book. This is accounted for by a brief reference, in that part of the Title where we might have expected to find this subject, to the extension of Roman citizenship under Antoninus (Caracalla) over the whole Roman world[49]. The *Latini* and *Dediticii* are accordingly, though their temporary survival may be explained in Gaius, omitted from the Institutes of Justinian[50].

Proceeding with the arrangement of the remaining Titles of Digest, Book 1, we have a pretty clear indication that the word *status was* limited, by the later Roman jurists, in the general sense above claimed (p. 484). *A priori* we might fairly have expected to find, under the head *de statu hominum*, besides the three Titles of which I have spoken (5, 6, 7), some account, in the same place, of the *public* conditions recognised by Law, which may have been occasionally, when

[46] Dig. 1. 6. De his qui sui vel alieni juris sunt; 1. 7. De adoptionibus et emancipationibus et aliis modis quibus potestas solvitur.

[47] They come with the text in the Codex Florentinus, ascribed by Teuffel and Krüger to the 7th or even the 6th century. The style of writing is singularly like that of the Codex Argenteus of Ulphilas, which is generally put earlier still.

[48] Austin[5], 13. 363; St. 172. See above, § 11, p. 461.

[49] Ulpian, Dig. 1. 5. 7. In orbe Romano qui sunt ex constitutione Imperatoris Antonini cives Romani effecti sunt.

[50] Compare Ga. 1. 13—25 with Just. 1. 4. 3. For Gaius' *silence*, on the other hand, as to *peregrini*, see above, p. 480.

there is no principle of classification in question, designated under the same term by "the Roman lawyers[51]." We do, as a matter of fact, find, first of all, a short notice of the different articles or subjects of Property[52] and then, thus separated from the three Titles on private conditions, a long list of dignities and official positions[53].

In this separation of Public and Private conditions, for an educational scheme of Law, I should certainly agree with the Roman authorities and Bentham, as against Austin in the unusual company of Blackstone[54].

Passing, from divisions of the Institutes and Digest, to individual passages, as illustrating the writer's application of the word *status*, I can only give the more significant among a very bulky list of quotations, in Austin or elsewhere. We find it used to indicate the conditions of liberty and citizenship, which are only permanently affected *in deterius* by the two greater *capitis minutiones*[55]; of family subordination or independence[56]; and also of connection with this or that agnatic group[57] which is apparently the force of the word in an obscure passage of Cicero[58]. Besides these there are also, no doubt, scattered passages, even in the Classical Jurists of the best period, in which *status* means a mere condition of *fact*; without any really legal bearing[59]. Hugo, in fact, on

---

[51] Austin[5], 42. 717; St. 361. Cf. Tab. and Notes, 942, 943.

[52] Dig. 1. 8. De divisione rerum et qualitate.

[53] Dig. 1. 9. De Senatoribus; 1. 10. De officio Consulis, &c., &c.

[54] See above, § 10, p. 442.   [55] Ulpian, Dig. 38. 17. 1. 8.

[56] id. Tit. xx. 11 and Dig. 28. 1. 15; Paulus, Dig. 28. 1. 14.

[57] Ga. 1. 162. See generally above, § 11, pp. 458, 459.

[58] De legibus, 1. 7. 23. Agnationibus familiarum distinguuntur status. "Nihil aliud dici," says Bake, p. 341, "nisi diversis agnationibus diversas esse familias." Savigny's interpretation (System, ii. Beil. vi. p. 451) does not add much to this identical proposition. ? Translate, "The *status* of individuals are determined by their agnatic conditions."

[59] Savigny, l.c. speaks of *status* in such passages as *bloss factisch*, not *wirklich juristisch*.

the whole, rejects any strict technical meaning for the word altogether in Roman authorities[60], for which view there is much to be said.

If I might venture on definition of so doubtful a term, I should say that *status*, which *may* mean generally *any* condition, and, in a legal treatise any condition legally recognised, is, in the Roman Educational scheme of Law, cut down, partly by the exclusion of Public conditions, and partly by that of Property relations, to Personal conditions which do in fact fall under the heads of Liberty, Citizenship and Family, but are not confined either to the last or to the mere question of Capacity in all three. It is a man's participations in these three conditions which make up his *Caput* or legal personality (§ 11, p. 459). But a loss of Public position, or *dignitas*, does not involve a *capitis minutio*[61].

Thus far, I have been speaking simply of the Roman uses of the word *status*. In its use by modern writers, the idea of *status*, singular or plural, is obviously governed by the Roman Institutional division, so that the word, with them, generally means what they consider was or was intended to be the subject of Gaius' first Book. It is therefore little more than a part of the individual author's theory as to the *Jus Personarum*, and is best considered with those theories, to which we may now return. A few detached definitions and distinctions on the subject will be noticed below (p. 490).

The theory of Savigny has the merit of possessing great clearness, and of attempting to shew a definite connexion, in subject-matter, between the different conditions actually treated in the first Book of Gaius. His assertion of the important part played by Family Law in the *Jus Personarum* cannot be contested: the proportion of the space occupied by that subject to the other divisions of *Personae* being

---

[60] Rechtsgesch[2], p. 118, cited in Savigny, l.c. p. 450.
[61] Just. 1. 16. 5.

that of two if not three to one (§ 12, p. 467). But, in his reduction of the entire *Jus Personarum* to the Law of Family Relations, he appears to me to disregard much that *is* in Gaius' first Book, and to read much into the Book which is *not* there.

Following that task for forced numerical symmetry which has been stigmatised, perhaps a little too severely, in the Roman Jurists (above, p. 480 and § 11, p. 453), Savigny subdivides Hugo's three conditions of Freedom, Citizenship and Family (above, p. 474) respectively into three more triads —*Liber, Servus* and *Libertinus*; *Civis, Latinus* and *Peregrinus*; *potestas, manus* and *mancipium*. Of these nine subjects, which would all naturally be included in our unlimited account of Capacity (or, as it may otherwise be put, of *personal legal conditions*), those *only*, says Savigny, are included in the *Jus Personarum* which are connected with the Family.

In the first division, slavery and the different degrees of *libertinitas* are represented to be introduced as part of Family Law, incidentally, as I understand Savigny, to the Family right of Patronage[62]. On this, I can only say that, if slavery *is* introduced as part of Family Law and *libertinitas* in particular *à propos* of *patronatus*, it is in no words preserved to us. The subjects are brought forward at the very beginning of the Book, before any mention of the Family at all.

The *Liber* of the first division, and the whole of the second division—*Civis, Latinus, Peregrinus*—are, we are told, omitted as being part of Public Law[63]. The reason is not very conclusive, nor is the fact exactly as stated here. I must refer on this subject to what has been said above (p. 480). For the omission of the *normal* conditions of *Civis* and *Liber,*

---

[62] System, i. § 55, p. 365. Cf. ii. Beil. vi. 6, p. 458.   [63] ib.

which does *not* present a difficulty in Savigny's explanation, I have endeavoured to account otherwise elsewhere (above, p. 472).

The third division, including the subjects of *potestas*, *manus* and *mancipium*, coincides pretty fairly with Savigny's idea of the general subject of the book. This subject is no doubt very fully represented in Gaius, and only the obsolete portions omitted by Justinian.

On Savigny's objection to the inclusion of *tutela* in *Jus Personarum*, under Hugo's theory of Capacity, I have spoken above (p. 481). The subject clearly comes under his own view as a matter of Family Relation resulting from a personal incapacitation of the ward to deal with his property —though perhaps a power over his person is strictly to be regarded as accidental[64].

Agnatio is, we have seen, brought in by Gaius incidentally to *tutela* (above, p. 468). That the subject is not treated more fully in the *Jus Personarum* is to some extent accounted for by Savigny's regarding it as coming under the least definite of the Family Relations, Marriage, Fatherly Power and Kinship—another of his rather gratuitous triads. It does not however seem to me that so much stress is laid by him, as is represented by Dr Moyle[65], upon the comparatively slight notice here of a legal condition the results of which upon the succession to Property are more important than upon an alternative title to *tutela*. For further observations upon Savigny's view of Family Law being the *exclusive* subject of Gaius' Book, see the part already referred to in Dr Moyle's Justinian.

The detached definitions and divisions referred to above, p. 487, are mostly due to one passage of an early exponent

[64] This power was therefore possibly too much relied on by me above. See on the whole subject Savigny, System, i. § 55. pp. 361, 362.

[65] System, i. § 54, pp. 354, 355; Moyle, Justinian[4], pp. 90, 91.

of the *Jus Personarum,* **Heineccius**[66]. They require but a brief statement, and that less from their intrinsic merit than from the notice attracted to them by Austin.

Status, according to Heineccius, is the *quality* by virtue of which men enjoy *varying* legal conditions. The latter part of this statement is very much the same as the theory that the *Jus Personarum* is the Law of Unequals, which we shall find worthy of some consideration (p. 492, also above, p. 474). The former part is a remanet from the old doctrine of occult qualities, of which Austin, in quoting Heineccius, falls foul. I need not here do more than refer to his, and Thibaut's, criticism of this doctrine, which has been sufficiently dealt with both by satirists and philosophers[67]. The "ideal base" of Bentham[68] is obviously open to the same objections as the occult quality. "A *status* or Condition is nothing fictitious or ideal, but a lot of rights or duties marked by a collective name and bound by that name into a complex aggregate."

A distinction of *status* as *natural* or *civil,* drawn by the same Heineccius[69], does not appear to be much relied on by that Jurist himself and is certainly useless in a legal treatise. So far as a *status naturalis* has legal consequences, it is a *status civilis*: so far as it has not, it does not concern the Jurist[70].

---

[66] Elementa, 1. 3. 7. Cited by Austin, in his note on *tria capita,* p. 724, as from the same author's Recitationes. See, too, Austin[5], 41. 697; St. 354.

[67] Austin, l.c. See, too, Whewell's Philosophy of the Inductive Sciences[2], ii. p. 294.

[68] Vue Générale, ch. 17 (Traités, iii. p. 329).

[69] Elementa, 1. 3. 76. It seems here merely brought in for the sake of the *slave,* who is, according to Heineccius, a *persona* by *natural* Law but not by *civil* (see § 11, p. 457). The distinction, however, is stated with some difference in the *Recitationes,* to which Austin refers, pp. 748, 749.

[70] See Austin's objections to the distinction, 42. p. 719, and Thibaut's limitation of the differences of Persons to such as have *legal* consequences, Austin[5], 41. 709, n.

Status civilis is further divided in Heineccius into the three leading subdivisions of Freedom, Citizenship and Family Relationship which are specially distinguished as *status principales*[71]. That these are the conditions treated in the Roman *Jus Personarum* is certainly the case (above, p. 487). What are or should be those treated in a modern Personal Law will be considered in a later section, where it will be my endeavour as far as possible to keep clear of this unlucky term *status*, with its many definitions and its question-begging character. To one particular complication of the subject, and the extra difficulties imported into it by Austin's attempt to explain a confusion between *status* and *caput*[72], I have already referred at quite sufficient length (§ 11, pp. 457—459).

Austin. I come now to consider more particularly Austin's theory of the *Jus Personarum* in distinction from the *Jus Rerum*, as he conceives that distinction to have been intended, though not logically carried out, by its Roman authors. With this theory is connected a limited or specialised meaning of the word *status*, which has passed from Austin into the phraseology of many subsequent Jurists and has contributed to darken what I believe to have been the design of both the Roman and the English Institutionalists in their first Book.

Status, in the Austinian sense, a sense which accords most nearly perhaps with Blondeau's theory of the *Jus Personarum* (above, p. 474), only applies to such of the conditions recognised by Law as require special consideration on the ground of their difference from that of the average or ordinary citizen. His Law of Persons, which should come *second*, as supplementary to the *Jus Rerum*, or Law General,

---

[71] Elementa, l.c.; Recitt. as quoted by Austin "Tria Capita," p. 724. Also Savigny, ii. § 59, p. 397.

[72] Austin[5], 12. 351, 352; 42. 719; St. 163, 361.

deals with *certain* classes, each of which only comprises a part of the Community[73].

The determination of a true criterion for *status* in this sense —that is, the decision *what* bundles of rights, duties, capacities and incapacities require special treatment, Austin finds, as others have found after him[74], a very great difficulty. His Law of Persons has, as was justly observed by the late Mr Poste[75], only the negative character of anomaly, i.e. of unlikeness to the larger portion of the Law. A positive characteristic was suggested by the same author in describing the *Jus Personarum* as the Law of Unequal Rights, which view is much the same as that of Blondeau and has much to be said for it, as a matter of inference from Gaius' actual treatment of his subject. Conversely, according to Poste, the *Jus Rerum* was the Law of Equal Rights, Austin's Law of Things or Law General. These headings are retained in the 4th and revised edition of Poste. I venture to think that the refusal to regard the *Jus Rerum* as the Law of Property is a mistake: but in other respects this edition is much improved both in intelligibility and general utility, by its omission of great part of the Austinian Jurisprudence formerly intruded into Gaius by Mr Poste.

Consistently with his distinction of special and general Law, Austin considers that when Hale and Blackstone included under their Rights of Persons such matter as rights of Liberty, Security, &c., which reside in every person to whom the Sovereign or State extends a particle of protection, they committed a gross error[76]. Taking the same view of

[73] Austin[5], 40. 690 ; St. 349, where he instances *inter alia* husbands and wives, parents and children. By the side of this the "comparatively narrow class" of 45. 720 sounds oddly, to say the least. A good deal of the latter Lecture is omitted in St.

[74] E.g. Holland[10], pp. 135—138.

[75] Gai Institutiones[4], p. 14; see too p. 124.

[76] Tabb. pp. 982, 983.

the design of the Roman Institutes, he censures the mode
in which that design is carried out, on the grounds partly
of confusion between the general and special Law, partly
of inadequate or inconsistent treatment of the different
heads of the latter. General rights and duties, he says,
("the Law as it relates to Things") are in innumerable
instances treated under special Law ("the Law of Persons"):
special rights and obligations ("Rights and Duties *ex statu*")
being also scattered up and down the other departments[77].
In the first Book of the Institutes, rights and duties arising
ex statu are put down, but not all of them: whereas, in a
mere enumeration or description of *status, none* of the rights
arising therefrom should have been included; in a full
account of *status, all* such rights should be included, those
which deal with Property as well as the rest[78]. In the
former alternative he however admits that there would have
been no such division as the Law of Persons and Law of
Things at all, but merely an introductory disquisition on the
several *status*.

The main part of this indictment rests upon what is in
my view a misapprehension as to the Roman principle of
division. If that really is between Personal and Property
Law, the cross division into General and Special clearly
cannot be observed: some general rights and duties falling
into the former department and some special ones into the
latter. Individual illustrations can be perhaps better given
à propos of the division into Personal and Property Law by
Blackstone; which, as I have remarked above, is carried
out more fully and logically in the English than in the
Roman Institutes.

What has been here regarded as the true principle of
division in both, is in a few cases apparently violated by

[77] Austin[5], 43. 739 notes (omitted in St.).
[78] Austin[5], 43. 739 (omitted in St.).

Gaius, in the way of commission, some slight notices of Property Law being no doubt introduced into his first Book: but I think it can be shewn that this is done secondarily, and incidentally to general Personal qualifications or disqualifications (above, p. 470). Here also may be taken into account a suggestion based on Dr Emerton's strict interpretation of the particles *vel...vel* in Ga. 1. 8 (see § 11, p. 453). The *Jus Personarum* is not so much an absolutely exclusive division of Private Law, as Private Law considered *primarily* from a certain point of view, and treated accordingly.

It is rather, however, on the *omissions*, from the first Book of Gaius' Institutes, that we find some justification for the view taken by Austin, as to the design of the Book, and for the strictures passed by him on the manner in which that design is carried out. The *inadequate* treatment of the rights and duties arising from or constituting the conditions actually dealt with in the *Jus Personarum* has been pointed out above (pp. 471, 474). It has, accordingly, been questioned whether the intention of the Roman authors may not have been to describe only the modes in which the conditions spoken of were acquired and lost rather than the rights, duties and capacities constituting them: and their treatment of the subject must be admitted to be not quite consistent with either plan. This general deficiency is, I think, traceable to the same cause as their more particular omission, almost *in toto*, of universal or normal conditions. I have above endeavoured to account for it (pp. 471, 472) on grounds which do not apply, and accordingly do not produce the same omission, in Hale and Blackstone. The *utility* of Austin's theory, as an independent classification falls to be considered hereafter (§ 14).

Holland. Law of Abnormal Rights. In Professor Holland's chapter on the leading classifications of rights (9), the section devoted to the "Law of Persons and Things" deals less with the *Jus Personarum* of the Romans than with his own conception of what the Law of Persons, in this antithesis, ought to be, and the order in which it ought to be studied. On both points he, in the main, agrees with Austin.

So far as I understand his view of the Roman *Jus Personarum* he considers it to have been intended to treat of Persons, i.e. Men, in respect of their legal condition, classed with reference to their position in the Roman Family. But it is only the *absolute* variations, notably in the *negative* direction of exemption or disability, caused by these conditions, which he regards as coming correctly under the title *Jus quod ad personas pertinet*; a view much the same as that of Blondeau, who styles this branch the Law of Incapables. It was therefore "unfortunate" that the Roman Jurists added "special *rights* belonging to personal relationships," including e.g. not only the incapacity or minor capacity of the wife in power, but the supercapacity or superior relative rights of the husband[79].

It is true, as a matter of fact, that the Roman Institutionalists do give their consideration primarily to conditions of deficient right and subordination; but also that, on the other hand, they do not entirely omit to notice the side of authority (see above, pp. 466, 468).

Variation in both directions, therefore, is probably what Professor Holland meant to include under the designation, which he himself prefers, for the *Jus Personarum*—of Abnormal Law. For this style would certainly seem to cover cases of extra right or authority, in *relative* positions, at least as well as that of *artificial* Persons, or Corporations, which come rather oddly after Infant, Feme Covert, Convict, Lunatic, &c., in an illustrative diagram of Abnormal Persons given by the same author elsewhere[80].

[79] Jurisprudence[10], p. 133.　　[80] ib. ch. 14, p. 320.

I have endeavoured above to reconcile the comparative omission of normal rights and duties with my own view as to the design of a *Jus Personarum*. The question whether Artificial Persons should come within that division belongs rather to the modern treatment of Personal and Property Law (see above, § 11, p. 462).

Sohm. Among later Institutional schemes of Roman Law the excellent work of Sohm has met, I think, with as much attention from English students as any. The system, however, of Roman Private Law which constitutes the second Part of his Institutes, is rather a rearrangement or suggested scheme of the author's own than an interpretation of the scheme of Gaius or Justinian. The Law of Persons is, as in Gaius, divided from the Law of Property and made to precede it, the former dealing with the Subjects, the latter with the Objects, of private right (see above, p. 482). But the treatment of this Law of Persons cannot exactly be reconciled with any of the theories of the *Jus Personarum* heretofore mentioned. It is defined as the Law of *Proprietary* Capacity and contains the general results, in this respect, of conditions coming under the three heads of Liberty, Citizenship and Family relation, accompanied however with a great deal of really Personal matter and of Investitive and Divestitive Fact belonging to the first two. The main treatment, however, of the Family, and the Investitive and Divestitive Facts connected with it, which play so large a part in Gaius' first Book, becomes, with the subject of Inheritance, a third separate Book in Sohm. The Law of Actions, on the other hand, under the heading "The Protection of Rights," is placed in a general part at the beginning of the Law of Property, after a description of Juristic Acts, this last including a very definite and comprehensive account of Capacity for legal action in general. The Books which follow, the Law of Things, the Law of Obligations, and

Family Law with the Law of Inheritance, bear some resemblance to the leading divisions, though not to the order, of Gaius' Books 2 and 3. But the whole system is rather, as has been remarked, matter of modern than of Roman Institutional arrangement, and I have mainly used it as a collection of extremely good separate essays.

Cuq, in the second volume of his Institutes juridiques des Romains, adopts, for the *droit classique*, the ordinary meaning and order of Gaius' classification. After Book 1, on the modes of formation of this Law, come Book 2 dealing with *les Personnes*; Books 3, 4, 5 with *le Patrimoine* et *les droits réels*, *les obligations* and *les successions*; Book 6 with *les actions et la procédure*. The same arrangement is followed more simply and directly in the *droit du bas Empire*.

Girard, too, in his admirable Manuel, expressly recognises the general distinction of Law regarding Persons as Subjects and Things as Objects of rights[81]; and moreover divides the Manuel, after a historical introduction (Book 1), into three parts corresponding to those of Gaius, viz. Persons, Book 2; Property (*Patrimoine*), Book 3; Civic Procedure, Book 4.

Karlowa. The unfinished second volume of Karlowa's Römische Rechtsgeschichte, was to have included Private Law and Civil Process, Criminal Law and Criminal Process. So far as the earlier part of the first of these four subjects (which is all that was published) throws any light upon his conception of Gaius' *Jus Personarum* he would appear to revert to the theory of Savigny. After a comparatively short Introductory Part, which includes however some account of Juristic Persons (*Collegia, Sodalitates*, &c.), we come to the Family and Rights of Family Authority as the great subject which precedes the Law of Things, Obligations and Inheritance. It is not necessary here to go further into the subdivisions of Karlowa's Private Law or its

[81] See above, p. 482, notes.

distinction between what was due to *civil* and what to *honorary* Law.

Résumé. I do not see, in any of the theories or objections above stated, sufficient reason to abandon my opinion, derived from a consideration of the first Book of the Institutes *per se*, undisturbed by modern requirements and conditions. Neither the idea that the *Jus Personarum* was merely Family Law, nor that it was merely the Law of Capacity, seems to me to cover the matter with which Gaius intended to deal in his first Book. His antithesis being between the Persons themselves and their Property, his purpose, in which he is substantially followed by Justinian, is first to treat briefly the several private personal conditions. ranging from complete subordination to complete independence, recognised by Roman Law amongst members of the Roman State, together in some degree with the conditions of relative authority, and to explain the respective modes in which they began and ended. These conditions are no doubt mainly but not exclusively derived from the ancient Family relations, and they certainly cannot all be brought under the head of Capacity without a very extended and strained use of the word. Capacity, where it occurs in the first Book in the special application of acquiring or disposing of Property, appears to come in rather secondarily as a consequence of personal condition. As between these personal conditions, Gaius undoubtedly lays much less stress upon what is normal or general and simple than upon what is special, mixed or intermediate. Such a result, however, might not unnaturally follow from this being an early, if not the first, treatment of Law as a system. The writer is influenced less by purely scientific or educational considerations than by *practice*, which tends to take what is normal for granted. I can, however, see no express intention in Gaius to confine the *Jus Personarum* to special or abnormal conditions—in fact in one passage (above, p. 466) he asserts the normal condition to be implicitly treated in the treatment of the abnormal—a somewhat questionable principle; recognised, however, by Austin and pushed rather too far in a passage omitted by the Student's Edition[82]. A more surprising fact is that, in the description even of the special conditions, the rights and duties constituting them are almost as much to seek, in Gaius' first Book, as those of the general ones. That Book does, in fact, come to very little more than an *enumeration* of the several personal conditions normal and abnormal legally recognised at Rome among members of the Roman State, and an account of the modes in which those conditions could begin and end.

[82] Austin[5], 42. 717, 718. He applies this principle of implicit definition to Blackstone's treatment or non-treatment of native born subjects in Book i. ch. 10 (see § 13, p. 510). Similarly his statement at the end of Lecture 43, p. 730, St. 366, that Blackstone's Absolute Rights are treated by "the Roman lawyers" in the Law of Things rests upon a very forced implication from the *Obligationes ex delicto* arising from violation of those Rights, which are as we know treated in the *Jus quod ad res pertinet*.

§ 13. THE ENGLISH RIGHTS OF PERSONS

Subject of section. On the general adoption, by Hale
and Blackstone, of the Roman division *Jus Personarum* and
Jus quod ad res pertinet, see § 12, p. 464. The subject of
Wrongs is most naturally connected, in a work mainly refer-
ring to Roman Law, with Gaius' third division, *Actiones*.
I have now to speak, somewhat more in detail, of the English
Rights of Persons, the subject of Blackstone's first Book.

Terminology. The wording of the antithesis, Rights of
Persons and Rights of Things, is due partly to the more
logical opposition of Rights and Wrongs (ib.), partly perhaps
to a misapplication of some civilian's or early common law
writer's phrases *jura personarum* and *rerum*, which more
probably meant, as first used, *principles or rules of law*
concerning persons and things[1].

---

[1] See Hale's Analysis of the Law, § 53. This use of *jura* is classical
though less common than in the sense of "rights." See above, § 7, specially
note 63. Austin says (43. 736), "by *jura personarum* and *jura rerum* the
Roman lawyers intended the *law*, &c."; but I do not think the Roman
lawyers ever used the plural in these combinations. Bracton, i. 6. 1 (cf. i.
12. 1) and Fleta, i. 1, copy the Roman *jus personarum*, but do not seem to
favour *jus rerum*.

The criticism to which this unfortunate antithesis has been subjected was obvious enough. It has been assumed that Blackstone and Hale meant, by Rights of Things, Rights belonging to Things; it has been asked how Things can have Rights, or what Rights there are which are not Rights of Persons; and the objection to these *jura* has been extended, with great carelessness and injustice, by Bentham to the correct *Jus Personarum*, &c., of the Roman Institutionalists[2]. I may note that the phrase more open to objection, Rights of Things, is shewn by a passage in Hale's Analysis to be intended as meaning Rights not *belonging* to but *conversant with* Things: while, with Blackstone, the Rights of Persons are such as are "annexed to the persons" of men; the Rights of Things those which a man may acquire in and to "external things unconnected with his person[3]." What we have to consider is, not the unlucky expressions, but the practical meaning and utility of the leading division into Rights and Wrongs (below, § 19), and the subdivision, with which I am at present concerned, into Rights of Persons and Things, mainly with regard to the former half.

In the course of their treatment of this subject, our English Institutionalists find it necessary to extend the heading Rights so as to include Duties, and the word itself is occasionally used by them in this extended and improper sense[4]. The actual connexion, or interdependence, of legal rights and duties will be dealt with hereafter (§ 20), but, from what has been said already, it would clearly be a convenience to substitute some less ambiguous expressions

[2] See Christian's note on Blackstone, i. 1, p. 122, and Bentham's Vue Générale, ch. 14 (Traités, iii, pp. 294, 295), somewhat laxly quoted by Austin in his notes to Lecture 42, pp. 724, 725.

[3] See Hale's Analysis, §§ 1, 23; Blackstone, ii. 1, p. 1.

[4] See Austin's remarks on this and the similar double, or ambiguous, use of the German *Recht* and *Rechtsfähigkeit*, 42. 710; St. 359. On Hale's "Rights of Duty" see below, p. 505.

in the English Institutional phraseology, both for Rights
and for Persons and Things.   In the antithesis of the last
two words, the former has been hitherto taken, as in the
Roman Law, to mean the individuals themselves, the latter
all that may be the *property* of those individuals: some
Law, or Rights, being regarded as more distinctly connected
with themselves, some with their property.

Blackstone's explanation is rather more explicit.   It is
perfectly clear that the Persons, to whom the Rights of his
first Book belong, are *men*, not *conditions*.   But he introduces a new element of explanation, by referring to *person*
in a different sense as equivalent to *body*, a sense in which
the word occurs also, though to a less extent, in Hale[5].   This
explanation tends unduly to narrow the legal rights and
duties which are undoubtedly meant to be included in
Blackstone's first Book.   Fully to describe them, we must
use the wider adjective *personal*.   And, to conclude this
question of terminology, I hold that Personal and Property,
or Proprietary, Law is the most correct and adequate style
for the subject-matter of Blackstone's first two Books; as I
believe it to be also of the Roman *Jus Personarum* and
Jus Rerum, the main principle of the two Institutional
divisions being the same.

Mode of treatment.   In the manner, however, in which
this principle is carried out, there are material differences.
Under the Rights of Persons, to which our attention is, for
the present, confined, we have a certain amount of general
matter—matter of universal Right—prefaced, which does
not occur in the Roman *Jus Personarum*; we have the

---

[5] Compare Hale (Analysis, § 1), "Such rights as immediately concern
the *persons themselves*, or such as relate to their goods and estate," with
Blackstone's (i. 1. p. 122) Rights "which concern or are annexed to the *persons*
of men" or "such as a man may acquire over...things unconnected with his
person."   Later, however, in the same section above cited, Hale speaks of
a man's interest in the safety of *his own person*, &c.

special or particular topics, which *are* common to both,
treated in a much less one-sided manner by the English
than by the Roman writers; and finally we have the subject
of *political conditions* included in the former but excluded
from the latter.

These differences will now be considered a little more
in detail, with principal reference to the scheme of Hale,
which deserves more attention than it has generally
received, overshadowed as it has been by that of his great
successor.

Certain personal rights which normally belong to every
free member of the community are, as we have seen, passed
over with scarcely even mention, because assumed to be
known, by Gaius.   These are placed by our Institutionalists
at the commencement of their subject: not exactly however
on the direct and intelligible ground of their being general
or universal, but as the result of two successive subdivisions.

Hale's Rights of Persons absolutely treated.   *Natural*
persons, to begin with, are distinguished from persons *civil
politic* or *artificial*, i.e. Corporations.   It is with the former
that Blackstone's Book 1 almost exclusively deals: the subject of artificial persons being relegated to a final chapter,
as it is by Hale to a final section of his *Jura Personarum*[6].
This is intelligible and reasonable: but the next distinction,
in the treatment of these "natural persons[7]" gives rise to
some difficulty.   They may be treated (*A*) absolutely and
simply *in themselves*, or (*B*) in some degree or respect of
relation.   In the former point of view they have Interest in
themselves, their goods and estate, and Capacity.   The
Interest in the goods and estate comes more properly
under *Jura Rerum* (see above, p. 501).   But the Capacity, to
take or dispose, together with the Interest which every

---

[6] Blackstone, i. ch. 18; Hale, § 22.
[7] See generally Hale, § 1, which is here quoted.

person has in *himself*, i.e. in his personal safety, his personal liberty, his name and reputation, belong to the *Jura Personarum*. This power of taking and disposing is presumed in law to belong to all persons not disabled, and a list is given of those who *are* under various disabilities, modifying the normal capacity—Aliens, Attainted, Outlawed, Infants, Feme Coverts, Idiots and Lunatics, persons under Illegal Restraint, Villeins (antiquated) and Bastards.

The only remarks that I wish to make on this part of Hale's scheme are two:

1. Proprietary capacity is coupled, as an abstract Right separable from any concrete dealings in Property, with such clearly Personal Rights as safety, liberty and reputation.

2. Conditions of disability in respect of this Capacity (unequal rights) *are* treated, but not to the exclusion of the normal condition.

Blackstone's Absolute Rights. The fancy of Blackstone, referred to elsewhere (§ 12, p. 478) as to the *origin* of his Absolute Rights in a state of Nature, does not really require any consideration here, as the actual principle of division is the same as that of Hale. Hale's proprietary "capacity" becomes with Blackstone the more Comprehensive Right of Property "which consists in the free use, enjoyment and disposal of all acquisitions, without any control or diminution, save only by the laws of the land[8]." But this, together with the Right of Personal Security, including the enjoyment of Reputation[9], and that of Personal Liberty, belong to particular men "merely as individuals or single persons"—as Hale puts it, "considered absolutely and simply in themselves"—whereas all other Rights of Persons are *relative*[10].

Absolute and Relative. This division of Rights of

---

[8] Blackstone, i. 1, p. 138.   [9] ib. pp. 129, 134.

[10] ib. p. 123.

Persons into absolute and relative, as understood by either of our English Institutionalists, does not exactly tally with the distinction between general and special. The modern philosophical description of a legal Right (or indeed *any* Right) as being intrinsically *relative*, i.e. dependent on obligations incumbent upon others (see below, § 20), was no doubt unknown to them. But, on the other hand, they considered the ordinary *citizens*, as we now rather prefer to call them, to stand primarily and properly, as *subjects*, in one universal *relation* to the magistrates or governors[11]. Consequently, a considerable part of what we should regard as normal or universal, in Personal Law, falls into Hale's *relative* division, where he treats of the Rights of Subjects, which are of two kinds, Rights of Duty (see above, p. 501), to be performed, and Rights of Privilege, to be enjoyed.   In Blackstone's arrangement of both, under Rights of Persons, the Rights of Privilege, of which Hale speaks in his 13th section, are mostly treated by Blackstone in the first chapter[12] as modes of securing his three principal Absolute Rights, while the Duties of Subjects come in a later chapter[13] together with some of the disabilities placed by Hale in his first section, those namely of Aliens.

The whole of this arrangement is certainly, as matters are considered in modern times, unnecessarily complicated and confused.   The Personal Rights and Duties of a general character, as belonging to the ordinary citizen, or subject, ought clearly to be all taken together, the special disabilities, in this respect, of the non-citizen being added as an Appendix to them.   I only wish here to insist that the former, so far from being omitted by the English Institutionalists, form a definite though small part of their Personal Law.

[11] See Hale, §§ 2, 13; Blackstone, i. 2, p. 145; 10, p. 366.

[12] Blackstone, i. 1, pp. 141—144.

[13] Ch. 10.   Of the people, whether aliens, denizens or natives.

Relative Rights. We pass now to the second branch of
the English Rights of Persons, that of *relative* and special
Rights, which constitutes by far the greater part of the
subject; as that which partially corresponds to it constitutes
almost the whole of the Roman *Jus Personarum.* The
difference, however, between the corresponding portions of
the two Institutional schemes is considerable, both as to contents and treatment. Gaius deals far less with the legal
conditions themselves than with the manner in which they
begin and end, dwells mainly on the aspect of subordination, and confines himself to Private Law. Hale and
Blackstone look at the subject of mutual relations *generally*
—giving indeed the side of authority rather the priority
over that of subordination: they then enter fully into the
rights and duties themselves, not merely into the modes of
investment or divestment: and they expressly include Public,
or as Hale calls them, Political Relations. Under the last
head comes the whole account of the Government or
Magistracy[14], ending with the section or chapter on the
People or Subject, of which I have spoken above.

The inclusion of **Public Relations** under the Rights of
Persons is the most striking difference between that branch
of our English Institutional system and the *Jus Personarum*
of the Romans. It results, of course, from the initial limitation of the Roman Institutes to Private Law (see above,
§ 10, p. 434); but, as an independent fact, constitutes, in
the view of Austin, a considerable superiority, in Hale
and Blackstone's Rights of Persons, over that Institutional
system and most others. This is not a view at all generally
accepted, either in literature or codification: but perhaps
the best criticism of the English Institutionalists' plan, as a
matter of present utility, may be gathered from the difficulties found in it by modern editors of Blackstone and the

[14] Hale, §§ 3—12; Blackstone, i. chs. 2—9.

rearrangements which they have thought it necessary to propose (see the beginning of next section).

Private Relations. At present we may leave the subject of Public Relations aside, and pass on to those of Master and Servant, Husband and Wife, Parent and Child, Guardian and Ward in Blackstone's Rights of Persons[15].

Of these, the three first might be truly described as belonging to the Family considered as a Household, and are accordingly styled *economical* by Hale. The last he classes with Ancestor and Heir, Lord and Tenant, Lord and Villein, as *civil*, a somewhat peculiar use of the word, apparently meant to indicate relations of a private character recognised by the State, but not, in his view, belonging to the Family or Household[16].

The question whether the relation of Guardian and Ward belongs rightly to Personal or Property Law has proved, as we have seen[17], one of the difficulties, or rather critical points, in determining the true character of the *Jus Personarum*. On the whole, it certainly appears to be correctly joined with purely Family relations and to belong primarily to Personal Law. Blackstone adds to his account of the Ward's personal incapacities, which are regarded by him as practically privileges, a certain amount of matter on incapacities and exemptions of *Infants* generally[18]. This, though undoubtedly part of Personal Law, would seem to come better under the first part, dealing with the rights and duties of the ordinary citizen in general (see above, p. 505).

The subject of Ancestor and Heir, on the other hand, belongs so predominantly to Property Law that the two or

---

[15] Blackstone, i. 1, chs. 14—17.
[16] Hale's Analysis, §§ 14—21.
[17] See above, § 12, pp. 480, 481.
[18] Blackstone, i. ch. 17, pp. 464—466.   See, too, below, § 15, p. 520.

three personal questions made into an independent section by Hale would be better taken with the general law of Inheritance in that second division. This, therefore, as well as the obsolete subjects of Lord and Tenant, Lord and Villein, is properly omitted by Blackstone from his "private economical relations."

Résumé. Besides the slighter differences of general treatment, between the Roman English Institutionalists, above referred to, we may note that the inconvenient interpolation of Public Relations, between the general and special parts of Private Personal Law, has broken their continuity and led to individual portions which should belong to the one being occasionally placed in the other[19]. But, subject to all these differences, I must repeat in conclusion that the English Jurists do seem to have had in the main the same definite purpose with their Roman predecessors: and that this was, not to place particular or special law, simply as such, in the first division, but to distinguish the Personal from the Proprietary Law. The predominance which the special or particular assumes over the normal in Gaius' first Book is no doubt a difficulty which I have endeavoured to meet as well as I can. But Austin is not justified in blaming Hale and Blackstone because they include under their first division of Rights those general ones which, though omitted by the Roman writer, are *personal*, as distinguished from rights directly connected with property. The occasional confusions and repetitions which occur in both systems are due to the inherent difficulties in the antithesis which their respective authors *did* recognise, not to their deviation from another which they did *not*. How far the time-honoured division can still be usefully employed will be considered in the next section.

19 See above, pp. 503—505.

Order of Treatment. Before taking leave of the subject as generally treated by Hale and Blackstone, I would add a word as to the *order* in which it has been suggested that Personal and Property Law should be taken by the student. We need not, perhaps, set much store by Justinian's or Hermogenianus' dictum above cited (§ 11, p. 460), though it does not seem unnatural that Personal condition might claim consideration prior to that of Property. Hale, on the other hand, recommends that, as a matter of study, the Rights of Things should come first, "for the former part" (Rights of Persons) "contains matter proper for the study of one that is well acquainted with those *Jura Rerum*[20]." Not a very enlightening reason, but naturally commended by Austin[21], according to *his* view of the distinction between the Law of Persons and of Things, on the ground that the general Code should come first, and the comparatively miscellaneous matters, which are properly a sort of Appendix, second. Now there is no doubt that, while the Rights of Things obviously belong to *general* law, the greater part of the Rights of Persons is actually special or peculiar, particularly if we take into account the large space devoted to Public Rights, which might not be considered useful preliminary reading for *all* students of Law. It is possible, therefore, that Hale's motive for the change of order from that of "the usual method of civilians and our ancient common law tractates," *was* the one suggested by Austin. But it does not, of course, follow that Hale meant by the *Jura Rerum*, as comprising the "interest of goods and estate," anything but Property Law.

Again, what Austin tells us, in the same passage, that Blackstone practically adopts Hale's change of order, is only true so far as this—that Blackstone, in his Rights of Persons, puts what is general (Absolute Rights) before what is special

[20] Analysis, § 23.   [21] Austin[5], 43. 727; St. 364.

(Relative Rights): but not true that he either attaches Austin's meaning to the two main divisions or that he recommends the second to be taken first.

I may notice here another misrepresentation, as it seems to me, by Austin, in support of his position that the rights and duties of ordinary citizens "are not considered in the Law of Persons." Blackstone, he maintains, in his tenth chapter, passes over the rights of native born subjects, "as being the principal subject of his whole treatise," to consider incapacities of aliens, &c.[22] It is true that Blackstone does in the chapter in question (p. 371) refer to the rights of natural born subjects as being the principal subject of *the two first books* of his Commentary: but it is also true that he at the same time occupies more than half of the same chapter with an account of their *duties*.

[22] Austin [5], 42. 718.

§ 14. AUSTIN'S LAW OF PERSONS AND THINGS

As the principle of a division of the Corpus Juris, depending on an antithesis of Person and Thing, is here maintained to be the same with the Roman and the English Institutionalists, I might proceed at once with the latter, and shew, as I hope to do, that their general plan may be still advantageously employed, with some modification, in an educational course of Law. But the fact cannot be ignored that the theory of Austin has gained a considerable reception not only as an interpretation of the Roman division but as a substantive counter proposal or substitute for the English one. It may well therefore be considered here, mainly in the latter point of view.

Bentham's Law General and Particular. The idea of Austin's Law of Persons and Things was possibly suggested in the first instance by the observed fact that the greater part of the *Jus Personarum* and its English equivalent was devoted to *special* conditions. But this idea was doubtless confirmed and strengthened by Bentham's suggested division of a Corpus Juris into (A) a General Code, (B) Special Codes, or bodies of Law specially relating to particular classes[1]. The expressions General and Particular, applied to Law by Bentham himself, are not suitable for English use as a main division, on account of the technical sense which *particular* has acquired in our law language[2]. But General and Special would be a much better style, for this assumed or proposed division, than the "Law of Persons and Things," which certainly requires a great deal of "snuffing," to use Austin's or Hobbes' quaint phrase[3], before it can enlighten us as to the intended meaning. The question, indeed, how the style *Jus Rerum* came to be employed by "the Roman Jurists" for the Law General, as Austin alleges, is answered by him in so obscure and inconsistent a manner that I content myself with referring to the passages in which his two different explanations occur[4], and giving the upshot as stated in the Student's Austin, as follows.

It has been seen that *res* or "thing," in its widest meaning, embraced the whole matter with which laws are conversant. Having for convenience singled out a department of law and called it "Law of Persons," it seems natural that the authors of these institutional treatises—familiar with the term *res* as wide enough to embrace all the subject-matter of law—should call the opposed department "the Law of Things."

In all the unwarranted assumptions made, and arbitrary

---

[1] See Austin[5], 40. 692; St. 350.   Also note to Lecture 43, on Bentham's Ideas of Method, p. 741.   The passage referred to is in ch. 1 of the Vue Générale (Traités, iii. pp. 189, 190).   See also ch. 19, pp. 332, 333.

[2] E.g. a *particular* custom.   See Blackstone, Int. 3, pp. 74, 75, which for the most part relates only to people *locally* determined.

[3] Austin[5], 42. 712.

[4] Compare Austin[5], 40. 685, 686 (and Tables and Notes, ii. 2, p. 932), with a lower paragraph on p. 686.   Most of the former passages are omitted in St. the statement in the text being taken, with slight variation, from p. 346.

meanings given to words, by Austin, throughout his reasoning on this subject, there may be perceived an underlying idea of some intrinsic and original *generality* in expressions connected with the word *res*[5]; to which attention will be drawn more particularly hereafter, in considering his explanation of the phrase *jus in rem*.   Besides the reasoning based on this idea, his identification of the *Jus Rerum* with the Law of rights and duties *generally*, is moreover backed by various quotations from Thibaut and Savigny; but they do not appear to me to give it much real support.

Austin's Law General and Special.   We may now, therefore, pass from Austin's version of the Law of Persons and Things " as conceived by the classical Jurists in their elementary or institutional treatises[6]," to the statement of the Austinian principle *per se*, and the peculiar meaning of the word *status* connected with it.

" Certain sets of rights and duties, and capacities or incapacities, are, for the sake of commodious arrangement, detached from the body of the Law, and placed in a peculiar department: and to those sets of rights, &c., which for the sake of arrangement and exposition it is found convenient thus to detach, the name of *status* is applied or is more particularly applied[7]."

This division, which may be better styled as one into General and Special Law, is not, it will be seen, based upon any intrinsic difference such as that of Personal and Property Law, or Family and other Law, but on empirical questions of convenience.   The conveniences alleged by its advocate are, on the one hand the brevity and clearness obtained by placing all rules of law, which are capable of being so placed,

---

[5] Cf. what he says of *Jus Rerum* in p. 941 of Tables and Notes, ii. 3, C. *b*, with p. 958, ii. 3, C. *d*, on *jus in rem*.

[6] Austin[5], 41. 696.   See, too, 13. 363, 364.

[7] Austin[5], 41. 697.

apart from any modifications to which they are subject by
the special rights or incapacities of any particular class of
persons; on the other hand the convenience to particular
classes of persons in having the special provisions relating to
them placed by themselves under a peculiar head[8]. Alternatives of arrangement combining these two principles are
suggested by Austin and rejected. All common matter
might be inserted under the head of each separate class
besides what is special. But such a Corpus Juris would be
most voluminous and involve the most unnecessary repetition.
Or, the special matter might be appended in each instance
to the general provisions which it modified or controlled:
but at the cost of brevity and clearness, as also of the
advantages which particular classes might derive from their
special law being collected to their hands[9].

All these are incontestable propositions but do not seem
to lead to very precise results. They are mainly due to
the suggestions of Bentham referred to in note 1. It is
not quite clear, from the very brief and sketchy manner in
which he treats the subject, whether the advantage, for the
particular *état*, of finding its particular law collected together,
is to be attained by little separate Codes or by an index to
the general one. But, in any case, a very wide list of such
états seems to be contemplated both by him and Austin.
"Father" e.g. is coupled with "Agriculturist" and "Trader"
the last being again divisible into a number of subordinate
heads[10].

Hale's suggested change of order. With regard to
order of treatment, Austin, who is more explicit on this
question than Bentham, and who has, in some sense, the
opinion of Sir Matthew Hale to support his view (see § 13,

[8] Austin[5], 40. 692; St. 350.
[9] Austin[5], 40. 693—695; St. 351.
[10] Bentham, l.c. p. 333. See Austin, p. 690.

p. 509), points out that what relates to the great majority
of the community—the Law General—ought to *precede*
what relates to specific classes of persons—the Law Special :
the latter being a sort of appendix—at any rate supple-
mental, and presupposing the former[11].

In respect of the particular advantage desiderated by
Bentham, much is no doubt already attained and more may
be, by good codification or well drawn consolidation statutes.
A large amount of Special Law for trading classes is provided in most of the Continental Systems, by the addition,
to general Property Law, of a *Code de Commerce*. In our
own case the knowledge required by individual classes is
generally supplied in text-books or separate treatises address-
ing themselves not to students so much as to men engaged
in the business of life and divided into callings, professions
or trades.

For the other advantages alleged by Austin—the brevity
and clearness, and, as far as possible, freedom from modifications (above p. 514), which are no doubt specially required by
the student in the beginning of an educational course—it
must be urged that the principal, if not the only, modifications in the Law General, with which the commencing
student need encumber himself, are matters of general
Capacity or Liability, perfectly detachable from individual
dealings (see § 13, pp. 503, 504), and consequently capable of
being considered, together with certain rights and duties, as
distinctly *personal*.

As to the question therefore of *order* of treatment or
reading raised by Hale, which undoubtedly arises, and
perhaps with greater strength if we suppose the matter of

[11] Austin[5], 43. 727, 728; St. 364; 44. 749; St. 369. The latter passage
rather appears, by the side heading, to be confined to the Law of Political
Conditions, but the argument is clearly applicable to Austin's Law of Persons
generally.

Public Conditions cleared out of the way, I can only say that the few *generalia* of capacity and liability, required for a consideration of Private Personal Conditions, may very well *precede* the Law of Property and Criminal Law, wherever we choose to take the quite separable subject of Constitutional Law.

Consequently there does not seem any very strong reason for departing from the "usual method of civilians" (Hale, l.c.) and putting a *Jus Rerum* first. But, whether the ordinary view or that of Austin be accepted, as to what the *Jus Rerum* is, we have still to face the questions *what are* the conditions proper to be included in Personal Law; or, according to Austin, what sort or amount of characteristics is enough to mark out a class which is to be exceptionally considered; *status* being, it must be remembered, in his use of the term, merely defined as *any* condition which requires special treatment and consideration.

How status are to be determined. This is the crucial difficulty in Austin's system, and his attempts to answer the above question, made at great length and with much repetition in Lectures 40—43, must be regarded as very unsatisfactory. He examines and rejects the criteria of a *status* which have been proposed by other writers, but fails to substitute any of which he can himself entirely approve.

Since I merely propose to consider this discussion so far as it actually bears on the true division between the first and second Book of the Institutional system, I need not repeat the objections to an *ideal base* or an occult quality (§ 12, p. 491) or to Capacity considered as an *exhaustive* description (ib. p. 480). The *status* with which we have to deal is simply, as Austin rightly holds, a lot of rights and duties *as well as* capacities and incapacities, marked by a common name as indicating a complex aggregate.

The question asked above has been varied thus: What is the principle of union which associates certain rights, &c., together, so as to make a *status* of them? According to Bentham, it is the identity of the Investitive Fact in virtue of which the *status* is possessed[12]. Austin justly denies the distinctive character of this test, because it is common to many other aggregates of rights and duties which are practically never treated as *status* (plural), as well as to so-called *singular* or *particular* rights[13]. On the same ground, of their non-distinctive character, other tests of the rights and duties constituting a *status* are rejected by Austin, and need not be particularised here—e.g. that they are commonly divisible into such as arise *ex statu* (more properly "from the generating fact") *mediate* and *immediate*; which is much the same as saying that *status* consist partly of capacities and partly of independent rights, &c.: or that they are the subject of a *jus in rem* belonging to the person who has the *status*, &c., &c.[14]

Austin's unsatisfactory answers. The tests upon which he himself would preferably rely are the following: 1. *Status* resides in a person as member of a class, not as being that individual person[15]. 2. The rights, duties, &c., constituting *status* belong *exclusively* or *specially* to the class of persons by whom the *status* is borne, although certain *consequences* may result to other people, e.g. in the case of *contracts* by an ordinary adult citizen with an infant[16]. 3. That class must not be such that it may comprise any or nearly any person whatever[17]. The first of these tests is little more than an identical proposition. The entirely gratuitous difficulties raised in the Tables and Notes, p. 949

[12] Vue Générale, ch. 17 (Traités, iii. p. 329).
[13] Austin[5], 41. 702—705; St. 356, 357.
[14] Austin[5], 41. 705, 706; St. 356.   [15] id. 40. 688, 689; St. 348.
[16] ib. 689.   [17] ib. 690; St. 349.

(Austin), might have been obviated by pointing out that a sole Sovereign, quâ Sovereign, is *generically determined*, though it may sound strange to call him a "member of a class."

It is in the application of his second test that Austin parts company with the division of Person and Property. A body of legal rights, duties, &c., may clearly be *personal* and yet general, although Personal Law, wherever there are different Classes or Orders recognised by the State, must consist largely of *special* bodies of rights, duties, &c., to which Austin's definition of *status* will apply (see § 15, p. 536).

Austin's third test is capable of an obvious *reductio ad absurdum*. In another passage, prudently omitted from the Student's Austin, he goes so far as to say that the rights, duties, &c., which are to be separately treated, must be such as specially regard a *comparatively narrow* class of the community[18], which will scarcely suit the cases, universally placed both in Special and Personal Law, of Father and Child or Husband and Wife. The proportion, in fact, borne by a class, whose legal condition would be placed in Special Law, to the whole Community is one of those which, as Austin himself practically admits, can never furnish a good line of demarcation. His own preferred tests are not regarded as satisfactory by himself. In the peculiar collections of rights and duties, which have been severed from the rest and called *status* (plural), he finds no common generic character; the distinction being purely arbitrary and the arrangement one of mere convenience, depending mainly upon the capability, which these collections have, of being detached from the bulk of the system without breaking the continuity of exposition[19].

The absence of this capability of detachment is alleged

[18] Austin[5], 42. p. 721.
[19] Austin[5], 40. p. 688; 41. 696; St. 348, 354. Also Austin, 42. 720.

by Austin as the reason for what he considers a difficulty in
the Roman Institutional system, i.e. the placing of the bulk
of rights and duties, which devolve on the heir (strictly the
heres) of a deceased person, in the general Law or Law of
Things[20]. As a matter of fact, the subject of succession or
inheritance *is* peculiarly capable of being treated as a detached subject, and its position in the Roman and other
systems is due to the real principle of division, which
Austin ignores, or endeavours in vain to identify with that
of his own invention.

Hale, Austin remarks, puts the rights and duties of
the heir "who is in some respects *successor universalis*"
inconsistently in the Law of Persons as well as in the Law
of Things[21]. But the usual, as well as the exceptional
arrangement, really depends upon the antithesis of Person
and Property. Succession, as a particular mode of acquiring
Property, is placed principally, by most authorities, in the
second division: the subject of Ancestor and Heir, with that
of Lord and Tenant, is briefly noticed, by Hale, in the first,
with obvious reference to the personal relations of feudal
status[22].

When we come to enquire what are the legal conditions
and relations, general or special, which are or ought to be
included under Personal Law, we naturally cannot make
much use of Austin's attempted definitions of *status*, as
understood by him. If, however, we consider the term as
applied to the varying *personal* conditions, which were much
more numerous, in the earlier Roman Law, as in our own,
than they are at the present day, a test which Austin first
adopts and afterwards discards is not without its value.
"The rights and duties, capacities and incapacities, which

---

[20] Austin[5], 42. 720, 721 (omitted, with much of this Lecture, in St.).
[21] Austin[5], 40. 695; 41. 703; St. 357.
[22] Hale, Analysis, §§ 18, 19 and §§ 30, 33.

constitute a *status* or condition, are commonly considerable in number and various in kind," or, as he puts it elsewhere, they are "indefinite in number and kind." They "impart to the party invested with them a conspicuous character and affect him in most or many of his social relations[23]." All this is a good deal whittled down, and tends to be more so, in levelling modern times, under what Sir Henry Maine describes as Progress from *status* to Contract (below, § 15, p. 536); but, as we shall see in the next section, there are still points of *personal* distinction which have their definite meaning and importance.

Holland, who takes, in the main, the same view of the Law of Persons as Austin (§ 12, p. 495), appears however rather to prefer the criterion of *status* which that author discards to that which he adopts. He himself suggests that "the personality recognised in that Law is such as modifies indefinitely the legal relations into which the individual invested with it may enter[24]." And it must be noted that when Holland proceeds to illustrate the distinctions of his Abnormal Persons (p. 495) from the Normal, the deviations from the normal type are all (except that of the *artificial* Person, the Corporation), of a personal character, e.g. Infant, Feme Covert, Convict, Lunatic[25].

Salmond. This is perhaps the most convenient place to note the views of Professor Salmond, though they indeed bear as much upon the subjects of §§ 11 and 13. The second Book of the Roman Institutes he distinctly takes to be the Law of Property or the Law of Proprietary Rights: the first, the Law of Personal Rights, or Status. He shews that Status in this sense includes or ought to include Rights as well as Capacities (see § 12, p. 476) and Duties

---

[23] Austin[5], 40. 688 (omitted in St. 348); Tables and Notes, ii. 3, C. *b*, p. 944.

[24] Holland[10], p. 136.   [25] ib. pp. 133, 137.

or Liabilities as well as Rights (see § 13, p. 501): but he evidently does not recognise any insuperable difficulty in distinguishing Rights, Duties and Capacities, as Personal, from Proprietary Law, as a general matter of Jurisprudence. His test of Proprietary Rights, by transferability, is very much the same as that applied in the definition hereafter attempted of Property[26].

[26] Salmond[2], § 82, pp. 209—213. On Property as Assets see below, § 16, p. 549.

§ 15. MODERN PERSONAL LAW

Re-arrangement of Blackstone by Stephen. In
looking at the English Corpus Juris, with a view to modern
Educational requirements, we must obviously take into
account not merely Blackstone's original scheme but the
re-arrangement, to a certain extent, of Blackstone's subject-
matter which has been found desirable—conspicuously in
the well-known and valuable work of Stephen.

It will be found that the lessons to be drawn from the
"Digest of English Civil Law," now on the point of
completion, are by no means disregarded here: but it
must be remembered that this Digest is not only limited
in *scope*, as compared with the comprehensive scheme of
the old Commentaries, but is advowedly and intentionally
modelled upon a recent foreign Code deviating to a considerable extent from the scheme of the Roman Institutes,
which scheme I take to have been, in the main, followed
by Blackstone, particularly in his Rights of Persons and
Things.

Public conditions better in Constitutional Law.
Returning, then, to this particular division of subject-
matter with a view, as has been said, to modern Educational
requirements, I think the first question is as to the proper
place and contents of what Austin calls the Law of Political
Conditions, and what has been spoken of above (§ 10, pp. 442,
447) as Constitutional Law in the wider or vaguer sense.
This, it has been assumed, might be advantageously omitted
from the "Rights of Persons" and studied by itself, whether
taken as Constitutional Law is, in our Cambridge Honour
Course, *before* the study of English Civil and Criminal Law,
and in connexion with Jurisprudence, or not.

Austin's objections.   The difficulty of distinguishing
Political Conditions, in general, from Private ones, in respect
of their author and purpose, which is objected by Austin[1],
appears to me, on his own shewing, very unreal.   With regard
to *authorship,* he does not seem to refer to any common origin
in the actual history of infant Law (in which reference it
may be sometimes difficult to make this distinction), but
rather to his general theory of *all* Law, legal rights and
legal duties, being the creation of the Sovereign or State.
As to confusion or coincidence of *purpose,* his reasoning
appears to be based upon philosophical assumptions as to
the ultimate objects of both kinds of rights and duties
being the same.   It does not appear to be so much this
modern reasoning as the varying language of the pre-
Justinian Jurists which led Thibaut to place *tutela* and
patria potestas in Public Law[2].   No practical difficulty of
the kind exists in modern Law, except perhaps in the single
case of Juristic Persons[3].

Particular case of Courts.   There is more to be said

---

[1] Austin[5], 44. 747, 748; St. 368.

[2] Austin[5], 44. 747, 748.   See above, § 10, p. 439.

[3] See § 11, p. 462, also below, p. 526.

for a separation of Courts and Officers of Justice generally, from other Political Conditions, on account of the natural connexion of the former with Procedure and of Procedure with Public and Private Wrongs. The arrangement of Blackstone in this respect (see § 10, p. 443) is retained by Stephen. I can only repeat what has been said above (l.c.) that there does not appear to be any real difficulty in separating the Courts themselves from their Procedure, so as to give a brief account of them under the head of Constitutional Law in the wider sense. This is done by Anson in the second volume of his Law and Custom of the Constitution (ch. 10), a work which forms a homogeneous body of English Public Law, in a rather more comprehensive sense than the term is used by Austin (see § 10, p. 442).

There is no particular difficulty in identifying the Political Conditions hitherto considered, to which the somewhat inaccurate name of Magistrates or Magistracy may be loosely applied (see § 13, p. 506), with real Persons.

Stephen's "Social Institutions." A more serious objection, than any yet noticed, against a classification of Rights, purporting to be *exhaustive*, as Rights of Persons and Rights of Things, is raised by Stephen; i.e. that such a classification fails to include what are termed the Social Institutions of the country, e.g. the laws relating to the Poor, to Highways, to Public Charities and the like. "For topics such as these the Analysis of Blackstone affords no proper place; and, when they are of too much importance to be neglected, expedients of an awkward kind are often devised to make room for them. Thus the Law of highways and turnpikes is made incidental to the office of parish surveyor, and the large and interesting subject of the poor law is dealt with by way of digression from the office of overseer[4]."

[4] Preface to the original edition of Stephen's New Commentaries on the Laws of England, p. xii.

This difficulty, however, can scarcely be regarded as insuperable, nor apparently was it so regarded by Austin[5]. It was got over to a considerable extent in the Index to Chitty's Blackstone by cross references, e.g. "Poor, see Overseer." Occasionally no doubt such subjects must for convenience have as their "heading" or title collective or abstract terms, which cannot be rendered by names of persons or even classes. For example, "the Social Economy of the Realm" forms Part 3 of Stephen's Book 4, which treats of Public Rights. This third Part—the first two being devoted to the Civil Government and the Church— begins with the laws relating to Corporations and passes through every conceivable case falling under the head of Social Economy, in which some portion of public authority is delegated to officials sole or corporate[6]. It is of course, possible, even in these cases, to look at the subject as identified with the administrative body; and accordingly the greater part of this matter *is* brought in under the head of Boards or Departments of Government in Anson's second Part, "The Crown[7]." In respect, however, of this particular branch of Public Law, I have found the arrangement of Anson's excellent work *less* clear and comprehensive than that of Stephen, on which last there are one or two further remarks to be made.

Corporations. Although it may seem rather a straining of the *style* Constitutional, the subject of Corporations does appear to belong more particularly to that main division of Law, as meaning the Law of Public Rights or Conditions

[5] Outline, p. 72.

[6] Put in the briefest terms, these are: Poor, Charities, Education, Asylums, Prisons, Highways, Navigation, Sanitation, Public Conveyances, Press, Public Houses, Professions, Banks, Registration of Births and Deaths.

[7] Local Government, e.g., comes under the general head The dominions and dependencies of the Crown, ch. 5.

and it has, as we see, been so classed in a practical Educational work on English Law. Notice is no doubt required *somewhere* on the gradual recognition of rights and duties, which seem at first sight peculiar to the individual, as applicable also to the juristic personality[8]; but this does not seem sufficient to draw the subject as a whole, if indeed at all, into Private Personal Law. Of a great and important part of the Personal Rights and Duties belonging to private individuals the *persona ficta* is obviously incapable[9]. Nor, on the other hand, can this subject be treated as belonging principally to the Property branch of Private Law. The original English conception of a Corporation is that of a Public or quasi-Public body. The extension of some of the features of Corporate Personality to private Commercial Enterprises is secondary and comparatively late[10]. Whether an original public character may also be predicated of the Roman Corporation is more difficult to determine. It would appear from a passage in Gaius' Commentary on the Twelve Tables that there were, at the time of that legislation, Unions or Fellowships (*Collegia, Sodalitates*)—perhaps very early Traders' Gilds[11]—whose internal arrangements were recognised as valid, provided they did not infringe on the " public law[12]." This does not however amount to what seems to be regarded by Gaius as the most distinctive feature of

---

[8] E.g. liability on trust reposed or for delict committed.

[9] See Savigny's contention that for Private Law the juristic person is *nichts als Vermögensfähige Subjecte*, System, ii. § 85, pp. 239, 240.

[10] See ch. 14 (On the Laws relating to Banks) of Stephen's Part 3 of Book 4 (of Public Rights). This chapter really belongs half to Public, half to Private, Property Law. As to the very recent amenability of Corporations to Criminal Law in England, see Kenny, Outlines, p. 62.

[11] See the legislation on this subject attributed to Numa, Plutarch, Numa, c. 17.

[12] Dig. 47. 22. 4. On the probable meaning of this expression, see above, § 5, p. 303. Compare, however, § 10, p. 438.

a *universitas*—that of having a common *actor* or *syndic*, through whom the common proceedings can be taken or other acts be performed, *as in a respublica*, i.e. a recognised municipal body; which special privilege, as an addition to common property and a common chest, requires public authorisation[13]. This is a quotation from Gaius' Commentary on the provincial Edict, included, with others from different Jurists, in the Digest Title on proceedings taken on account of or against a *universitas*[14]. On the whole, it would appear that the *universitates* specially intended by this Edict, or its probable original at Rome, were quasi-Public bodies, as requiring special recognition, distinct from the directly political *Municipium*, *Curia* or *Civitas*, but borrowing from it the special feature of a Corporation[15].

As my present object is merely to consider the proper *place* of Corporations in an Institutional system of Law, which place I consider to be, on the whole (see above, p. 525), *outside* Private Law, I must refer for further notice of Juristic Persons to §§ 37 and 38 of Sohm's Institutes, in which will be found, besides the Roman history of the developement of corporate unity, a good deal of reference to the modern discussion as to the *real* or *fictitious* character of these "legal Persons." That question is not, of course, meant to be begged here by the technical use of such terms as *persona ficta*[16], but is simply outside my present subject.

---

[13] Dig. 3. 4. 1, 2. Quibus autem permissum est corpus habere collegii societatis sive cuiusque alterius eorum nomine, proprium est ad exemplum rei publicae habere res communes, arcam communem et actorem sive syndicum, per quem tamquam in re publica, quod communiter agi fierique oporteat, agatur fiat.   See too on Legacies to a Collegium or Corpus, Paulus, Dig. 34. 5. 20.

[14] Quod cujuscunque universitatis nomine vel contra eam agatur.

[15] See Lenel, Edictum[2], § 34, pp. 99, 100.

[16] See P. and M. i. 469—495. Also an article by Sir Frederick Pollock in L. Q. R. xxvii. pp. 219—236, on the question whether our Common Law did really receive the fiction theory of Corporations.

Further, on the *place* of Juristic persons in some modern Codes, see below, pp. 533, 534.

Several of the subjects which come under Stephen's "Social Economy of the Realm" (above, p. 525), obviously include, or have correlating with them, important rights and duties attaching to the ordinary private citizen as distinguished from the official. It will suffice to instance the long-established system of poor relief and the comparatively recent one of compulsory education. These rights and duties, which are by way of being much increased since the simpler days of Blackstone, would seem now to require some express notice, as an addition to the subject of absolute rights (see § 13, pp. 501, 505). This, however, is only part of a more general question.

Absolute Rights and Duties. Returning to Stephen's re-arrangement of Blackstone's Rights of Persons, as a practical test of how the subject of Personal Law can be now most advantageously treated, we find a second important point to be noticed is the *bisection* of the Private part of that subject. In accordance with the suggestion of Hale above referred to (§ 13, p. 509) as to the advisable prior study of *Jura Rerum*, Stephen, transferring the last of Blackstone's Absolute Rights—the Right of Property—to a second Book, includes with it Property Law, and places the whole before the Rights in Private Relations of Master and Servant, Husband and Wife, Parent and Child, Guardian and Ward. The reason given, that it is in the nature of the Relative Rights to *presuppose* the Absolute ones of Life, Liberty, Personal Security and Property[17], will be considered below (p. 535).

Except as to this shifting and re-classing of the Right of Property, the Normal rights of the ordinary citizen are left to form, as they ought to form, the beginning of the

[17] Stephen's Preface, p. vii.

whole work. The part of Blackstone dealing with these
Normal rights might probably be re-written with advantage; regard being had to modern legislation, which has
undoubtedly added some, and infringed upon, or permitted
the infringement upon, others[18]. But the mere existence
of such an opening Chapter is a great improvement upon
the deficiency of this subject in the scheme of the Roman
Institutionalists.

There is more difficulty in the question whether we
should not require, in the Book on Personal Law, some
opening statement of **Absolute Duties**, to which phrase
two, if not three, different meanings have been attached.
What Blackstone calls by this name are *Moral* Duties,
which are not expected to be either explained or enforced
by any law of Human Society[19]. With Austin, Absolute
Duties are *legal* Duties, incumbent *upon* the individual
normal citizen, but only due *to* the Community at large.
This general conception may be taken, for the present,
practically to cover all the different sorts of Duty enumerated
by him in Lectures 17 and 18. The individual cases will
require, and receive, further consideration, with regard to
their respective objects and purposes, in the later section
on Particular Duties: at present we have principally, as in
Austin's Lectures 45 and 47, to do with their *place* in a
Corpus Juris.

On the whole Austin would apparently prefer to state
Absolute legal Duties partly under the Law of Political
Status, partly as a preface to Criminal Law. As a matter
of actual literary treatment, we do find their enunciation,

[18] Perhaps the circumscription of the Absolute right of Liberty, due
to the Trades' Disputes Act, should be rather called an abrogation or de-
rogation of the Duty to respect such Liberty (see below, p. 530). On the
subject generally see an article of Mr S. C. Basak, L. Q. R. xxvii. pp. 292,
306, 297, 415. Also Stimson' Popular Legislation, ch. 11.

[19] Comm. i. 1. pp. 123, 124.

if any, to occur mainly in statements of the Crimes or Public Offences which are constituted by their violation[20]. They are often created or imposed in no other than this implicit manner, by the Law declaring that such or such a punishment shall follow such or such an act[21]. This implicit enactment, however, is not confined to the case of Absolute Duties; Relative Rights as well as Duties being, as Austin points out, created, e.g. in the Praetor's Edict, by the sole expression of *remedies* provided against violation[22].

It certainly seems somewhat inconsistent to place the Absolute and Primary Rights of the citizen in the first part of the first main division of an Institutional work, but to relegate his Absolute Duties, which are equally Primary, to quite the end, as subsidiary or explanatory to the subject of Public Wrong.

Hitherto we have had very little direct statement of Absolute Duties in the Personal Law either of Codes or Institutionalists. Such maxims as *sic utere tuo ut non laedas alienum* (see § 17, p. 587), or the simpler *alterum non laedere,* occur occasionally in juristic literature, and express in a general way the universal duties correlating with normal or universal rights—such duties being, in fact, tacitly assumed in the statement of those rights[23]. These might not unreasonably be called, from their general and

[20] Austin[5], 47. 786.

[21] Austin[5], 45. 793, 794; St. 377, 378. "Act" of course includes forbearance or intentional omission; Absolute Duties belonging both to the negative and positive class, e.g. to abstain from drunkenness in public, as well as to pay rates and taxes.

[22] Austin[5], 45. 769.

[23] See § 14, p. 505; § 19, p. 616. Compare also Blackstone, i. 1. p. 123, with Stephen, On Personal Rights, vol. i. pp. 78—86. In several of the directions indicated in the present section Mr Jenks' revision varies from the original one of Stephen.

impersonal relativity, Absolute Duties: but they are *not*, I think, what Austin means by that phrase. *His* are Duties owed generally to the Community, but the violation of which does *not* interfere directly with any individual person's Private right[24]. Even these are nevertheless, in the view of some of our Institutionalists, *relative* duties; to some extent directly represented as such, under the old-world idea of allegiance due to the Sovereign[25]; but, for the most part, comprised implicitly under a general obligation to obey the laws and comply with the requirements of legally appointed public officers[26]. This is the private citizen's position with relation to the minor Public Authorities with whom he is brought more immediately in contact, referred to above (p. 528). There is an increasing number of subjects, besides Poor and Education, in which the tendency of modern legislation, more particularly perhaps in our own country (see § 4, pp. 171, 192), is to introduce new Absolute Duties, or turn previous matters of pure Custom, Etiquette or Philanthropy into legal obligations, in the life of the ordinary citizen. Some general statement of such additional Duties, as well as of any additional Absolute Rights conferred on the citizen, would seem to require, for the first chapter of Personal Law, a revised version of Stephen's Personal Rights, Book 1, taken together with the first chapter of Book 2, "as to Property in general"; Rights being understood to cover Rights and Duties (see § 13, p. 501), or that phrase being substituted for it.

With regard to the proposed contents of the chapter "as to Property in general," I shall have to speak a little further presently, in treating of the Right of Private Property[27].

---

[24] See on Particular Duties, § 21, p. 647.
[25] Blackstone, i. 10, pp. 367—369.
[26] See Hale, § 13, and generally, above, my § 13, p. 505.
[27] § 17. See also above, § 13, pp. 503, 504.

That right, with its correlative duties, being in fact little or nothing but a Capacity, may, it is assumed, be separated, as Hale does separate Capacity, from particular Interests in goods and estate[28], and placed, with other more obviously personal rights and duties, under the head of Personal Law.

Capacity alone cannot, as has been shewn[29], be considered adequately to describe a legal *status* or condition. In such a *status*, there may be and generally are direct rights and obligations besides: although, as in the above case of Property, the distinction between some rights and obligations themselves, and the Capacity for their enjoyment or incurrence, is not very easy to draw. The term was, as we have seen, confined by Sohm, at least in his account of Roman Private Law (above, § 12, p. 497) to *proprietary* Capacity: but it should certainly be extended to the case of rights and duties, and legal action, in general.

In this sense, Capacity forms a very important part of Personal Law, and that too in the very first branch, i.e. the Rights and Duties of the individual ordinary citizen. This Capacity is, in all civilised systems acquired or modified by circumstances or distinctions applicable to all—age, sex and intellectual faculty. Such modifications and distinctions, therefore, are scarcely to be described as *abnormal*: at any rate the conception of them does not exclude, but rather assume, the conception of ordinary legal capacity[30].

Foreign Codes. I may here cite, as instances of what has been adopted in modern times, for the natural beginning of a legal system, the French Code Civil, which has formed the model for so many others in Europe, and the more recent, and independent, *Bürgerliches Gesetz* of Germany. Neither, it is true, has any substantive description of the rights and duties of the ordinary citizen, which

[28] See above, § 13, p. 503.　　[29] See above, § 12, pp. 478, 479.
[30] See above, § 12, p. 480.

must probably remain, in general, rather matter of institutional literature than Codification. The French Code, however, begins with the *acquisition* of these, by birth or naturalisation, and their loss; the public record of birth, marriage, or death; the recognised legal residence (*domicile*) of the Citizen, and provisions for the case of his disappearance[31]. The German Code deals at once with general legal Capacity, or Incapacity, in point of age, mental condition or conduct, the rest of the sections on Persons Natural being mainly occupied with questions of residence, change of residence, declarations and presumptions of death or life[32]. Directly after this, there follows a detailed treatment of Juristic Persons, first belonging to Private, second to Public Law, preceded by a number of directions common to both[33].

Place of Corporations as fictitious Persons, &c. This position and treatment in the German Code may be perhaps connected with the modern tendency, particularly in Germany, to recognise, in Corporations, a *natural* Capacity of Willing and Dealings belonging to a *real Gesammtperson* or *être collectif* as distinguished from the earlier conception of *êtres intellectuels* or *imaginaires*, which is scarcely yet extinct in France. It is true that the French Code does not expressly recognise the existence of *personnes juridiques*; but that of *personnes civiles* does appear in later French legislation, and the existence of such Persons is held by some French Jurists to be implicitly recognised in the Code (see M. Levé cited in note 34). The subject is very fully discussed by M. Planiol, according to whom the subject of

---

[31] The first four Titles.

[32] Bürgerliches Gesetzbuch, the first Titel, §§ 1—20.

[33] The second Titel, §§ 21—100. For further remarks on the Introductory Part of the German Code, or the English Digest modelled on it, see the end of this section.

fictitious personality is not, in reality or in proper place, an addition to the class of Persons, but is a form of Property, being one mode of possessing goods in Common[34].

In a very interesting article on legal personality, being an inaugural Lecture by the new Vinerian Professor, Dr Geldart, at Oxford, an increasing belief is alleged of a *real* personality in Corporations—a personality not absolutely bound by the literal terms of an original Trusteeship, an original contract, or even of an original purpose. The recognition of an implied inherent power of developement might well, it is suggested, be held competent to himself by a *judge*, who believed in such a personality. Any such belief, however, or recognition, appears to me to assume a reference to considerations of public policy and interest which may justify my own view as to the *position* of Corporations in a Code or Educational Scheme, i.e. that they should come rather in the Law of Public Conditions than in either that of Private Persons or of Property. From his concluding remarks, upon Trades Unions, in the same article, I may perhaps infer that the same view would probably be held by Professor Geldart[35].

Relative Rights and Duties. In the view of Stephen, that the *Relative* Rights *presuppose* the *Absolute* ones of Life, Liberty, Personal Security and *Property* (above, p. 528), the last term is made to include the whole of Property Law. On slightly different grounds, Blondeau, we are told, with "many German expository writers," placed domestic conditions bodily in the "Law of things," immediately before the law of Succession, because the latter cannot be understood

---

[34] Planiol, Droit Civil[4], pp. 970—992, particularly note 1, p. 971. He remarks, by the way, besides the German legislation, that of Spain, as giving to *personas juridicas* a definite recognition, p. 973. This comes, as in the BGB, in Personal Law. See Levé, Code Civil Espagnol, p. 8.

[35] L. Q. R. xvii. pp. 90—108.

without adverting to them[36]. I cannot see that these
reasons adequately justify such a transposition in our own
case. The *generalia* as to Property, arising out of the
domestic relations, which are all that ought to be placed in
Personal Law, are extremely simple, amounting to little
more than certain modifications of Normal Capacity. The
application of these *generalia*, in detail, to Property Law
may, with perfect convenience, be left to that department,
in which, however, Succession is a complete and self-con-
tained subject.

But, in Germany, whether from a traditional connexion
of feudal personal relations with Land, or from adherence to
a national school of thought, the view of Blondeau and those
who agree with him, has been practically followed. In the
Code, Family Law is placed, together with Succession, *after*
the two Books on Property Law, being, I suppose, regarded as
unintelligible without previous treatment of that subject
in toto[37].

In the French Code Civil, on the other hand, after the
Titles on legal Residence and Disappearance (above, p. 533),
we have an account, much fuller than the Roman one, of
all the Personal relations and conditions of the Family,
including Guardianship, with what is practically *Cura* (*l'In-
terdiction*), Minority and Majority generally[38]. Then comes
the Law of Property, and its various modes of Acquisition,
the first of the latter being Succession, which it has here at
any rate been found possible to treat apart from the Personal
Law of the Family.

[36] Austin[5], 42. 721. He himself objects to the arrangement of Blondeau
on much the same ground as that suggested in the text.

[37] Book 2 contains the *Recht der Schuldverhältnisse*; 3, *Sachenrecht*;
4, *Familienrecht*; 5, *Erbrecht*. (On these subjects and their order I shall
have to speak hereafter.)

[38] Code Civil, L. i. Titt. 5—11. The effect of *Marriage* on Property comes
under Contract generally, in L. iii.

Status and Contract. In attributing the "Absolute Rights" of Blackstone to the "ordinary citizen," it was not considered necessary to refer to the old-world condition of Ranks or Orders in a Community, under which the personal Rights, Duties and Capacities of individuals might vary, not merely according to their own age, sex, &c., or their relation to another person, but accordingly as they belonged to this or that Rank. We have, in fact, *started*, in the present enquiry, with the comparatively "clearcut simplicity of the Roman Law" under the later Republic, or rather the middle Empire, as distinguished from that earlier system, once presumably universal, at least among our own Teutonic ancestors, of which the Anglo-Saxon *Rectitudines singularum personarum* preserve a record[39]. In respect of such archaic differences of Persons, it would be more correct to say that *status* has *disappeared* than that it has given place to contract. In the subsisting personal conditions, on the other hand, of a more definitely *relative* character, the dictum of Sir Henry Maine[40] has a considerable direct application. The old relation of owner or patron to slave or freedman, of lord to tenant or villein[41] may be considered as replaced by the contract of master and servant, although, under the special obligations somewhat onesidedly imposed by recent legislation, we might almost recognise a return to a statutory *status* of *employers* and *employees* generally.

The contractual arrangements, with regard to the *property* of intending *spouses*, have certainly in our own modern Law, followed, though *longo intervallo*, the Roman emancipation from the "good old rule" of *manus* and its English equivalent.

[39] See Schmid, Gesetze der Angelsachsen, pp. 370—376; Liebermann, pp. 444, 445, &c.; P. and M. i. 5; Maitland, Domesday Book and Beyond, p. 327.

[40] "The movement of the progressive societies has hitherto been a movement from Status to Contract," Ancient Law, ch. 5, p. 170.

[41] See Hale, §§ 19, 21, pp. 38, 39.

But there are still, and I think, always must be, certain Rights and Duties, capacities and incapacities, which can, according to the view here taken, be regarded as Personal, resulting from the conditions of Husband and Wife, Parent and Child, and, to a certain extent from that of Guardian and Ward. These together with the fundamental Rights, Duties and Capacities of the ordinary citizen, and with the Investitive or Divestitive Facts of the conditions concerned, constitute a considerable body of Personal Law, which does *not* concern only a comparatively narrow class[42], but of which it is important that everybody should know something, and which so many legal systems, both educational and statutory, have succeeded in detaching from their Property Law, and thought proper to be prefixed to it.

There does not appear to me to be much serious question of including any other class or condition in Private Personal Law, except perhaps in the case which forms the subject of the last paragraph of this section. I may, however, briefly refer to two classes which Austin is on the whole inclined to place in our first, or his supplementary, division.

Trades and Professions. The convenience of detachment, which Austin, it will be remembered (§ 14, p. 514), makes the principal or one of the principal conditions or advantages of *his status* (plural), is, I suppose, the reason why the law which relates to Traders "ought to enter into the Civil Code, under the Law of Persons[43]. In the present point of view, the Trader generally, or rather Trade, comes under the head of Contract in Property Law, but the particular applications of the principles of Contract in this case may, to a considerable extent, be conveniently brought together, and that is, of course, the ground or motive of the Commercial Codes, the separation of which from the

[42] See above, § 14, pp. 517, 518.

[43] Austin[5], 43. 740, note.

main body of the Law, though condemned by Austin, l.c., is, it must be presumed, found to be of real practical utility.

The privileges and duties of a *professional* man have, no doubt, a more truly *personal* character than the legal position of the Trader. With a view, however, to retain the *generally* applicable character (see above, p. 537) of our first Part, it might seem more convenient to couple these special privileges, &c., with the powers and duties of the various *licensing bodies*, to use the most general term; these last belonging obviously to the Law of Public Conditions.

The Chapter on the Laws relating to Professions, which is therefore very properly included by Stephen in his Social Economy of the Realm (above, p. 525), contains, or should contain, by implication, most part of the Personal Rights and Duties of the professional man. What more might with advantage be added—particularly in the item of Duties— could come perhaps only under the very general and vague heading with which I must conclude this section.

Trustees. In using this word, I must be understood as speaking rather to general questions of Jurisprudence than confining myself to the technical meaning of the term in any particular legal system. We have not, therefore, to do with the growth of Trusts in the English Law of Real Property[44]—or of English Equity in general; nor with the variable and debateable matters of fact which constitute the imposition or acceptance of a Trust. What we have rather to consider is whether there are certain rules of conduct— matter of Duty rather than of Right—definitely separable from any particular dealings with Property and peculiar to the position of Trustee: rules, therefore, which it might be desirable to state in connexion with, and distinction from,

[44] It was possibly rather with regard to the *cestui que trust's* so-called equitable *dominium* in land that Gierke's remark to the late Professor Maitland applies. Maitland's Equity, p. 23.

the Personal Rights and Duties of the ordinary citizen: seeing that this is a condition which he may, in the ordinary course of things, very naturally undertake. Or, to give the question a wider scope, beyond the direct acceptance of a trust *eo nomine*, might it not be possible to lay down some general principles of Personal Duty, in the department of Personal Law, which would apply to every case in which a fiduciary relation towards other persons is recognised or imposed by Law? In this view, I would quote the guarded language employed by a great writer on English Law; guarded, even when he is attempting to define a direct and positive Trust. "When a person has rights which he is bound to exercise upon behalf of another or for the accomplishment of some particular purpose, he is said to have these rights in trust for that other or for that purpose and he is called a trustee[45]."

When it comes to a general guide of conduct with regard to *property*, apart from the obvious adherence to the particular commission or authorisation, and the qualification of perfect disinterestedness, the Trustee's duty seems to be simply to play the part of a prudent owner or man of business[46]. The "diligence," however, required from him must be of an *absolute* character: i.e. measured rather by general external opinion than by his own practice otherwise. On the other hand a somewhat minor, or at least a different sort of, diligence and care for the interests of the other party may be required, where, as in certain cases, e.g. of *bailment*, the position of the bailee is rather said to partake of the nature of a Trust than to be a Trust proper: but such a relation would be more naturally attracted to and treated with the special proprietary transaction, in Property Law[47].

[45] Maitland, Equity, p. 44.   [46] Maitland, ib. p. 98.
[47] See Stephen, Book ii. "Rights of Property," ch. 5, "Title by contract," for the duties of innkeeper, carrier, &c.

There are also certain *negative* duties, e.g. of silence, or strictly limited communication, which partake of the fiduciary character, in cases of professional confidence: but these would appear to come rather under the special obligations of the professional man, which we have seen reason to place elsewhere than in Personal Law (see above, p. 538).

In this last case we are, indeed, quitting the domain of Private Law altogether for that of Public Conditions. And it is possibly in the light of a quasi-public character that the Trustee, simply as such, that is as regards his general Personal duties, would be best considered. See above, § 10, p. 437, for the quasi-public position of *Tutela*, which had certainly become something very like an English Trust, in the later Imperial Roman Law. The whole conception of the Title and Rubric *De excusationibus* (sc. *tutelarum*) proceeds upon the same idea[48]. Some of the considerations taken into account in the case of Corporations (above, p. 534) are also applicable to that of Trustee.

Conclusion. I have endeavoured to shew that the style and plan of Blackstone's First Book follow that of Gaius more truly than Austin's Law Special, and are, of course, more suited to the purposes of an Introduction than what Austin himself regards as properly matter of Appendix or Supplement. Whether, for the same purposes, some more complete modification or replacement of Blackstone's Rights of Persons than what are suggested by Stephen, is desirable, may now be very briefly considered.

The "Personal Law" sketched in the present section (which is, in several points, a return from Stephen to Blackstone) has been conceived mainly with the intention of presenting a general view of the Capacities, Rights and Duties inherent in the ordinary citizen, with the modifications which may be due to age, sex or the ordinary domestic

[48] See Dig. 27. 1. 3.

relations. Such a treatment of such a subject would appear to me to have considerable intrinsic utility besides serving as the introduction to a Code or Educational Course. But the latter object may of course be regarded as the more proper and predominant one. Under this aspect we find, for instance, in the new Digest of English Civil Law, modelled on the German Civil Code, the following subjects coming, in the Introductory Part, after Persons, Natural or Artificial: Things, Legal Acts (including Capacity), Time, Limitation of Actions and Self-help. These are, no doubt, treated in as general and elementary a manner as possible. Nevertheless, with the exception of Capacity, they would certainly seem to come better elsewhere—the first with Property Law, the rest with that of Remedies or Procedure.

§ 16. PERSONAE, RES, ACTIONES. RES

Res, Singular and Plural. According to the view here taken of the two members of the antithesis *Personae, Res*, the Personae are the individuals themselves considered with reference to their legal condition, the Res the Property belonging to them, also considered of course from a legal point of view. There is more general agreement among Jurists (Austin and his followers excepted) as to this second branch than as to the first. The various theories which have been held, as to the contents and scheme of the Institutional Book 1, have been considered above. As to Book 2, most people, I think, who look at the Roman Institutes themselves, apart from modern theory, will allow that the framers of the distinction under consideration meant by their second division what may be correctly described as Property Law.

Res, in Gaius' antithesis, is a plural, but in one of its earliest appearances as a legal term, or a Latin word at all— in the Twelve Tables—we find it used in the singular with a collective sense to indicate the whole of what a man leaves behind him at his death[1]. According to the more approved etymological signification of the word, it originally meant wealth or substance in general, and it apparently came down afterwards, though still very early, to signify the particular items which make up a man's wealth or property[2].

These items of Property would, of course, come to form the subjects of suits at law, and, in another passage of the Twelve Tables, the word *res* would appear to have attained the meaning of *suit* or *case*[3]. But there does not seem to me satisfactory ground for holding, as has been held by several good etymologers, that this was the *first* meaning of the word. On its use as signifying item of Property in the phrase *in rem*, see below, § 23. That the *res* of the Institutional division *are* the items which make up a person's Property is admitted in so many words by Sohm, and practically, though not so expressly, by Moyle, Goudsmit and

---

[1] Tab. V. l. 3; Gneist, xv.; Muirhead[2], App. p. 436. Here the dative or genitive *suae rei* covers, I believe, *all* the testator's belongings, the *familia* as well as the *pecunia* : see Schöll, pp. 13, 127.

[2] As to the derivation, *Res*, according to Benfey, is connected with RAI or RAS, meaning wealth, from Skt. RA, to give. This etymology is adopted, with some hesitation, by Skeat, s.v. Real. Brugmann, too, takes *Res* = Skt. RĀS, possession, treasure, property, i. 136; ii. 482. The derivation is rejected by Corssen[2], i. 478, 479, who takes a root indicating *recognition* or *consideration*, to furnish the origin and ground meaning not only of *Res* but of its alleged parallels, *thing* (English) and *Sache* (German) (A.S. *sac*), with their cognate verbs *reor*, *think* (*denken*, *Dinge*), and *say* (*sagen*). Corssen's view of *Res* might, *inter alia*, give some explanation of *reus* as the person under judicial consideration. But it is full of etymological difficulties (see *denken*, *Dinge*, and *Sache* in Kluge) and must be rejected in favour of *Res* = Wealth.

[3] Rem ubi pacunt orato, Tab. I. l. 6; Gneist, xii.; Muirhead[2], App. p. 434. For Corssen's derivation see n. 2.

other moderns[4]. A good many of the particular difficulties and objections raised by Austin in his 13th Lecture and elsewhere, on *Res* as opposed to *Personae*, may, I think, be obviated at once by adopting this view. Its adoption, however, does entail upon us some attempt to define what we understand under the term Property, in the "vague, vulgar and unscientific sense," coming seventh among the eight meanings of that word enumerated by Austin in his 47th Lecture[5].

Property, as the aggregate of a man's *res* or *means* is there well compared by him with the English "estate and effects," or preferably with "*assets*." How it is that the latter term comes to furnish the best expression for a man's Property, as an aggregate of Right separable from himself or his *person*, will be shewn directly by comparison with terms in Roman Law. These mostly belong to a comparatively late period, but it may be interesting to enquire what traces we have, in earlier names and formulae, of expressions for a man's property collectively.

Familia pecuniaque. The oldest of these appears to be that which is found in Gaius' form for the *testamentum per aes et libram* (2.104). The first word *familia* most probably meant *household*, in the sense of farm-land and agricultural stock proper, including, that is, slaves and beasts of draught or burden: the second, *pecunia*, covered grazing stock and other moveables. This phraseology belongs to a very early time, and is of great interest and value, with other words of the same date, in discussing the history of heritable and deviseable property. But it does not give us a common name for a property at large, which, however, it has been assumed above, had already been roughly developed in the time of the Twelve Tables under the vague term of wealth, *Res*.

---

[4] Sohm[2], § 58, p. 319; Moyle[4], p. 187; Goudsmit, Pandects, p. 89, &c.
[5] Austin[5], 47. 791; St. 385.

To pass to later expressions, **Bona** = *goods*, a word of almost hopeless derivation[6], has an established meaning clear enough—that of beneficiality or enjoyment.   This principle of beneficiality (*commodum*) covered all interests which entitled a man to exclusive possession of a material object, whether he was owner or not, and even the potential possession involved in a right of action to recover it.   Further—and this brings in rights *in personam*—*bona* includes any interest whatever for which a man has a present right of action, he being considered to have in his possession (*apud se*) what he can at once recover by procedure[7].   But neither a contingent interest, nor anything which can *now* be taken from a man's possession by eviction, is *in bonis*[8].   Under this phrase *in bonis*, coupled with *habere* and *esse*, the same idea of beneficiality appears very prominently in the various interests protected or created by the Praetor, e.g. where the interest in question is contrasted with the bare Quiritarian title, as of a *legitimus heres* against whom the Praetor has given possession to another, or of a person intending to convey a *res mancipi* who has only delivered, not mancipated, it.   In these cases, besides the legal ownership *ex jure Quiritium*, a practical one is predicated of the person who is said *in bonis habere*, though, to speak strictly, he has only a right to

[6] Quod beant, hoc est beatos facient, says Ulpian. *Duonus*, as the original form of *bonus*, seems to be established by the Scipios' monument (c. 250 B.C.).   Whether this can be traced to the *gu* or *gau* of *gaudeo*, &c. (see Curtius, § 122, p. 172), is doubtful.   The transition from *gu* (before a vowel = *gw*) to *b* direct would have been easier (Corssen[2], i. 88).   Brugmann takes *duonus*, with some hesitation, from a root *dau* = that which is held in honour or acknowledged (i. 150; ii. 150).   Pianigiani works back, through a Sanskrit root, to Ulpian's *beo*!

[7] See Modestinus, Dig. 41. 1. 52; Ulpian, Dig. 50. 16. 49, 143, and generally Karlowa, ii. 962, and Moyle[4], Int. to Just. Book 2, pp. 189, 190. The fullest enumeration of *bona* is that in the first cited passage of Ulpian, from a book (59 ad Edictum) which appears to deal specially with *bonorum emptio*.   See Lenel, Edictum[2], p. 397.

[8] Paulus, Dig. 41. 1. 42; Celsus, Dig. 50. 17. 190.

possess. This, however, being ripened into legal ownership by the short period of usucapion, the subsisting *nudum jus* of the other party is not taken much account of by the classical Jurists[9], though it was not until Justinian's time that it was expressly merged in the *dominium bonitarium*, as it is sometimes called from the δεσπότης βονιτάριος of Theophilus[10].

Facultates is a less common expression for much the same idea as that of *bona*. The word, of course, means literally *powers*, and is exactly translated by the German *Vermögen*, except that the Latin plural would seem rather to express the individual items and the German singular the aggregate[11]. This word, on its German rendering, appears to have suggested Savigny's somewhat fanciful definition of Property Law or Right (*Vermögensrecht*) as consisting of the relations which extend the power of the Person entitled, beyond the natural limits of his being. This idea, of an extension of the individual's power over the external world, is rather cursorily noted in Sohm and, I believe, in Karlowa. Savigny treats as *secondary* the idea of *beneficiality* (or conversely *well-being*), which I think most people would regard as *principal*, in the conception of Property[12].

Of such scientific or quasi-scientific attempts to define what is meant by Property as an aggregate, or Property as a general right, we find little trace in the practical law either of ancient times or modern. A popular antecedent

[9] Cf. Ga. 2. 40, 41, with 3. 166 and 1. 54.

[10] Cod. 7. 25. The phrase of Theophilus comes in his long paraphrase, and extension, of Just. 1. 5.

[11] The meaning and immediate derivation of *facultas* are so obvious that it is unnecessary to go into difficulties about *facio* (e.g. in Corssen, Beit. 45). *Ver*, in *Vermögen*, has the *intensive*, which is quite as well established as the *destructive*, meaning of that particle.

[12] Savigny, System, i. § 53, pp. 339, 340; see the note *b*; Sohm[2], p. 163. I cannot now retrace the passage, which I perfectly well remember, in indexless Karlowa.

of *bona* comes to us from early days in the supposed meaning of such ancient formulae as that of the *testamentum per aes et libram* (above, p. 544): in later law we come nearer to a general term in Ulpian's enumeration (above, n. 7), made apparently with reference to what we shall find to be the most distinctive case of a person's Property *en bloc* being transferred and separated from that person's self.

The cases enumerated by Gaius of acquisition or transfer of a Property, *per universitatem* (see below, p. 564), as distinguished from acquisition or transfer in individual items (*per singulas res*) are four: succession according to the old customary or the early statutory law (*hereditas*): succession granted by the Praetor (*bonorum possessio*): purchase of insolvent's goods (*bonorum emptio*): and *arrogation* i.e. adoption of a male not in power, or taking of a wife *in manum*[13].

Bona as descendible, hereditas, patrimonium. One suggested definition of Property as an aggregate is "whatever descends to a person's general representative at his own decease." This is, I think, what is generally meant by the English "estate and effects" (see above, p. 544): the words, if separately assignable, being roughly intended to correspond respectively with the landed property and the non-landed, which used to go, in our law and legal phraseology, to the *real* and *personal* representatives respectively, of the deceased.

Descendibility is what is indicated in the expressions *hereditas*, as an aggregate (see below, p. 565), and *bonorum possessio*: *bonorum possessio* being merely an equitable or Praetorian succession over-riding or supplementing the civil or, as we may say, the Common Law one.

According to some this descendibility is what is indicated by the Latin word *patrimonium* which is in a good

---

[13] When considering these acts in law for our present purpose, we may omit the last, in which the person and the Property pass together.

many passages simply equivalent to a man's property as an aggregate. In others, however, it sometimes means property in possession as distinguished from debts due to one; in others, absolute ownership; in others, private or individual human ownership generally[14]. In the first use above-mentioned the idea was evidently that of the total belongings of a living *pater familias*, which use is an argument against the erroneous view sometimes maintained of a joint ownership with, or a trusteeship of, the *pater* during his life.

To return, however, to *bona* as equivalent to *universum jus* of the deceased:—the idea of beneficiality might *prima facie* seem to exclude *liabilities* from the descendible *bona*. But it was a well-established principle, whether due to an old doctrine that the deceased's personality was continued in his successors, or to general principles of equity in the Praetorian Law, on which *bonorum possessio* depends, that the disadvantages of the inheritance must be taken with the advantages, the debts as well as the credits. The totality of a man's *hereditas* might be zero, or even a minus quantity, the last being called *damnosa*[15]. Karlowa (l. c.) alleges that the term *facultates* is said of the *active* rights, to the exclusion of the *passive* liabilities: but I doubt whether this limited meaning can always be maintained. With the particulars of action to be brought, as a matter of procedure, by or against the *bonorum possessor*, through the *fictio* or legal assumption that he *is* the *heres* of the deceased person, I have not here to do[16].

[14] E.g. Dig. 46. 6. 9; 10. 2. 10, and Ga. 2. 1, compared with the next two sections, and with § 9 as restored from Dig. 18. 1. pr.

[15] On this result of the Property being "treated as an abstract" see Savigny, System, i. § 56, pp. 375, 376; Karlowa, ii. 963, and ll.cc. especially Ulpian, Dig. 37. 1. 3. pr.   Also Austin[5], 42. 710; St. 359, and above, § 12, p. 483.

[16] See Ga. 4. 35.   For the suggested *form* of the action, Lenel, Edictum[2], p. 178.

Bona as Assets. Besides interests, however, which can descend or pass by succession, it would seem reasonable that the aggregate, a man's Property, should also cover such as are only good for his life but can during his lifetime be alienated by or transferred from him. In the case of the Roman *ususfructus*, this life-interest cannot, it is true, be transferred so as to put the transferee exactly in the place of the usufructuary, but its enjoyment *can* be sold or let[17]. If this could be done voluntarily by the usufructuary for his own benefit, it would be unreasonable that it should not be done compulsorily for the benefit of creditors, on the sale of a bankrupt's goods[18]. At any rate such interests do not appear anywhere to be mentioned as exceptions from the general effect of the *bonorum venditio* which followed on what we may roughly call an act of bankruptcy. Possibly the introduction of the *actio Rutiliana* for recovery of sums due to the bankrupt, by the *emptor bonorum*, as an improvement on the old *fictio* in which the same emptor was treated as the bankrupt's *heres*, may indicate that *hereditas* had been found an incomplete specification of a property as compared with Assets[19]. But this change may have been due to the obvious justice of exchanging the total liability of a *heres*, to the respective creditors, for a liability only to a certain dividend[20], on the part of the *emptor*.

There were, yet, in Roman Law, certain interests, literally external, but yet so personal, or at least so strictly confined

[17] See for the strict law Ga. 2. 30. The passages relating to transfer of enjoyment are collected by Roby on Dig. 7. 1. 12. 2, p. 83.

[18] Possibly done by a sale *nummo uno*, as of a *hereditas fideicommissaria* in Ga. 2. 252, or by a *cautio passurum se uti frui*, Marcellus, Dig. 24. 3. 57. The *fact*, as to *ususfructus*, is stated by Ulpian, Dig. 4. 2. 5. 8. Even a bare *usus*, which could not ordinarily be leased or sold, might (*semble*) be thus made available for creditors. See Paulus, Dig. 10. 3. 10. 1.

[19] See Gaius, 4. 35.

[20] "Jusqu'à concurrence du dividende convenu," Girard[5], 1048, n. 3. See too Lenel, Edictum[2], § 218, p. 412.

to the *family* of the deceased, as to be untransferable to outsiders (*extranei*) as *heredes*, and *a fortiori*, it must be presumed, to creditors—e.g. the services of duty or respect, as distinguished from mechanical labour, owed by a *libertus*[21]. Leaving, however, out of the question these interests, which *might* no doubt be vaguely called *bona*, I think that the English "Assets"—what is applicable to the discharge of a man's obligations on bankruptcy—will fairly cover every conceivable item of his Property: and this is perhaps the best account of the aggregate described by that word in what Austin calls the wide and vague sense; though it may seem rather too special a case to bring so prominently into a general definition.

Divisions of individual Res, per se. It has been already suggested (above, p. 544) that a fundamental conception of individual *Res*, whether called Things or not, as Items of Property, will obviate some of the difficulties raised by Austin on the nomenclature of this division of Roman Law. But, as there are other difficulties, mainly of scheme or arrangement, which are not due to Austin's peculiar views, but descend directly from the Roman Institutionalists and their modern followers, I have found it necessary to speak here, at some length, upon the subjects collected together in Lecture 13 of the Student's Austin, on Things and their relation to Rights, following however, as far as possible, the treatment of Gaius and Justinian. The "Lecture" referred to really consists partly of Austin's Lecture 13 on Person and Thing and partly of his Lecture 46, which goes most conveniently with the former, on certain distinctions among Things. It is a motley *cento*, coupling together some main divisions, which have actually been or at least proposed as such, with other quite subordinate distinctions of mode or

---

[21] See Ga. iii. 82 ; Ulpian, Dig. 38. 1. 29 ; and Lenel, Edictum[2], p. 417.

form, and adding or premising certain philosophical definitions
of very questionable utility.

We may begin with distinctions which purport to constitute divisions among Things *themselves*, and therefore post-
pone the first of Gaius' dichotomies (see § 10, pp. 436, 437),
into Things which are or are not matter of Private Property,
to a section where that subject will be specially treated, as
it is by Austin, in a separate Lecture (52).

The next principal division of Gaius, the postponement of
which by Justinian will be explained below (pp. 568, 569),
is the widely recognised one of **Res Corporales and Incorporales.** The former are defined as perceptible by the senses,
par excellence by that of touch[22]: the latter are not so perceptible, being such as " consist in a Right," as for instance
Inheritance, Usufruct, Obligations however contracted. "Nor
does it matter that in an inheritance things corporeal are
comprised, for the fruits too which are gathered from an
estate are corporeal, and that which is due to us on account
of some obligation is generally corporeal, as an estate, a slave,
money; because the right itself of succeeding, the right itself of
using and enjoying, the right itself belonging to the obligation is incorporeal. In the same class are the rights belonging
to landed estates in city or country, which are also called
servitudes[23]." In this passage, which I have translated rather
in full, because it seems to be sometimes misunderstood, it

---

[22] Ga. ii. 12, 13, supplemented from Dig. 1. 8. 1. 1. Theophilus, on
the parallel passage in Justinian (2. 2. 1.) adds *sight*, " ὃ ἀφῇ καὶ θέᾳ
ὑποπίπτει," possibly following, and misunderstanding, the *cerni* of Cicero,
Top. 5. 27. That all sensations are modifications of the sense of touch
is not such absolute " jargon " as Austin makes it out, 13. 361; St. 168.
See also 40. 685.

[23] Ga. 2. 14; Just. 2. 2. 2.   The words *jure*, or *in jure, consistunt*
(Theophilus, ἐν δικαίῳ συνίσταται), are translated in Poste, " have an
existence simply in law." I think the sequel justifies the translation given
in the text, which is practically that of Moyle, Abdy and Walker.

will be observed that there is a confusion between *heredi-tas* meaning an aggregate of things, descending from the ancestor, and *hereditas* meaning the right to succeed to that aggregate, the word being first used in the former and secondly in the latter sense.

This time-honoured distinction, as used for the purposes of Law or Jurisprudence, must be admitted, on examination, to be an illogical comparison of disparate objects. It is not correctly described merely as a division into Things and Rights. If reduced to a common denomination, it amounts to setting Rights of complete ownership in material objects against all the other Rights which make up a man's Property. It is obvious and natural that the former class of Rights should be identified with the material objects themselves; and these would, no doubt, be, in the remote days of nascent Law, the only items of such Property. But, as Law and legal Rights begin to develope themselves, Property neces-sarily comes to consist, in an increasing proportion, partly of lesser Rights in or over material objects, of which some other person is the more nearly complete owner, and which may be classed, together with his, as Proprietary Rights or more exactly Rights of Ownership; partly of payments or performances due *from* others, under a legal obligation, which are conveniently, though again somewhat inaccurately, styled Obligatory Rights. The fundamental distinction here indi-cated has been stated by modern Jurists as an actual division of the Roman *Jus Rerum* into *Dominia* and *Obligationes* (see below, § 24).

From the multiplication of Rights other than complete ownership of material objects, and their frequent compli-cation with these, it naturally results that the apparently fundamental distinction of *res* as Corporeal and Incorporeal does not come to much account in the Roman Institutes. In the *actio in rem*, for instance, *res* most probably did at first mean a material item of property, such as a slave or a farm, held in complete ownership. But, as the phrase and the action were, it is evident, early extended to apply to rights in or over material objects belonging to another person, such as a Usufruct or a Servitude over a farm, the scope of *actio in rem* does not coincide with *res corporales* as against *res incorporales*, many of which (being *dominia*) will be coupled together with Corporeal Things by this common remedy[24].

The distinction of *res corporales* and *incorporales* as a division of items of property, is, in Gaius, almost immediately followed and combined with a different classification according to modes of alienation or acquisition (see below, p. 566). In the English Institutes it is from the first subordinated to other divisions (Real and Personal, Hereditaments and Tenements), which are so definitely matter of particular national history and practice that they can with difficulty be brought under principles applicable to Jurisprudence generally. What is to be said here on the subject will be found below under the head of Realty.

Austin's Things strictly so called. Before proceeding to the distinction of *res* as *mobiles* or *immobiles*, which is naturally connected with the subject just referred to, I must give some notice here to a *definition* of Austin's, if only for its connexion with inaccurate and paradoxical statements as to Roman Law. This definition certainly borders much on the "Metaphysic," from which its author professes to abstain. "A Thing," he says, "strictly so called, is a *permanent* external and sensible object *not a person*." The purpose of the first qualification added to the Roman definition of *res corporalis*, is to exclude from the list, of Things proper or

---

[24] See the parallel drawn by Maitland with the *Thinglike*, or rather Landlike, Incorporeal Things of Blackstone (below, n. 39) and *their* recovery by *real action*, P. and M. ii. 123, 124, 130, 146, and generally the whole article, ch. 4, § 6.

strictly so called, Facts, Events, or Incidents, *some* of which are also external and sensible but are *transient*. Among the latter are Human Acts and Forbearances. These—the only Facts with which Austin is here concerned—are alleged by him to be included by "the Roman lawyers," besides Things "strictly so called," and Persons treated as Things, among *res corporales*. His reasoning depends upon the peculiar meaning given, by him, to Subject (i.e. subject *matter*) and Object with reference to Rights (see above, § 12, pp. 482, 483). It appears to be as follows: Human Acts and Forbearances as being the *object* of Rights and Duties are to be distinguished from the Rights and Duties themselves. But the *res incorporales* of the Roman lawyers consisted of Rights. The *objects* of these Rights and Duties, therefore, must be included in the other branch, together with the Things "strictly so called," which are their subject-matter. The strange paradox above stated, seems to cast some doubt upon the wisdom, if not the truth, of this sharp line drawn between Rights and their objects[25]. The limitation, again, of a Thing "strictly so called" as *not a person* introduces an unnecessary subdivision into the Roman *res corporales*. The Slave, who is no doubt a Person, as has been shewn above (§ 11, p. 547), is also a *res corporalis*—a material object which may be in complete ownership —in just the same sense as any other. Indeed Austin himself in treating of *jus in rem*, admits generally that whoever is the "subject" of a right which resides in another person, and which avails or obtains against a third person or persons, is placed in a position analogous to that of a Thing, and might be styled, in respect of that analogy a Thing[26]. The

[25] This seems to be the explanation of the statement in Austin[5], 13. 361. See also 16. 393. In the former passage the words "or objects," line 10, should, I think, be deleted.

[26] Austin[5], 15. 385—387; St. 187, 188. See also the expression *Recht auf eine Person als auf eine Sache*, quoted from some German Jurist in T. and N. 940, which is perfectly intelligible. This is *not* the case with

partial application of the term Thing to human beings, i.e.
to the Slave and not to the *filius familias in potestate*, imputed by Austin to the Roman Jurists, is *not* matter of
caprice.   The passages where the word is thus used generally speak of slaves, but there are a few references to legal
remedies, fast dying out, which point to that harsher time
when the son was still a chattel.   Probably in the time of
Gaius, and more probably in that of Ulpian, the son *had*
quite ceased to be regarded as a *res*.   Still, the quotation
from the latter author by Austin is by no means so conclusive as he represents it, for Ulpian does in point of fact
go on implicitly to agree with Pomponius that a father can
still bring the *vindicatio*, or real action, for his son by express
reference to the old Law[27].

Res mobiles or immobiles (res soli).   A distinction of
res even more natural or obvious than that into Corporeal
and Incorporeal may be mentioned here, though it is not
employed as a division of Property by the Roman Jurists.
Where they do use the distinction *moveable* and *immoveable*,
they mean by the latter *land* (*solum*) or what is literally
attached to and goes with land[28].   This principle of attach-
ment is much developed and extended in modern systems,
mainly in those based on Roman Law, so that in the case for
instance of *biens immeubles*, under the French Code Civil,

various other phrases, e.g. *dinglich-persönliches Recht, jus realiter personale*,
&c., quoted by Austin as meaning the same thing, which it is by no means
clear that they do.

[27] Austin[5], 15. 388; St. 189, quoting Ulpian, Dig. 6. 1. 1. 2.   See also
Ulpian, Dig. 47. 2. 14. 13, and Paulus, Dig. 47. 2. 38. 1, as to *actio furti* for
son, or other free person, stolen.

[28] Uncut crops, houses or other permanent erections, and their fixed
appurtenances, &c., see, *inter alia*, Dig. 41. 1. 60; 6. 1. 44; 19. 1. 15,
17. pr., 17. 7; 50. 16. 242. 2.   As to *mobiles*, note, by the way, that the
puzzling *moventia* in a *passive* sense, which gives rise to the question in
Celsus, Dig. 50. 16. 93, may be explained by Ulpian's *res mobiles aut se
moventes* opposed to *res soli*, Dig. 50. 16. 93.

which are said to be such by *destination* (as distinguished from *nature*), the phrase almost amounts to a technical term, the contents of which could not have been guessed by the ordinary lay mind[29].

Austin, in treating of this distinction, speaks of things physically moveable but immoveable by institution, e.g. an heirloom[30]. The particular thing instanced is not very happy in its selection; Blackstone expressly designating it as a *mere moveable* though *inheritable*. This last point is, of course, a reference to feudal tenure: as a matter of fact, the heirloom is possibly rather a creature of old Customary Non-Feudal than of Feudal Law[31].

The English Realty. This conception appears to be truly based, in the first instance, upon a physical distinction of things *per se*, but it is also extended, at the outset of Blackstone's definition, so as to take in a quite different idea, of feudal relation. Things real, he says, are such as are permanent, fixed and immoveable, which cannot be carried out of their place; as lands *and tenements*. Things Personal are goods, money and all other moveables, which may attend the owner's person wherever he thinks proper to go[32]. The latter part of this definition may possibly account for the

[29] Code Civil, 2. 1, §§ 517—526. Practical consequences of the difference may be found at § 2118.

[30] Austin[5], 46. 778; St. 14. 169.
The distinction of moveable and immoveable does not occur in Hale's Analysis. It is used in the French Code, the latter class signifying primarily land and buildings, but both classes being extended beyond their natural meaning by "distinction" or "object." (See Code Civil, L. ii. Tit. 1, chs. 1, 2. For the comparatively slight notice of this distinction in BGB., see § 90 of the Code, with Neumann's Notes, Handausgabe[2], i. p. 37. See, however, Scherer, i. p. 104.)

[31] Blackstone, ii. 2, pp. 16, 17. For the Customary character of the heirloom see Elton's Origins[2], pp. 198, 199. The French *préciput*, by the way, which Elton compares, is clearly connected with the Roman *legatum per praeceptionem* (Ga. 2. 216, and see Code Civil, § 919).

[32] Blackstone, ii. 2, p. 16. Hale gives no definition.

original use of the term *personal*, but is out of the question for any later conception of Personal Property: which I propose for the present to regard merely by negation, as all that is not Real. The Reality of *Land* is explained by good modern authorities to lie in the fact that it can always, in the nature of things, be recovered or restored *in specie*[33]. This invariable possibility of recovering the *real thing* depends, of course, upon the physical *indestructibility* of land, which is, according to the above explanation, the true essence of its *reality*, though it was not, I think, what was understood by Blackstone's *permanence* (see the application of that term to *tenement* and below, n. 34). In other substantial or material Property besides land, recovery *in specie* might be attempted to be ensured, either by magisterial intervention, which was probably the case in the earliest, as it undoubtedly was in the latest, times of Roman Civil Law, or by the alternative of the defendant's having to pay a very highly estimated value, in the intermediate period: but it might, in spite of all authority or penal valuation, have been rendered impossible, by destruction.

The inclusion, however, by Blackstone, of *tenements*, and, shortly after, *hereditaments*, under Things Real, renders it necessary to supplement the above natural or physical distinction by one based upon Feudal Custom. *Tenement* comprises *anything*, substantial or not, which may be *holden* by one man of another, provided it be of a permanent[34] nature;

[33] See Joshua Williams' Real Property[21], ch. 1, p. 230; Littleton, in Co. Litt. 284 b, § 492, is to a like effect—" Action of wast is in the realty, because the place wasted shall be recovered"; see Coke's note. It may, however, be questioned à *propos* of the word *shall*, in this last note, whether the non-restitution of moveables was so much the result of possible destruction or of an option allowed to the defendant, in their case, from the first, by an English Court, see below, § 23, p. 725.

[34] What Blackstone exactly meant by this *permanence* has been disputed and the propriety of employing the expression in this definition questioned, see Preston, Estates, i. p. 10. Blackstone, ii. 24, p. 384, is in favour of

e.g. not only land but rents, offices, advowsons, rights of common, &c. And *Hereditament* may cover anything which will descend to the person feudally determined as *heir*, e.g. the heirloom above mentioned, or a condition the benefit of which descends to a man from his *ancestor*.

In accordance with this extended and technical conception of Things Real (or Hereditaments as they are preferably termed by Blackstone) they have to be subdivided by the English Institutionalists into Corporeal and Incorporeal; the phrase being borrowed from Gaius or Justinian, and used in the same illogical manner (above, p. 552) and with less excuse; for absolute ownership of land, which might, by a natural freedom of expression, be identified with the land itself, is not competent, in our legal theory, to an ordinary citizen or *subject*: he can only hold an estate or interest in it, and *all* such are, strictly, Incorporeal[35]. The above identification *is*, however, practically made both by Hale and Blackstone, of certain estates in land: the other branch of Things Real they assort on varying and arbitrary grounds, though the interests comprised come to be much the same. With Hale, Things Real Corporeal appear to be different kinds of landed Property *in possession*, with certain incidents and appurtenances. Then comes an intermediate class of Things "not in their own nature incorporeal" such as reversions, remainders, and "the estate of land," whatever that may mean. Finally, Things "which *are* in their own nature incorporeal" such as Rents, Services, Advowsons, Tithes, &c.[36].

---

indestructibility, but see above. According to a modern suggestion *permanent* is "as compared with the life of man," Joshua Williams, R. P.[21] p. 11.

[35] See Austin[5], 40. 686; St. 13. 168.

[36] Hale, Analysis, § 24. He strangely calls Corporeal Things Real *Manurable*, explained by Runnington "capable of cultivation," which *would*, apparently, be the etymological meaning of the word (Skeat, s.v. Manure). Hale's third class, coinciding with Blackstone's "Incorporeal

Blackstone's Corporeal Hereditaments "may all be comprised under the general denomination of land." His Incorporeal are rights which are described as a sort of *accidents* inhering in and supported by the Corporeal *substance*: to which language "of the logicians" he adds the distinction pointed out by Justinian (after Gaius) between the profits produced and the rights which produce them (above, p. 551). The actual Hereditaments so called are specifically stated as "principally of ten sorts, Advowsons, Tithes, Commons, Ways, Offices, Dignities, Franchises, Corodies or Pensions, Annuities and Rents[37].

In the majority of these cases of Incorporeal Realty the Things in question can clearly be regarded as rights and profits annexed to or issuing out of Land, and would be without difficulty treated as such from the point of view of General Jurisprudence. They are very properly so styled in Mr Jenks' Law of Property[38]. Where this can *not* be predicated of them, their position in English legal systems is accountable for, on historical grounds, by their close similarity, in mode of creation, conditions of enjoyment, or forms of remedy on dispossession, to rights which are so annexed[39].

Hereditaments," are generally now described as *purely* Incorporeal Hereditaments which, "unlike a reversion remainder or executory interest, *never* assume a Corporeal form," Joshua Williams, R. P.[21] p. 421.

[37] Blackstone, ii. 2, 3, pp. 17, 20, 21.

[38] Digest of English Civil Law. See below, p. 561.

[39] In P. and M. ii. ch. 4, § 6, the close analogy of rents, offices, advowsons, and such like Incorporeal rights generally, to *land*, is well shown with reference to proprietary and possessory remedies (see particularly pp. 134, 135, 146, 147).

Peers' Titles, which are now always (except in the case of Lords of Appeal and Bishops) conferred so as to give an *hereditary* Honour, were once annexed to some place, though this has long ceased to be the case. See Co. Litt. 20[a], n. 3, and Stephen[14], vol. ii. pp. 581—584. This undoubted Incorporeal Hereditament cannot, from its inalienability, be considered a species of Property. It is best placed, as by Stephen (Bk. iv. pt. i. ch. 9), among Public Rights.

There is a special difficulty in English Law; viz. how a *term of years* has come *not* to be Realty, into which I cannot here enter, further than to say that this arbitrary distinction is traced with much probability by Maitland to a comparison of the English term with the Roman Usufruct, and the acceptance of a dictum of Paulus that Usufruct is no part of Dominium; the fact being that Usufruct, whether part of Dominium or not, was certainly a subject of the proprietary *actio in rem*[40].

Except so far as taking the distinction of English Realty to be based originally and fundamentally on Land, I have no intention of attempting a definition or pursuing the subject further. Austin, in a note to his Outline (i. p. 57) suggests as the nearest generic description of the two kinds of Property in England, that Real Rights (as meaning Real Property), when transmissible to representatives, devolve *ab intestato* to *heirs*, Personal to *administrators* or *next of kin*. But a correct definition, he adds, would involve a complete description of the several or various rights which belong to the two classes respectively. The above "generic" difference is, no doubt, the main practical reason, as distinct from avowed history, for retaining our very artificial English distinction of Property rights or interests. Even this difference, however, has for certain purposes been abolished by recent legislation (see the Land Transfer Act 1897), and the tendency of our time seems to be to break down the Feudal barrier between Realty and Personalty and to assimilate the estates interests and modes of acquisition between

---

[40] See P. and M. ii. 36, 114—116; also i. 215. Whether *ususfructus* was *pars dominii* or not is discussed at length by Roby, on Dig. 7. 1. 4, where Paulus takes a somewhat different view from that expressed by him in the passage Dig. 50. 16. 25. pr., cited by, or rather referred to, in Bracton, 220[b]. This last passage certainly appears to recognise *seisin* of the *termor* as a possible suggestion. See, however, id. 167[b], where *possession* is denied to both termor and fructuary.

the two. As a matter of legal education, even in the earlier
days when Austin taught, the seven Lectures following that
on Distinctions between Things contain *inter alia* an attempt
to reduce some of our English estates and interests (mainly
in Land), by comparison with the Roman Institutes and
other systems of Law, into generally applicable terms of
Jurisprudence. A practical contribution to this result must
be recognised in the recent Digest of English Civil Law
(above, p. 559), reference being particularly made to Mr
Jenks' partial re-arrangement of English Property Law
"strictly so called," i.e. exclusive of Obligations, in comparison with the *Sachenrecht* of the new German Civil
Code. In styling this re-arrangement *partial*, I mean that
the English division of Landed from other Property is still
retained, as a matter of fact and practice, whereas in Austin's
scientific or theoretical Classification of "primary rights *in
rem* as existing simply" (Lectures 47—53), it is ignored and
the English estates are merely treated as a model or instance.
To the latter subject I may return hereafter, but shall ab-
breviate Austin as much as possible, these being not main
divisions of the whole body of Law but only subdivisions
of a part, and much complicated, even in Austin's treatment,
with matter purely of English Law.

English Personalty was left above as a mere residuum
= Not Realty. Some remarks however may be made here
which have a little bearing, not exclusively on the difficulties
of our Feudal survivals, but on matter of general Jurisprudence.

It is not necessary, from this point of view, to go into
the origin of the word *chattel* generally, or to trace the
process by which the chattel *real*, now confined to a term
of years in land, came to descend to the executor rather than
to the heir[41]. Although this form of property is assimilated

[41] See P. and M. ii. 116, 149, 329, &c.

to other chattels, as regards liability for debts, and succession, by our Law, it is certainly most conveniently treated, for purposes of general consideration, as an interest in Land, and is taken together with Real Property not only in Stephen's general edition of Blackstone's Commentaries but in separate modern works on this special branch[42].

With regard to Chattels Personal, we seem, at first sight, to have the illogical distinction of Corporeal and Incorporeal Realty merely repeated in other words, under the name of Choses in Possession and Choses in Action[43]. But, apart from this somewhat academical objection, it must not be overlooked that the latter expression, as designating the *residuum* of Personalty, is rather misleading. Choses in *Action* are not, as it might seem, simply identical with Obligatory Rights (see above, p. 552).

"Debts and Contractual Obligations" enter, no doubt, principally into this branch of English Personal Property: but there are frequently other important items, classed under the same head, which must be placed distinctly among Rights of Ownership, or *Dominia*[44]. This will be more

[42] Stephen, Bk. ii. pt. i. ch. 5; Joshua Williams, Of Personal Interests in Real Estate, R. P. pt. iv.

[43] Austin[5], 46. 776.

[44] See above, § 16, p. 552. On Choses in Action there is a good note in Anson's Law of Contract[13], p. 274, n. 1. Neither Hale nor Blackstone's definition is satisfactory for modern times (see Hale, Analysis, §§ 22, 23; Blackstone, ii. 25, pp. 389, 397). In particular, Blackstone's position "that all property *in action* depends entirely upon *contract*, express or implied," has been long challenged, in earlier editions of Stephen, and the term extended to *damages* for a *wrong*. The last editor also includes under Choses in Action "Incorporeal things which have only a *notional existence*, such as debts, stocks, shares, debentures, patent and trade mark rights." Stephen[14], Bk. ii. pt. ii. ch. 1, p. 8. Most of these might perhaps be fairly interpreted as *jura in personam*; but patent, trade mark and copyright belong to a different class (see below, § 23, pp. 704, 705), and compare the proposed heading of Choses in Action under "Law of Property" in the new Digest of English Civil Law, particularly Titt. IV—VII.

apparent when we come to treat specifically of Rights *in rem* and *in personam*.

On the general scheme of Hale and Blackstone's Property Law, its merits and demerits in comparison with the Roman *Jus Rerum*, &c., I leave what is to be said to the end of this section.   At present I return to Austin's Divisions of *Res*.

Genus and Species.   Among the mass of heterogeneous distinctions collected by Austin in Lecture 46 (see above, p. 550) are two to be mentioned here; one of which, though not a distinction of Things *per se*, cannot be passed over altogether, on account of its place in Gaius' arrangement of his *Jus quod ad res pertinet*, while the other, though in no sense applicable as a division of Property Law at all, deserves notice from the difficulty of its terms.   I refer to Things as taken *singulae* or *per universitatem*, and to Things as *generically* or *specifically* determined.   In the latter, which I shall dispose of first, the main difficulty is a peculiar meaning given to the words *genus* and *species*.   In this sense the two words do not mean a larger and a smaller class, but by *species* is meant that last or smallest class of all[45]—which is really no class—the *individual*, i.e. a thing individually determined; while *genus*, in this antithesis, means a thing (or *quantity*) determined by the class, large or small, to which it belongs.   However the words are to be truly explained, the ultimate meanings, of subject-matter generically or individually determined, for *genus* and *species*, are clearly to be recognised in the writings of the classical jurists[46].

[45] This is the best attempt at an explanation, in unphilosophical terms, which I can give of the obvious source of the antithesis in question, viz. Aristotle's ἔσχατα εἴδη and τελευταῖα γένη ἐπὶ τοῖς ἀτόμοις.   See Metaph. 1. 995ᵇ. 30 ; 3. 998ᵇ. 16 (Bekker), and other passages where the ἄτομον itself is spoken of in terms justifying its Latin description as an *infima species*.

[46] See Julian, Dig. 45. 1. 54. pr. Cum species stipulamur...quotiens

Subject-matter of the former class is said to admit of *performance* or *discharge* (*functio*) in its kind or sort[47]. Hence has been formed the base Latin word *fungible*, performable or dischargeable (i.e. by some other similar amount of the same material), a clearer expression of which idea is given by the German *Vertretbar*, "representable."

I have somewhat digressed on this subject, which is on the whole very well stated by Austin, on account of the difficulty that I have always felt in explaining the above legal terms with reference to the natural and original meaning of the words[48]. This, as has been said, is no true division of Things *per se*. Of course, it may be applied to Proprietary Rights of Ownership, by way of description or designation: but its more frequent application is in the case of Obligatory Rights, to *performance*, where the specific *mode* of performance is of the essence. The subject, therefore, comes indeed into Property Law, but mainly as a special case of Obligation.

Singulae res—universitas. The last remark also applies, in some degree, to the distinction between *singulae res* and a *universitas rerum*—at least in the cases instanced by Austin[49], which actually turn on performance of Contract. The more frequent use of this distinction by the Roman Jurists is to describe the *acquisition* of a person's Property *per universitatem*, i.e. *en bloc*, as distinguished from the acquisition of individual *res*[50]. The most important case is that of general

autem genera stipulamur; Ulpian, Dig. 30. 30. 6, where *Corpora legata* and *quotiens species legatur* are distinguished from *ea quae pondere numero mensura continentur*; Paulus, Dig. 12. 1. 2. pr. *Mutuum damus recepturi non eandem speciem quam dedimus...sed idem genus.*

[47] Ulpian, Dig. 12. 1. 2. 1. *Quia in genere suo functionem recipiunt per solutionem quam specie.* Mommsen notes a suggested emendation of *quia* into *quae*; *quae tam* appears to me to be required.

[48] The passage of Austin[5], 46. 778—780, is transferred in St. to 13. 1 0, 171.

[49] Austin[5], 46. 780, 781; St. 13. 171.　　　　[50] Ga. 2. 97; Just. 2. 6.

succession by *inheritance*, with which *bonorum possessio* is closely connected.

We noted above the double meaning of *hereditas*, to indicate the aggregate of Things, to which a *heres* succeeds, or his right of succession. The former is an instance of *universitas* as opposed to *singulae res*: the latter comes practically to be the heading of a main division in Property Law.

The subject, in fact, which we may call generally Inheritance, taken with that of *bonorum possessio*, extends from Book 2. § 97 of Gaius, and Tit. 9. 6 of the same Book in Justinian's Institutes, to Book 3. § 76 Gaius and Tit. 9 Justinian. The remaining *acquisitiones per universitatem* do not take up much room in the older work (Ga. 3. §§ 77—87) and, being in great part obsolete or repealed under Justinian, are very briefly disposed of by him in the Short Titles 10, 11, and 12, which are directly followed by the compact mass of Obligations.

This distinction of *singulae res* and *universitas*, as a matter of general application, is not, I think, one which would occur to the mind as naturally a leading division of *res*, or even as a leading distinction between modes of acquisition. I am therefore inclined to suggest, as the motive for what seems to me rather a second thought in Gaius (who is followed by Justinian), the wish to make his substantive treatment of Inheritance[51] practically a separate homogeneous division of Property Law, coming between the other Rights of Ownership and the fundamentally different Rights of Obligation (above, p. 552).

With the exception of *res mancipi* and *nec mancipi*, which will be treated directly, it is unnecessary to go further into the distinctions of Things *per se*, as noticed by Austin,

---

[51] Compare the brief notice on the mere mode of acquisition in Ga. 2. §§ 34—37 with the great mass of 2. § 97—3. § 87.

or into the somewhat arbitrarily devised ones, which Austin himself admits to be misapprehensions, of Bentham, in the Chapter *des choses* of his *Vue Générale d'un Corps complet de législation*[52].

Beside the material division of *res* as Land and Not-Land, there is also to be somewhere taken into account the legal position of **Sea** and **Sea-shore**; in very recent times that also of superincumbent **Air**. The former two of these subjects, together with their corollary or complement of so-called Divine and of Public ownership, come in the earlier sections of Gaius and Justinian's Book 2[53]. I have found them to be most conveniently treated, so far as they come into Private Law, under the heading of my following section— the Right of Private Property. I therefore now pass on to a very artificial and technical classification of *res*, which is obviously incapable of any modern or general application, and is mainly important in the Roman system on account of the real and practical divisions of subject-matter which it nominally introduces.

Modes of alienation and acquisition. After the passage of Gaius translated above (p. 551), on *res incorporales*, there evidently came, in a part of the MS. largely illegible, some detailed enumeration of *servitutes*, in the strict sense, i.e. *praediorum*: the so-called *personal* servitude of *ususfructus* had been mentioned before. This matter is immediately followed by a fragmentary line or two (which can however be confidently restored from Ulpian's Regulae) stating a new division of *res* as *mancipi* or *nec mancipi*[54].

That division was, no doubt, historically based on a distinction in the property itself. The *res*, which required the

---

[52] Traités, iii. pp. 262—267.   See Austin[5], 46. 781.
[53] Ga. 2. 1—11 ; Just. 2. 1. 1—10.
[54] Ga. 2. 14, 14ᵃ ; Ulpian, Regulae, 19. 1.

special form of acquisition or alienation known as *mancipium*, evidently belonged to what is the most probable meaning of *familia* in the Twelve Tables (above, p. 544), i.e. a man's agricultural plant or estate, by which he was originally ranked in the *census*, and transfer of which therefore required special publicity. But, in the later terminological sense of this division of *res*, it is one depending simply, as Austin puts it[55], on form of Conveyance, and as such belongs to the principle, broadly followed and continually referred to by Gaius, of classification of property by modes of alienation or acquisition.

This, which is not perhaps quite so correctly called a classification as a recurring note of difference, is connected, though not on any definite plan, with the distinction of Corporeal and Incorporeal Things, and further complicated by a considerable separation of modes of *alienation* which were specially matter of old Roman Law, from *acquisitions* on what is called *natural* principle, the latter coming, in the main, second[56].

A sort of appendix, on restraint of alienation by a *dominus* and power of alienation by a *non-dominus* (§§ 62—64), which is interpolated between these modes, seems to go more properly with a similar one, treating of a like restraint upon pupils and women (§§ 80—85), with which it is now placed by Krüger and Studemund[57]. It is followed by the common (though more strictly Old Roman) subject of acquisition through persons in power, &c. (§§ 86—96), after which comes

[55] Austin[5], 46. 778. It should be noted that the paragraph dealing with this subject has been, in the larger editions, pitchforked into the middle of that on *genus* and *species*, with which it has nothing whatever to do. The error is corrected in St. 13. 171.

[56] Ga. 2. 14ᵃ—61; 65—79. Note the change of phrase in §§ 65, 66. With the exception of *traditio*, which is common to both classes, the *natural* acquisitions are mostly *original* rather than *derivative*.

[57] Coll. Libb. Jur. Anteiust.[5] i. pp. 59, 60.

oddly that distinction of acquisition *per universitatem*, the motive for which I have suggested above (p. 565).

Justinian, in this part of his Institutes, follows the main divisions of Gaius so far as to take Inheritance and Obligation at the end of Property Law, but deviates from the original scheme a good deal, as to the earlier part.

After the sections on Public &c. or Private Property (above, p. 566) he places the whole subject of Acquisition by *natural* Right or Law as being *vetustius jus*[58]. This reason, however fanciful, is from Gaius himself, who in his Res Cottidianae (Matters of everyday practice) put the Natural modes of acquisition first, probably rather because even then they were beginning to supersede the Civil ones[59]. All these natural modes appear to be acquisitions of material things, nor would it seem that any other *res* were contemplated in Justinian's Second Book until Tit. 2, which begins with sections corresponding to Gaius, §§ 12—14 (above, p. 551).

The brief enumeration of servitudes in Gaius above referred to (p. 566) is now enlarged by Justinian's compilers, drawing matter from Gaius' other works as well as from those of other Jurists[60], into a considerable account of *res incorporales* or Rights, such as *Servitutes, Ususfructus* and *Usus*, consisting a great deal of the manner in which these were created, transferred or extinguished. *Usucapio*, which follows at considerable length (Tit. 6), and *donatio* (Tit. 7) which, in despite of its *natural* appearance, is expressly coupled with *usucapio* as a subsisting mode of *civil* acquisition, refer again

---

[58] Just. 1. 11—48, corresponding generally with Ga. 2. 65—79.

[59] See Gaius, Res Cott. ii. (Dig. 41. 1. 1. pr.). The Title here cited (De acquirendo rerum dominio), with one exception (l. 54), deals only with the natural acquisitions of material things.

[60] Gaius' Res Cottidianae, his 7th book *ad edictum provinciale*, Ulpian, *ad Sabinum*, &c.

to the acquiring of material things[61]. Titles 8 and 9, 1—5 correspond to Gaius' appendix mentioned on p. 567. The introduction of *hereditas* has been stated above (p. 565).

As to the part of the Second Book which precedes the last named subject, it is very difficult to reduce Justinian's arrangement to any consistent scheme. The main beginning of the Book and the enormous first Title generally, appears to be taken up by material things considered as subjects, *sensu Austiniano*[62], of complete private ownership, followed by a full account of the Natural modes of acquisition, which had at Justinian's time, and partly by his legislation, in all but a few cases, superseded the old Civil modes, in respect of these interests[63].

Incorporeal Things, or rights in material objects less than complete ownership, together with their acquisition and determination, are certainly the subject of Titles 2—5. But the surviving modes of Civil acquisition come in after this, as means of producing complete ownership in material things. On the placing of Inheritance and Obligation I have spoken sufficiently already.

Hale and Blackstone's Book ii. In considering the plan of this part of the Roman Institutes as followed to some extent by our English Institutionalists, we must remember that the latter had only Justinian before them; with, *possibly*, the Epitome of Gaius preserved in the *breviarium Alarici*, and published in some old editions of the Corpus Juris[64]. This, although prior to Justinian, is obviously modified by comparatively late Imperial practice, and accordingly omits all the specially old Roman or "Civil" modes of alienation and acquisition. We may fairly take it that practically the sole model

[61] Just. 2. 5. 6.
[62] For this phraseology see § 12, p. 482, and below, § 20, p. 639.
[63] See Just. 2. 1. 40 on *Traditio*, and Moyle's note.
[64] See Teuffel, § 488. 2 (vol. ii. p. 542).

of Hale and Blackstone was here, as for the main division of
Personal and Property Law, so also for the subdivision of
the latter, Justinian's somewhat confused arrangement of the
matters comprised in his Second Book. Their variances,
however, are considerable. First of all, they adopt, or affect
to adopt, a much more definite recognition and discrimi-
nation of the different parts or stages in Justinian's treatment generally. For, what they propose in their Rights of
Things is to deal separately and successively (1) with the
Things themselves; (2) with the Rights which may be
enjoyed in those Things; (3) with the manner of acquisition
or alienation of those Rights[65].

This is not, as it might seem, an arrangement based on
the Roman distinction of Res Corporales and Incorporales,
which is *literally* copied by our Institutionalists, in all its
illogicality of correlating rights with material objects, but
confined to one branch, Realty, of the English Property Law.
Enough has been said on that subject. But we must note that
there is necessarily a *duplication* of the treatment proposed
to themselves by Hale and Blackstone, due to the great dual
cleavage of English Law, which must always be, as we shall
see directly, a source of considerable repetition. I cannot of
course go into details of the unavoidably confused material
which it is Blackstone's great honour to have reduced into
anything like the order and readability of his Commentaries.

[65] The main parts of Hale's Analysis here referred to are §§ 23, 26,
pp. 44, 52, 54. Blackstone's Book ii., which requires more particular
notice, runs thus : ch. 1, Introductory on Property in general; 2, 3, Real
Property ; 4—12, Feodal System, Tenures and Estates ; 13—23, Titles to
Things Real ; 24, Things Personal; 25, Property in Things Personal ;
26—32, Titles to Things Personal.

In comparing the statement of Blackstone's Scheme with the latter part
of Austin's "Arrangement which seems to have been intended by Sir
William Blackstone" (Tab. VIII., opposite p. 984; St. 472), we must note
that the comparative simplicity of the original is a good deal obscured by
Austinian interpretations.

As to the general merits or demerits of our Institutional system, compared with the Roman, for purposes of modern study, we may certainly, at the outset, claim some superiority for the former, in the attempt to disentangle the Rights or interests themselves from the Titles or modes of acquisition. How far an entire separation is possible, or advantageous, will be considered hereafter under the head of Titles.   It is expressly adopted in the scheme of the French Code, under rather a different name[66].   In two important points, however, Blackstone's system shews a distinct inferiority to the Roman—Succession, or Inheritance, and Obligation.   We have seen above (p. 565) how the former subject is allocated by Gaius and Justinian to a final place in Rights of Ownership, pointedly disconnecting that department from Rights of Obligation, and how it is made, as in almost every system but the English into a homogeneous mass, to be taken by itself.   Whether it should include all Family Law is another matter (see above, § 15, pp. 534, 535).

But there is, in the most recent reproductions of Blackstone, as in his original editions, nothing corresponding to this compact and homogeneous mass.   Succession still appears, according to our Commentaries, under three different heads— of Title by descent, by alienation in the way of devise, by testament and administration[67].

Obligation also, whether considered as an element in acquisition (see below, § 23, p. 716), or as a substantive Right and Duty, is far less clearly conceived and marked off by the English than by the Roman Institutes.   In Hale's Analysis, brief subdivisions of Things "Personal in Action,"

[66] See below, § 25, for the modern use of this term, and for the real or nominal adoption of a separation, similar to that of Blackstone and Hale, in modern Codes.

[67] Blackstone, ii. chs, 14, 23, 32, pp. 200, 373, 489 ; Stephen, Bk. ii. chs. 11, 20, of pt. i., ch. 7 of pt. ii.

"Propriety (i.e. Property) in Action," and "Acquisition of Property by Contract," meet us at different places in the part devoted to Rights, but the largest amount of matter on Covenant or Contract comes under Wrongs[68].

In Blackstone, while the *name* of Obligation is confined to that of Bond (in the English sense of Deed), and the subject is treated briefly in the department of Right to Things Real under the head of Alienation by Deed, the whole subject of Contract is contained (together with Title by Gift and Grant) in a single Chapter of Rights to Things Personal[69]. This deficient and ancillary treatment of Contract is fairly accounted for by Blackstone's editor of near a hundred years ago—Chitty—as due to the immense increase in the English Law of Contract since Blackstone's time. That treatment is of course enlarged and improved in Stephen, though the subject is still very unsatisfactorily placed and styled, among Things Personal, under the old heading of Title by Contract[70].

The treatment of *obligationes ex delicto* apart from *obligationes ex contractu* in which the English Institutional scheme compares favourably with the Roman, depends upon the English division of the whole Corpus Juris into Rights and Wrongs, and is considered in later sections on that subject. To the same part of this work I must refer (under "Duties") the Roman definition of *Obligatio* and the questions connected with it.

[68] Hale, § 23, p. 45 ; § 26, p. 52 ; § 28, p. 56 ; § 41, p. 83.

[69] Blackstone, ii. ch. 20, pp. 341, 342 ; ch. 30, pp. 442—470.

[70] Stephen, Bk. ii. pt. ii. ch. 5. See the Prefatory Remarks (vol. ii. p. 55).

§ 17. THE RIGHT OF PRIVATE PROPERTY

Among the various meanings of the word Property which are enumerated in the summary at the end of Austin's 47th Lecture, and with most of which it is perfectly unnecessary to trouble the reader, we have hitherto considered only that of an aggregate—a man's Property as separate from himself— with a view to the determination of Proprietary as distinguished from Personal Rights. I have now to speak of Property as a Right in the abstract, a sense on which Austin casts considerable scorn, but which must, I think, be generally admitted to be a real and definite conception, the Right of Private Property. On the word itself, as indicating this idea in a narrower and more specific sense—the sense in which Austin identifies Property or its Latin original *proprietas* with *dominium*—I shall have something to say later on. At present I have to deal with the more general subject; which may be treated (see above, § 16, p. 566) as arising out of the Roman distinction of *res publicae* and *res privatae*, ranged by Austin somewhat oddly under the head of *jura in re alienâ* [1].

Gaius begins his second Book with a general distinction between *res* which *are* within our Patrimony and those which are *regarded* or *treated* as outside it. Read with a later section this comes to a division into *res* which are capable of being owned by individual men, and *res* which are, at least conventionally, incapable of being so owned [2].

Certain *res* are accordingly placed under the ownership of Heaven, and excluded from that of any individual man, by regular public consecration; in others this may result from an act of private burial [3]: others again, on the walls and gates of a city, are similarly incapable of individual ownership as being in some sort divine property, because *sanctioned* against human interference by penalties similar to those enacted in the sanctioning part of a law [4].

The second of these cases has no representative that I am

---

[1] Austin [5], 52. 840—844 : St. 51, 52. pp. 403—405.

[2] Ga. 2. 1, 11. The difference between *sunt* and *habentur* cannot be disregarded in a writer like Gaius. It was evidently noticed by the authors of the Epitome, though they predicated the *regard* or *recognition* rather of the *human* property. Nostri juris sunt quae in proprietate nostra esse *noscuntur* (Epit. 2. 1. § 2). On *patrimonium* as an *aggregate*, see above, § 16, p. 548. It may be noted, by the way, that the *fundi patrimoniales*, of which we may hear occasionally, are not estates capable of Private Property in general, but parts of the Emperor's private property in particular.

[3] See Ga. 2. 4—7; Just. 2. 1. 7—9. As to the translation of *juris* in this and similar passages, see § 12, p. 466, and below, n. 10. It is unnecessary to go here into the differences of *sacrum*, *religiosum* and *pro sacro* or *pro religioso*.

[4] Ga. 2. 8; Just. 2. 1. 10. As to *sanctio* used for the *whole law*, see Const. Deo Auctore, § 2, &c.

aware of, in modern times, and cannot, one would think, have survived to any great extent in that of Justinian.[5]   In the first and third, Austin, consistently with his general principles, makes out that the objects in question are practically nothing but a division of public property reserved or destined by the State to certain definite uses.

The *res divini juris* of Roman Law, and it must be presumed, their modern equivalents, are, in his view, *national* property *conceded* to public or political persons on trust for the particular uses in question[6].   I am not here concerned to enquire into this " concession," by the State, as a historical fact.   It may have been fairly true in past times and can be proved, for occasional instances, in present.   With regard to most modern religious property it is entirely false.

But, however acquired, and by whatever objects discriminated or, as a matter of feeling, consecrated, it will probably be admitted that *res divini juris* have been and are mostly property vested in Corporations so important as to demand recognition and, to require surveillance by the State (see below, p. 576).   This amounts to a case of property held, or administered, by persons in an official or quasi official position.   As a matter, therefore, of arrangement, or convenient position in a Corpus Juris, with which we are at present most directly concerned, the subject will fall into the Law of Public Conditions, whether that is treated as part of the Rights of Persons or as part of Constitutional Law, in the wider sense of that term (see above, § 15, p. 523).

This will appear more obviously, if we consider some previous arrangements.   Hale's initial division of Things as Ecclesiastical and Temporal (Analysis, §§ 22, 25), which is a mere repetition of the Roman distinction of Things as *nostri*

---

[5] Witness the elaborate provisions for Christian dedication in Cod. 1. 2. See, however, Girard[5], p. 242.

[6] Austin[5], 52. 842—844 ; St. 405.

juris aut divini, is not adopted by Blackstone : but the latter's own treatment of the Clergy in one place (i. ch. 11) and advowsons and tithes in another (ii. ch. 3) necessarily involves very inconvenient repetition. This is avoided in the plan of our later Institutes, by taking Church and Church property *together,* under the head of Public Rights[7].

The same reasoning applies to *all* property in a State, vested in persons, single or corporate, for public purposes. We need not, therefore, go into detail about city walls and gates, theatres and racecourses, which are incapable of individual ownership either from their quasi consecrated character described above (p. 574) or because they are believed to belong to the whole body (*universitas*). These last are Gaius' *res publicae* which are *humani juris*[8]. I have specially compared the section of Gaius with the passage added, in Justinian's Institutes, from Marcianus, because the word *universitas* appears to be misunderstood by Austin, who takes it to mean a *subordinate* Corporate body, to whom the State concedes the property in question, on trust. In such cases, there *will* generally be some intermediate body—not always very clearly determinable, which shews the advantage of treating such institutions in the abstract (see above, § 15, p. 525) as matters of the Social Economy of the Realm. But, as a matter of translation, *universitas* means here simply the State itself, as may be seen from comparing the passages in

[7] Stephen, Bk. iv. pt. ii. " The Church." In Anson " The Churches " are similarly treated as part of Constitutional Law. See The Crown, ch. 9, " The Crown and the Churches." This would seem a natural place for the subject in any system, whether our own connexion of it with the particular member of the Corporate Sovereign is retained elsewhere or not. See, on the modern English Institutional treatment of these Public Rights in general, above, § 15, p. 525.

[8] Ga. 2. 11; Just. 2. 1. 6; Marcianus, Dig. 1. 8. 6. 1. *Civitas,* I may, however, remark, in Just. § 6, simply means *city,* a meaning established as early as Ulpian, Dig. 1. 8. 9. pr. Sive in civitate sint (sacra loca) sive in agro.

Gaius and Justinian.   The mistake is, however, of no great importance.

What Austin goes on to remark is obviously true.   A State may concede the *res publicae* which are "in its patrimony," i.e. which are, however they have become so, State property, to an individual or a Corporation for their own private purposes as well as for public e.g. as lesees.   In this case the State is like any other landlord and the concessee like any other tenant[9].   How the State comes to have private property is another matter.

The special case of *heriditas vacans* I defer to a later part of this section (pp. 590, 592, 593).

Besides these *res publicae*, in which the question of ownership is between a State and its individual members, there are Things and Rights which are said to be common, or *public, as of universal right*[10].   In the confused *mélange* inserted by Justinian between the second and third sections of Gaius' Institutes, Book 2, mostly from the same author's everyday practice (*Res cottidianae*), but partly from other sources, we read of air and running water, sea and consequently sea-shore, as being common to all : of rivers and harbours as being *public*, so that anyone may fish in them : the same being true as to the temporary *use* of river *banks*, for mooring and landing cargo, the *property* of such banks being of course in the owners of the adjacent estates[11].   That of the *sea-shore*, on the contrary, can be no one's private property,

[9] Austin[5], 52. 842, 843 ; St. 51, 52. 403.

[10] I must apologise for what may seem a perverse avoidance of translating *jus* "law." But, while passages like Dig. 1. 8. 5. pr. (Riparum usus publicus est jure gentium) seem simple enough, when the undoubted reading is juris (as in Just. 2. 1. 4 ; Dig. 1. 8. 4. pr., &c), something like the above cumbrous rendering is inevitable. In such cases, *jus* must, it appears to me, bear the meaning of *right*, and in fact, that of individual or particular right, approximating to ownership. See § 12, p. 466, n. 6.

[11] Just. 2. 1. 1—4 ; Gaius, Dig. 41. 1. 7. 5, is not really contradictory to this, but merely speaks of the river generally as *alveus*.

though anyone may put up a hut there for shelter, drying nets, &c.[12] A somewhat inconsistent direction to all such fishermen to keep off from more important edifices, by a rescript of the Emperor Antoninus Pius[13], is not inserted in the Institutes of Justinian.

In Austin's view of these last-mentioned *res communes* or *res publici juris*, as legal rights can only emanate from a State, we are compelled to regard all rights of the kind referred to as relating only to parts of the territory of a State in which the State allows the right of user, in a limited and temporary degree, to its subjects (*semble*, to people in general when passing over such territory). With the open sea he does not appear to deal, though of course he takes the opportunity to gird at the supposed Natural Law and *jus gentium* which is regarded as giving rights independently of a State, &c.[14]

In these particular cases, the *gentes* might possibly be regarded as a sort of territorial appellation for what were simply parts of the comprehensive Roman Empire, and, so long as that existed, Austin's view would be fairly tenable. I believe, however, that the word, as used by the Roman jurists, had a more universal meaning, and that, in this case, *jus gentium* is practically identical with, or anticipatory of, a certain part of modern International Law (see § 9, p, 429). In modern times the old doctrine of the *sea's* universal *community* is somewhat modified by the recognised rights of bordering nations over what is sometimes called their maritime territory : the same modifications, *mutatis mutandis*, applying to frontier *rivers* or rivers which flow through different countries ; while any common right in those entirely comprised within the territory of a State is generally abandoned[15]. These are all matters falling distinctly within

12 Just. 2. 1. 5. 13 Marcianus, Dig. 1. 8. 4. pr. 14 Austin[5], 52. 842.
15 See Hall's International Law, pt. 2, ch. 2 ; Westlake (Peace), ch. 7.

the province of International Law, to which must now also
be added questions of *aerial* transit. They are, however,
from their quasi-territorial character, subject also to some
amount of control or administration by Municipal or National
authorities—who have obviously, in the last case of rivers,
a *sole* independent power. This control being necessarily
vested in some *public* person or persons, comes, in my view,
most conveniently under the head of Constitutional Law
in the wide sense[16], whether it be classed as an abstract
subject of Social Economy or passes under the name of some
determinate administrative body.

In Gaius' Institutes, nothing whatever is said of these
common rights of all mankind, the matter in Justinian being
borrowed mainly from the former author's Books on Practice[17].
But I must return to the subject of Gaius' *res universitatis*
(above, p. 576) because the principle of State ownership would
appear to apply to the important subject of Public Land
Ways, although Public *Water* Ways might be considered,
in Roman Law, matter of universal right.

These particular objects of Public Right may also be
looked at, from the point of view of their *user* by the private
citizen : a power or capacity which ought to appear, however
briefly, in the chapter of Personal Law devoted to his normal
Rights and Duties. This side or aspect, however, of the
particular *res publicae* now under consideration, comes practically more under our notice in statutory legislation against

[16] See § 10, p. 442 and § 15, p. 523. It comes, as being historically
deduced from the Royal Prerogative, under that head in Stephen, Book 4
(Of Public Rights), pt. 1, Civil Government, ch. 6. So, in Anson's Constitutional Law (Crown), the main part of the subject is treated, under the
head of Ministers of the Crown, in the sub-divisions Admiralty and Board
of Trade ; while the connected specialties of Jurisdiction fall elsewhere,
under Courts.

[17] I prefer the style of *Res Cottidianae*, as more probably the original
one. Aureon, βιβλία ἑπτά, no doubt occurs in the Florentine list of the
Digest books ; but it must surely have been some admirer's synonyme.

interference[18], or in statements as to the restriction of neigh-
bouring proprietors in their ordinary rights of ownership[19].
Most probably, indeed, the major part of the subject, as
treated in law, will be found in the public regulations of
Land and Water Ways (Land und Wasser *Strasse*) in the
interests of national defence or general traffic, to quote
the words of the German Constitution[20]. The powers
statutorily given to this or that public authority may, of
course, be comparatively detachable and simple. But it
will certainly appear desirable, to anyone who has endeavoured
to follow the unavoidable cross references, if the entire subject of such half private, half public rights, beyond a brief
statement of normal capacity (above, p. 579), together with
any special jurisdiction thereunto pertaining, could in every
system of legal education be consolidated under some common
head in "Public" or "Constitutional" Law. This is the
more possible where there is such a nucleus of detailed
Statutory Law as, e.g. with ourselves in our Highway and
Navigation Acts.

In dealing here, mainly, with the best *arrangement* of
the subject-matter before us, I do not propose to spend much
time in considering the theory of *ownership* in the bed of a
navigable river on the ground of a public road. For the somewhat debated "Sovereignty" of an individual modern State

[18] Such as the Interdicts in Dig. 39. 1, and generally in Lenel, Edictum[2],
§§ 241—244.

[19] See the notes in Scherer, &c., on BGB, §§ 903, 904, which, in
themselves, are merely very general statements of the ordinary rights
of individual ownership: also below, n. 22.

[20] Reichsverfassung, Art. 4, no. 8. The principle is developed in more
detail by Artt. 41—55 (nos. vii., viii., ix.). It may be noted that, by the
last number, the whole Mercantile Marine comes under treatment, which
might not seem at first to be intended. See Art. 54, and generally Laband's
notes on these numbers, Staatsrecht, iii. § 73. On the somewhat ambiguous
opening of Art. 54, as to the Mercantile Marine, see Laband, Staatsrecht, iii.
§ 80, p. 245. On nos. vii. and viii. generally, ib. §§ 73, 74.

in its "maritime territory," its "littoral" seas and gulfs, I
would refer altogether to works of authority on the International Law of Peace[21]. In the more obvious cases of internal
land and waterways the modern German and French doctrine
agrees with the Roman that the material objects in question
are *not* susceptible of private property but belong to the
State[22].

In English Law, on the other hand, the presumption as
to highways is that, apart from special legislation, or evidence
to the contrary, the *ground* of the road belongs to the adjoin-
ing proprietor—if two, between them, *usque ad medium filum
viae*[23]. In a navigable "public" river, above the flux and
reflux of the tide, the bed is, in like manner, *primâ facie*
vested, together with the fishery, in the *riparian owners*,
as of course in private waters, over which the public have
merely acquired a right or easement of navigation[24]. Into
the question what extent of tide constitutes a river *public*
I shall not enter here. Within the said flux and reflux the
bed is vested in the Crown for the use of the subjects of the
realm.

Res publicae in Austin's largest sense. The *res
publicae* hitherto quoted from Gaius and Justinian are such,
according to Austin, in a *narrower* sense which he contrasts
with a *largest* sense of this expression. In the latter, *all
things within its territory* belong to the State, in the former,
res publicae are such things as the State *reserves to itself*. Of
this claim to universal state ownership we find little, if any,
definite assertion, whether under the style of *res publicae* or
otherwise, by the Roman Classical Jurists or even by the

[21] E.g. Westlake, ch. 9; Halleck, ch. 6, &c.
[22] See Holzendorff, Encycl. i. 569 (Kohler); Scherer on BGB, l.c., n. 16
(vol. III. 93); Code Civil Français, § 358. Distinguish the *servitude* of the
banks, &c., § 650.
[23] Halsbury, Digest XVI, Rights of owners of soil, pp. 51–59.
[24] Law of Waters, Coulson and Forbes, pp. 81, 82.

Roman Emperors. It is best considered under its post-Roman aspect and title of Eminent Domain.

With regard first, however, to the *res publicae* which are as Austin says *reserved to itself* by the State, out of the objects of its universal ownership, there are one or two consequences of Austin's rigid definitions which may require a little preliminary clearing away. The right, for instance, of absolute ownership claimed for the State in these articles of its "*patrimony*," its private or quasi-private Property, is not according to the Austinian definition a *legal* one, not being conferred or enforced by any superior power. The articles in question are accordingly, in one passage, most paradoxically spoken of as having *no owner*, and a servitude e.g. a right of way granted over land in the patrimony of the State is only a *quasi-servitude*[25]. *Sed haec hactenus.*

Before speaking of Eminent Domain, I am obliged in the view here taken throughout, as to the true origin of Right and of the State, to proceed in a different order of treatment from that of Austin. Assuming, as he consistently does, the State to be the fountain or ultimate source of all Right, with which Jurisprudence is concerned, he naturally regards the rights of Ownership, amongst others, as conceded or allowed to private persons out of the supreme ownership of the State. In the contrary view here taken, Eminent Domain is *not* correctly regarded as a supreme or an original State Ownership, and ought to be preceded by some enquiry into the origin and nature of the Right of Private Property.

The Right of Private Property, or the Right of Property *tout court*, placed, as we have seen (§ 12, p. 478), by Blackstone among the Absolute Rights of Individuals, may

---

[25] Austin[5], 49. 804 ; 52. 841, 844 ; St. 390. I do not know the authority either for the last statement above, or for the expression. Quasi-usufruct is an entirely different thing. The idea of Austin probably arises from a misapprehension of Ga. 2. 31.

be broadly described as the legally protected power to enjoy for one's self, and to exclude others from enjoying, all that is comprised in Property as an aggregate.   Different modes and degrees of ownership will be considered hereafter ; at present we deal simply with the Right generally, having a little to say as to its possible origin but more as to its actual limitations.

According to Austin what Blackstone meant by the Right of Private Property was either *nothing* or *all* rights soever which are the subject of his Commentaries.   So, too, the same author says :   when speculators on political government and society tell us that the end of every government is to institute and protect Property, and when people speak of the " Institution of Property " or the " Security of Property " as arising from this or that form of goverment, they mean by Property legal rights and faculties *of any kind*, since, if it only means such legal rights as come under the meaning of *dominion* it would exclude from the proper scope of civil protection or creation all such rights as are the effects of contract or quasi-contract, e.g. "*jura in personam*[26]."   Now, as to what Blackstone meant by the Right of Private Property, although of course all the Rights of Things in Book ii. ultimately depend upon it, it is in itself quite clearly distinguished by him both from them and from the other Rights, Absolute or Relative, contained in Book i.

The other conclusions too of Austin are equally paradoxical.   They arise, partly from his misconception of *Jus Rerum*, or the Law of Property, as Law General; partly from his choosing here to ignore the fact of a *jus in personam* being so far a *jus in rem* also, that it will be protected by legal remedies against the possible interference of third parties, although the remedy may not be formally an *actio in rem*

---

[26] Austin[5], 47. 791, 792; St. 385. Also 6. 292 (St. 123), note. The passages referred to in Blackstone are Comm. i. 1, p. 138; ii. 1, pp. 1—3.

(see below, § 23, p. 703).   The aggregate, a Property, includes rights which arise from Contract, as well as those which do not; and the Institution, Protection, &c., spoken of in such passages as those cited above, is certainly to be understood as extending to the whole subject matter of Blackstone's Book ii., and Gaius' Books 2 and 3, so far as *obligationes ex contractu.* I shall have to discuss elsewhere (§ 18) the illogicality, but practical convenience, of including *obligationes ex delicto* together with those *ex contractu*, as similarly items of Property, in the Roman System. Blackstone excludes them at the outset from that category, by his fundamental division of Rights and Wrongs.

Although, however, in discussing Blackstone's Right of Private Property, we need not be forced into the dilemma of either unduly extending or absurdly narrowing the scope of that right, from what it is naturally understood to be, by Blackstone and most other people; there is no doubt that the reasoning and speculation about the right does, in general, refer more particularly to the narrower or more specific of the two senses of *proprietas* or *dominium* which Austin attributes to the Roman Jurists (see below, § 24, p. 739). We may, therefore, in considering the Right of Private Property, confine ourselves, for the present, to the case of complete ownership, as representative of the whole subject.

Only, before taking leave of these particular criticisms or paradoxes at the end of Austin's 47th Lecture, I may note the statement that " in English Law the term Property is not applied to rights in *immoveables*[27] ". It is true that in Hale and Blackstone the term is apparently confined in scope to things or chattels *personal*, explained as *moveable*[28]. The

---

[27] Austin[5], 47. 790; St. 384.
[28] Hale's Analysis, §§ 26, 29, pp. 52, 57; Blackstone, ii. 24, 25, pp. 388, 389.

difference, of course, springs from the dogma well established in the time of our Institutionalists, that in England there is no true ownership of land except in the King. But modern English lawyers have long spoken of Real (i.e. *landed*) as well as Personal Property, and the accidental and particular narrowing of the word in accordance with English theory has certainly no meaning for general jurisprudence.

The Right of Private Property is one of those which Blackstone styles Absolute, which would belong to Man in a State of Nature, independent of relation to any other person, and of Society generally. This, however, is only put forth as a " probable " origin, the same author presently admitting that the right, in its present conservation and modifications, is entirely derived from Society[29]. It is, therefore, unnecessary to enter into the very hypothetical State of Nature, or the difficulties arising from reference to it, which are duly pointed out by Austin[30].

No general theory as to the origin of Private Property can be attributed to the Roman Jurists. The nearest approximation to one is to be found in *occupatio*, the taking,

[29] Comm. i. 1, pp. 124, 138.

[30] Austin[5], 32. 574; 43. 729; St. 292, 365. There is undoubtedly some confusion, both in the above cited passages from Blackstone's Commentaries and in p. 47 of his Introduction, between the idea of a savage " state of nature " and that of a " natural society " not yet developed into a civil or political one, or State.

But I think no fair-minded person can read through the latter passage, on the origin and nature of society, without feeling that the attack in Bentham's Anonymous Fragment on Government, ch. 1, was grossly unfair, as a mere matter of logical criticism.

On the question of historical investigation, or theory, there is, in the opinion of the present writer, a great deal to be said, and much evidence to be adduced, in favour of something very like Blackstone's " natural society "; held together by general moral feelings expressed in the administration of a common justice, which forms the foundation of the ultimate Austinian State. See § 5, pp. 292—294, 300, 301.

so as to exclude others[31], of the wild creatures, belonging to no one, in earth, sea or sky, which may, no doubt, have been the first objects of individual ownership[32]. Capture from an enemy, which was considered as conferring such ownership in an eminent degree[33] can scarcely have been regarded, even among the *bellicosi* Quirites, as the *sole* proper origin of ownership, and is, after all, like *traditio, derivative*, therefore *secondary*, rather than original. A discussion of the import of such words as *herus, heres* and *heredium* belongs to the detail of early Roman legal history : but I may here just briefly advert to a point arising from the last of these words in particular. The old Socialist doctrine *la propriété c'est le vol* is sometimes revived now-a-days, more particularly with reference to *land*, the "*nationalization*" of which, though mainly based on modern grounds of alleged utility, is with some people supported by appeal to very doubtful facts of early history. As to the latter argument, it must be distinctly noted that so far as the meaning of ancient forms and words coupled with prehistoric tradition (e.g. in the case of *heredium*) can be relied on, there is evidence in most old nations of private or individual ownership *in land* existing from the earliest times, whether by the side of communal or not[34].

Passing, however, from the right of Private Property, in respect of its remote origin, to the same right in the view of modern jurisprudence, we may proceed to notice two general qualifications of this right. One is its alleged restriction by

[31] I suggest this as a probable meaning of the compounded preposition *ob*.

[32] Ga. 2. 66, 67 ; Just. 2. 1. 12.

[33] Ga. 4. 16.

[34] See evidence to be adduced in a subsequent Part under *Gens*. Also P. and M. on the Manor and the Township, i. 594—624, and Maitland's "Domesday-Book and Beyond," pp. 340, &c., on "the Village Community."

the principle "*sic utere tuo ut non laedas alienum*[35]":
another is its subordination to what is called Eminent
Domain. By the former maxim I understand not so much
the non-interference with the special rights of other persons
in the same subject-matter, as the limitation of an absolute
owner's power, to do what he likes with his own, by the fact
that he must not exercise that power in a manner prejudicial
to the person or property of his neighbour. It is put in this
very general form by Bentham as the obligation *de ne faire
de la chose aucun usage nuisible à autrui*[36].

This maxim cannot be taken absolutely, exceptions being
continually allowed to it not only in juristic writings but in
practical modern Law. In England, for instance, damage
resulting to one's neighbour from the use of one's own
property in the exercise of common or ordinary rights has
been repeatedly regarded as *damnum sine injuria*, giving no
right of action[37]. A malicious *motive* appears to be immaterial, provided that what is done is not of an excessive or
very unusual character. In this the Roman law is different,
the *animus nocendi* giving a right of action to the neighbour
who suffers damage. The motive is also taken into account
by the German Code in cases where there *can* be no other
object than to injure the neighbour[38].

Austin points out that in this and a similar maxim, *qui jure
suo utitur neminem laedit*, if the *laesio* is taken in the natural
non-legal sense of mere *damage*, the assertion is in fact

[35] I give this maxim in what was probably its original form—a mediaeval
hexameter—*utere* being considered to be second person future, " So shalt
thou use thine own as not to damage another's."

[36] Cited by Austin, 48. 828. See, however, the original, Traités, iii.
p. 287.

[37] See generally Pollock on Torts[9], pp. 151—161.

[38] Marcellus, Dig. 39. 3. 1. 12, speaks of diverting another's source of
water by digging on one's own estate. For the German doctrine see BGB,
§ 226, Die Ausübung eines Rechtes ist unzulässig wenn sie *nur* den Zweck
haben *kann* einem anderen Schaden zuzufügen.

untrue: if it means *such* damage as a man is *legally bound* to abstain from inflicting on others, such maxims come to little more than a truism—the right must be used so as not to produce a wrong. But his remarks on this subject belong on the whole rather to the more general restrictions on the power of indefinite user by an owner, indicated, e.g. in the French Code[39], than to the particular limitation alleged in the maxim *sic utere*, &c. I do not think the latter can be pressed much farther than as putting an owner on his enquiry, when use of his own property is, as a fact, likely to prejudice his neighbour, whether such prejudice has been previously recognised as allowable. We may pass, however, now to a much more definite limitation of private ownership.

Eminent Domain (*dominium eminens*) is literally a supreme ownership considered to reside in the Sovereign or State over all property in its Territory[40]. As such, it has been identified by some writers with the ultimate feudal ownership (of land), which in English legal theory belongs to our King[41]: but this is clearly, as is pointed out by Westlake, a mistake[42]. It is better regarded as a *right*—a quasi-legal right according to Austin (above, p. 582)—residing in the Sovereign but only of occasional application[43].

Every State, feudal or not, has the right, or at least exercises the power, to "*expropriate*" private property for

---

[39] Code Civil, § 554: La propriété est le droit de jouir et disposer des choses de la manière la plus absolue, pourvu qu'on n'en fasse pas un usage prohibé par les lois ou par les règlements.

[40] The idea, if not the term, is as old as the days of Seneca (Orat. 31, ap. Heffter, tr. 133). Grotius, 2. 14. 7, calls it *supereminens dominium*, but in 1. 1. 5, 6, more correctly according to my view, an *eminens facultas*.

[41] See below, pp. 590, 591.   [42] International Law (Peace), pp. 85—88.
[43] See Halleck, ch. 6 (vol. i. p. 124).

public purposes : but the right is not necessarily based upon a supposed ownership. In general parlance, the power in question is, no doubt, designated by the technical term, Eminent Domain, more particularly when it is exercised for *total* conversion to public use in cases of great emergency, but the principle also applies to any *partial* alienation or subjection, e.g. to rights of road, &c., for ordinary purposes of public utility[44].

On the same principle of public utility depend the *restrictions* which have been placed, in England as elsewhere, upon the *disposal* of private property for certain purposes, and upon the destruction or alienation in general, by their owners, of certain objects possessing an exceptional national interest[45].

I must here repeat (see p. 584) that most of the present remarks about the Right of Private Property, and its restrictions or qualifications, are principally directed to Rights of Ownership over material objects ("Rights *in rem* over Things properly so called," as Austin styles them). They are in principle applicable, *mutatis mutandis*, to Rights

[44] See Code Civil (Français), § 545, *pour cause d'utilité publique, et moyennant une juste et préalable indemnité* (*préalable* means payable before *dépossession*, Sirey, Code Civil, i. p. 443). Of course the equitable principle embodied in the last words of the section will generally be acted on by present governments. How far it will stand against the later Socialist doctrines may be questioned. See, on the abuse of land taken for public purposes in America, Stimson, Popular Law-making, 129—133. Also on this, and the wider principle of general levelling, § 4, pp. 280, 281.

[45] E.g. lands in *mortmain*, historical monuments (45 & 46 Vic. c. 73 ; 63 & 64 Vic. c. 34), famous works of art, &c. A somewhat sweeping opinion is quoted by Holland from Lord Holt, in Hargrave's Law Tracts, to the effect that whenever private property is affected with a public interest it ceases to be *juris privati*. The quotation, so far as I can identify it, seems only to refer to Ports. It is in Part 2, ch. 8, p. 89, of the Treatise de portibus maris—attributed, by the way, not to Holt but to Hale. See, however, Holland[10], p. 201, n. 2.

in personam also, which enter into a man's Property: but I do not propose to discuss that rather more difficult application here. I should add, before proceeding to discuss the literal acceptation of Eminent Domain, that certain other restrictions upon the Right of Private Property are touched upon by Austin in the same part of his work (Lecture 48) with those above mentioned. These, however, belong partly to the subject of what he calls Status and what is here treated as Personal Law (e.g. the Incapacities of Infancy, &c.), partly to that of *limited* or *fractional* Rights of Ownership. And this latter subject, together with the proposed scientific definition of *complete* Ownership, are too much complicated by Austin with peculiar English Law to be treated in full here (see below, § 24, pp. 741, 742).

The State as residuary : *Dominium Eminens* has been hitherto treated rather as an over-riding power, and a restriction or limitation of the Right of Private Property than as a true ownership residing in the State. Such an ownership, however, has been expressly claimed, under the same style, in many legal systems, for the State or the individual Sovereign, but only in a sort of residuary character: and this seems the best place for considering the subject.

In its broadest form, the principle relied on does not come to more than this: that *bona vacantia*—property without an owner, falls to the State or the Sovereign as representing the State. It must not, however, be forgotten that *bona*, an inclusive term in general jurisprudence, is sometimes, notably in *our* older legal phraseology, taken as confined to moveables. Land, therefore, must in an English view of the subject, be *primâ facie* taken into exceptional consideration. Now, in land, there is, according to the received English theory, no full private property, the only *absolutum et directum dominium* belonging in this case to the personal Sovereign[46]. Such Sovereign we may now regard as representing the State : so that here we seem to have a genuine supreme State ownership. But it must be remembered that, as distinguished from the *dominium eminens* which means a present and over-riding power (above, p. 590), this, as to actual effect in modern English Law, is only a right of ownership dependent on the previous failure of all entitled parties, so that it may be loosely described as that of an *ultimus heres*, although the Lord is really "in of his own right" not by way of inheritance[47].

In the case of *forfeiture*, on account of crime, the penalty apparently is one which might be inflicted by *any* Sovereign, independently either of feudal tenure or of any claim to a general State ownership: the consequences, on the other hand, usually resulting from *attainder* (*escheat propter delictum tenentis*), depend solely on such feudal tenure, the Lord taking in virtue of his own ultimate ownership. In the majority of cases, consequently, upon the Statute *Quia Emptores* (18 Edw. 1, 1289) the right of escheat came to belong to the Crown, and was surrendered with other part of the revenue by 12 Car. 2, 24. Criminal escheat has now been abolished[48].

But I find myself here entering too much upon the English subject of *estates* in land, and generally upon that of a succession of interests in the same property, which, if treated at all in an introductory work, must be taken under the

[46] Blackstone, ii. 7, p. 105. On the growth and real age of this theory, see P. and M. ii. 2—11.

[47] See Austin[5], 51. 836. In this passage he seems rather arbitrarily to allow the name of absolute property in land to the owner in fee where the Crown's property right was the *only* one expectant on the determination of his estate, though not, of course, where the estate of a *mesne lord* was interposed.

[48] 33 & 34 Vic. 23. See on the whole subject Stephen[14], 2. 1. 12, Vol. i. pp. 251—254 ; Halsbury, Digest, s.v. Vol. vii. &c.

heading, "Rights of limited duration" in Austin's proposed scientific classification of part of the Law of Things. It is rather with reference to moveables or "personal chattels" that the Sovereign's or State's right to *bona vacantia*, owner-less property, is in the main, applied by Blackstone : though the doctrine of the King being general owner and Lord Paramount of the soil crops up curiously enough in his account of "Estrays"[49].

The main principle relied on by him, and backed by a quotation of Bracton, is drawn from an alleged *new jus gentium*, as being matter of positive law in most of the modern Constitutions of Europe, over-riding the "natural" right of the first finder, or *occupant*, whereas that right "continued" under the Imperial (Roman) Law[50].

The general Roman law on this subject is more correctly stated by these earlier authorities than by Austin in his 52nd Lecture. He, it would seem, from his use of the technical term *fisc*, and other brief references to the law of the Empire, takes the view that, in that law, the Sovereign was regarded as the *original owner* of *bona vacantia*, and the *occupant* as a concessionary from the Sovereign[51]. And indeed, this view *is* rather in accordance with the language of Justinian in the particular case of Treasure Trove[52]. But the words, though referring to a Rescript of Hadrian, may be merely a piece of later grandiloquence as to any Imperial legislation. The actual Rescript, as represented by

[49] Blackstone, i. p. 297.

[50] Blackstone, i. pp. 298, 299. The particular passage in Bracton (i. ch. 12, fol. 8ᵃ) does not necessarily refer to anything but Waifs and Strays. In iii. ch. 4, fol. 120ᵃ, however, the same change of right, by *jus gentium*, is alleged of Treasure, and perhaps generally of *res nullius* (see Fleta, i. 43). To this modern *jus gentium* a comparatively definite meaning is given by Grotius, as matter of positive law obtaining generally among the nations of Europe, from their common German origin (Grotius, 2. 8. 2, 7).

[51] Austin⁵, 52. 845.   [52] Just. 2. 1. 39. Ei *concessit* qui invenerit.

Hadrian's biographer, Spartianus[53], would appear simply to have regulated the relation between the finder and the owner of the land; and, while the subsequent Imperial enactments vary, they by no means bear out Austin's doctrine of a supreme ownership, *primâ facie* residing in the Sovereign.

In the case of things *abandoned*, and so without owner, which go to the first occupant, there is, as late as the time of Ulpian and Paulus, no talk of State's or Sovereign's ownership[54]. In fact, the Roman lawyers rather say that certain things are regarded as no man's property, because they belong to the State as a whole, than that things in general belong to the State, when they happen to be, for the time being, no individual's property. The former are what Gaius refers to as *res publicae* : of the latter he gives an instance in *res hereditariae antequam aliquis heres existat*[55]. The particular expression *bona vacantia* is, with the classical Jurists, mostly confined, if not exclusively applied, to *caduca*, property which, by the disqualifications of the *lex Julia* and *Papia Poppaea*, or the *lex Junia*, has *fallen*, from the person primarily intended as *heres* or *legatarius*, to the first in succession qualified to receive it, and, failing any such person, is *presented* (*defertur*) to the people, i.e. the national treasury or later to the Emperor's privy purse[56]. This ultimate

[53] Vita Hadriani, c. 18. See other passages cited in my article, Archæological Journal xliii. pp. 350—357.

[54] Dig. 41. 7. 1, 2.

[55] Compare Ga. 2. 10, 11, with 2. 9 as restored from Dig. 1. 8. 1. pr. The reference obviously is to the strange *possessio pro herede*, or frankly *possessio pro possessore*, which was allowed in ancient times (Ga. 2. 55—57; Ulpian Dig. 5. 3. 11—13. pr.) though reprobated by later (Ga. ib. and 4. 144; Just. 4. 15. 3). The still stranger idea, to the ordinary mind, of a deceased person's property *generally* becoming *res nullius*, has been recently advanced by a modern author as a ground for the State's interfering, on these occasions, to redress the inequality of fortunes, Sir R. K. Wilson's Province of the State, pp. 198, 240.

[56] See Ulpian, xvii. 1, xxviii. 7; Ga. 1. 24; Juvenal, Satt. 9. 86—88; and generally Girard[5], pp. 875, 876.

devolution, as matter of express statutory enactment, may with much greater propriety be referred to a *dominium eminens* in the sense of an over-riding power (above, pp. 588, 589) than to a supposed supreme ownership[57].

Dominium indeed in the latter sense, as applied that is to the State or Sovereign, appears to be, at the outside, rather implied than expressed in Roman Law: this use of the word only occurs in the later Imperial times and for special cases[58].

In modern law, leaving out of the question the admitted general over-riding *power* over all private property, and the special feudal theory as to land, I proceed to consider the claim of State *ownership* in *bona vacantia*.

In England this question will, of course, only apply to Personal Property. Here I must not omit to mention a sweeping contention from Coke's Reports which seems rather *pro tanto* in favour of Austin's view as to *dominium eminens*[59]: that by *our old law* the King was entitled to *seize* upon the goods of an intestate, as being the *parens patriae* and general trustee of the Kingdom. It is possible, however, that there is here some confusion between the very ancient *right* of a lord to take a *heriot* for himself, and a *duty* to divide a deceased's property generally among his wife, children and near kinsmen[60].

---

[57] Not much historical weight can be given to the fancy of Tacitus (Ann. 3. 28) that, "where individuals hang back from the privileges of parentage, the people, *as the parent of all*, should keep the ownerless goods." As to claims of *creditors* on property, where there is no lawful successor, see Ga. 3. 78; Callistratus, Dig. 49. 14. 1. 1; Cod. 7. 72. 5; and Lenel, Edict[2], § 207, p. 401.

[58] See Dirksen, s.v. § 4.

[59] Rep. 9. 38, as cited by Blackstone, ii. 494. The idea is probably Coke's own. At least I cannot find it in the passages of Plowden, &c., referred to in the Report. There is nothing on this particular point in Coke, Instt. 176[b].

[60] See Cnut, ii. 70; (Schmid[2], p. 308). Compare Bracton, 2. 26 § 2,

As to *bona vacantia* on intestacy, the Crown is, no doubt, at English Law, beneficially entitled in one very exceptional case, of a *bastard* dying without a will, and leaving no wife or lawful issue, though the right is not in recent times strictly enforced[61]. This would seem to come fairly under Blackstone's general principle stated above (p. 592) as to *bona vacantia*, the motive alleged being " to prevent strife and contention to which title by occupancy might give rise." The rule of English law is accepted and stated in Halsbury's Vol. vii., being applied there generally to the failure of beneficiaries or trusts[62]; but it does not appear that either these or any other matters of Royal Prerogative in England amount to a claim of general ownership such as that alleged by Austin in his *dominium eminens*.

In modern legislation by the two leading representatives of Grotius' "nations of German origin" (above, n. 50) the Austinian view is so far adopted as to allege a *residuary* or *supplementary* ownership in the State.

Under the French Code goods (*biens*) *vacants et sans maître*, and those of persons who die without inheritors (*heritiers*), or those to which the succession is abandoned, belong to the *domaine public* (in the original version of 1804 *à la nation*). Elsewhere it is laid down that goods which have no master belong to the State[63]. The above mentioned *domaine public* should be *domaine de l'état*, according to Sirey and Gilbert, who define the former as matter *not susceptible of private ownership*, while the latter is

fol. 60 b, and generally P. and M. on Intestacy, ii. 6, § 4. Possibly the passage of Tacitus above cited (n. 57) may have been present to the mind of the learned writer.

[61] See Blackstone, i. 459, n. 27; Stephen[14], Bk iii. ch. 3 (Vol. ii. 345).

[62] Halsbury, Title Constitutional Law, treats of the Revenues of the Crown now forming part of the Consolidated fund (p. 110), including those arising from Prerogative Rights, *inter alia* to *bona vacantia*, pp. 209, 210.

[63] Sections 539, 713.

composed of *the same biens* as those which do constitute private properties [64].

Again in § 768 (*Code Civil*) the succession to an ordinary private property is spoken of on failure of the inheritors there specified as *acquise* à l'état[65]. Planiol does call this not a case of heritage but a right of Sovereignty[66]: in which view there may seem to be an alleged ownership by the State, though only as residuary, possibly in imitation of Roman Law.

In the German Code, a similar succession of the State to an Intestate's property, on failure of relations or lawful wife, is represented by Dernburg as matter of Statute following a previous Common Law (*gemeinrechtlich*) acceptance of the Roman right of the *fiscus*, which was likewise statutorily established under Augustus[67]. A question had been raised whether the State was not, in this case, simply a privileged occupant, but the contrary view has prevailed, that of a residuary inheritor by Statute, so that the conception of an heirless heritage no longer exists[68].

Apparently, therefore, in these cases we have Imperial Statute Law of Rome copied, as establishing a State succession, *against* the primary right of first occupancy : and this is possibly the nearest approximation to Austin's supreme general ownership as the true meaning of Eminent Domain.

On the other hand, the right of the first occupant to ownerless moveables is allowed by the German Code, where the original ownership has been clearly abandoned[69].

---

[64] Code Civil, i. p. 422, on § 537. Compare Ga. 2. 8, res *quodammodo divini juris velut muri et portae*, with ib. 2. 10, 11, res humani juris...quae universitatis esse creduntur.

[65] Sirey et Gilbert, Code Civil, i. p. 626.

[66] Planiol, Droit Civil, iii. p. 377.

[67] Bürg. Recht, 5. 51, on B. G. B., § 1936 ; see too above, p. 593.

[68] Scherer, v. 41, and Dernburg, l.c.

[69] B. G. B., §§ 958, 959.

In the French law it is questionable whether they do not come under a general claim of ownership by the State, as succeeding to previous seigniorial rights[70].

The law of Treasure, which is defined by the German Code as a thing which has been so long hidden that the owner cannot be ascertained, follows, both in that Code and in the French, the equitable legislation of Hadrian (see p. 592) and makes no claim for the State. It is to the alteration of this law, through the Sovereign's claim of ownership, that the reasoning referred to on the same page, about a modern *jus gentium*, particularly applies. Both the justice and the expediency of this rule, attributed by Grotius to the nations of German origin, and adopted by ourselves amongst others, may, in my opinion, be questioned. See the article above referred to (note 53).

As against modern Socialism I do not propose to enter the lists here, but take the liberty to regard Private or Individual Property, subject to the limitations heretofore mentioned, as still a healthy subsistent institution, even in Land.

It might seem natural to conclude these Sections on Res, or Property, with some notice of the main Subdivisions of Property Law which have been adopted as convenient in Educational Courses or Codes, as also of the different principles of classification suggested by Austin. But I have not found it possible to make these subjects at all clear without frequent reference to the definitions and distinctions

---

[70] On this subject the last clause of the Code Civil, § 717, refers to *lois particulières*, for which see Sirey, Code Civil, i. p. 603. There is also a reference to C. C., §§ 2279, 2280 (as well as to the general § 539 referred to above, n. 63) on a sort of *prescription* in such cases.

See Sirey, l.c., and Planiol, i. 821, on the vague meaning and doubtful law of *épaves*, literally *strays*, but applied to *tout objet mobilier égaré par son propriétaire*. Such are distinguished by the latter author from *res derelictae*, as to which, and game, *alone* he considers that *occupation* still exists in French law (p. 816).

of which I have spoken above, § 1 p. 31, as necessarily postponed to the last part of the work. These again have an obvious connexion with the English division of Rights and Wrongs, which may be regarded as based, though not quite so obviously, on the Roman juxtaposition of the *Jus quod ad actiones pertinet,* by the side of the *Jus Personarum* and the *Jus Rerum.*

§ 18. PERSONAE, RES, ACTIONES. ACTIONES

JUS quod ad actiones pertinet, 599. Meanings of *agere* and *actio*, 600—602. Modern criticism of Gaius' arrangement, 602, 603. Coupling or separation of Obligatory *ex contractu* and *ex delicto*, 603, 604. Appendix to *Jus actionum*, 604, 605. Blackstone's Book iii. generally, 605, 606. Compared with French and German Codes, 606, 607. Place of Procedure in an Educational Course, 607, 608. Substantive and Adjective Law, 608, 609.

Jus quod ad actiones pertinet. In Gaius' triple division the attention is naturally directed at first to the question what was meant by *Personae-Res*; but this order is a matter merely of convenience, for the position of the third term requires an equal and independent consideration. This third term, Austin, it will be remembered, criticises as *disparate*, and maintains that it ought to be distributed over the first two instead of being co-ordinated with them[1]; proceeding to attack Blackstone, for his division of "Rights and Wrongs," on somewhat similar grounds.

In the view here taken, the three terms of Gaius' division may be correctly rendered: (1) the law relating to Persons (in a private capacity) *themselves*; (2) the law relating to the Property of these Persons; (3) the law relating to their Legal Procedure, as private Persons. But the exact scope of the third term cannot be investigated without some enquiry into the different meanings, in Roman juristic phraseology, of the word *actio*.

[1] Austin[5], 43, 726, 727. He here follows Thibaut. N.B. there is a misprint "rights" in the 9th line from top of p. 727, which is rightly corrected to "wrongs" in St. 363 but retained in the 5th larger edition of Austin.

These are, undoubtedly, rather difficult to bring under
one common head, and they have led to some confusion
in Gaius' treatment of the subject. This confusion again has
resulted in a sort of revised version (which I myself consider
an improvement) of the *Jus Actionum*, made by Blackstone,
and a still further revised version, of more questionable value,
set up by Austin.

Meanings of agere and actio. *Agere* was originally a
transitive, not a neuter, verb, and probably meant, in its first
employment as a law term, to *drive* or *press* one's Right.
However that may be, I think the fundamental idea of *actio*
and *agere* is, not the ordinary exercise of a Right, but
the taking of some remedial proceedings, by a private
person[2] whose Right is questioned or endangered. All the
cases enumerated by Moyle in his note upon Justinian
4. 6. pr.[3] may be fairly explained on this principle, and
the slight modifications of it, or deductions from it, which
I shall now briefly notice.

Actio, for instance, is occasionally said—mainly in the
phrase *legis actio*—of certain proceedings not really remedial
but belonging to what is called the "Voluntary jurisdiction"

---

[2] In the face of the strongly expressed opinion of Voigt (Die xii
Tafeln i. 516, 518) and others, I hesitate to deny that *legis actio* may be
predicated of the Court, but certainly in nine cases out of ten it is predicated
of the Suitor. In Modestinus, Dig. 1. 7. 4 (cited by Moyle), it is merely suggested by Neratius that a magistrate, before whom *legis actio* can be
performed, can perform the same *legis actio* as a private person, technically
before himself. When an officer is said, under the Empire, to have the *legis
actio* or to have it given him, these phrases only mean that the *legis
actio* can be performed before him. See Paulus Sentt. 2. 25. 4: Ulpian Dig.
1. 20. 1 and Mommsen Sr. i. 189, n. 4.

[3] Moyle[4] (on Just. 4. 6. pr.) 540, 541. Cf. Salkowski, § 24 p. 120 and
Sohm[2], p. 242. In both the last, the idea of having the *judicial* machinery
placed at one's disposal is perhaps too exclusively pressed. *Pignoris capio*,
for instance, is a legal remedy involving no use of judicial machinery. See,
however, Ga. 4. 29.

of the higher magistrates, e.g., Adoption, Manumission, *In jure cessio*[4]. In these cases, however, it must be remembered that the *vindicatio*, which comes in, *is* formally an Action for the recovery of Quiritarian property. It was probably also from a formal reason that *praejudicia*, which were simply ascertainments of fact, were, though with some question, called *praejudiciales actiones*, and regarded as a sort of *actiones in rem*[5]. The Stipulations directed by the Praetor, which Ulpian says are called Actions " as filling their place," and Interdicts, which also "are comprised under the same style," were liquidated recognizances to obviate the necessity of a subsequent judicial estimate, or precautionary measures to protect rights which were questioned or menaced[6].

With a few exceptions like these, which scarcely are exceptions, *actio* properly signifies *remedial procedure*—remedial procedure undoubtedly, in a wide sense—not merely, as Heineccius put it, the *means* of pursuing[7], but also of defending one's Right. It will, therefore, cover Exceptions and Interdicts (as well as Actions in the narrower sense); also execution, and indeed any other self-help recognised or allowable by law[8].

There is also a vaguer or laxer view of *actio* taken in Celsus' definition, which Justinian embodies in his Institutes, and according to which *actio* is the *right* to take such remedial

---

[4] See Dig. 1. 7. 4 and compare Ga. 2. 24 (idque legis actio vocatur) with the use of *vindicatio* in the other cases mentioned.

[5] Just. 4. 6. 13. On this subject see below § 23, pp. 707—709.

[6] Dig. 44. 7. 37. pr. Actionum instar obtinent...actionis verbo continentur. In Dig. 17. 2. 65. pr. *actio* covers both *judicium* (= *actio* proper) and *stipulatio*, but the word has possibly here the general meaning of *conduct*. On the Praetorian Stipulations see Moyle on Just. 3. 18. pr.

[7] " Actio non est jus sed medium jus persequendi " cited by Austin[5], 45. 765, I suppose from Heineccius' Recitationes. Both meanings, however, are given in the Elementa 4. 6. § 1126.

[8] See Moyle[4], p. 541 c.

procedure[9], the sense in which a person is said *actionem habere* and similar phrases. Here we have the beginning of Austin's Sanctioning Rights (see below § 19, p. 617). In one passage of a little used writer, Macer, *actio* almost approaches the English meaning of the Wrong from which a right of action arises[10], but this is not a sense of the word used in Gaius' or Justinian's Institutes. In a Constitution of Constantine, A.D. 319, *actio fisci* is the *record* of a debt due to the *fiscus*, a use which I only mention as possibly leading to a somewhat similar use of the French word *actions*, in the case of a company[11].

Modern criticism of Gaius' arrangement. It is only with the first two meanings of *actio* that we are at present concerned, in speaking of Gaius' third Institutional division. That division, as regards its carrying out, has been somewhat severely criticised, since Austin's time, for comprising under one head the rights of action and the actions themselves— for giving, in fact, a larger treatment to the Remedial or, as Austin terms them, Sanctioning Rights than to the actual Remedies, the Procedure proper[12].

As an application of Austinian analysis, this charge may be successfully brought. But it is more fair to say that, in Gaius' Institutes, Actions are, to some extent, distinguished by scope and object, as well as by form, than to blame him for ignoring the new idea of Sanctioning Rights interposed by Austin between the Wrong and the Remedy— a middle term, the utility of which may be strongly questioned (see below, § 19, p. 618).

[9] Dig. 44. 7. 51. Just. 4. 6. pr. Whether Celsus was only referring to *actio in personam* (as seems probable) or not, does not affect Justinian's use of the quotation. See Moyle l. c.

[10] Macer, Dig. 48. 1. 7.

[11] Cod. Just. 10. 1. 6. See Littré, s.v. No. 14. For an instance, Code de Commerce, 1. 3. 34.

[12] See e.g. Moyle⁴, p. 504 : Poste⁴, pp. 14, 444.

Gaius' primary intention, in the *Jus quod ad actiones pertinet,* is to treat of the " civil " or private legal remedies for Wrong, of course inclusive of the right to take those remedies, but not necessarily of the Wrongs themselves, which gave occasion both to the remedial right and to the actual remedy.

Incidentally, subjects still further from the primary one are here and there discussed. For instance, the question of the original liability of a master or *paterfamilias* for acts of those under his control comes in implicitly in §§ 69–81 of the 4th Book. This matter, which might no doubt have been better treated as an independent subject under Obligations in Book 3[13], is introduced under Actions *à propos* of some statement in a lost part of Gaius as to the particular *form* of Action *de peculio*[14]. But the main point at present is that Gaius' plan is not based on any substantive treatment of the Wrongs, to which his Remedies apply, in the department of Actions. In fact, the subject of Private Wrongs in general is, with one exception, not treated directly in his Institutes at all : it has to be gathered either from his statement of the remedial procedure or from his account of Relative Rights and their corresponding Obligations[15]. The exception is in the case of the *obligationes ex delicto,* where certain violations of normal and Absolute Rights *are* specifically defined, together with some ancillary notice of the Actions available. It is undoubtedly true that the Absolute Rights themselves are here assumed, but scarcely correct to say, as Austin does[16], that they are " implicitly treated " under the head of Delicts by " the Roman Lawyers."

[13] See Moyle[4], 504.

[14] The contents of the illegible pages, 210, 211, of the MS. are supposed to have dealt with the subject-matter of Justinian's Instt. 4. 6. 36—38.

[15] See Austin[5], 47. 785 on this subject, and on the exclusion of Absolute Duties or Duties due only to the Community (see below, § 21, p. 648) from these Manuals of Private Law.

[16] Austin[5], 45. 768, St. 366.

Coupling or Separation of Obligations ex contractu and ex delicto. I do not propose to enter here into the patently illogical coupling of Obligations *ex contractu*, which do not arise originally from a Wrong, with Obligations *ex delicto* which do ; nor into Austin's grounds for approving of the treatment generally of those two subjects by the Roman Institutionalists in the case of the latter, and disapproving of it in the case of the former[17]. There is certainly the merit of simplicity in their classing together all benefits of Obligation, however arising, as items of Property ; and in keeping these Rights, whether *primary* or *secondary* (§ 19, p. 618) apart from the procedure by which they were to be ultimately made available. Thus much at least is clear, that the Wrongs, or occasions for remedy, so far as they come at all in Gaius' Institutes, do *not* come in his third division of *Actiones*.

The transfer of the subject of Obligation *ex delicto* by Justinian into his 4th Book, where it very abruptly introduces *his* Law of Actions, has been variously accounted for. It is possible that the change may indicate a feeling as to the impropriety of classifying *obligationes ex contractu* and *ex delicto* together, and the necessity of giving the latter a more markedly independent treatment. Some reason may also be found in the great change which had taken place as to Procedure, and the smaller amount which could be learned on that subject in Justinian's time, from an Institutional work based originally, as to this part, on obsolete Law[18]. The idea, therefore, of making up pretty nearly equal amounts of matter for the different Books, may come in here, as it occasionally appears to do, in the divisions of the Digest[19].

[17] Austin[5], 45. 710, 769 : St. 378 : also notes 3 and 4 to 43. 739, 740.
[18] See Moyle[4], 505 (Int. to Book iv.).
[19] See Roby, Int. xxxiv. (on Book v.) and xl. (on Book xxii.).

Appendix to Jus Actionum. There needs but very little more to be said about the *detailed* contents of the *Jus quod ad actiones pertinet.* The subject of checks on vexatious litigation seems to come in rather abruptly after a hiatus in the MS. of Gaius[20]. But both this and the remaining six sections are a natural Appendix to a Law of Actions. So too is Justinian's following Title 17, De Officio Judicis, dealing with sentence and execution. The brief concluding notice De Publicis Judiciis (Tit. 18) is nominally introduced *à propos* of the dissimilarity between these *judicia* and the private ones. But it is more logically accounted for by Justinian's intention to make his Institutes an introduction to the study of the whole body of Imperial Law, Criminal as well as Civil[21].

Blackstone's Book iii. generally. On Blackstone's main division into Rights and Wrongs, and subdivision of the latter into Public and Private, I shall have to speak more fully in the following sections. At present I only wish to compare his treatment of Private Wrongs and their Remedies with the subject-matter of Gaius' *Jus Actionum.*

Blackstone's third Book contains a very multifarious collection of matters. First comes a brief notice of certain extra-judicial remedies and of redress by suit in Court generally (chs. 1, 2, 3): second, an account of the several Courts and the different departments which come under their cognizance (chs. 4—7): third, a detailed statement of the different private wrongs recognised by English Law and their remedies described generally (to this is appended a chapter on the anomalous case of injuries proceeding from or affecting the Crown) chs. 8—17 : last, the actual proceedings in Court and their sequel (chs. 18—27).

In this medley there is a good deal of repetition and confusion, as well as what seems to me misplacement. The

----

[20] Ga. 4. 171—181.   [21] Const. Tanta, § 11.

first part, with its archaic survivals of self-help, and the few *automatic* remedies of our Law, forms certainly a natural introduction to redress by process in Court. The account, on the other hand, of the Courts themselves belongs properly to Public Law, whether we regard it as part of Constitutional Law, in the wider sense of the term, or as coming under Public Conditions or Relations in Personal Law, see § 15, pp. 523, 524. The final chapter, however, of this part (chap. 7), intended as a connecting link with what follows, ought rather, perhaps, to be taken with chapters 8—17, of which I have next to speak.

The great feature, whether merit or not, of Blackstone's arrangement now under consideration, is that, while he gives Civil Procedure a distinct place, he prefaces it with an independent account of the Private Wrongs or Civil Injuries which it is intended to redress. This arrangement is peculiar to Blackstone, who is, however, in point of fact, merely following out the idea of Hale (see § 19, p. 610). On the modifications of it, in the later treatment of Stephen, I shall have to speak in the next Section.

Compared with French and German Codes. This independent treatment of Wrongs does not, as we have seen (above, p. 603), appear at all definitely in the Roman Institutes: neither does it in the European Codes, which in their general scheme follow the Roman Institutes. The principle may indeed be considered as represented, to some extent, by the *substantive* heading of *Délits et quasi délits* which comes in the French Code Civil (L. 3, Tit. 4), under the general head of non-Conventional Obligations, after Quasi-Contracts, like the *Obligationes ex delicto* in Gaius: whereas, in the Contracts and Quasi-Contracts, the Causes, or originating occasions of Action, are to be gathered from the primary Obligations themselves, which have been disregarded.

In the German Code of Private or Civil Law (*Bürgerrecht*) Delicts similarly follow on continuously after Contract and Quasi-Contract. In the earlier and larger amount of the Law of Obligations there is much detailed subdivision, and the fault or breach has to be gathered, in the main, from the particular Duty: in the later part the fault, which is the originating occasion of the Obligation, is more independently stated[22]. In neither Code does statement of a particular Wrong depend on reference to its particular Remedy (see below, § 19, p. 621); Procedure being kept entirely distinct in the *Prozess-Ordnungen* of the German and the *Codes de Procédure Civile* and *d'Instruction Criminelle* of the French system.

Place of Procedure in an Educational Course. As a matter of the historical development of Law, the consideration of Procedure will generally take a very early place. But, for purposes of legal education, the desirability of treating this subject separately, and late, seems obvious.

When Austin speaks (above, p. 599) of the propriety of distributing the subject-matter of Gaius' third head under the other two, he must apparently be thinking rather of the Wrongs than of the remedial Procedure. Whether from a view to the natural order of reading, or to the generally succinct treatment of a Corpus Juris, Procedure should come last, and by itself. It is necessarily technical, and not required by the ordinary reader nor by the legal student until entering on practice. Again, the same process will often be found applicable to several distinct Wrongs : so that the common remedy should, for mere avoidance of repetition, be kept apart from its various provocative occasions.

[22] The second Book, on Obligations (*Schuldverhältnisse*), contains nearly 600 Sections on Contractual and Quasi-Contractual matter, about 30 on Delictal. The meaning and order of the following Book (*Sachenrecht*), the separate treatment of Family Law (Book 4) and of Inheritance (Book 5), have been or will be noted elsewhere.

This is recognised by Austin, who also points out how not only may the same remedy be applicable to different Wrongs, but the same Wrong may be a complex violation of several distinct Rights or Duties[23]. The latter point is a decided argument in favour of Blackstone's recognition of Wrongs as a substantive heading, reference being made, in each case, to the particular remedy applicable, out of the appended modes or forms of Procedure. But to make a third or rather fourth department, as indicated by Austin, of Sanctioning Rights and Duties arising out of Wrongs, apart at once from the primary Duty, the Wrong itself, and the treatment applicable to it, is a flagrant instance of the over-*morcellement* which Austin himself so often justly deprecates.

Substantive and Adjective Law. Bentham's division of Law into the above heads (which, however, I doubt whether he intended for an actual dichotomy) at first sight simply expresses the separation of Procedure from the rest of a Corpus Juris[24]. The criticism of this division by Austin consists mainly of objections to its phraseology, based upon an interpretation of his own.

Adjective, he says, meaning *instrumental*, not only Procedure but all the secondary Rights and Duties which arise out of Civil Injuries and Crimes, as well as some original or primary Rights and Duties, which have an instrumental character with reference to others, ought to be included in the second and excluded from the first division[25].

The above was certainly not what Bentham, as I understand him, meant by Adjective Law. If, however, there be, as I am inclined to think there is, some ambiguity about

[23] Austin[5], 45. 767, 771, 772 : St. 378.   The whole, however, of his views on the practical advisability of the divisions now under consideration seems to me extremely variable and undecided.   See further on these subjects § 22, pp. 673, 674.

[24] Traités iii. p. 188 (Vue générale, ch. 1).

[25] Austin[5], 45. 765, cf. 763 : St. 375, 376.

the meaning of this term, among those who employ it, this certainly seems to be a conclusive reason against the introduction of terms of classification not adopted, to my knowledge, in any actual system[26].

Apart from these considerations of phraseology, the idea of an *exhaustive* division of Law into Substantive and Adjective—by the latter being meant simply Procedure—is only open to the slight objection that it does not very clearly include certain other parts of the *machinery* of Law, like Conveyancing, which now requires more distinct treatment than its occasional notice in the Roman Institutes (see § 16, p. 567).

As a question of Codification, there does not appear to have been any difficulty in framing two distinct Appendices of Procedure, Civil and Criminal.   For a Student's elementary course, both are equally matter to be postponed, together with Conveyancing and, in my opinion, the entirety of the large and difficult subject of Evidence, which belongs really more to Procedure than to any other branch of Law (see below, § 19, p. 623).

[26] Holland (Jurisprudence[10], p. 347) quoting Bentham (Works, ii. p. 6) for the meaning of Adjective Law, seems ready to extend the term a little, in the line of Austin; but appears actually to use it (pp. 86, 161), as did Bentham, simply in the sense of Procedure.

§ 19.   RIGHTS AND WRONGS

Hale and Blackstone.   The desirability of recognising
Wrongs as a head of subject-matter distinct from Remedies
has been briefly referred to above (§ 18, p. 606).   This is,
however, only a subdivision in the view of that larger antithesis, devised by our English Institutionalists, between
Rights and Wrongs, of which some direct notice is now
necessary.

The origin of this antithesis is not improbably to be
traced to a misapprehension of medieval phraseology by
Sir Matthew Hale (above, § 13, p. 500).   The peculiar
difficulties, arising from Blackstone's use of it, are mainly
due to his inclusion of Criminal Law, that subject not being
included, or only included by reference, in Hale's Analysis
of the *Civil* Part of the Law.   This Analysis—less known
than it deserves to be—is divided into three heads: (*a*) Civil
Rights or Interests; (*b*) Wrongs relative to those Rights
or Interests; (*c*) Relief or Remedies applicable to those
wrongs[1].

[1] Analysis, § 1.   The word Civil has, even in the short space of this
Analysis, several different shades of meaning, as it has, perhaps to a still

As compared with the Roman Institutional system, the first head corresponds directly to Gaius' Books 1, 2 and the greater part of 3; the third to Book 4. With the second head there is nothing that corresponds directly in the Roman system; but the *obligationes ex delicto* (Ga. 3. 182—225) do so partially and implicitly (above, § 18, p. 603). Criminal Law, which forms no part of Gaius' Institutes, is separately treated by Hale in his Pleas of the Crown. This last subject is included by Blackstone under *his* antithesis of Rights and Wrongs, which is extended by him so as to cover the whole subject of Municipal, i.e. particular National Law[2].

A slight inconsistency must be here remarked in Blackstone's language as to the origin of legal Rights and Wrongs. On the page referred to in the last note, we have Rights and Wrongs first explained as right pieces of conduct commanded, and wrong pieces of conduct forbidden, by the laws of England. The rightness or wrongness here is in reference to an anterior moral standard, which has been reinforced, in the particular cases, by a legal sanction[3]. But, a few lines down, Rights, though not defined, are treated without any such reference, simply as legal powers or advantages, and Wrongs simply as the infringement of them. The latter is

greater extent, in Roman Law (see §§ 7, 22, pp. 365—367, 684, 685). In the present use the signification of Civil Rights is apparently the general one of Rights enjoyed by a person as member of a Civitas, a Social or Political Community. In "the Civil Part of the Law," ib. Civil is opposed to Criminal.

[2] Blackstone, 1. 1, p. 122. For the explanation of Municipal see above, § 9, p. 430.

[3] See below, § 22, p. 665. The quotation *jubens honesta et prohibens contraria* is rather from Bracton (1. 3, fol. 2ᵃ) than Cicero's Philippics, xi. 12. 28. Against this description, as applied to Law generally, see the objection of Christian (or Chitty), in Blackstone, Int. p. 44, n. 5, who would substitute "what shall be done, or what shall not be done," practically from Cicero, de Legg. i. 6. 18.

the view taken by Hale, and, on the whole, preferred by Blackstone.

Hale's Analysis, not purporting to include Criminal Law, deals only with Private Wrongs, which of course can be truly represented as infringements of the Private Rights belonging to individuals considered as individuals[4]. He does however somewhat inconsistently *mention* certain Criminal Wrongs, without indicating any violation of Rights, "which, as Criminal or Public, are to be distributed under the Title of Pleas of the Crown[5]." Blackstone, when he comes to speak of Public Wrongs; on the principle that *all* particular Wrongs are the privation of Rights, defines these as a breach of Public Rights and Duties which affects the whole Community. The King therefore, in whom centres the Majesty of the whole Community, is supposed by law to be the person injured and so the proper prosecutor for every public offence, whence Criminal Law came under the old style Pleas of the Crown[6].

With the adequacy of the above distinction between Public and Private Wrongs I am not at present concerned. But the treatment of the former as infringement of Rights of the individual Sovereign, though of high antiquity, and still maintained, to some extent, in English theory, must be regarded, in the view of general Jurisprudence, as a mere legal fiction[7] peculiar to certain systems at certain stages of development.

[4] Blackstone, iii. 1. 2.

[5] These are Wrongs of *temporal* conuzance, as distinguished from others only visited with ecclesiastical censure. Analysis, § 39. See generally below, § 22, p. 670.

[6] Blackstone, l.c. and iv. 1. 2.

[7] See § 21, p. 646, n. 18. On the general doctrine Stubbs, C. H. i. 7, p. 187; Stephen, General View, 58, 59; Markby[6], § 600, p. 295; P. and M. ii. 517, 570, rather, perhaps, on the difficulty of regarding this as really the original distinction.

Wrongs to be regarded as breach of Duties.   All the absolute legal Duties, so called by Austin, may as we shall see (§ 21, pp. 642—648) be reasonably resolved into Duties to the Community, which can therefore in a sense be said to have Rights.   But, as it is not always easy (see below, p. 616), nor particularly profitable, to set forth such Rights, beyond a mere converse statement of the Duties, it seems better, with Austin (in Lect. 18), to regard legal Wrongs, taken as a whole, more as violations of legal Duty than as infringements of particular legal Rights.   The former is really the original meaning of the Latin word *delictum*.   *Injuria*, too, is correctly, so far, taken by Austin to be, in its original signification, rather the opposition to Right generally than to an individual Right[8].

The acceptance of this point of view, however, as to legal Wrongs, does not at all necessarily involve the admission of Austin's reference of all Right and Duty to express Command, nor does it oblige us to accept his dictum that Right in general is merely an abstraction from particular Rights. It does rather involve the assumption that every particular Right correlates with, or is dependent upon, some Duty; as will be pointed out below, § 20, p. 635, in the definition of a Right which I venture to add to the previous attempts enumerated in Austin's 16th Lecture.   For the present, what I have to say, about the Absolute Duties above mentioned, is that they are to be clearly distinguished from what Blackstone designates by the same name.   His Absolute Duties are purely moral or religious ones, which man, he says, is bound to perform considered as a mere individual, i.e. not as a member of any human Society[9].   Austin's Absolute Duties are *legal* Obligations, enforceable by Courts of Justice, but having no individual Rights to correspond—

[8] See below, § 22, pp. 666, 667, as to *injuria* and *delictum*.
[9] Blackstone, 1. 1. 123; 4. 4. 41.   See Austin[5], 17. 401, n. 59; St. 194.

none at least which can be stated without involving some violation of his fundamental principles, and occasionally some obvious absurdity (see below, § 21, p. 643).

Taking it for granted, then, that Wrongs are, in general, better described as violations of Duty than infringements of particular Rights, we may come to consider a little more in detail the style and contents of Blackstone and Hale's dichotomous division.

Rights as a main division to include Duties. Their own ambiguous use of the term Rights may be here taken into account. Whether we choose to refer the ambiguity, with Austin, to a common origin of Right and Duty in Command, or as is here suggested (see below, § 20, pp. 625, 629) to a fundamental idea of Rightness or Wrongness, it is certain that both Blackstone and Hale are occasionally obliged to apply the term Right to what is more commonly called a Duty, and to include in their first department, of Rights, some notice of Duties also. Thus Hale, when he comes to Subjects (i.e. ordinary Citizens), treats of their "Rights of Duty to be performed, as of Privilege to be enjoyed," and Blackstone, under his Rights of Persons commanded to be observed by the Municipal Law, speaks first of such as are due *from* every citizen, which are usually called Civil Duties, adding however, as a reason, that some Right in another person must correlate with every Social Duty[10]. What correlating Rights can be made out in the case of Austin's Absolute Duties will be considered below (p. 616). Thus much seems to be established by experience that any reasonable treatment of legal Rights opposed, as a

[10] Hale, Analysis, § 13; Blackstone, i. 1. 123. The use of Right as equivalent to Duty occurs in the earliest English. See the beginning of Caedmon's Genesis, " *Us is riht micel thæt*," &c., where "our bounden duty" is nearer the meaning than "very right." Austin calls this use "good Saxon English" (Tab. i. n. 6, p. 956), though at present it is confined to the vulgar if it occurs at all.

main division, to Wrongs, must deal, at the same time, at least with some legal Duties.

Relative Duties taken with Rights strictly so called. Which of these Duties can, and should be, treated together with Rights or, as I would rather express it, under the head of Rights *and* Duties ? The object, at least of the Institutionalist, is the complete and intelligible treatment of one subject in one place, and the consequent avoidance of repetition. This object—possibly, it is true, a counsel of perfection—is duly kept in view by Austin in his 45th Lecture *ad finem* ; but his contributions to it are rather in the nature of depreciatory criticism than of positive suggestion (see below, p. 620).

All Rights called *par excellence* Relative (see § 15, p. 528) have obvious Duties corresponding to them, and the two will naturally be stated together. To this class of Rights belongs a considerable portion of Personal Law, and, in Property Law, the whole subject of Contractual and Quasi-contractual Obligation. On the other hand Obligations *ex delicto*, though coupled by the Roman Jurists, as also items of Property, with those *ex contractu*, depend upon violations of Duty where the violation is so much more prominent than the Duty that, apart from other considerations, they might of themselves more naturally be classed under the head of Wrongs.

Absolute Rights of Blackstone and Duties of Austin. The Absolute or, as I should prefer to call them, the Normal Rights, of Blackstone (see above, § 15, pp. 528, 529), have, as we shall see in the definition of a particular Right, Duties of forbearance or regard corresponding to them, and incumbent upon all members of a social Community other than the individual clothed with the Right. These Duties are in general simply *assumed*, as ancillary to the Rights concerned, in Institutional works on Law, except perhaps in some such general maxim as that of *alterum non laedere* in Just. I 1. 3[11].

It is upon the Absolute Duties of Austin that the question of intelligible explanation mostly turns. These, which were formerly considered rather as correlating with Rights belonging to Authorities, civil or religious, may be now generally regarded as Duties to the Community. In many of the individual additions which have from time to time been made to their number, even by modern legislation, the primary or original Duty is only defined implicitly in the penal or recuperatory procedure provided for violation[12], as, in old legislature generally, early Statute Law simply provides for violations, whether of individual Right or of Absolute Duty, previously recognised as such by Custom or Moral Sanction only.

When the violation of an Absolute Duty is evidently, from the character or competence of the Remedy provided (see § 22, pp. 677, 678), meant to be treated directly as a Public Wrong, it might seem to come most properly under that head, the violation attracting to itself, or comprising, the statement of the Duty[13].

When the Duty to the Community, on the other hand, corresponds to Rights or quasi-Rights conferred upon specific bodies or individuals simply in a ministerial or public capacity, it would seem more natural and convenient to place such Duties, as Austin suggests, in the Law of Political Status, together with the Rights which are merely instrumental to their enforcement[14].

But it may be questioned whether, in both these cases, some general statement of the Absolute Duties incumbent

[11] Austin[5], 43. 729; St. 364, 5.

[12] Austin[5], 45. 768, 771, 772; St. 377, 378, also Outline, 66, and generally below, § 22.

[13] Austin[5], 47. 784, 786. [14] Ib. 786. See also § 15, p. 531.

upon the ordinary citizen (particularly when of a positive[15] character) ought not, as a matter both of policy and common sense, to be inserted, together with his Absolute or Normal Rights, at the beginning of Personal Law.

A statement, certainly, of the Duty, *for the first time*, in the remedial or punitive Procedure, seems open to an objection which I have felt somewhat strongly against a not uncommon arrangement of legal study. Teachers, I know, of high experience have sometimes preferred to take the Criminal Branch first in the educational treatment of English Law, from its comparatively simple and what is considered to be its specially interesting character. To my mind, this order of study has somewhat of the repulsive : and accordingly in a Code, or at any rate in an Educational scheme, I would prefer to shew the student his right course first, rather than leave him to pick it out among the rocks and shoals of the wrong one.

Sanctioned and Sanctioning Rights. A division of Rights as above, which is strongly pressed if not invented by Austin, although merely intended by him for a subdivision of his "Law of Things," or Law General, may well be taken under a wider bearing in considering the scheme of Blackstone. This distinction of Rights, it is true, like Holland's similar one of Antecedent and Remedial, does involve some special questions of principle, as well as of phraseology. But, as a matter of scheme and arrangement, it depends on much the same points as are raised by Blackstone's main division of Rights and Wrongs, compared with the arrangement of the Roman Institutes.

[15] E.g. to pay rates and taxes, serve in a militia or army, give notice of births, deaths, contagious diseases, &c. See Austin[5], 47, p. 785. Negative Duties, too, of the less obvious character, e.g. to abstain from cruelty to animals, might certainly be stated with advantage. On the general negative Duty corresponding to Absolute or Normal Rights, besides what has been said above (p. 615), see § 22, pp. 669, 670.

Austin divides his "Law of Things" into (*a*) Law regarding Rights and Duties which do not arise from Injuries or Wrongs directly or immediately; (*b*) Law regarding Rights and Duties which do arise directly and immediately from Injuries or Wrongs: in other words (*b*) Law enforced directly by the Tribunals or Courts of Justice and (*a*) Law which they only enforce indirectly or by consequence[16]. Instead, therefore, of speaking of Rights and Wrongs, Austin speaks of Rights and Duties Primary or Sanctioned and Secondary or Sanctioning. Now, while there is no great objection to the terms Primary and Secondary, or their explanation, I fail to perceive, either in practice or theory, any superiority in the new division over the old one. It seems to me far more reasonable to make the Wrongs themselves the antitheton of the original Rights or, as I should prefer to say, Rights and Duties, and to treat all "secondary" Rights, together with the means of enforcing them, as consequences of those Wrongs. Some Injury or Wrong is, according to Austin's definition, essential to all his Sanctioning Rights[17]; so that we are surely justified in taking, for title, the generating fact, the conception of which must, as he himself admits[18], precede that of the Secondary Rights generated.

Why, then, does Austin go out of his way to suggest this new classification? Mainly, it would seem, for a reason worthy, no doubt, of consideration, as Austin's reasons always are, but which cannot be admitted without question.

The term Sanctioning is here used to express the proper *purpose* or object, as conceived by Austin, of the Secondary

[16] Austin[5], 45. 764; St. 375. I insert these pairs of letters for the sake of cursory readers, having repeatedly observed the most absurd blunders caused by Austin's puzzling use of the order or *figure*, as the Grammarians call it, Chiasmus (*A. B : b. a*).

[17] The apparent exceptions are disposed of by Austin himself in 45. 766; St. 376, referring to 25. 474—6; St. 233—235.

[18] Ib. 771.

Rights and Duties to which he applies that term. This
purpose he considers to be the *deterrence,* or the prevention
of future Wrongs: *redress,* or reparation to the injured party,
is, in his view, only a subordinate object[19].

Austin's view on this subject will scarcely be generally
accepted. It may, of course, be maintained, in the case of
those more serious crimes, where Blackstone complacently
observes that we seldom hear any mention made of satisfaction to the individual; the satisfaction to the community
being so very great[20]—which satisfaction, we may remember,
in former times took away all *means* of reparation. It may
also be maintained, though not so positively, where the civil
right to sue is recognised as practically available, but is
suspended until a criminal prosecution has been carried out
or attempted[21]. But this postponement of the civil remedies
of the injured party is not universally the case, even in
English Law, and it is too much connected with certain
peculiarities of that system to be adopted as a general
principle of Jurisprudence. I certainly think that, in the
case of civil injuries, most people, as against Austin, would
hold the main object of the secondary Rights to be *reparation* rather than prevention (see further below, § 22, p. 675).

Induced, no doubt, by considerations such as these,
Holland would substitute the style Remedial in place of
Austin's Sanctioning[22], though I imagine he would treat
the division more as an academical than a practical one.
In fact the point to be considered in an Educational scheme

[19] Ib. 762—764. Very slightly given in St. 374. For a thoroughly
Austinian reason why Sanctioned is preferred to Primary, see 768.

[20] Comm. iv. p. 6.

[21] Blackstone, ib. and iii. pp. 119, 120.

[22] Holland[10], 9. 141; Markby (Elements[6], §§ 840, 841, p. 412) speaks of
intermediate and ultimate Sanctions, the former corresponding to Sanctioning
Rights, or rather Duties, the latter to bodily pain, imprisonment and forfeiture.

is rather one of intelligible arrangement than of principle or terminology. *Ex vi termini* neither Austin's Sanctioning nor Holland's Remedial Rights can properly include the Wrongs from which they arise. On the question where the Wrongs *should* come, Austin's answer is, as has been suggested above (p. 615), of a very inconclusive character. We find him blaming the system of Gaius, or giving an exceptional approval to that of Blackstone, by subjecting the one or the other to principles and distinctions of his own[23], which were not recognised or known by either. But no uniform or consistent principle is laid down by himself.

On the whole it certainly seems to me that Blackstone's broad distinction of Rights and Wrongs is decidedly superior, on general grounds, both to the Roman Institutional Arrangement, and to that of Austin so far as any substantive suggestion is attempted by the latter.

Detail of Wrongs in modernised Blackstone, &c. It seems however to depend upon varying circumstances of legal developement, and the consequent variances of literary treatment, whether an express specification of Wrongs *per se can* always be made, so as to constitute the second department of a student's course or educational Digest, or of an intelligible Code: the remedies being in each case referred to in general terms, but the technicalities of Procedure postponed.

In this particular matter of arrangement, that of the two main modern Codes considered in the last section (pp. 606, 607) certainly appears to me confused and confusing. That of Blackstone may now be considered more in detail, and, of course, in the light of the modernised version of Stephen and Stephen's successors.

Crimes and Torts. The division of Public and Private Wrongs is the main subject of a later section: but I may anticipate so far as to say that, on the present question, as

---

[23] Austin[5], 45. 768—770; St. 378, 379.

to a substantive statement of Wrongs, there is no difficulty with Crimes, nor with the minor violations of Absolute Duty called Torts : the really difficult case for consideration is that of breaches of Contract. Here the question, whether the breach can only be expressed, if I may say so, *implicitly*, as simple neglect of Duties, which ought to come in the division of Rights; or can be separately stated as a Wrong, depends, I think upon the history, and survivals of history, in the particular legal system. Where the general principle of Relief or Remedy has been crystallised into certain Forms of Action, and still retains in practice a classification dependent on, or motived by, those Forms (though the Forms themselves may be discontinued or abolished), it will probably be possible and serviceable to formulate a specific Wrong. Thus, in the latest treatment of Stephen's modernised Blackstone (Ed. 14), under the statement of Civil Injuries in Book v., which corresponds to Blackstone's Private Wrongs in his Book iii., we find the Wrongs remediable by the old Actions of *debt, covenant* and *assumpsit* still capable of independent statement, as well as the more obvious cases of Tort, *detinue, trespass,* &c.[24]

Breaches of contract. In other Injuries generally described as " affecting Things in Action[25]," the Wrong would seem to be most naturally treated as the mere violation or neglect of Duties, to be set out in the department of Rights, under Contract. The Wrong, or the measure of damages, is simply the value of the performance to the plaintiff. But here again, by the side of the general rule that for the *breach of contract,* in so many words, an action will lie, more specific forms of remedy have been developed for particular contracts of common occurrence which compel us practically to look to the Remedy for a definition of the Wrong.

[24] Stephen, iii. p. 385.
[25] Id. Compare ii. p. 96 with iii. 441—445.

Cases for Equitable Relief. In the large class of cases requiring Equitable Relief, which can often be scarcely called Wrongs at all, there is certainly much difficulty in finding a proper place for them, as indeed for the subject of Equity in general. It does not come very satisfactorily in the excellent chs. 8—12 of this Book v in the new Blackstone.

Place of Equity generally. I ventured in a previous section (15, p. 539) to question whether certain rules of conduct, peculiar to the condition of Trustee, might not be stated, under that head, in Personal Law. But Trust, taken in the widest sense, does not include the whole subject of Equity—not of course signifying here a mode of Interpretation or a principle in the Administration of Justice (see § 3, pp. 114, 115) but a definite body of supplementary Law. In this sense Equity is undoubtedly "a collection of appendixes between which there is no very close connexion[26]."

Trust and Constructive Trust, more particularly the latter, might conceivably have been brought, in Justinian's Institutes, under his comprehensive Title of Obligations *quasi ex contractu* (Instt. 3. 27. 5); specific Performance directly under Contract. Partnership too, which belongs largely to modern Equity, is some argument for treating the subject as an appendix to the Law of Obligations. On the other hand, quite an equal number of the subjects "over which Equity has jurisdiction" enumerated in the chapters of Stephen to which I am now referring[27], have to do specially with Rights of ownership in Land. Administration of deceased persons' estates, too, belongs to the earlier half of Property Law (see § 17, pp. 551, 552), while the Wardship of Infants comes partly under Personal.

In spite, however, of this multifariousness I think that in the interest of legal education there ought to be made, or

[26] Maitland, Equity, p. 19.
[27] See particularly Stephen's Blackstone, vol. iii. p. 457.

at any rate there always will be made, some attempt at a statement of "the general principles of Equity" (such as is given in Stephen, ch. 9) for the sake of the English student. The question to which I have at present digressed is, where that statement will best come.   Equity is not connected with Crimes, and very little with Torts.   It would seem, at first sight, most suitable for an appendix to Property Law.   But the application of its principles is so continually occurring throughout Property Law that it would almost serve better as a preliminary notice than as an appendix.   At the risk of uttering a paradox—a risk against which every adapter of Austin must be on his guard—I venture to suggest the subject as an appendix to the article on Trustee, at the end of Personal Law.   Trust is practically, as well as historically, the leading matter of Equity, and the other subjects of that Jurisdiction, if they are to be collected together at all, may well be collected round that nucleus.

Conclusion.   New Digest of English Civil Law.   Except in this large and important addition of Equity, which is in great part a growth since Blackstone's time, the Book on Civil Injuries, in our modernised Institutes, follows generally the original order, of Wrongs, Remedies, Procedure: Injuries by and to the Crown being brought under the last subject towards its close and a chapter on the existing Limitations of Actions being interpolated just after the digression on Equity.   To this retention of Hale and Blackstone's principle I presume to add my hearty approval, subject to the postponement of Procedure.

In the last respect I may claim the support of the new Digest of English Civil Law: and, that, as I understand, not on any fanciful reason of Procedure being "Public Law" (see above, § 10, p. 438), but on the practical one, of avoiding unnecessary anticipation of technicalities, for the student (see too, § 18, p. 607).

In other respects, too, this Digest will be frequently cited hereafter, on account of its important endeavours to recast the educational treatment of English Law in a more scientific or more generally intelligible form. But, as the work is, by its prescribed plan, bound to follow the fundamentally different scheme of the German Civil Code[28] it is scarcely worth to compare it here with Blackstone's main division of Rights and Wrongs. I pass, therefore, to consider the elements of that division more in individual detail.

[28] The following is a brief comparison of this Digest, as proposed and partially carried out, with the *Bürgerliches Gesetzbuch.*

Dig. i.   General. BGB. *Allgemeiner Theil.*

   ii.   Obligations (Contract, quasi-Contract and Tort). *Schuldver-hältnisse.*

  iii.   Property Law. *Sachenrecht.*

  iv.   Family Law. *Familienrecht.*

   v.   Succession. *Erbrecht.*

§ 20. RIGHT, WRONG AND DUTY.
PARTICULAR RIGHTS

Ideas to be analysed. Austin. In speaking of the main division of a Corpus Juris adopted by Blackstone, I have necessarily assumed Rights, Wrongs and Duties to be matters popularly understood or apprehended in a loose general way. We now come to consider them more closely, to analyse the popular apprehension of them, and to compare it with the definition of Austin. Definition is scarcely the word for the very inconclusive remarks at the end of his 16th Lecture. But it is only fair to say that his Lecture would seem to have come down to us in a very fragmentary state.

With **Austin** Rights, Wrongs and Duties, like Law, all come from Command. Every Right depends upon a Duty —a Duty incumbent upon others relatively to the person invested with the Right. Duty is merely liability to the evil which must result on disobedience to the Command of a Superior able and prepared to inflict such evil. A Right and a relative Duty signify the same notion considered from different aspects. Hence the word Right is occasionally used in the sense of Duty—the latter idea, of something which is commanded or directed, being in fact the primary one[1].

In treating of Jurisprudence, Austin only concerns himself directly with legal Rights and Duties, where the Command referred to is that of the person or body which is Sovereign in some given Political Society. Whatever *natural* Rights and Duties he recognises he would refer to *divine* Command, as does Blackstone (below, p. 628). *Moral* Rights and Duties must be referred to rules of Positive i.e. *human* Morality. The former, however are not, *per se*, enforced judicially: the latter, not proceeding from a determinate Superior, are not subjects of command, and therefore, strictly speaking, not Rights at all[2]. Whether as *against* a Sovereign, or as between two independent States connected by a Treaty, there can only be these Rights improperly and analogically so called, or, as Austin would prefer to say, no Right at all. Conversely a Sovereign can have no *legal* Rights against his subjects[3].

Duties have hitherto appeared mainly as ancillary to Rights. But Duty is the wider term of the two. All Rights depend upon Duties incumbent *on* others: but there are Duties which do not create Rights *in* others, at least not in determinate persons (see above, § 2, p. 59). The latter class are termed by Austin Absolute, the former Relative Duties[4]. The different use by Blackstone of the term Absolute Duty has been already pointed out (§ 19, p. 613). The common characteristic of Austin's Absolute Duties will be shewn hereafter (§ 21, pp. 642—646). Finally,

---

[1] Among the many passages from which this statement is made up see particularly Austin[5], 16. 395; 18. 409 and note 69; 24. 466, &c.; St. 192, 198, 199, 228.

[2] See Austin[5], 12. 343, 344; 16. 401, 402; 18. 409; St. 160, 192, 198.

[3] Austin[5], 6. 282, 283; St. 116, 117.

[4] Austin[5], 17. 401, 406; St. 194, 197.

Wrongs are violations of Duty. A *legal* wrong is an act of forbearance or omission which amounts to disobedience to the Command of a Sovereign[5].

His Right in the Abstract. What Austin has to say upon Right and Wrong, as distinguished from *a* Right and *a* Wrong, is naturally confused and difficult to those who do not belong to his school of philosophy. Usually he means by the word Right, when he does employ it without an article, a general expression embracing all particular Rights—in other words a particular Right defined in the most general manner—which he terms "Right considered in Abstract[6]." To me, as I suppose to many others, this is a question-begging expression: I believe that the process of *abstraction* (or collection) is, even with Austin, nominal rather than real, while in the theory of Right maintained by those who differ from him it has no place whatever[7].

Blackstone, and objections to Austin. With Blackstone, the Right and Wrong, whether singular or plural,

---

[5] Austin[5], 18. 409; St. 198.

[6] Compare Austin[5], 16. 394, 396; St. 191, 2 with 17. 400.

[7] Elsewhere (6. 285; St. 118 n.) Austin distinguishes between the particular Right, which is a "faculty" or power, and Right the adjective or substantive, which means *just* or *justice*, justice being apparently an *abstraction* from just particulars, like Right in the abstract. (For a slightly different view of justice see the latter part of note *s*, Austin[5], 6. 268; St. 108.) In the note at the beginning of Lect. 18 (Austin[5], p. 409; St. 198), which starts with an erroneous etymology, he identifies this adjective *right*, as well as the adjective *just*, with that which is *commanded*—a view supported by extremely questionable statements as to the Roman *aequum* and the Greek δίκαιον. There are, it is true, in this amazing note, expressions pointing to a more correct appreciation of the original metaphorical meaning of Right and Wrong; but as, immediately above, Austin goes out of his way to derive *right* from *directum*, I cannot but think that the idea of what is *directed* or ordered, rather than of what is *stretched* or straight, is the one present to his mind, and that I am justified in representing his view of the fundamental meaning of Right and Wrong as conformity or disobedience to Command (see P. J. 26, 27).

general or particular, which precede human enactment and are reinforced by it (see above, § 19, p. 611) are the result of Natural Law which is dictated by God[8]. Here too, therefore, all Right, Wrong and Duty depend ultimately upon Command; so that, as to the present point, we need not recur to Blackstone's change of view when he comes to *legal* Right and Wrong, or his peculiar use of the term *Absolute* (ib. pp, 612, 613), but may just note the absence of any idea of the philosophical process of *abstraction*.

Austin's theory on these subjects is so complete in itself, and so consistent with his view of Law in general, that it cannot but command attention, even with those who fundamentally differ from it. In fact, like Hobbes' dictum "no law can be unjust[9]," most of Austin's apparently paradoxical conclusions are mere truisms or mathematical demonstrations, if his fundamental propositions be accepted. But it must be admitted that such fundamental propositions, which are from time to time represented by him as matter of analysis or abstraction, are often rather *postulated en bloc* from the beginning than *collected* from any comparison of actual phaenomena[10].

I must venture therefore here upon a brief return to the province of Morality, because it seems to me that moral considerations do really bear, more properly than Austin's literal "Command," not only upon the true conception of Rights and Wrongs but, what is more to the present point, upon their serviceable treatment in an Institutional course of Law.

---

[8] Blackstone, Int. 41, 54, 55; Comm. i. 1. 121, 123.

[9] Austin[5], 6. 268, note *s*; St. 108.

[10] In some cases they seem to have been mainly based upon the epigrammatic generalities of Bentham. Compare, for instance, the subject of the preceding pages with the beginning of the Principes du Code Civil, Traités, i. 145, 146 (Hildreth, 93, 95), or of the Vue Générale, chap. 2 (ib. iii. pp. 192, 193), and the long note (apparently Bentham's) in the Oxford "Principles," pp. 224, 225.

Jus and *Right* belong, according to the view maintained in a previous section, to a class of terms expressing the ideas of moral approval or disapproval which have indeed an imperative form or character, but do not depend upon any assignable Command and are not conceived as dependent upon Command. For the probable origin of these ideas and their connexion with the growth of the oldest Law, which I take to be based upon popular feeling or conscience, I must refer to §§ 3 and 7, pp. 131, 135, 136 and 347. What we are here concerned with is the true relation of a particular Right or *Jus* to Right or *Jus* in general, and the question how this relation bears upon the practical operation of Rights and the true conception of Wrongs.

Moral Rights. With Austin, as we have seen, Right (singular) is an "Abstract" expression, secondary to individual or particular Rights. In the view preferred by the present writer, which is that of a greater Jurist than Austin —Hugo **Grotius**—and of not a few moderns, the first conception of an individual Right is derived from the idea of that which is Right or Just in general, as being that which is Right for, or in reference to, an individual person[11]. And this idea carries with it a common disapproval of interference with that individual Right, or, in another point of view, a common feeling of Duty to respect it[12]. These

[11] Grotius, 1. 1. 4. The definition is given more fully below, in note 15. His reasoning is only on the word *jus*, but I may add that the same order of meanings, deriving what is right for a particular man from what is right in general, occurs in the Greek θέμις, the French *droit*, the Italian *diritto*, and the English *right*. See P. J. pp. 46, 86. In p. 26, n. 36 is cited a good early instance (Plautus) of *jus* passing from the general to the particular meaning. On the German philosophical distinctions as to the use of *Recht* see below, p. 637.

[12] See Salmond[2], pp. 182, 183, quoting also Windscheid. So Savigny, in his view as to the operation of an individual Right in practical life, says *mit unserer Einstimmung herrscht*, which Guenoux renders *du consentement de tous*. See below, pp. 637, 638, n. 26.

Moral Rights and Duties, protected and enforced, so far as they are protected and enforced, by what I venture to call "the common Conscience" of a human Society, are the only Natural ones of which I can discern any real existence. The Absolute Rights of which Blackstone speaks as pertaining to individual human beings in a State of Nature (see § 12, p. 478), in which they have no relation to other human beings, will now be generally discredited, on the ground that such a State of Nature is inconceivable or unproveable for any but the most exceptional and accidental cases.

Salmond, who agrees in deducing particular Rights from Right in general, or from some rule of Right, identifies the latter ultimately, in the passage above quoted (note 12), with a principle of general utility to mankind. This view of natural or moral Rights differs but slightly from Austin's reference to the tacit commands of the Deity, to which commands general utility is an Index (above, § 2, p. 66, § 3, p. 96). Any conscious reference to general utility is, however, a purely modern idea. Nor does this view take into account that direct sanction of moral Rights, lying in a common feeling of absolute approval or disapproval, which there is ground for believing to be the historical basis both of Morality and Law—whether it be a gradual development out of the general Social Instinct of Man, or a more specific faculty distinguishing the human animal from his earliest existence (above, § 3, p. 98).

Social and relative character of all Rights. Whatever be the psychological origin of the feeling above referred to, we must see that its practical effect, in determining conduct, is *social*. Every particular Right is really *relative*: it postulates an association of human beings within which it exists, and upon the common feeling of which its existence depends. Blackstone's Absolute Rights, apart from any question about his State of Nature, are more *intelligible* in their conception by Austin, as relative to Duties incumbent upon a Society at large. And it is to this relative Character of Rights that we may most probably, as has been suggested above (§ 19, p. 614), attribute that ambiguity in our Institutionalists' language by which the term a Right is sometimes used in what is called an *onerous* rather than a *lucrative* sense. A particular Right being that which is right for a particular person, it may, in Hale's language[13], be right for him to enjoy or to perform something. Both are in the general sense *right* or deserving moral approbation: the negation of either is *wrong* or deserving moral disapprobation. It is however the former alone which we most usually call a Right and the latter a Duty.

Moral and Legal Rights. The *social* and *relative* character of a particular Right is, to my mind, its primary feature, and the one which ought therefore to appear most prominently in the attempt to define it. The substitution of a *legal* for a *moral* sanction is an external matter of expediency or necessity, not affecting that inherent and fundamental quality.

There are, as we have seen above (§ 4, pp. 164, 165), two divergent opinions as to the *raison d'être* and first origin of a State or Political Association. The one to which preference has been given here is that, as an original Society extends in number and space, the effect of the common conscience becomes less immediately applicable, Rights less safe and Duties less efficacious, against the selfishness of the more wealthy or influential: so that first an occasional and then a permanent organisation of the joint force of the Society becomes necessary for the Administration of Justice. But I hold that the idea of Justice can be proved *prior* to the State, and that the first recognised Rights and Duties

[13] Analysis, § 13.

have been previously Moral ones, the original disapproval of interference with the individual Right being replaced by protection or redress on the part of the Common authority.

In Austin's point of view, who, as we have seen (above, p. 627), has very little to say of Right in general, the only individual Rights to be considered by the Jurist are *legal* ones. Whatever their previous existence, if any, they are, for him, creatures of the Sovereign's Command, dependent upon corresponding Duties imposed by the Sovereign's authority. And, in many cases, Austin's account of the origin of Rights is perfectly true. Rights and Duties, on matters which, at least before, were morally indifferent, are daily created by legislation. In others, a previous Moral Right and Duty is protected and enforced by political authority. But whether we consider the particular Right as arising from the common feeling of a Society or from Sovereign command, its fundamentally *relative* or *social* character is the same. It is therefore inadequate to define Rights without clear reference at the same time to Duties which are their complement, and of which the corresponding Wrongs are violations.

Definition of a Right. We may therefore leave out of account not only those older quasi-philosophical attempts to define a Right which are discussed by Austin and Holland[14], but also those more modern ones which treat a Right *merely* as an interest protected or a power recognised by Law (see below, n. 18). This same fault of omission appears also indeed in many of the older definitions, over and above a tendency to bring in that convenient "occult quality" which did medieval philosophers such yeoman's service whether in physics or metaphysics (see above, § 12, p. 490, n. 67.

Grotius. For instance, a Right was, evidently, not mere

14 Austin[5], 16. 397—400; St. 193; Holland, ch. 7.

physical ability. It was, therefore, according to Grotius, a *moral* (by which he means simply a non-physical) *quality*, belonging to a person for the rightful enjoyment or performance of something[15].

This definition has the merit, to begin with, of indicating the *beneficial* character of a Right, which many of the modern definitions do not indicate. That the "enjoyment or performance" must be *rightful* looks rather like the common fault of including, in a definition, that which is to be defined. It should perhaps, however, be rather regarded as an insistence on referring particular Rights to a prior conception of Rights in general. But the negative or fictitious "moral quality" would certainly be better replaced by some specific statement of the *mode of operation* of a Right, i.e. of its guarantee and basis (see below, p. 635).

The omission of this statement is the fault of several later definitions of a Right, while it is too exclusively relied on by others. It comes prominently forward in the account of a Right cited by Austin from Mühlenbruch, which appears to me to have otherwise very little merit, and is, in fact, queried by Austin himself. "Right we call a condition and power of doing or not doing. Hence arises the fact that to a Right there always corresponds a Duty of others, which Duty is either common to *all*, and is determined merely by the rule that no one is to injure his neighbour, or is

---

[15] Grotius (De Jure Belli ac Pacis, 1. 1. §§ 3, 4) after the general statement, Jus hic nihil aliud quam quod justum est significat, proceeds...Ab hac juris significatione diversa est altera, sed ab hac ipsa veniens, quae ad personam refertur. Quo sensu jus est qualitas moralis personae competens ad aliquid juste habendum vel agendum.

I purposely omit a division which follows, of Rights into more or less perfect. This is based upon the Aristotelian (or perhaps, in its origin, Platonic) division of *justice* into several kinds. (See Nicomachean Ethics, 5. 2—5.) The philosophers' reasoning is contested, in certain points, by Grotius, who practically abandons the distinction and the subject of *imperfect* Rights altogether.

peculiar to definite persons, arising from that Right by which individuals are bound to individuals[16]."

In a long quotation, on the other hand, from Mackeldey's Lehrbuch we are merely told that "Right in the *subjective* sense (see below, p. 637) indicates the *moral* (opposite to *physical*) possibility either to be at liberty to do something one's self or to require that another should do or pretermit something on our behalf[17]. And, to come to later authority, Jhering's definition of a Right simply as an Interest protected by Law[18] is, beyond an apparent denial of the existence of any but *legal* Rights, merely a general indication of beneficial character.

Austin cites from "certain writers," referring, as far as I can make out, to Bentham[19], what purports to be a definition of a Right as "that security for the enjoyment of a good or advantage which one man derives from a Duty imposed upon another or others." To which the only objection which I have to make is that it wrongly identifies the protected power or faculty with the protection. Similarly, the nearest

[16] Austin[5], 16. 399, 400, Notes, omitted in St. (see however, St. 32. 292), Jus vocamus conditionem facultatemque faciendi aut non faciendi; ex quo nascitur ut juri semper respondeat aliorum officium; idque aut commune est omnium, quod eo solo cernitur ut ne quis alterum laedat, aut certorum hominum proprium, scilicet eo jure oriundum quo singuli singulis obstringuntur.

The *sequitur* expressed by the words *ex quo nascitur* is not very intelligible. See Markby[2], § 152, p. 93, on this passage, particularly the *non faciendi*, which is justly criticised by him as involving a most undesirable confusion of ideas. This particular criticism is, however, omitted in later editions, e.g. 6th, p. 83.

[17] "Die moralische Möglichkeit (? = facultas) entweder etwas selbst thun zu dürfen, oder zu verlangen dass ein Andrer zu unserem Vortheil etwas thue oder unterlasse." Austin[5], p. 399 (see Mackeldey, Lehrbuch[12], § 2, p. 3).

[18] Ein rechtlich geschütztes Interesse, as cited by Holland in ch. 7 from Geist, iii. § 60 (p. 339). For other modern definitions see the same chapter.

[19] Austin[5], 16. 397; Bentham, Principes, i. p. 128 (Hildreth, p. 84); Le droit est la garantie; la faculté est la chose garantie.

approximation at which he himself arrives at a Definition appears to be that "a Right is the Capacity or power of exacting from another or others Acts or Forbearances." Since he only deals, in effect, with *legal* Rights, he adds that the authorisation by Law to exact such Acts or Forbearances, or the Sanction enforced by the State, should be also expressed[20].

In all this, as appears from Bentham's own words (n. 19), the guarantee or basis of a Right is confused with the Right itself. The definition which I should prefer is a modification of Mühlenbruch and Mackeldey; framed moreover so as to include more distinctly that important distinction of Rights, which must be taken into account from the first, though whether it can be made a main division of the Corpus Juris, as proposed by Austin, is certainly matter of question.

Every good or advantage which we call a Right may, as it seems to me, be resolved into a Power either, on the one hand, of doing or enjoying something, in the widest possible sense of the words, or, on the other hand, of having something done for one, which, in both cases, corresponds to and depends on an Obligation incumbent on others. The Obligation in the former case is one incumbent upon all members of the Society wherein the Right is enjoyed (other than the person enjoying it) to forbear from interference : in the latter case it is incumbent upon some determinate individual, among such members, to do what is required by the Right.

Rights in rem and **in personam.** This difference in the incumbency of the Obligation or Duty, corresponding to a Right, constitutes the distinction as stated by Austin between Rights *in rem* and Rights *in personam.* "A Right

---

[20] Compare Austin[5], 16. 398; St. 193 with Thibaut, ib. 400, who correctly regards the "power of exacting," &c., as *auxiliary* or *necessary* rather than *principal.* Jedes Recht führt, als solches, die Möglichkeit des Zwanges *mit sich.*

in rem resides in a determinate person or persons and avails against other persons universally or generally. Further, the Duty to which it correlates is *negative*, that is to say, a Duty to forbear or abstain. A Right *in personam* resides in a determinate person or persons, and avails against a person or persons certain or determinate: the Obligation with which it correlates may be negative or positive, that is to say an Obligation to forbear or perform[21]."

"The phrase *in rem* denotes the *compass* and not the *subject* of the Right." (*Compass* apparently means field of operation: on *subject* see below, p. 639.) "It denotes that the Right in question avails against people generally, and not that the Right is a Right over a thing. For many of the Rights in question are either Rights over or to *persons*, or have no subject, person or thing[22]." The phrase *in personam* is an abridged or elliptical expression for *in personam certam sive determinatam*. Like the expression *in rem*, it denotes the *compass* of the Right, i.e. that the Right avails *exclusively* against a determinate person or determinate persons[23].

With regard to these definitions, the comparatively simple question whether a Right must necessarily reside in a determinate person will be considered in the next section under the head of Duties (§ 21, p. 648). In a later section I shall endeavour to distinguish the use of the phrase *in rem* and *in personam* by the Roman Jurists from the distinction based on them by Austin, and to shew that the latter is not suitable for a principal division of a Corpus Juris. At present I must conclude my consideration of Particular Rights with an attempt to explain some difficulties of terminology.

[21] Austin[5], Outline, 44, 45; Lect. 16. 394, 395; St. 192.

[22] Austin[5], 14. 369, 370; St. 176. Outline, 46, 47 quoted in Lect. 47. 786, 787; St. 381.

[23] Austin[5], 14. 370. The above definitions give the exact words of Austin, though not all from any single passage.

Recht subjectiv and objectiv. The German *Recht*, while undoubtedly retaining its general moral meaning, has developed this meaning into that of Law on the one hand and of a particular Right on the other. The former developement has not been fully arrived at in England, or at least not retained; for designations, in our earlier Laws, of the Rights and Duties collectively pertaining to particular Classes approximate very nearly to it[24]. As to the latter, a particular Right is often called by the German Jurists Recht in the *subjective* sense (see the Index to Jhering's *Geist*). By the antithetical expression, Recht in the *objective* sense, they are understood by Austin[25], who strongly reprobates the use of either phrase, to mean Law strictly so called. I doubt whether this use of the phrase does quite so definitely exclude the moral meaning. Literally, the designation *objective* would seem intended to express an external or independent existence, as distinguished from reference to, or inherence in, a particular person. Not to repeat the argument of § 3, I venture as against a strong modern school (see above, p. 134) to identify Recht in this so-called *objective* sense with Right in general, as popularly recognised, and partially expressed in Law, rather than *merely* with the latter.

The ambiguity or, from another point of view, the moral significance of the German Recht is prominently brought out in Savigny's description of *a* Right, in the subjective sense, as depending, in actual life, on the agreement of others, and descending ultimately from that Positive Right which lies in the common consciousness of a People[26].

[24] E.g. in the *Thegn-riht, eorl-riht, folc-riht,* &c. of the *Rectitudines* above referred to, § 15, p. 536.

[25] Austin⁵, 6. 285, 286, note v; St. 118; 42. 713 (omitted in St.).

[26] Savigny, System, i. § 4, p. 7. Betrachten wir den Rechtzustand im wirklichen Leben, so erscheint uns darin zunächst die der einzelnen Person zustehende Macht, ein Gebiet worin ihre Wille herrscht, und *mit unserer Einstimmung* herrscht (Guenoux translates *du consentement de tous*). Diese

The two passages referred to clearly indicate one point of view here taken as to an ïndividual Right, i.e. that it is a creature of Society, depending on, or at least backed by, surrounding admission and originating in a common social feeling. The term *positive* applied by Savigny to the Right which "lies in the common consciousness of a people," I take to indicate the *active* and *efficient* feeling of common approval or disapproval, to which I have so frequently referred the origin of Law. It is, in fact, Austin's "positive Morality" *plus* the distinctive character, the special scope and force, which he appears to me to ignore in his use of the word (see above, § 3, pp. 86, 87).

In Savigny's *genealogy* of a Right, referred to in the last note, we may remark a statement of the Right's immediate ancestor as *Rechtsverhältniss* Legal or *Rectal* (if I may coin a word) Relation, a convenient expression for Right *and* Duty, superior to Hale and Blackstone's occasional archaic use of Right in the latter sense (above, § 13, p. 501). It is an expression objected to by Austin[27] as implying, he says, that not only every Right, but every Obligation is Relative, which Blackstone does in fact endeavour to make out (see § 19, p. 612, 614). The subject of Absolute Duties, in Austin's

nennen wir ein Recht dieser Person, gleichbedeutend mit Befugniss: Manche nennen es das Recht im subjectiven Sinn. Compare too the genealogy of a Right, as traced by Savigny, ib. §§ 5, 7, pp. 7, 9, 14 and §§ 52, 53 generally (see above my § 3, p. 132). Jhering (Geist, i. 107, 108), in an obvious reference to the passage above cited, dwells on the *subjective* Right, or Will, in the *individual*, as the fountain-head of Roman Private Law, but appears rather to ignore the *consentement de tous*. The principle of Self-help does undoubtedly enter very conspicuously, as he shews, into the developement of that Law; but it is surely Self-help as recognised by the Community to be allowable or maintainable. This is, in fact, admitted in a later passage of the Geist iii. 1. 329.

[27] Austin[5], Table i. note 6, pp. 925, 926. The objection does not, to my mind, outbalance the convenience. *Schuldverhältniss* is a similar comprehensive word; and in *Rechtsfähigkeit* competence to incur Obligation, as well as to enjoy Right, is clearly intended.

sense, will be more fully treated in the next section; but it must be noted that Savigny, in the passage just now referred to, was only speaking of particular *Rights*, which have been shewn (above, p. 630) to be *all* relative.

Subjects and Objects of particular Rights. Apart from the question whether *objective* Right, in German, means Law in the strict Austinian sense or Right in general, the meaning of the other expression *subjective* is fairly clear, and obviously connected with the German use of the word Subject as indicating the *person* in whom a particular Right is vested, in antithesis to Object, the Thing in or over which the Right may exist. These meanings have been sufficiently illustrated above (§ 12, p. 482), but I must for a moment revert to the different sense in which Austin proposes to use the same pair of terms, to the German use of which he objects as conducing to the confusion which he finds in the antithesis of Subjective and Objective as applied to Right individual and Right general or Law[28]. In his objection to these adjectives as somewhat confusing and unintelligible I entirely concur, without necessarily accepting Austin's reasons for doing so[29].

In Austin's own use of Subject and Object, with regard to a particular Right, the former is the Thing (which may of course be a human being or person), in or over which a Right of Ownership (see § 16, p. 552) exists, the latter the acts(?) or forbearances, on the part of others, to which the Right entitles its possessor[30]. This use of the term Subject might be accepted as intrinsically intelligible and convenient enough, but for its general acceptance otherwise by a consensus of Jurists: that of Object is extremely confusing and objectionable, when we consider the constant use of the word, mostly in connexion with the epithet *material*, to

[28] Austin[5], 41. 712, 713. [29] See Editor's note on St. p. 175.
[30] Austin[5], 41. 712, 713; St. 175. See also 46. 776.

indicate a *res corporalis*, in which sense it is used by Austin himself, in his definition of a Thing (above, § 16, p. 553). My own preference therefore is to take Subject and Object in the sense in which they are generally understood, and not to trouble about Subjective and Objective Right.

Holland in his valuable chapter on Rights, to which I would generally refer the student, is in agreement with what has been said above, so far as basing an individual Moral Right upon a general feeling of approval.   He also speaks of the *object* of a Right in the same sense generally as that in which the word is used here "whether it be a physical thing or what the Law chooses to treat as such." But instead of considering, and calling, a person, as taken above, the *Subject* of a Right, he prefers to introduce a distinctive reference to the corresponding Duty and to speak of two persons, one of *inherence*, one of *incidence*[31].   These terms, as explained by him, are intelligible and expressive. My only objection to them is to the introduction of a new technical phraseology, not absolutely necessary.   The matter however will come better under the discussion of Rights as *in rem* and *in personam*.

[31] See Holland[10], 7, pp. 76, &c.

Duty and human Sanction.   Upon the idea of Duty,
as a matter of Psychology, it is not within my province to
enlarge.   In the matter of general feeling, just as this idea
has been, throughout the ages, one of the highest motives
to human conduct, so deep is the aversion and reluctance
from treating Duty simply as the result of Command.   If
the notion of Command at all is to be inferred from certain
expressions in this or that old language, it is the command
of Deity.   The feeling of Obligation is certainly conceived
as anterior to any human imposition[1].   That feeling is here
regarded as belonging to the same powerful and peculiar
appreciation of conduct as Right or Wrong which is specially

---

[1] See above, § 3, p. 100, and compare the usual explanation of χρῆ (upon
which, however, I cannot rely with any certainty).

characteristic of the human animal and is presumably derived from the fundamental principle of Man's essentially
Social Instinct.

That the feeling of Duty, in many minds, derives its
strength from self-regarding considerations alone, must be
admitted; though the possibility of its original developement
in the mind of an absolute solitary is, to me, as little conceivable as the case itself. With the majority, however, of
mankind, this feeling is undoubtedly backed by the Sanctions
of Positive Morality, in the ordinary meaning of the latter
word, or by the more definite but not always the more
powerful ones of Law. It is with these two cases, or rather
with the last alone, that Jurisprudence has to do. We may
therefore pass by Blackstone's Absolute Duties (above, § 19,
p. 613), as well as Cicero's *officia*, which are purely Moral
Duties, and such moreover as would probably be only
recognised by philosophers of a certain school[2].

Austin's Absolute Duties. Of particular legal Duties
those which have principally been considered hitherto are
complementary or ancillary to particular Rights, i.e. are
Relative (§ 20, pp. 626, 630). Such Duties will naturally
follow the classifications and subdivisions of the Rights with
which they are respectively connected. The proper place
for Austin's Absolute Duties in an Educational System, and
the frequently *implicit* mode of their creation, were briefly
discussed above, §§ 15, pp. 529, 530. With regard to the
Duties themselves, they may, to speak generally, be considered either as correlating with Rights belonging to the
particular Community at large[3], or as Duties to the Community simply without any mention of Rights at all. But

---

[2] See Madvig's note on De Finibus 3. 17. 58. There is no definite use
of the word, in this sense, by the Roman Jurists. They generally mean by
officia services or attentions legally due from a freedman to his *patronus*.
For Austin's arbitrary use of the word see below, § 23, p. 721.

[3] So Salmond[2] 185; see further below, p. 648.

as they are of somewhat various kinds they require a little more examination in detail.

Austin divides them roughly into cases where there is either no other person, individual or complex, to or in respect of whom the duty is to be observed; where there are such persons, but they are uncertain or indeterminate; or where the person towards, or in respect of whom, the duty to be observed is the monarch or sovereign number[4]. The first of these categories is divided into two heads in Lecture 17: one where the duty is to, or in respect of, the party to whom, on Austin's theory, the Command is directed, i.e. is a Duty to one's self; the other, where the Duty imposed is not a duty towards *man* or *person*. A cross classification towards the end of the Lecture would appear, rather grotesquely, to class together, under this last head, Duties towards the Deity, "lower animals" and infants[5].

The point, however, of the discussion turns upon what Austin terms the *proximate* end of these different absolute Duties; their *ultimate* end—the general interest—being the same in all cases[6]. This may be slightly otherwise stated in the words of one of Austin's *proximate* ends, as "the good of the community or mankind at large."

Whether we can point to any conscious adoption of the extensive philanthropy in the last words or not, we may, at least in modern civilised nations, accept the "good of the community" as the ultimate end of all *legal* Duties whatever[7]. In most cases of recent legislation, the motive is, or

---

[4] Outline, 65, 66.

[5] Austin[5], 17. Compare pp. 401, 402 with 407: St. 194, 198. The common point is, I suppose, the want of Austin's "test of a Right," i.e. capability of being enforced in a Civil action, 16. 398 (omitted in St.).

[6] Quoted from the distinction (or non-distinction) of Public and Private Law, p. 404. The *proximate* end referred to is on p. 406.

[7] Markby[6], ch. 4, § 150, p. 93 speaks of Rights belonging to "society at large": this does not, however, probably mean more than Salmond's

professes to be, simply and solely the attainment of this end: in a few, particularly in old survivals, an apparently different immediate object requires, as has been said, some consideration in detail.

Self-regarding Duties. A *moral* Duty *to* one's self is a conceivable, though not a very logical, idea, one's mental or psychical personality being considered as divided, and the inferior portion as under obligation to obey the superior. A Right *against* oneself I do *not* apprehend as equally conceivable either morally or legally[8]. There are however certain Duties, legally recognised, *about* or *regarding* one's self, the proximate object of which may at first sight appear to be the advantage of the party obliged.

In the peculiar case of *suicide* instanced by Austin as violation of a Duty towards self[9] Blackstone's "interest of the King in the preservation of all his subjects" may be construed into a sort of Right in (and Duty to) the Community, though the old forfeiture has been abolished and the only legal censure on a *felo de se* remaining in the English Law is the posthumous one on his reputation,— involved in the deprivation of Christian rites[10].

In other cases where there is any talk of self-regarding Duty, it is generally fairly obvious that the conception of a *legal* Obligation does not occur until the interests or the feelings of "the public" are directly concerned. It is not for instance from drunkenness pure and simple, but from drunkenness which prejudices or annoys the community that a man is legally bound to abstain[11]. It must be admitted,

---

statement in note 3 above. Holland[11], ch. 9, p. 129, definitely attributes Rights, in these cases, to the State.

[8] See, on the latter, Austin[5], 17. 407.

[9] Ib. 406, referring to Blackstone, 4. 14. 189.

[10] See the Felony Act of 1870, and the Interments Act of 1882.

[11] See for this and other cases Austin[5], 17. 407: Blackstone, i. 124: iv. 41. The old enactment of James I. (4. c. 5, § 2) repealed by the Licensing Act of

however, that, as "social questions" are more studied and more widely known, so does the tendency increase to visit with legal prohibition or constraint conduct hitherto regarded as merely erring in point of morals or prudence[12].

Much the same reasoning applies to Austin's legal Duties not regarding *men*, primarily Duties to the Deity. I am speaking here, it must be remembered, mainly of quite modern legislation[13]. Ancient Law often appears to begin with penalising *sins*, though generally, I believe, as bringing a curse on the Community. Much the same idea enters, no doubt, into certain forms of medieval legislation, which may, however, nominally impose Duties and Penalties for the "honour" or "glory" of God. But, in the general modern view, it is a Duty to the Community which is understood to be violated in the case of legal offences against God and religion which are classed by Blackstone (among others) as "Either directly or by consequence injurious to Civil Society[14]."

So too the interest of Society in the prevention of cruelty to *animals* is shewn by Bentham as a ground for the prohibition which makes, in an increasing number of modern legislatures, abstinence from such cruelty a legal Duty[15]. The statement of "demoralisation of the people," as one of the evils to be obviated, by our first Statute on this subject, points to the same bearing of this Duty[16].

1872 (35 & 36 Vic. c. 94) gave prominence to the *sin*: but the evil results to the Community were also enumerated among the matters to be remedied.

[12] E.g. questions of heredity, "unfitness," &c.: a culminating point is indicated in the American word, and thing, "sterilisation."

[13] Not of *all* modern. The old puritanical legislation of New England is, to a great extent, obsolete: but there are still traces of it even in the South, see Bryce, New Ed. ii. cxi. 782, 3.

[14] Blackstone, iv. 42, 59.

[15] See the end of the excellent chapter on "Limites qui séparent la morale et la législation." Traités, i. ch. 12, p. 43 (Hildreth, p. 66).

[16] Preamble of 5 & 6 Will. IV. ch. 59. Compare too the allowance of

Duties towards the Sovereign are very briefly enumerated by Austin in his summary at the end of Lecture 17, with Duties to persons indefinitely: and, when the latter mean the Community at large, they really come in effect to much the same thing[17]. But the two are, on Austin's theory, clearly distinguishable; and there is also a further distinction drawn by him, which has some practical value, while his main position has the unreal, though logical character, which affects so much of his reasoning on Law.

Duties towards the Sovereign then are, according to Austin, Absolute, because a Sovereign can have no legal Rights against his own Subjects[18]. But in Persons who are "Members of Sovereign Powers" he admits the possible residence of legal Rights, and consequently of relative Duties towards such Persons[19]. It is not quite clear whether the latter are, in this case, supposed to be in a private capacity, and their Rights, therefore, merely those of ordinary individuals, or whether the Rights are conferred for the general good[20], in which latter case the "member of Sovereign power" clearly represents the public or community. Modern legislation will generally be express enough on such matters; but there is some confusion, of ideas and language, in technical survivals of Right to a Sovereign who was in former times really *sole*, but is now become merely part of a Corporate Sovereignty[21].

vivisection, for purposes of public benefit, with the checks on unnecessary publicity of its performance (39 & 40 Vic. ch. 77).

[17] Compare Austin[5], 17. 407 with 402: St. 197.

[18] See above, § 20, p. 626, and ll. cc. in note 3: also Austin[5]: 16. 396: St. 115. In the latter quotation from Austin (omitted in St.) he speaks of the *absurdity* of a Sovereign conferring a Right on himself. Historically this is not always very evident, e.g. in the case of the Septennial Act. See generally, § 4, p. 234.

[19] Austin[5], 17. 407, n. 68. [20] Austin[5], 17. 403: St. 195.

[21] Above, § 19, p. 612. On the case of *Misdemeanors* in English Law being treated as infringements of a Right in, or Duty to, the Crown as an

Duties to persons *indeterminate*, or to persons indefinitely, Austin explains to be Duties "the proximate purpose
of which is the advantage of the Community at large or
mankind in general[22]. Now this, except perhaps as to the
last words (see p. 643), appears to me the *ultimate* purpose
of *all* Absolute Duties as *legally* recognised. What is meant
by the Duty being, in its *proximate purpose*, a Duty towards
the Community at large or, as Austin says elsewhere, towards
the members generally of the given independent society,
requires a little explanation. I take it that he means a
Duty to abstain from acts *generally* prejudicial or to do
acts of precaution against *general* danger or prejudice[23],
where the danger or prejudice can *not* be regarded as
immediately interfering with any other individual person's
Rights. He does *not*, I think, here refer to those Duties
of forbearance or regard, which correspond to the Absolute
or Normal Rights of every member of a Social Community
and are incumbent upon every other member[24]. In the
case under consideration there is no assignable individual
Wrong: the Wrong is conceived as purely *public*, and must
therefore be necessarily and exclusively sanctioned, as Austin
says[25], by *Criminal* proceedings.

Austin's Absolute Duties, which are Duties to the Community in general, are styled and regarded by him as
Absolute on the express ground that they have no Rights

individual, see F. J. Stephen's General View of the Criminal Law of
England[1], pp. 57, 58 and Hist. ii. 204.

[22] Austin[5], 16, 396.

[23] Of these two obligations the negative one may be illustrated by the
English Common Law liability for Common Nuisance (see Blackstone, iv. ch.
13, p. 167) in addition to the cases of Arson and Treason instanced by Austin[5],
17. 407: St. 197. Positive obligations of this class are not, for the most
part, *legally* recognised until made matter of statutory imposition. See
above, § 19, p. 617, and Bentham on *Culture de la Bienveillance*, Traités, ii.
ch. 16, p. 308 (Hildreth, 427).

[24] See above, § 19, p. 614.   [25] Austin[5], 17. 406: St. 197.

corresponding to them. This depends upon the Austinian position that every Right must necessarily reside in a *determinate* person[26], which is, after all, rather an arbitrary point in Austin's definition than a self-evident fact. Enforceability, for instance, by an individual's legal process, which is sometimes taken to be the test of a private Right, has been, in legal history, continually recognised as competent to an individual representing the public (see below, § 22, pp. 677, 678).

Professor Salmond, who lays it down generally that there is no Duty without a corresponding Right, points out that at any rate Rights residing in the Community are perfectly conceivable (above, p. 642, n. 3). In his view it would be better to dispense with the term Absolute altogether from the list of legal Duties. I should prefer to retain it, understanding it however to include not only Austin's Absolute Duties, all of which I regard as Duties to the Community, but also the Duties which correspond to the Absolute or Normal Rights of every individual member of the Community (above, p. 647).

Roman obligationes. The present has been found by me the most convenient place for considering the Roman *obligatio*, although the use of that term by the Roman Institutionalists, as confined to Property Law (see below, p. 650, and § 24, p. 739) is narrower than Austin's conception of Duty generally, and it may be unavoidable a little to anticipate the subject of the later sections, 23 and 24.

It may be inferred from what has been said above (§ 16, p. 552), and will be made clear when we come to deal with the distinction of *in rem* and *in personam*, that the Roman *obligatio* is only understood, in general, by the Roman jurists as a tie between individuals. It is not applied by them to the Duties of forbearance or regard spoken of

---

[26] See above, § 20, p. 636. Austin[5], 17. 401: St. 194, &c.

above, or as Austin puts it, to Duties which correspond to
Rights *in rem*[27]. But the suggestion that these Duties
might be distinguished from *obligationes* proper, by the term
officia, does not accord with the general Juristic use of that
word and leads to unnecessary confusion[28].

The conception of Obligation has been again, with some
authors, rather narrowed by an exclusive connexion with
Contract, which may be roughly defined as an Agreement
producing legal Obligation. Definitions come late in the
developement of this as of most subjects. Nothing in fact
that can be regarded as a full definition of Contract is ever
arrived at in Roman Law or, until very lately, in English.
Obligation, on the other hand, has been defined by Justinian,
probably quoting the words of some Jurist belonging to the
earlier time, in Instt. 3. 13. As preface however to this and
other Roman authorities I have to say a few words upon an
important modern definition, which appears to enter more or
less into most later writing on the subject and contributes to
illustrate—sometimes to obscure—the meaning of *obligatio*
in the Roman Institutes.

Savigny. Obligations are, according to Savigny, one
branch of Rights. A Right may be over some Thing—some
portion of "Unfree" Nature—or it may have for its object
(*Gegenstand*) outside (*fremde*) Persons. (I do not propose to
enter again (see § 16, p. 553) into the definition of a Thing
(*Sache*), or the exact import of the word *unfrei*. It appears
here to signify "wanting in human volition[29]"; *fremde* is
explained by what follows.)

Among the Relations classed under his second head of
Rights, there may be, says Savigny, an absolute control

[27] Austin[5], Outline, 45, Lect. 22. 445. The censure passed on Austin
by Moyle, at the beginning of Exc. v. to Justinian's Institutes, is scarcely
fair, but see below, p. 650, n. 32.

[28] See above p. 642 and below, § 23, p. 721.

[29] See Holland[10], ch. 8, p. 97, n. 2.

(*Herrschaft*), in which case the other Person is simply a Thing; or a partial control, only extending to individual acts or lines of conduct (*auf eine einzelne Handlung*). It is this Relation of partial control which we call Obligation[30].

Upon this definition many comments and variations have been made. Occasionally even statements of Roman Law seem to be based upon it[31]. But the definition is modern, not Roman, and I refer to it mainly by way of caution against its employment as a true account of the old Institutional *obligatio*. That of Savigny, so far as the above definition goes, is confined to the idea of a Right: the Roman *obligatio* means sometimes a Right sometimes a Duty. Savigny's Obligation, on the other hand, is not confined to Property Law; for he proceeds to include under it Family Relations, which certainly fall within the Roman *Jus Personarum*, where the Roman Jurists do not, as a rule, speak of *obligatio*, which they treat merely as an item among *Res*[32].

Two meanings of **Obligatio.** *Obligatio*, in the use of the word by the Roman Jurists, varies, as has been said, between two meanings: perhaps we might express the ambiguity better by saying that it is sometimes looked at from one point of view and sometimes from another; sometimes on the advantageous side as a Right, sometimes on the disadvantageous side as a Duty[33]: the former meaning is more in accordance with the scheme of the Institutes, as indicated at the beginning of Gaius' Second Book[34]; the latter is that expressed in the definition of Justinian.

[30] System, i. § 53, pp. 338—340: Obligationsrecht, i. 4. 305: see Holland[10], ch. 12, p. 235: Salkowski, p. 24: Girard[5], p. 388.

[31] See e.g. Karlowa, ii. 808, 809.

[32] System, l. c. pp. 340—342. Also above, § 16, pp. 551, 553: Salmond[2], § 165, pp. 427, 428.

[33] Austin has various notices of this double meaning; e.g. Outline, p. 45 note: Lect. 24, p. 466: and particularly Tab. i. note 6.

[34] Ga. 2. 14. The resultant value is more definitely stated shortly after,

Obligatio *as a Right.* In the Roman Institutional arrangement and, I think, generally in Roman Juristic writing—the exceptions being stray metaphors—*obligationes* fall within the *jus quod ad res pertinet.* This we have taken to mean Property Law, and the individual *res* to mean items or articles of Property, amongst which *obligationes* belong to the sub-division *incorporales.* In their mode of alienation, which is Gaius' main basis of classification as to *res,* they differ materially not only from *res corporales* but also from the rest of *res incorporales*[35]. This and other reasons—among them perhaps some recognised closer connexion with Actions—might sufficiently account for the position of *obligationes* at the end of Gaius' second division, without recourse to Austin's assumption that "the Roman lawyers" distinctly intended a sub-division of general Rights into *dominia* and *obligationes* corresponding with his own *jura in rem* and *jura in personam*[36]. My present point, however, is merely that, in the general scheme adopted by Gaius, *obligationes* are regarded from the advantageous side, as Rights, which are items of Property.

Reducible to money value. In this point of view we may take into account the statement of Ulpian, which, though made on a very special case, seems to be generally true, that, at Roman Law, all matter of *obligatio* must be dischargeable in, and therefore reducible to, a money value[37]. This fact, which is represented as being of the essence of an "obligatory Right" by some modern writers[38], is, I think,

as "quod ex obligatione nobis debetur." For Justinian's definition, see below, p. 655.

[35] Ga. 2. 14, 28—30.

[36] See above, § 16, p. 552. On the position of Obligations in the French and German Codes, § 23, p. 728.

[37] Dig. 40. 7. 9. 2. Ea enim in obligatione consistere quae pecunia lui praestarique possunt: libertas autem pecunia lui non potest, nec reparari potest.

[38] E.g. Sohm, § 73, p. 379. See also below, p. 652.

more truly regarded by Moyle[39] as a result of deficient procedure or machinery.   It was the case, down to Ulpian's time, with *actio in rem* also, where the plaintiff's only means of getting specific restitution of his property was by the imposition of a heavy pecuniary alternative[40] : for the reference to physical transfer under the judge's order, attributed to that Jurist, is generally supposed to be an interpretation from the " extraordinary procedure " of a later time[41].

The genuine dictum, however, of Ulpian first cited has its significance, in more ways than one.

1.   It would appear to exclude, from the category of *obligationes* in Roman Law, all Obligatory Rights, which might otherwise come under Savigny's definition, but are so distinctly personal that they cannot be conceived as reducible to a pecuniary value, e.g. the Rights and Duties of family relationship so far as they have emerged from the barbaric condition of simple ownership by the *paterfamilias*; the *operae officiales* of a libertus, as distinguished from the *operae fabriles*; the gift of *libertas* itself[42].

2.   It more easily accounts for the classing together of *obligationes ex contractu* and *ex delicto*, objected to by Austin in Lect. 45 (see above, § 18, p. 604), if we consider that both, being alike reducible to a pecuniary value, are regarded equally as items of a man's property.

3.   Ulpian's statement also makes rather more intelligible the technical use of the words *creditor* and *debitor*.

---

[39] Justinian[4], Exc. v. p. 476 and Exc. x. p. 649.

[40] Ib. and on Just. 4. 6. 31 (Actiones arbitrariae).

[41] See Ulpian Dig. 6. 1. 68 as cited by Moyle, p. 559.   On the alleged interpolation, see Roby Int. 206; R. P. L. 2. 441, and Girard[5], 1024, n. 2. On the enforcement of specific performance of an *obligatio*, see Lenel Ed.[2], De eo quod certo loco, § 96, p. 234.

[42] See Dig. 38. 1. 9. 1: 40. 7. 9. 2 (note 38): also Moyle, 440: Salkowski, 194: Anson, Law of Contract[11], p. 7.   On Austin's *officia* above, p. 649, and below, § 23, p. 721.

Etymologically *debitor* (*de-habere*) is the man who *has from* another, the *borrower*; and, although *creditor* perhaps had, in point of derivation, the more general meaning of placing trust or confidence[43], there is little doubt that the pair of words were rather specialised, in ordinary language, to lending and borrowing. In the language, however, of the Jurists, *creditor* may be said of anyone to whom anything is *due* on any ground, not merely of contract but even according to Ulpian of delict[44]. He is rather more strictly defined by the same author elsewhere as a person having a right of action not barred by an exception; so that a merely *natural* Obligatory Right does not make a man or *creditor*, or only so by a misuse of language[45]. The technical use of these words may no doubt have arisen, as Savigny holds[46], from the fact that the oldest Contractual claim specifically recognised at Rome was for money lent, but it may well have been maintained and emphasized by the reducible character of all obligations to money, alleged by the classical Jurists.

Paulus' Definition. The same *advantageous* view of *obligatio* is taken in a fragment of Paulus' Institutiones which, besides the fact that it comes nearest to a definition of *obligatio* by one of the classical Jurists, is worthy of special

---

[43] Curtius, 254; Corssen, ii. 410, &c. The derivation from giving one's *heart* (Cuq i. 388. 3) is a piece of modern sentiment which would have been meaningless to the Roman, who generally meant by *cor* what we call *brains*.

[44] Gaius and Ulpian Dig. 50. 16. 11 and 12. pr. creditorum appellatione non hi tantum accipiuntur, qui pecuniam crediderunt, sed omnes, quibus ex qualibet causa debetur; ut si cui ex empto vel ex locato vel ex alio ullo debetur. sed et si ex delicto debeatur, mihi videtur posse creditoris loco accipi. See Moyle[4], Exc. v. p. 474.

[45] Dig. 44. 7. 42. 1. Creditores eos accipere debemus, qui aliquam actionem vel civilem habent, sic tamen, ne exceptione submoveantur, vel honorariam actionem, vel in factum. 50. 16. 10. Quod si natura debeatur, non sunt loco creditorum: also Julian Dig. 46. 1. 16. 4. Licet minus proprie debere dicantur naturales debitores, per abusionem intellegi possunt debitores et, qui ab his pecuniam recipiunt, debitum sibi recepisse.

[46] System, v. Beil. 14, p. 513, nn. *a*, *b*.

attention for its bearing on the cognate subject of *actio in rem* and *actio in personam* (see below, § 23, p. 695). " The essence of Obligation consists," says Paulus, " not in its giving us the ownership of some material object or some servitude (*personal* servitudes are here intended) but in its binding down another person to us (or ' for our benefit') to assure some property or perform some service or generally make something good[47]."

Two points are particularly to be remarked in this passage. 1. It shews clearly the distinction between the Rights resulting from Obligation and those which consist in different degrees or modifications of Ownership.   2. It indicates, perhaps not quite so clearly, that what the Romans intended by *Obligatio* was a constraint or control incumbent on, and for the benefit of, ascertained or *determinate* persons. The Roman *obligatio* only contemplates Duties which are in the strictest sense Relative, not those which Austin terms Absolute (see above, pp. 642, 643). This Relative character is well shewn by the fact that, in strict Roman Law, a promise by A to B, to do something for C, confers no right on C[48]. The definition or explanation of *solutio*, in the sense of performance, by the three technical terms *dare, facere* and *praestare* will be considered presently.

Obligatio *as a Duty.*   Coming to the other meaning of this term, as used by Roman writers, we find, in the well-known definition of Justinian (3. 13), the converse view taken, to that of Paulus :—*adstringimur* as against *nobis obstringat*, and *obligatio* signifying the *disadvantage* of the

---

[47] Dig. 44. 7. 3. pr. Obligationum substantia non in eo consistit, ut aliquod corpus nostrum aut servitutem nostram faciat, sed ut alium nobis obstringat ad dandum aliquid vel faciendum vel praestandum.   See below, § 23, p. 710.

[48] Ga. 3. 103 as to Stipulation.   Paulus (Dig. 44. 7. 11) speaks more generally of "Quaecunque gerimus."   See the notes in Poste[4], 344—346 and Moyle[4] on Just. 3. 19. 4; also id. Int. to Book 3, p. 346.

control under which the person subject to it lies, *release* from such control being the original idea of *solutio*.

I may remark by the way, on Paulus' *nobis obstringat*, that the relation between the parties in *obligatio* does not appear to be fully expressed by the neutral idea of mere mutual connexion, which was rather Sir Henry Maine's view as to the *juris vinculum* of Justinian[49]. Without pressing unduly the force of the compounded preposition *ob*, as signifying that A is bound *towards* or *for the benefit of* B[50], we can positively assert the one-sided direction or bearing of the *obligatio*, from the datives with which it is connected[51]. It is a Right as looked at from the point of B; a Duty as looked at from the point of A: not merely a tie between the two.

Obligatory Rights. The ambiguity in the use of the Latin *obligatio*, to which Austin not unreasonably objects (above, n. 33), is sometimes avoided, as we have seen, by translating the word, in its advantageous sense, an Obligatory Right, in its disadvantageous sense an Obligation[52]. The expression Obligatory Rights or Rights of Obligation serves also for a sub-division of the Roman Property Law (whether definitely intended as such by the Roman Jurists or not) in distinction from Real Rights or as I should prefer to call them Rights of Ownership[53].

I now proceed to the details of Justinian's definition which, as above suggested (p. 649), is probably, in the main,

[49] Ancient Law, ix. 324.

[50] See Roby, Grammar, § 2023. *Ad*stringimur may possibly have something of the same meaning. Austin's conception of being tied to a given place (22. 452), whether suggested by *ob-* or *ad* is certainly very questionable. I cannot agree with Cuq (i. 331) that the meaning of *obligatio* was ever *physical*, as *nexum* (or rather *nexus*) may have been. See too Mommsen, Strafr. 326, n. 3.

[51] Nobis...ei, in Paulus l. c. Ga. 4. 2 and Just. 4. 6. 1.

[52] See Salkowski, 24: Sohm, 326, 279.

[53] See § 16, p. 552.

a quotation from some Classical Jurist, though I cannot trace it, in its entirety, to any extant source.

Obligatio est vinculum juris: it is a *legal bond*, not a moral or physical one, and a matter of *constraint* not merely of connexion; *quo adstringimur*: through which we are constrained (as to the possible force of *ad* see n. 46), *necessitate* by the necessity—there must be no *option* or alternative allowed to the *obligatus*[54]—*alicujus solvendae rei*: of rendering some thing or performing some act[55]; *secundum nostrae civitatis jura*, in accordance with the laws of our State. These words, although they *read* next to the clause expressing performance, are, I think rightly, connected by most English translators with the word *astringimur*. The propriety of the performance is involved in the propriety of the obligation to perform. In the translation, however, of Poste, who connects the words as above, I should enter a caution against the rendering "*by* the law of the State (power of the Sovereign)" as a gratuitous and misleading Austinianism[56].

The plural *jura* must not pass without remark. In the time of the Classical Jurists it means either the bodies or systems of law belonging to different individual States, *jura singularum civitatium*, or rules and maxims of non-statutory Law at Rome. The latter is, at least, as I have endeavoured to shew elsewhere (§ 7, p. 374), the most satisfactory

---

[54] No *si volam*, Pomponius, Dig. 44. 7. 8: no "licet aliud facere," Modestinus, Dig. 44. 7. 52. 7; and, of course, the obligation must not be by way of joke, Paulus, ib. 3. 2. For an apparent but not real reference to the *obligatus*' decision, *an sit obstrictus*, see Ulpian, Dig. 18. 1. 7. pr. and Hunter on that passage (Roman Law, p. 382).

[55] The former translation, by Sandars and Abdy and Walker, is better, I think, than the latter by Moyle, *res* being taken in the vaguest and widest sense. But both are inadequate: indeed the original can only be made clear by rather a lengthy explanation (see below, pp. 658, 659).

[56] It is corrected in Mr Whittuck's edition (4) "in accordance with the law of the State."

interpretation in the difficult phrase *condere jura*[57]. But, in later times, e.g. those of Diocletian and Maximian[58], *jura* seems to mean quite generally "the laws" or "the law," which is the best translation here.

The exact purport of this clause is not very clear. Theophilus, the Greek translator of the Institutes, who connects it with the words immediately preceding, and translates as if referring to the mere payment of money due (below, n. 65), adds, by way of illustration, that such payment must not be made to a Pupil without the Tutor's authorisation. This narrowing of what is evidently intended as a perfectly general definition, is a strong reason for preferring the connexion of the clause in question with *astringimur*. My own view of its purport is that the intention was to exclude *obligatio naturalis* and confine the definition to *obligatio civilis* in the rarer and wider sense of the phrase, i.e. *any* obligation enforceable at Roman Law by positive Action[59]; not merely pleadable by way of exception, or otherwise allowed a certain subsidiary and ancillary effect, as distinguished again from other obligations of morality or good faith which are entirely inoperative[60].

The word *civilis*, it is true, is used directly below by Justinian in its more common meaning, as distinguished

---

[57] Ga. 1. 7: 4. 30. In the *jura populi Romani* of 1. 2 this plural might seem to have much the same meaning as in the passage of Justinian. But the reading, though confirmed by the latest editors, was questioned by the scholar-like judgement of Huschke, who suggested constat autem *jus civile* populi Romani from some archetype i c p r, see Huschke's Gaius 1873, p. 24: Muirhead's Gaius, p. 2.

[58] See their const. in Cod. 8. 35. 5 "jura permittunt."

[59] So this clause is understood by Abdy and Walker, Justinian, p. 282, note 1. This is the meaning of *civilis obligatio* in Aristo apud Ulp. on the "innominate" contracts: "hinc nasci civilem obligationem" Dig. 2. 14. 7. 2.

[60] See on *naturalis obligatio*, Salkowski, § 114, pp. 541—549: Moyle, Exc. v. pp. 476—479: Girard[5], 640—644.

from Praetorian: obligations springing simply from the Praetor's jurisdiction being called by the latter name, in contrast with those which are established by Statute or at least approved by non-statutory Roman Law[61]. But both classes are equally enforceable as above, whereas *naturalis obligatio* is not. This last subject is too difficult and too much a matter of individual cases and relations to be entered on here. I shall therefore return to the part, in Justinian's definition, of *obligatio* which was left for further explanation (above, p. 656).

Solvere rem, in the untranslateable *alicujus solvendae rei,* is only explicable by reference to the old Roman law of Debt. *Solvere,* etymologically to loosen away (*se luo* Curtius 368), was no doubt first said of releasing the *person* bound, as in the old formula of *solutio per aes et libram,* where the *nexus* was once literally a bondsman[62]. But when the expression *nexus* came, by the operation of the *lex Poetelia,* to lose its literal meaning, and to be applied to the *money* not to the *man,* the idea of releasing became, in this important and typical case, equivalent to that of *paying*[63]. Hence, in the end, *solvere,* originally to set free, was said of paying or rendering anything due under an *obligatio*[64]. This is probably the very general meaning of

---

[61] This wide expression will, I suppose, cover such general recognition of Real and Consensual Contract as cannot be directly referred to the Praetor, and all results of the *auctoritas prudentium,* see above, § 7.

[62] Me a te solvo liberoque, Ga. 3. 174. The immediate example is of a *judicatum*: but the form is also applicable to the *nexus* (see § 173).

[63] See Livy, 8. 28: Festus F. 165, nexum aes. I am somewhat anticipating conclusions worked out in the subsequent history.

[64] Gai. 3. 168 solutione ejus quod debetur: Paulus, Dig. 46. 3. 54 solutionis verbum pertinet ad omnem liberationem quoquo modo factam magisque ad substantiam obligationis refertur, quam ad nummorum solutionem. Ulpian, Dig. 50. 16. 176 solutionis verbo satisfactionem quoque omnem accipiendam placet. Solvere dicimus eum, qui fecit quod facere promisit.

res intended in Justinian's *alicujus solvendae rei,* the "thing" covering a material object, a service, or even a forbearance.

The explanation, therefore, of *solutio* by mere reference to money *payment,* and to the accidental and temporary fact that the *condemnatio* in the formulary system took that form (see above, p. 651), does not appear to go to the root of the matter or the fundamental meaning of the word, although it is evidently adopted in a general way in Justinian's *solvendae rei* and more particularly in Theophilus' version[65]. In the modern words, too, derived from *liberare,* rather fanciful physical meanings of that word have been occasionally resorted to instead of what is here suggested as the true source of the whole class of ideas—the personal release of the Roman *nexus*[66].

Dare facere praestare. The objects of *obligatio* stated by Paulus (above, p. 654) may be here considered as a statement of the different forms of *solutio.* The words are no doubt derived, as Moyle suggests, from the old forms of personal action[67] : perhaps a little more distinctive meaning may be made out of them than he allows. *Dare,* above translated "to assure," is to give so as to make the thing given the property of the recipient, *facere accipientis*[68]. Once

---

[65] καταβάλλειν τὸ ἐποφειλόμενον.

[66] The meaning of the middle age Latin *liberare,* Fr. *livrer,* is derived by Littré (s.v. *ad finem*) directly from the physical idea of *letting go.* See too Pianigiani's explanation of *liberare* as from *cessar di ritenere.* Skeat correctly recognises, for *deliver* (s.v. Livery) an intermediate meaning to *give, to give freely.* I would rather say to *pay,* derived again from the old idea of *release* as above. *Liberare* being once established in the sense of to hand over or deliver, we have from it *Livery,* the suit or badge delivered at stated periods by a feudal superior to his retainers, and the *liberatura* or commons delivered to the scholars at a college buttery.

[67] Moyle, Just. Exc. v. 475, cf. Ga. 4. 2. The Excerpta Probiana (Coll. Jur. Antejust.[5] ii. p. 146, no. 13) only prove *dare facere.* *D. f. p.* however occurs in the Lex Rubria, c. xxii., followed by *restituere.*

[68] Ga. 4. 4: Just. 4. 6. 14: Paulus, Dig. 50. 17. 167. pr.

or twice, indeed, it occurs in legal language with the sense of mere physical transfer: but the ordinary technical meaning is the one given above. I do *not* think that the idea of Quiritarian *dominium* is to be specially pressed in the ownership produced by *datio*[69]. *Facere* evidently covers every *positive* service.

Praestare is not an easy word to explain, in point either of etymology or historical use. It is always, I think, an *active* verb with the classical Jurists; and it so often indicates the idea of guaranteeing, making good, or producing, that it almost seems as if they must have derived it, in thought, from the personal security *praes*, with which it has only a remote collateral connexion[70]. It has been taken to be strictly and properly said of compensation for a wrong, in action *ex delicto*, but without sufficient proof. It is used with *operas, actiones*, etc., in a multitude of cases in which there is no notion of performance of a delictal obligation. I take it to have been a residuary term, added in procedure, and thence in juristic writing, to *dare facere*, in order to cover not only all positive performances which could not very clearly come under those words but perhaps also negative action or forbearance which could not logically come under those words at all[71]. The difficult phrase, *jus rebus recte praestari*, speaking of the right of defendant in a real action, or *stipulator* in a *verbal* obligation, to be secured against

---

[69] As Poste in Ga.[2] 3. 88 (probably following Ortolan's Propriété Romaine T. ii. § 1179). Omitted in Ed.[4] (Whittuck).

[70] Corssen's long note (2. 549. 550) is only on *praesto* (adv. or adj.) and *praesto esse*. It seems inevitable to regard praestare, with Littré s.v. *prêter*, as *verbe neutre passé au sens actif*. See too Pianigiani s.v. *prestare*.

[71] See Poste's Gaius[4], p. 447 and Mu. Ga. on 4. 2, p. 267 n.: Girard[5], 443. 1, and Roby on Dig. 7. 1, p. 156. As to Savigny's remark on *praestare* not being found in any extant *intentio*, see above, n. 66, and note that this is clearly not regarded as conclusive by Lenel in his reconstructions of the Edict, e.g. Edictum[2], §§ 80, 108, 109, pp. 202, 280, 287.

liabilities attaching to the property concerned, throw no light on the above question, except as shewing that the secured indemnification is prospective and contingent[72].

Place of Obligations in Corpus Juris.

From the view of general Jurisprudence we are more concerned with the above subject than with the *sub-divisions* of Obligations or Obligatory Rights either in Gaius and Justinian or in modern systems—with one exception, to be noted hereafter.

The question whether Obligatory Rights in general come naturally and conveniently before or after those of Ownership, is answered by the framers of the German Code in a manner rather startling to the English legal student— *Schuldverhältnisse* (Obligatory Relations) coming second after the General Part, and *Sachenrecht* (Property Law, according to the English Digest) only third (see § 19, p. 624). I much prefer the Roman Institutional order, but would consider more fully the merits of the division generally and the possible reason for the German arrangement in § 23, under Austin's heading of *in rem* and *in personam* regarded as the main division of a Corpus Juris, to which again I prefer, for simplicity and practical convenience, Blackstone's Rights and Wrongs (see § 19, pp. 610—614). This English principle of division necessarily involves a distinct separation between the two sources of Obligation recognised by the Romans— Contract and Delict—the distinction being practically over-ridden, at least in Gaius, by both Obligations being classed together as items of Property (see § 18, p. 604). As to the desirability and possibility of a substantive statement of Tort, and its connexion with Crime, see above (ib. p. 606); on breaches of Contract, § 19, p. 621.

Any further detail as to the classification of Obligations, by the occasions of their contraction or incurrence, is so

[72] See Dig. 6. 1. 19 and 50. 16. 71. 1. Also Roby's R. P. L. i. 442.

much matter of particular national history and practice that it can only belong to a more advanced study of Jurisprudence than is contemplated in the present work (see above, § 1, pp. 18, 22, 38).

The distinction between Civil (in the narrower sense) and Praetorian, which is occasionally extended, from its more common use, as between Actions, to Obligations, is not employed, as a basis of classification for the latter, by the Roman Institutionalists. In point of recognition both were taken into account together, as are legal and equitable claims with ourselves, since the recent Judicature Acts, and similarly subject to certain survivals, in treatment, from an original difference in modes of relief, though not, as with us, in separate Courts. A place in the educational system which seems to be required, in English Law, for a separate statement of Equitable principles has been, with some hesitation, suggested above, § 19, p. 623.

The partial and indirect recognition of Natural Obligation, by Roman tribunals, has been compared with the treatment of certain Imperfect Obligations in English Law. The parallel, however, does not extend very far, and the cases cited go rather to disprove the direct enforcement of moral obligations in England, unless based on a previous receipt of some valuable consideration by the obligor, than to illustrate the Roman defensive use of *Naturalis obligatio*[73].

[73] See Poste's Gaius[4], p. 318 and Anson on Contract[11], pp. 117—120.

§ 22. RIGHT, WRONG AND DUTY.
PARTICULAR WRONGS

Wrongs violations of Duty. It was shewn above how
Blackstone's inclusion of Criminal Law in his Institutional
work, as distinguished from that of Hale, necessitated an
extension of Hale's treatment of Wrongs as violations of
individual or particular Rights : Crimes, or Public Wrongs,
having now to be defined, somewhat artificially, as infringement of the Rights of the individual Sovereign. It was
therefore maintained that, for a comprehensive view of
Wrongs generally, it is better to regard them as violations
of Duty: there being some Duties, called Absolute by
Austin, in which, although they may be fairly regarded as
due to the Community, and the Community as having
corresponding Rights, the violation of an individual or
particular Right is simply a legal fiction[1].

Legal references to a Moral Standard. In all this,
reference is exclusively made to Rights, Wrongs and Duties

[1] See § 19, pp. 612, 613 ; § 21, p. 646.

recognised as such by Law. But I would now revert for a moment to the consideration of an anterior Moral Standard, which is, as we have seen (§ 19, p. 611), recognised by Blackstone himself in his first definition of Rights and Wrongs.

A particular Wrong he there obviously takes to mean a "wrong piece of conduct," which, whether also forbidden or not by the laws of England or any other given country, has an independent recognition in popular feeling, springing directly from the general idea of Right, Wrong and Duty, and is by no means necessarily confined to the violation of particular Rights.

A reference to this anterior Moral Standard is obvious in certain serious cases of English Criminal Law, where the intrinsic Wrongness of the Act, according to Current Morality (independently of its visitation with a legal sanction), has been in English judicial practice expressly held material to the question of its perpetrator's liability as affected by his mental condition.

The English legal term *malice*, under all its extended and varied applications, scarcely ever entirely loses its original signification of *wickedness*. Criminal Justice, it has been justly said, is based upon Morality, and there are reasons of practical utility for retaining in Law those moral terms to which some lawyers affect a professional objection. Indeed Austin's exclusion of a moral standard, in the ordinary sense of the word *moral*, seems to do away with any reasonable justification of that generally received Canon of legal liability for wrong, "Ignorance of the Law excuseth none[2]."

Moral Wrongs, like Rights, are here assumed, whether from a general recognition of Duty to others, or from their ultimate dependence upon a *common* feeling or conscience,

---

[2] At least in Criminal cases. See my Analysis of Criminal Liability, pp. 61—63. Also, Austin[5], 25. 485; St. 240. On "*Malice*" and the reason for retaining it, F. J. Stephen's General View[1], pp. 82, 83. See, however, Ed.[2], p. 75.

to be the creatures of a Social existence (see above § 20, p. 638, § 19, p. 615). They are also Legal or not accordingly as they are recognised *merely* by such common feeling, or by the organised power of a Community besides; Jurisprudence only dealing directly with the latter class.

Legal Wrongs. It is not, of course, claimed that *all legal* Wrongs are previously *moral* ones. Duties, Absolute or Relative, are daily Created, on matters morally indifferent, by legislation (see above § 20, p. 632). The question of the moral wrongness of an act, previous to its visitation with a Criminal Sanction, is indeed rather matter for consideration by the Legislator or Reformer than of fact for the Jurist. The converse case, of the efficacy of legal prohibition in creating moral disapprobation, is an interesting subject touched on by F. J. Stephen in his General view of the Criminal Law of England, pp. 82, 83, but scarcely entering into our present consideration.

Legal Wrong generally, being a breach of legal Duty, is obnoxious to the unfavourable notice at the least—*animadversio* is the euphemistic Latin expression—of the judicial authorities of the Community. It is the particular *manner*, in which these authorities act or are put in motion, that is on the whole held to constitute the more practically applicable distinction of Public and Private Wrongs, as compared with a distinction by their effects and tendencies, or by the end and purpose of their respective modes of treatment.

The division of Wrongs expressly into Public and Private, being a specially leading feature in our English Institutional system, is best considered primarily with reference to English Jurisprudence and secondly to the same division as observable or inferable in Roman Law. I shall however preface both with a few remarks on the Roman Jurists' definition and treatment of legal Wrongs generally.

Injuriae. *Injuria* is a word bearing a number of various senses in Roman Law, as may be seen at once from Justinian 4. 4 pr. which comes directly from Paulus' book De injuriis[3]. Austin asserts the fundamental idea to be opposition to Right or Law generally rather than negation of a particular Right[4]. This is fairly in accordance with an explanation of the word by Paulus (l.c.) as *omne quod non jure fit*, and by Ulpian as *non juria* (sic), i.e. *quod jure et justitia caret*, the particular case in the last reference being the *iniquitas* or unfairness of Magistrate or *judex*. The derivational meaning of the word is simply non-Right, German *Unrecht*[5], and the adverbial ablative in the *lex Aquilia* or elsewhere clearly signifies *wrongfully*, unjustifiably or inexcusably, by no means always in the definite sense of *unlawfully* or *illegally*.

As somewhat narrowing the above wide meaning given by Austin to *injuria*, it must be recognised however, on the one hand, that the word is scarcely ever used, by any accurate Roman juristic authority, in the case of a *public* wrong; on the other that Paulus, in the passage above cited (note 3), seems to regard *injuria* as always a wrong done to some individual person, as well as being *contra bonos mores* generally[6]; while, in a well-known extract from the Twelve Tables, *injuria* was taken by the Roman Jurists in an obviously concrete sense, as that violation of a particular Right which is involved in an outrage on some one's personal security or dignity[7].

[3] Cited in Collat. 2. 5. 1 (Coll. Jur. Antejust.[5] iii. 144). See also Ulpian Dig. 47. 10. 1. pr. ; Dig. 9. 2. 5. 1 and the somewhat unsatisfactory note on Dig. 9. 2. 3 in Monro's generally excellent *lex Aquilia*.

[4] Austin[5], 18. 409 ; 24. 463, 464 ; St. 198, 199, 228 etc. The idea of *Contrariety to Command* which intrudes itself in some of these passages is quite unjustifiable.

[5] See Curtius, p. 151.

[6] Collat. 2. 5. 2. See Muirhead[2], 21.

[7] Paulus in Collat. 2. 5. 5. Qui injuriam alteri facit quinque et viginti sestertiorum poenam subite. Gellius, however, reads (20. 1. 12) Si injuria

On the whole therefore *injuria* does not seem a very happy expression for general disobedience to Law[8], apart from the fact that it has come, at least in Modern English, to mean little more than simple *harm* or detriment, and where it is used in an approximately technical sense by legal writers (as by Christian, see below, p. 672) it is rather confined to *private* Wrongs.

Delicta. *Delictum* is, in itself, like *injuria*, a very general term. Derivationally, and therefore originally, it signifies Omission of Duty, the leaving of something undone which ought to be done: and in some old formulae, where *deliquerunt* for instance is opposed to *fecerunt*[9], this negative meaning is maintained. As early, however, as the time of Plautus it was used of *positive* transgressions, and so, coming to mean either non-fulfilment or violation of Duty, it *prima facie* answers fairly to Austin's definition of Wrong. In the ordinary usage of the word the Duty violated may be religious, military or legal[10]. In Juristic writing *delictum* is mainly breach of *legal* Duty; but with the important exception (due no doubt to the Institutional antithesis which we have shortly to consider) that it does *not* seem to be said of the violation or neglect of such Duties as arise from Contract or quasi-contractual relation. It is so far, therefore, narrower than Austin's legal Wrong or Injury, which includes the violation of these Duties also[11].

Publica and Privata. The expression *privatum delictum*

alteri faxsit which might indicate an adverbial use of injuria and an omitted accusative of the actual outrage. The German use of *objective* and *subjective* as applied to *injuria* is, I agree with Monro, l.c., much better avoided. See for instance Jhering's employment of the two terms Geist. 1. 129, n. 28[a].

[8] As Austin would prefer to use it. See Outline 45 and Lect. 45. 764; St. 375.

[9] See Liv. i. 32.

[10] Horace, Delicta majorum immeritus lues. Odd. 3. 6. 1. Paulus D. 5. 26. 2. Militare delictum.

[11] Austin[5], 18. 409; St. 234, etc.

occurs, though not very often, in the later Imperial legislation, the Delicts in question[12] being obviously opposed to the subjects of the *publica judicia*. I do not know that the expression *publicum delictum* does occur in juristic language, the epithet *public* being used rather of the procedure than of the Wrong. The significance of this distinction will be seen when we come to the subject of *crimina* in Roman Law and the distinction of Public from Private Wrongs in English.

Obligationes ex delicto and ex contractu.   In Gaius 3. 88 and Justinian 3. 14 pr. we have a main division of *Obligationes* by the occasions from which they arise; from Contract or Delict, to which two heads are added by Justinian from Gaius' *Res Quotidianae*, namely the supplementary ones of Quasi-Contractual and Quasi-Delictal obligation.   The propriety of co-ordinating obligations, which arise in the first instance from Wrong, with those which do not, has naturally been subjected to severe criticism by Austin and by various other modern authors, as a matter of general Jurisprudence[13].

The primary reason for the Roman arrangement was that it is part of the general Institutional scheme to treat both sets of Obligations or, as they might here be more conveniently called, Obligatory Rights, together, as being both items of a man's *Res* or Property (see above § 16, pp. 551, 552). To this must be added the fact that breach of Duty was pursued under the same general forms and in the same Court in both cases.

Whether on these grounds, or simply from an early following of the Roman Institutional arrangement, several modern Codes still couple Obligations *ex contractu* and *ex*

---

[12] E.g. by the Emperor Zeno in Cod. 9. 35. 11 ; by Justinian, Cod. 1. 17. 2 (Tanta circa) 8, as contrasting the subjects of Dig. 47 and 48.   The Rubric to Dig. 47. 1 is of later authority.   See Mommsen, Str. p. 11, nn. 6, 7.

[13] See Austin, Lect. 45 and above, § 18, p. 604 ; § 19, p. 615.

delicto[14]; the "Digest of English Civil Law" also, in this respect, following, according to its general plan, the *Burgerliches Gesetzbuch*[15].

Definition of Delict. The distinction of Delict from Crime will be considered presently. Of Delict as opposed to Contract no definition occurs in the Roman Jurists, though they give here and there individual points of difference. The principal of these is of course the negative one that delictal obligation does *not* arise from any previous contract or relation recognised by Law as quasi-contractual, like that between Tutor and Pupil[16]. *Positive harm* seems to be regarded by Gaius as universally true of Delict[17]. Where this harm consists merely of damage to property, it must have been inflicted with no right or wrongfully—*nullo jure, injuria*[18]. Theft and personal violence or insult obviously do not require this qualification.

Since I must not anticipate the division of Rights, as being *in rem* or *in personam*, by describing Delict as violation of the former[19]; I can only here suggest the following as a rough definition. Delict is generally the violation of one of those normal or universal Rights, to the enjoyment of personal security, reputation and property, which are secured to each

[14] See Code Civil, L. ii. Tit. 4. 2 ; Italian Code, L. iii. Tit. 4, § 3 ; B.G.B. §§ 823—851.

[15] Tort is coupled with quasi-contract in Book iii. Part iii.

[16] See Just. 3. 27. 2. The actions *quasi ex contractu* between Tutor and Pupil must not be confused with the *actio* spoken of in Just. 1. 26. 3, i.e. the *postulatio suspecti tutoris*, the indictment of a Guardian whose honesty or competency is questioned. Probably the former of the two grounds was alone contemplated by the Twelve Tables, the procedure being called a *crimen* (*ib.* pr.). General unsuitableness, however, which might be merely ignorance or incapacity, is recognised as a ground of application for removal of a *tutor suspectus* by Ulpian, D. 26. 10. 3. 18. As to this proceeding being *popularis* see below, p. 681.

[17] Noxiae (? noxae) appellatione omne delictum contineri, D. 50. 16. 238.

[18] Just. 4. 3. 2 ; D. 9. 2. 4. pr., 5, etc.

[19] See Austin[5], Outline, 61, 62 ; St. 455.

individual by obligations upon every other individual in all States where any Justice is administered[20]. But I must observe that the Editors of the Digest of English Civil Law give up the idea of any safe generalisation on Delict, as represented by the English Tort, and content themselves with adding an enumeration of particular cases to the negative characteristic, absence of contractual relation.

Public and Private Wrongs. Hale and Blackstone. The Wrongs treated in **Hale's** Analysis are infringements of the Rights of individuals: whether he regards those treated in his Pleas of the Crown as infringements of the Rights of the Crown or not, his division of the two classes depends mainly on the mode in which they are prosecuted. On the subject of Ecclesiastical Wrongs[21], indeed, he approaches for a moment to Blackstone's distinction by effect or tendency. Wrongs *temporal,* however, which alone concern us at present "may be divided into two kinds: (1) such as are criminal or public wherein the wrong doer is proceeded against criminally —and these are to be distributed under the title of Pleas of the Crown, (2) such as are civil or private; wherein, at the suit or prosecution of the party injured, he has reparation or right done" (see below, p. 691).

With **Blackstone**, on the other hand, as we have seen (§ 19, p. 612), Public Wrongs are distinguished from Private primarily by their intrinsic character and tendency, as being violations of the public rights and duties due to the whole Community in its social aggregate capacity: that they are to be prosecuted by the Crown is a consequence rather than an original condition.

Austin. For the above distinction Blackstone is taken to task generally by Austin who urges that most Public

---

[20] See §§ 13, pp. 504, 505; 20, pp. 630, 631; 21, p. 647.

[21] In § 39 (of Hale), Ecclesiastical Wrongs Criminal, are *public scandals* (see my § 21, p. 645).

Wrongs are also violations of Private Rights and immediately detrimental to determinate persons: and that even the Wrongs styled Private are in their remote consequences mischievous to the community[22]. There are obviously a good many exceptions to the first objection[23]; and both might, I think, have been admitted by Blackstone himself without giving up his main line of difference.

Austin also alleges, in particular, as an objection to Blackstone's distinction, the different points at which, in different countries and times, the line has been drawn between "Civil" and "Criminal" (l.c.). This objection suggests the correction necessary in Blackstone's statement. It would be a strong one if the respective tendencies of actions were a matter of absolute fact: but, as they are mainly matter of opinion, to deny the distinction by supposed difference of tendencies, because opinion has varied as to the point of difference, is like denying that there has been any historical Morality, or rule of Right and Wrong, because different acts have been approved and censured in different countries and times. Blackstone's statement, as to the respective effects or tendencies of Crimes and Civil Injuries, is really a statement of the *belief* which induces States, from time to time, to treat some actions Civilly and others Criminally. They do believe (to use the words which Austin rejects) that the mischief of crimes (as a class) is more extensive than that of Civil Injuries as a class: and this is doubtless the reason why, where the completed Act is considered a Crime, the criminal or penal treatment is sometimes extended to *attempts*, which may be perfectly innocuous, whereas in the other case, an injury must have been committed, i.e. harm or detriment actually caused[24].

[22] Austin[5], 27. 501; St. 249, 250.

[23] The religious offences, which are historically among the first acts to be regarded as Crimes, are an old instance. In modern times, I suppose, treason or smuggling will serve.

[24] Austin[5], 27. 507 (om. in St.).

Distinction by different objects of treatment. Belief as to the tendency of actions is, of course, closely coupled with the end or purpose of their respective treatment by a State, in which some authors place the main distinction between Public and Private Wrongs. " Where," say they, " the injury is a Crime, the end or scope of the sanction is the prevention of future injuries. The evil inflicted on the individual offender is inflicted as a punishment, or for the sake of warning or example. In other words, the evil is inflicted on the individual offender in order that others may be deterred from similar offences. Where the injury is Civil, the end of the sanction is redress to the injured party[25]."

So the Roman Jurists tell us of this or that procedure being adopted on grounds of public or private utility; where modern authors speak more specifically of prevention of future wrongdoing or redress to the injured party. And this distinction is the one taken by Christian in his note to Blackstone, 4. 1, p. 5. After stating that the distinction between public crimes and private injuries seems entirely to be created by positive legislation he goes on: " In positive laws those acts are denominated Injuries for which the legislature has provided only retribution or a compensation in damages: but when from experience it is discovered that this is not sufficient to restrain within moderate bounds certain classes of Injuries, it then becomes necessary for the legislative power to raise them into Crimes and to endeavour to repress them by the terror of punishment or the sword of the public magistrate."

As against this distinction Austin maintains that even if redress of the injured party is admitted to be always *one* object of a civil proceeding, its remote *and paramount* end is, as in a criminal case, the prevention of offences generally. Nor does he make the above admission unreservedly; for he

[25] Ib. 503; St. 251.

holds that in civil actions styled *penal* the action is given to the party, not for his own advantage, but for the mere purpose of punishing the offender[26].

That, in cases of Civil proceeding where the result, if such can be conceived, is *mere restitution*, the *paramount* object of such proceeding can be represented as the prevention of offences, is an obvious absurdity. The question might however be fairly asked, in such a case, where *was* the sanction of the original legal Duty which is assumed to have been violated?

Austin's answer to this question, and his argument for these Civil proceedings, amongst others, being in their remote object preventive, is this: that the evil doer, besides being stripped of every advantage which he may have happened to derive from the wrong, is subjected to the expenses and other inconveniences of a suit (l.c.). In this case, then, the payment is apparently assumed of *some* Court or professional *Costs*, which are at present an invariable incident of Civil proceedings with us[27]. It is manifestly unjust that any part of them, but what has been unnecessarily incurred, should be paid by the person wronged, and it is generally regarded as inexpedient that the whole should be borne by the Public[28]. But as this view has not always been taken in ancient systems, and might possibly not be taken in the future of modern ones, the sanction of Costs should I think be considered as an accidental rather than an essential feature of Civil proceedings. What must always remain is the *nullity* of the encroacher's dealings with his neighbour's property, and the disappointment of his own expectations[29].

[26] Austin 27[5], 504; St. 251, 252.

[27] See Stephen, General View[2], ch. 1, p. 2.

[28] See Markby[6], ch. 19, § 837, n. 1. on Bentham's proposal to that effect. Also Sir R. K. Wilson, Modern English Law. 145, 155, 156.

[29] See above (§ 2, pp. 78, 79), on the Sanctions of Nullity.

But neither this, nor the "salutary fear inspired by the prospective liability" to a suit, which Austin represents as the object of a certain rule of Roman Law[30], appears sufficient to support his view as to the paramount end of civil proceedings being the prevention of future offences.

Roman penal actions. Under the heading *penal actions* we have to comprise two different cases, to one only of which does Austin's reasoning (above pp. 672, 673) apply. Indeed he would appear, in the light of later research, to start with a misconception of the fundamental notion of *poena* which invalidates a good deal of his reasoning upon the Roman Law of this subject.

Poena, in its primary signification, which may be clearly traced in much of its later use, does not so much indicate *punishment*, i.e. the infliction of penalty or suffering upon the offender, as *his satisfaction* of the offended person, whether by enduring suffering or by making payment. In the rough Code of the Twelve Tables, where it occurs as a pecuniary compensation for personal injury, it is evidently a commutation of the vindictive satisfaction known as *talio* —an eye for an eye and a tooth for a tooth[31]. In the later formulary actions called *penal*, it is a pecuniary satisfaction distinct from simple restitution or reparation, the action in question being called, in respect of the former *poenae*, in

---

[30] That a *pactum de non petendo* in case of a contemplated delict—it cannot apparently apply to breach of contract—is void; the reason *alleged* (*sic*) being the removal of the salutary fear, etc. Austin[5], 27. 504; St. 251. No reference is given.

[31] For Austin's reasoning see, amongst other passages, the note on p. 1051 on "punishment" and "penal." But *poena* had, I have no doubt, the original meaning of *satisfaction*, whether it be derived, with Corssen, from an Italian root *pu* (cf. *purus, putus, putare*) meaning *clearance*, or taken, as a *loan-word*, from ποινή, which, whatever its own derivation, may generally be translated ransom or satisfaction. *Talio* is here taken in the sense which it certainly seems to have borne with Roman Jurists and antiquarians. See Gell. 20. 1. 15; also Muirhead[2], 102, n. 12.

respect of the latter *rei, persecutoria. Res,* it must be remarked, in this particular use means generally that which is one's *due,* as matter of strict reparation, rather than that which is literally one's *own.* The inclusion of Obligatory Rights under the word has been noted above (§ 16, p. 552). In fact the *res,* in these phrases opposed to *poena,* approximates to what has been called, in English legal language, *efficient redress,* i.e. damages *plus* costs, the *poena* being something more than both[32]. Actions to recover what is, or is alleged to be, already one's own property—which I will assume to be the general meaning or object of *actiones in rem*—are never, we are told, penal[33]. As to *actiones in personam,* it is unnecessary here to go in detail through the different cases where the action is purely penal (*furti, injuriarum*) or partly penal and partly recuperative as in proceedings under the *lex Aquilia,* or where, though the proceedings do not arise from Delict, denial of liability subjects the defendant, if cast, to double payment. The ground and degree of the penalty may be reasonably attributed to the gratuitous and aggravating character of a delictal wrong, to a flagrant breach of trust, or the vexatious contesting of a very patent obligation[34].

In these cases an ulterior object, of discouraging such conduct for the future, may no doubt be recognised or suggested. But, as the earlier *poenae* were, it would appear, mainly imposed as a commutation for the vengeance of a rough Self-help (see below, p. 687), so all of them seem primarily, if not entirely, intended for the satisfaction, in money, of the person offended, to whom alone they go, and at whose sole discretion they are enforced.

[32] See Ga. 4. 6—9. On "efficient redress" see Kenny, Outlines[5], p. 16.

[33] Just. 4. 6. 17. See however below, p. 676.

[34] E.g. Furtum, injuriae, damnum injuria datum; depositum "miserabile" (Just. 4. 6. 17) and depensum; judicatum and its equivalent legatum per damnationem.

The statement above that Actions *in rem* are *never* penal, is made without qualification in Justinian; the meaning being that restitution, if made in the fullest sense (cf. *consequential* damages, &c.), is all that is required from the unsuccessful defendant. Whether this was or was not all that is meant to be covered by the double payment, under the old *sacramental* procedure, for intermediate produce unjustly received, it was at any rate for the exclusive benefit of the plaintiff and recoverable, as in the other *poenae* above mentioned, at his sole discretion. Both these statements apply to all the wagers, counter-wagers, and other securities mutually given and taken by litigants in the later system, which may perhaps be regarded as to some extent representing our Costs (see above, p. 673). The Sacramental Deposit itself did *not* go to the profit of the successful litigant. It was not a true wager but must be regarded ultimately perhaps as Court fees, but originally, I believe, as atonement for the sin of a false oath.

Comparison with some English cases. The Roman *penal* Actions may be compared with the cases in English Law where the plaintiff in a Civil or private suit is awarded a compensation much exceeding any material loss or detriment which he has sustained by the defendant's act, under the style of Exemplary Damages. This expression does no doubt support *pro tanto* Austin's contention as to the remote object of such proceedings generally. Yet, when we consider that the proceedings in question are entirely in the option of the aggrieved person, we must conclude that the satisfaction of an aggravated sense of wrong, and sometimes possibly the deterrence of repetition *as between the parties*, is rather the true object than example to such members of the Public as may be tempted to inflict similar wrongs.

Before passing to a different class of Roman actions I may say that my present criticism has been confined to

Austin's view as to the object of proceedings on Private Wrongs. In the case of Public Wrongs, I of course admit proceedings to be taken, in Austin's words, for the prevention of repetition, generally. But as this, though a chief object, is but one with others which are coming to be more and more widely recognised[35], I think it might be safer or more accurate to define these objects generally in the vaguer Roman manner (above p. 672), as Public utility or satisfaction.

Populares Actiones. Very different in effect and object from the *poenales actiones* treated above is another class of Roman Actions which might properly be called, as they sometimes though rarely are, *poenales*, from their express object being the recovery of a penalty usually offered by some Statute. The proceedings however for such recovery —in form civil actions (see below, p. 684) before an ordinary *judex*—were competent to *any one*, and were, as such, or as brought to protect the interests of the Public, called *populares*[36]. The former ground, of being open to any of the People, is the explanation given or selected by Justinian for the term *public* in the proceedings similar as to *promotion*, though not as to *form*, called *publica judicia*[37].

English Penal Actions. Blackstone[38] applies the term *popularis actio* to suits which can be prosecuted at the discretion and for the benefit of a " common informer." This *style* has a professional or semi-official look, such as we sometimes find attaching to the word *accusator* in Latin, but the part may be played by any member of the public. The point in these proceedings, as in the ostensibly *criminal* ones to be noted hereafter, is that whether initiated by

[35] See Kenny[5], Outlines, 29—35, on Deterrence, Prevention and Moral Retribution.

[36] Ulpian, Dig. 9. 3. 1. pr. and 5. 5. Cf. Dig. 47. 23. 1.

[37] Just. 4. 18. 1. See below, pp. 685, 686.

[38] Blackstone, 3. 9. 161.

common informer, or public prosecutor, or some other member of the sovereign body[39], or by any private person, the proceedings are taken and the penalties imposed for public purposes, and are *not* at the discretion or in the interest of the person injured by the penalised act, simply *as such* ; for of course there is nothing to *prevent* his being the initiator (see below, pp. 681 and 688).

The Roman *Penal Actions*, then, in the ordinary use of that term, which are brought at the option of the party injured and may therefore be justly regarded as for his interest alone, must be distinguished from those which bear the same name in English Law and to which Blackstone is referring in the passage last cited. The latter were initiated, as their old name (*qui tam*) indicates, partly no doubt for the prosecutor's interest, but as much for that of the Public represented by the King. They were, indeed, in some cases only competent to officials, and when brought by private persons were early forbidden to be compromised[40]. They are not much employed in modern vogue and, as Sir James Stephen says, cannot exactly be described as a part of the Criminal Law, though very nearly related to it. But they fairly illustrate the true distinction of a Public Wrong.

Distinction by remissibility. It will have been recognised that the distinctions of Private from Public Wrongs, on the one hand by their effects and tendencies, on the other by the respective objects of their treatment, though generally true and somewhat perversely criticised by Austin, are neither of them capable of very exact application. The second was adopted by the great authority on Criminal Law

---

[39] A distinction by Austin between the prosecution by the Sovereign or a member of the Sovereign body (27. 501), is rightly treated as a distinction without a difference, and omitted, in St. 250.

[40] See Kenny[5], Outlines, 14. Stephen, General View[2], pp. 2, 3, etc.

Penal, or *qui tam*, actions were so called because the plaintiff acted tam pro se quam pro Domino Rege.

just referred to (Sir James Stephen), in the first Edition of his General View, but with the addition of words which make more clear what seems the best or at least the most available line of division. Speaking of the Sanctions of Civil and Criminal Law he says "In the first case the Sanction is imposed *entirely* for the sake of the injured party: the enforcement is *in his discretion* and for his advantage. In the second case the Sanction consists in suffering(?) imposed upon the person disobeying. It is imposed for public purposes, and has no direct reference to the interest of the person injured by the Act punished. Punishments are thus Sanctions but they are Sanctions imposed for the Public, *at the discretion* and by the direction of those who represent the Public[41].

It follows that the proceedings and the Sanction are, in the case of Private Wrongs, *remissible* by the injured party (and by him only, see below, p. 680), whereas, in the case of Public Wrongs, they are only remissible by the State or Sovereign. This is Austin's distinction between Private and Public, or Civil and Criminal Wrongs[42]; the latter pair of terms, which will be explained presently, referring rather to the different *modes* or *forms* of proceeding than to the tendency of the wrong, or to its remissibility.

The merit of the distinction is that it rests upon a generally observed *fact* of actual treatment, and not upon tendencies, motives or objects, which must be more or less matter of *opinion*, nor simply upon form of procedure, a distinction with which the Roman *popular* and the English *penal* Actions are inconsistent.

In another passage[43] Austin gives some rather unnecessary exceptions and explanations which may be briefly disposed

[41] General View[1], p. 4. In the second edition this is omitted and a Crime is simply stated to be, in the strict legal sense of the word, an Act forbidden by Law under pain of punishment.

[42] Austin[5], 17. 405 ; St. 196.

[43] Austin[5], 27. 502, 503 ; St. 250.

of. The incapacity of the Infant to pursue, or his Guardian to remit, a Wrong done to the former, is merely part of the general Law as to the Condition of Infancy. The case of a Sovereign issuing *letters of protection*, against the prosecution of a private wrong or the enforcement of a private liability, certainly seems inconceivable at the present day. But the instance cited in the note is capable of some explanation[44]. The "analogous" case of Wright as stated by Austin (l.c.) is different. This, as put, is the remission of a Public Wrong, on which the informer had brought, formally, a Civil Action, for a statutory penalty. The Crown's power of pardon being not exercisable after the action was commenced and an interest vested in the Plaintiff, an Act of Parliament was employed— certainly an extremely high-handed measure and distinctly unconstitutional though, according to Austin, not *illegal* (see his remark on Acts of Attainder 6. 273). The case does not, however, appear to be quite correctly stated, so that Austin's sympathy for "poor Wright" may be a little misplaced[45].

The mixed character of an English Penal Action will

[44] It is that of Lord Cutts, to whom a Writ of Protection was allowed "against action by his Taylor, for a year, for that he is detained in our wars in Flanders" (Lev. 3. 332); so that the case bears some slight resemblance to the freedom of Members of Parliament during the customary period, from arrest.

[45] Proceedings against clergymen for non-residence under 21 Hen. 8. c. 13 and 13 Eliz. c. 20 were "stayed," although already commenced, under 41 Geo. 3. c. 102 and 42 Geo. 3. cc. 30, 86, and an amending act, 43 Geo. 3. c. 84, having "given occasion to many vexatious Prosecutions," 54 Geo. 3. c. 6 (1813) gave leave to apply for a similar "stay." But the various actions brought by Wright and reported in Taunton, 5. 304, and 6. 46—55, in the years 1814, 1815, appear to have been fairly argued and decided on the interpretation of these statutes in the usual way. Nor does the voluminous statute 57 Geo. 3. c. 99, which *inter alia* repeals so much of the previous Acts as relates to the residence of clergy in their benefices, contain any such unjust retrospective effect as is alleged by Austin with regard to "poor Wright." Query was this person Bentham's "Mr Wright" whose house was an "emporium of politics" in 1801? (See Bentham's Works, by Bowring, 10. 361.)

account for two of the exceptions to Austin's distinction noted by Dr Kenny, viz. that, in these Actions, we have Sanctions of Civil Procedure remissible by the Crown (before an Actual Suit is commenced), and Sanctions against a Public Wrong not remissible by the Crown (after an actual suit is commenced). His other exceptions may, I venture to think, be explained without any great stretch of Austin's general principle[46].

Concurrence of Public and Private Wrong. The distinction between Public and Private Wrongs of course does not prevent the same Act belonging to both categories. Breach of those Duties styled Absolute by Austin, which can be reduced simply into Duty to the Community, is *only* Public Wrong, and is necessarily, as Austin says, sanctioned *Criminally* (see § 21, pp. 643, 647). But in all other conceivable cases of Public Wrong there must be some Private one also. The Act will ordinarily be one of those violations of Normal or Universal Right known as Delicts (see above, p. 669), though it is quite possible that certain breaches of Contract, or of quasi Contractual Obligation, may come to be regarded as of sufficient public detriment to justify public prosecution[47].

The recovery of private compensation on satisfaction in these cases varies much in different systems of Law and does not appear to furnish any definite line for the division of a Corpus Juris by subject matter. The statement of Blackstone

[46] See Kenny, Outlines[5], 15, 16. The unabated nuisance is (semble) a continuing offence; that specified under the Habeas Corpus Acts is a very special provision of particular Constitutional Law limiting the powers vested in one part or member of the Corporate Sovereign.

[47] There are possibilities of this kind in modern Law arising out of the vast organisations of employees and the obscure doctrine of Conspiracy; a more established case is that of fraudulent trusteeship. The last may be compared with the Roman *postulatio suspecti tutoris* on which Just. 1. 26. 3 says "sciendum est quasi publicam esse hanc actionem, id est omnibus patere." See above, n. 16.

that, according to English Law, in the more atrocious cases the private satisfaction "is swallowed up in the public"[48] rests practically upon the rule of total forfeiture of goods for treason or felony. Now that this forfeiture is abolished by an Act of 1870, the old doctrine of our Law, that Criminal proceedings have nothing to do with Compensation, has been somewhat modified by the power given to the judge or magistrate of awarding costs and compensation, up to a certain amount, out of the prisoner's goods, both in felonies and minor cases. In other systems a claim for compensation may be made concurrently with the "public action," i.e. the Criminal procedure, in the same Court and before the same Judiciary. This is not the case in England, where the two proceedings are moreover distinguished by the fact that, in the more serious cases known as *felonies*, Civil action by the person aggrieved is postponed until a Criminal prosecution by him or some other person has taken place[49]. The right, concurrent or alternative, to take Civil and Criminal proceedings at Roman Law, will be considered shortly: as we now come to examine more closely the distinctions actually *expressed* by the terms Penal, Civil, and Criminal, which have been somewhat cursorily anticipated in the last page or two.

Penal Law. It has been shewn that, in Roman Law, *penality*, that is some suffering inflicted on or payment exacted from the offender, outside of simple restoration, reparation or indemnification, does not constitute the distinction between Public and Private Wrongs. In modern parlance, the adjective *penal* and the substantive *penalty* may no doubt be often confined to such suffering or payment when imposed for public purposes. But to call the division, which deals with Public Wrongs and their treatment, by the

[48] Blackstone, iv. 1. 1.

[49] See on the whole subject of Concurrent Private and Public Wrong, in respect of Compensation, Kenny, Outlines[5], 488, 489, 435, n. 2 and 96. Also on the German *Nebenklage*, below, p. 689.

name Penal Law which was suggested by Bentham and has been adopted by most modern Codes of the Latin nations seems rather to invite misconception.

The German *Strafrecht* more nearly, I think, indicates the Law of "Evil inflicted by public authority," which is Mommsen's definition of *Strafe*: but he apparently includes under that term the *poenae* of Delict, although they were, as a matter of legal developement, taken separately from Criminal proceedings, and have only a brief notice actually devoted to them in his Römisches Strafrecht[50]. He does not at any rate insist at all clearly on what has been here regarded as the true criterion of a Public Wrong (above pp. 678, 679). This may, as has been said, be considered as practically recognised in the German Empire, by the separation of a distinct body of substantive Law and Procedure under the head of Strafrecht. The distinction, however, here intended is much better expressed, as a matter of significant terminology, by the term Criminal as opposed to Civil.

Civil and Criminal Law. In considering the derivation and original meaning of this antithesis, it may be well to advert once more, very briefly, to the much discussed phrase *jus civile*. The explanation of this phrase as the Law proper to any particular *Civitas* or State (and, when none is specified, to the writer's own, i.e. the Roman) is familiar, from the beginning of the Institutes of Gaius, who apparently derives the adjective from *Civitas*[51]. This derivation is impossible: *jus civile* can only have meant originally the Law of the Citizens (*cives*), as distinguished from that administered between

---

[50] Mommsen, Strafrecht, 1, 5 and generally the 4th section of the 2nd Book (Der delictische Privat-prozess). *Strafe* is rendered by Kruge's translator " punishment, penalty, fine." It is a very isolated High German word, on the etymological meaning of which no argument can be safely founded.

[51] Gaius 1. 1, quoted in Just. 1. 2. 1. With Cicero, too, *national* is, I think, the more frequent meaning of the word *civilis*. For very modern uses of " Civil Law " see below, pp. 690—692.

foreigners, or citizens and foreigners (see § 7, pp. 365, 366), and, in the antithesis now under consideration, *civil* refers to the individual or *private* citizen as distinguished from the *populus* and the Magistrate or other person representing the *populus*. The antithesis is one of prosecutor and procedure. It does not quite tally with that between Public and Private Wrongs, because, as we have seen (above p. 677), a Civil or (formally) Private Action might be *popularis*, open to any one, and brought to protect the interests of the public. On the other hand, the proceedings said to be taken *Criminaliter* were always Public, both in form and object[52].

Crimen is generally connected with κρίνω[53] and so might originally mean any matter for judicial enquiry. (It may be remembered that the private *judex* or Declarer of Right is rather by way of being an Arbitrator or Awarder than a magisterial investigator.) In its earliest extant usages[54], however, we find the word already established with the limited scope and the ethical colouring of *charge* or *blame*.

Accusation is its most ordinary meaning in Cicero and the classical Jurists, though there are a certain number of

[52] When Gaius (3. 208) speaks of the *fur impubes* as *obligatus eo crimine*, he *may* vaguely call *actio furti* a *crimen*, but it is possible that criminal proceedings proper were already beginning to be competent *to the person aggrieved*, in this case. They do not seem to have been actually *public* in Ulpian's time (see Dig. 47. 2. 93. In spite, however, of Monro's scholar-like note on this difficult passage, I am inclined to question whether *agentium* does not, after all, mean the *thieves*). The word *civiliter* occurs, earlier than Ulpian, in the sense "like a private gentleman," as opposed to an official dignitary. See Juvenal, Sat. 5. 112. Poscimus est coenes civiliter.

[53] Max Müller, however, takes it rather from the root of Skr. *sru* "repute" (see Vaniçek, 1096). It may possibly be a loan-word from Magna Graecia, though no κριμεν can be found—only a κριμνον = groats. The word seems to mean that which is *sifted* as *semen* is that which is *sown* (see Curtius, 156).

[54] E.g. Plautus Pseud. 1. 5. 12; Trin. 3. 3. 11. See generally Mommsen's Strafrecht, 10, n. 4.

passages in which it must obviously be translated *guilt*[55]. Where it is occasionally applied to Private Wrongs[56] the word seems merely to bear a general ethical meaning without any special reference to an exceptional use (*privatum* or *extraordinarium*) of *crimen* in the strict sense. *Crimen* in this untechnical sense of *guilt* is not apparently said of such Private Wrongs as relate to mere disputed property or breach of Contractual obligation, but only of Delicts, which are naturally and intrinsically matter of moral disapprobation, as breaches of those general and fundamental obligations under which each individual lies to all others in any ordinary civilised State (above, p. 670). In the majority of cases, however, *Crimen* indicates the treatment of the matter rather than the Wrong or Imputability—it means *accusation*, i.e. the handing in (*delatio*) of a person's name as an offender, as distinguished from *Civil Action*, going to law or joining issue *with* him (*jure* or *lege agere cum aliquo*) in the manner prescribed by the Twelve Tables or settled by the practice of the Praetor's Court. The Roman antithesis, then, of Civil and Criminal is, as has been said above, one of prosecutor and procedure—rather more of the latter: it does not *directly* indicate whether the proceedings are competent on the one hand to the person injured *alone*, and on the other to the Sovereign, the State or members generally of the State. It is the crossing of the two distinctions, by form and competence, which causes some difficulty in the explanation of *publicum judicium, popularis actio* and *privatum crimen*, which have been to a certain extent explained above. A few remarks may be added here, from the historical

---

[55] Cicero, Pro domo, 35. 95; id quod mihi crimini dabatur...peccatum non erat; epp. ad Div. 7. 3. 6. Sunt qui...criminis loco putent esse quod vivam.

[56] As in Ga. cit. note 47. See too 3. 197 ; 4. 178 both of *furtum* ; Paulus, Dig. 9. 2. 30. 3 of damnum injuria datum (dangerous burning of thorns or stubble). See, however, Momms. Str. p. 10, n. 4.

point of view, as somewhat qualifying Austin's criticism of Blackstone (above, pp. 670, 671), so far, at least, as relates to the Roman conception of a Public Wrong.

Publica judicia. The Criminal Law of Rome can, I think, be proved, if not to have been developed out of cases of offence against the national religion, at least to have been first employed for such cases, as involving a pollution on the community ; which therefore had to be purified either by minor expiation or, as in the chief offence *parricidium*, by the *devotion* of the offender. Later, so far as we can judge from legend and tradition, though still very early, came the recognition of a secular offence *perduellio*, which is often translated *treason*, but is literally "making war on the wrong side," and which was undoubtedly taken, in historical times, to cover any violence endangering the safety of the State[57].

These acts, which were, it is plain, regarded directly as committed against the public interest, were "tracked" and, according to what is now the more generally received opinion, capitally sentenced and punished by state officials, the *quaestores parricidii* and the *duumviri perduellionis*.

When, at the outset of the Republic, all capital sentences, by *civil* as distinguished from *military* authority, were made appealable to the *populus*, these previous powers of direct sentence became practically accusations on a capital charge before the Popular Assembly as a Court. But the *publicae causae* were, it is probable, so called, in the first instance, rather from their seriously concerning the interest of the community than from their being tried before the people[58].

[57] I must leave details on *parricidium* and *perduellio* to a later part of this work. Both are treated at length in my Early Roman Law, §§ 6, 7, 16, 17.

[58] Mommsen Str. 180. 2. The other view which was, until lately, accepted in the main, is taken by Austin, 34. 604 ; 44. 778; St. 370. Sir Henry Maine practically accepts the same explanation of *judicium publicum* in A. L. ch. x.

Hence there is the less reason for surprise in the fact noted by Austin that the *publica causa*[59] or *publicum judicium* retained its name when these and other Public Wrongs, which came to be recognised as such by Statute, were no longer brought before the *populus* but delegated to special Commissions; these ultimately becoming standing Courts of Criminal Investigation (*quaestiones perpetuae*).

A great deal of what is now regarded as Public Wrong (e.g. Theft and Personal Outrage) was, as is well known, left by the earlier Roman Law to private prosecution and therefore to private remission. These deficiencies in the Criminal Code appear to have been gradually supplied not so much by the *populares actiones* mentioned above (p. 677), which only involved a money penalty, as by special or additional grounds of accusation (*Crimina extraordinaria*) which were added to the original *publica judicia* at the close of the Republic and under the Empire. In Justinian's time, or indeed by the time of Macer, c. 200 A.D. (see Sources, p. 142), the expression *publicum judicium* appears to have become identified with such Criminal procedure as was specially provided by Statute[60]. The clashing of two different criteria is the explanation of *plerumque* in Justinian's statement that these proceedings are *generally* open to any one of the people[61], in which we have the true distinction of Criminal proceedings proper, though it is considered to be incorrectly given as the original explanation of the style *publica* (see n. 58).

Cuivis ex populo. In taking this as the crucial distinction of Criminal Procedure in Imperial Rome, we regard the informer as practically replacing the earlier magisterial

[59] This seems the older term. It is used by Cicero, pro Sex. Rosc. § 59, and is distinguished by him from a *privata causa* as arising *ex crimine* not *ex controversia*. See 2, De Orat. 24, 104.

[60] Macer, Dig. 48. 1. 1; id. Dig. 47. 15. 33.

[61] Just. 4. 18. 1. 1. Publica autem dicta sunt quod cuivis ex populo executio eorum plerumque datur.

prosecutor in the Public Judicia[62]. The point is immaterial, provided we allow that the legal machinery may be put in motion by any private person who is aware of the facts, whether he be or be not the party aggrieved, so that there is no possibility of any effective remission by the latter.

This principle is, I think, generally admitted in modern legal systems as to more serious offences affecting the Public safety or security: but in those which are less so, it does not by any means constitute the recognised difference between Public and Private Wrong, and the practical initiation of proceedings varies considerably.

In England, for instance, though the principle enunciated by Austin is generally true (see above, p. 679), restrictions on the universal right of indictment have been imposed, in the case of certain Crimes peculiarly open to false accusation, by the Vexatious Indictments Act and other Statutes[63].

With regard to foreign legal systems I do not propose to consider any statutory definitions of Crime depending upon degree of punishment[64], or difference of Court, etc., but simply whether the legal machinery may be put in motion by any private person who is aware of the facts, be he or be he not the party aggrieved, so that there is no possibility of *remission* by the latter.

The French Code d'Instruction Criminelle expressly recognises the non-effect of a renunciation of the Civil action to stay or suspend the Public one, and the obligation on any one who has been witness of an attempt upon public security or the life or property of an individual to give information[65]. But there appears to be a wide and very undefined discretion in the *parquet,* or public officer generally, whether

[62] See the latter part of § 3 in Book ii. of Mommsen's Römisches Strafrecht.

[63] See Kenny, Outlines[5], pp. 441, 464.

[64] As e.g. in the French Code Pénal, Art. 1.

[65] See Sections 4 and 30.

the person aggrieved and (*semble, à fortiori*) a person not aggrieved, may *require* public action to be taken, except in the more serious cases[66].

As to the German *Strafprozessordnung* I have found it specially difficult, as an outsider, to determine what appears to be the *principal* object of a comparatively recent foreign Code in regulations on this subject, and I fear I can only profess to give a general impression derived from commentators.

It would appear that until recently the theory of an *official monopoly* of instituting proceedings prevailed in German Criminal Law, except in an important class of cases, which could not be publicly prosecuted without private initiation by the person injured or his representative[67]. A proposal was made to supplement this and other cases of possible failure of prosecution by a general subsidiary *actio popularis*, but this was not adopted by the Imperial Legislative Commission. Under the present Law, cases of the above class involving personal outrage or bodily injury can be prosecuted by an ordinary Private Action on the part of the injured person without any previous invocation of official authority, while, on the other hand, the Law recognises *no* public offence (*verbrechen*) on which the right to take proceedings is *exclusively* allowed to the person injured. The *joinder* of such person, in what is called a *bye suit* (*Nebenklage*), *together with* the action by the public prosecutor, in cases where the life, health, liberty, personal *status*, or property of the former has been affected or menaced, is a matter of justice, less clearly developed in our own legal system, but does not seem to bear on the general principle of competence *cuivis ex populo*[68].

[66] See an Article in Journal Soc. Comp. Leg. N. S. xii. (1911) by M. Léon de Montluc on Criminal Procedure in France and England.

[67] Holzendorff Rechtslexicon i. 123.

[68] See Str. P. O. §§ 156, 158, 168—170, 414, 456, etc. For the above general opinion I am quoting Birkmeyer's Deutsches Strafprozessrecht, § 53, particularly p. 304, n. 27.

I do not propose to follow further the very partial and incidental treatment of the subject now under consideration in Continental Codes, but will return, for a moment, to some illustrations of it in late Roman Law which I have myself found extremely puzzling.

Occasional Roman meaning of praejudicium. From the late introduction, at Rome, of criminal proceedings for offences, which had previously been treated simply as Private Wrongs, there evidently occurred, for some time, difficult questions arising from the fact that, if such proceedings were only, or mainly, competent to the person aggrieved, he might *prejudice* or exclude them, to the detriment of public interest, by preferring his civil remedy. So long as this was the case, the offences in question were clearly not yet treated in the full sense as Public Wrongs. But the upshot of the slightly conflicting passages in the Digest on this subject, from the period of Ulpian and Paulus, seems to be that both procedures came to be allowed to the person wronged; the property, out of which his civil compensation might be made, *not* being absolutely exhausted by the penalty on the criminal charge (see above, p. 682): but that, while *he* had the first right to bring such charge, if he neglected or refused to do so, it was open to the general public[69].

Civil, as an educational division of particular National Law. In connexion with our discussion of the antithesis of Civil and Criminal, it may be desirable to give some further explanation of the term *Civil Law* when used as one of Bentham's three main divisions of any system, referred to above, § 10, p. 449, in a sense which may not improbably pass into general acceptance.

Sir Matthew Hale, in the Preface to his Analysis, when he speaks of the method or terms of "the Civil Law"

[69] See Dig. 9. 2. 23. 9 : 9. 2. 5. pr. and the notes of Monro (Lex Aquilia) on these passages. Also above, p. 684.

evidently means the Roman Law generally (see above, p. 683), a sense in which this expression is still frequently used by modern writers. The same author, however, when he comes to the distinction of Public and Private Wrongs evidently connects the Civil Action *eo nomine* with *Civis* the Private Citizen. The former Wrongs are proceeded against, he says, Criminally and come under the title Pleas of the Crown : the latter as Civil or Private are proceeded against at the suit or prosecution of the party injured (above, p. 670).

Coke had similarly, before Hale, described the Common Pleas as synonymous with Civil, being *common* to all *citizens* as distinguished from Pleas of the Crown[70].

So far the distinction of Civil and Criminal is one simply of Procedure and competence of Procedure, on which, and its consequences in the way of remissibility or non-remissibility, enough has been said. But, besides some occasional uses of the word Civil, as opposed to Ecclesiastical Jurisdictions or Economical Relations (see § 13, p. 507), Hale also speaks generally of the Civil part of the Law, the subject of his Analysis, apparently as a residuary term meant to cover the *whole* of English Law (including Public Conditions) less Criminal. In comparing this meaning of Civil Law with the same phrase as adopted by Bentham for his triple division of a Corpus Juris, into Civil, Penal and Constitutional, we may remember that Bentham probably intended to remove the law of Public Conditions to the third head ; that, at any rate, it would seem better for us to do so, with a view to an Educational order of study (§§ 10, p. 447 and 15, p. 523). A further modification, with the same view, of Hale's Civil Part of the Law would be the omission or postponement of Civil *Procedure*, which has been above recommended, on account of its difficult or technical character (§ 19, p. 623).

---

[70] Co. Litt. 284ᵇ. *Placita communia seu civilia—Placita Coronae* or *Criminalia.*

What remains, will be, as near as may be, the German Bürgerliches Recht, the Law which deals with the Rights, etc., of the Bürger, the Civis or Private Citizen, less Procedure, and which is copied as to general Contents by the partially completed Digest of the "English Civil Law."

Division of Civil and Criminal Procedure. The question of the best place for Procedure generally in an educational course has been suggested elsewhere (§ 18, p. 607). A subdivision of this subject between the two classes of Wrong to which the Procedures respectively belong will generally be found necessary, partly from intrinsic differences, partly from the matters being so often treated in differently constituted Courts. The rules moreover as to the admission, etc., of Evidence may vary much, as they do, notably, in our own Law; though here it may be possible to take this difficult subject (which in any case should come late in legal study) mainly in connexion with Civil remedies, the special rules for Criminal Procedure being treated as exceptional[71]. In the Foreign Codes which have been more particularly compared with our own the two are distinctly separated— the *Code d'Instruction Criminelle* from the *Code de Procédure Civile*, and *Strafprozessordnung* from that of *Civilprozess.*

[71] As by Dr Kenny in the third chapter (26) of his Book 3, On Modes of Judicial Proof (Outlines of Criminal Law[5]). "Our Law of Evidence," says F. J. Stephen (General View[1], p. 68), "is the same in Civil and Criminal proceedings," and, although the subject is, of course, treated in relation to Criminal Law, the points of variance in that behalf are scattered and occasional. (See however ed.[2] ch. 16, pp. 185—188.) The same is more conspicuously the case in Bentham's Treatise on Judicial Evidence.

§ 23. *IN REM* AND *IN PERSONAM*

General use of the distinction by Austin. We have now come to the end of what appear to me the best main divisions of a Corpus Juris, viz. 1. Personal Law, which may or may not begin with Constitutional. This corresponds with the first Book of Blackstone, and the Private part of it with the first book of the Roman Institutes. 2. Property Law, corresponding with the second Book of Blackstone, the second and main part of the third Book of Gaius, the second and the whole of the third Book of Justinian. 3. Private Wrongs and the Procedure on them,

corresponding to the third Book of Blackstone, the end of
the third Book of Gaius and the whole of the fourth Book
of Gaius and Justinian.   4. Criminal Law or Public Wrongs
and Procedure, which do not come into the Roman Institutes, but constitute the fourth book of Blackstone.   On the
special treatment of Procedure advisable for the modern
beginner I must refer to what has been said in § 19, p. 623.

An entirely different recasting of the whole subject is
suggested by Austin, who, while he recognises a main distinction of Rights as Primary (or Sanctioned) and Sanctioning,
which corresponds fairly well with Blackstone's Rights and
Wrongs[1], would divide the former principally as *in rem* or
in personam, and treat what is here called Personal Law as
matter special or exceptional, constituting an Appendix or
second part to Law general[2].   In a later part of this section
I shall endeavour to shew how, according to Austin's own
admission, the distinction of Rights as *in rem* or *in personam*
cannot constitute a main division of Law, but will require
continual re-appplication in the several divisions otherwise
constituted.   This principle is, in fact, practically adopted by
Austin in the remaining Lectures (46—57), which are all that
is, in any degree, completed, of his originally intended course.
Assuming that the Law of Things (by which he means the
Law General) should come first[3], and naturally taking (within that Law) the primary before the secondary Rights, he
proceeds to subdivide these primary Rights into *jura in rem*,
jura in personam, and combinations or complex aggregates
of the two[4].   Of these subdivisions (except in certain dis-
jointed fragments) we have no more than the first.   It is
treated primarily, no doubt, with reference to Roman Law,
but contains so much illustration by the special English Law
of Real Property in Austin's time, that it is, as a whole, of

[1] See § 19, p. 618.   [2] See § 14, pp. 513—515.
[3] Austin[5], 43. 727, 728.   [4] Austin[5], 46. 773.

questionable utility for an elementary study of general Jurisprudence.   I have therefore ventured very much to abridge
and generalise Austin's more detailed treatment of "Rights
in rem as existing simply or as not combined with Rights *in
personam*[5]."   On the main distinction itself, to which Austin
attaches so much importance, I am obliged to dwell at greater
length.

The distinction of *in rem* or *in personam*, as applied to
Rights, comes very little into express account in Roman Law,
being mainly due to modern Civilians.   Its consideration,
therefore, in this application, and the utility of employing
such a distinction as a leading division of Law, are rather
questions for modern Jurisprudence, questions treated at
great length and with somewhat fatiguing repetition by
Austin in Lectures 14, 15 and 46.

In Roman Jurists primarily a distinction of Actions.
I have, however, at present to consider his statements and
opinions as bearing on the use of the phrases *in rem* and *in
personam* by the Roman Jurists; and may begin by saying
that this distinction, although slightly extended towards the
close of the Roman juristic period, was in its original and
main use one merely of civil procedure and confined to
Property Law (see below, p. 706).   It constitutes the first
broad division noted by Gaius in the actions of his own
time, but must have been already recognised in principle
during the preformulary period.   Whether the phrases *in
personam* and *in rem* were then in use or not, the normal
forms, under the *legis actiones, aio te mihi dare oportere* and
hunc hominem meum esse aio[6], involve a definite recognition
of the principle.   In the corresponding procedure of the later
system, originating, of course, much earlier than the time of

[5] Austin[5], 47. 784.
[6] Cf. Ga. 4. 16 with Notae Probi 4. 1 in Girard's Textes or Coll. Libb.
Jur. ante Just., Bk ii.

Gaius, the *intentio* or charging part of the formula shews a similar variation, "if it appear that the defendant is bound to pay or convey to the plaintiff" and "if it appear that a certain article of property belongs to the plaintiff[7]."

The first authorities which we have, other than inference from these Court Forms, for a division of actions as *in rem* or *in personam*, are Gaius' Institutes (c. 161 A.D.) and Ulpian's Regulae, a work written some 50 years later[8], and mainly, so far as we can judge from the fragments preserved to us, following the same general arrangement as that of Gaius:

An action *in personam*, says **Gaius,** is one by which we go to law with some one who is under obligation to us either from contract or delict; that is, when we contend (*intendimus*) that such a one is legally bound to convey, do or make good: an action *in rem* is when we contend either that some corporeal thing is ours or that some right belongs to us, as for instance (various interests in or easements over another's property are here specified), or when an action is competent to our adversary denying such rights[9]. The last words, I may note, do not refer to a defendant's *reply*, but to an original action brought by the owner of an alleged servient tenement, who is the person called *adversarius*, denying that it is so servient.

It might seem, from Gaius' order of explanation[10], as if the *actio in personam* had been institutionally regarded as preceding the *actio in rem*. **Ulpian** however, in a very

---

[7] Ga. 4. 41.

[8] See my Sources, pp. 125, 136.

[9] Ga. 4. 2, 3. The reading *aut cum*, before *actio est ex diverso*, adopted in Poste's Gaius and in K. and S. seems to me much better than Muirhead's (Gaius, p. 267) which omits those words. On the explanation of the last clause, briefly indicated above, see Ulpian, Dig. 8. 5. 2. pr. and the notes in Poste[2], pp. 448, 449.

[10] Ga. l. c.: cf., however, §§ 16, 41.

important passage from his Regulae preserved by the Digest[11], inverts this order, as it is supposed to have been inverted in the Edict[12].   After stating that actions are divided into two classes, *in rem* and *in personam* called respectively *vindicatio* and *condictio* (see below, p. 700), he proceeds:

"An action *in rem* is one by which we seek our property (*rem petimus*), which is in the possession of another; and it is always against such possessor: an action *in personam* is one by which we go to law with him who is under legal obligation to us for some performance or conveyance; and it is always against the same person." (For the addition in Justinian 4. 6. 2, see below, p. 709.)

This passage, we see, to begin with, explains the reason why an *actio in rem* was specially called a *petitio*[13].   *Petere*, whatever its first derivational signification may have been[14], had no doubt reached that of trying to get a thing into one's possession long before the noun *petitio* was applied to the *actio in rem*.   Why the term was introduced when the Romans already had the word *vindicatio*, I cannot positively say: perhaps because the forms properly designated by that word were only retained in the Centumviral procedure[15], the ordinary real actions in later use being the *formula petitoria*, or the formula following a *sponsio*.   The word *vindicatio* was however used for these later proceedings also.

Actio in personam certam.   But the important part of Ulpian's definition lies not so much in the terminology as in

[11] Dig. 44. 7. 25. pr.   In rem actio est per quam rem nostram quae ab alio possidetur petimus; et semper adversus eum est qui rem possidet. in personam actio est qua cum eo agimus qui obligatus est nobis ad faciendum aliquid vel dandum : et semper adversus eundem locum habet.

[12] Lenel, Edictum[2], Einleit., § 2, p. 35.

[13] Papinian, Dig. 44. 7. 28.   Petitio in rem infertur ; Ulpian, Dig. 50. 16. 178. 2.   Petitionis autem verbo in rem actiones significari videntur.

[14] To *fly at* a thing, like a bird of prey !   Curtius, 210.   See, however, Pianigiani, s.v. *Petente*.

[15] See Ga. 4, §§ 31, 92—95.

the manner whereby the defendant is ascertained or determined, which he makes the criterion of *actio in rem* or *in personam*. This has been the main point relied upon by modern Jurists, who have extended the Roman antithesis of *actions* to one of *rights* generally, and have pressed the fact of the *persona*, in the phrase *in personam*, being *persona certa sive determinata*, while they have either slurred over the phrase *in rem*, or given it various fanciful and unsatisfactory explanations to which Austin certainly contributes his share[16].

As to the Roman use of the antithesis, with which I am at present exclusively concerned, Ulpian, in the first of his two cases, clearly means that the defendant is the person, whoever he may be, for the time being in wrongful possession of the property : in the second (*actio in personam*) he would seem at first sight to mean that the defendant is an individual fixed or determined previously and independently of any wrongful conduct. This is clearly true in the case of an action arising from breach of *contract*, where the person who *must* be defendant is determined by the existing relation between the parties, before any breach takes place. When, however, an action arises from some wrong *independent of contract*, the defendant is not so originally determined, but *anyone* may be placed in that position, as Ulpian afterwards[17] shews, by his own particular wrongdoing, just as, in the *actio in rem*, by wrongful possession of the plaintiff's property. If therefore, Ulpian's two classes be meant to include *all* actions, and therefore *inter alia* actions *ex delicto*, the determinate character of the defendant in the *actio in personam* requires a little further explanation. The statement that the

[16] Austin[5], 14. 369, 370; T. and N. 941, 959, 960; St. 176, 177; 185, 186.

[17] Dig. 44. 7. 25. 1. Ex facto actio est, quotiens ex eo teneri quis incipit quod ipse admisit, veluti furtum vel infuriam commisit vel damnum dedit.

action is always against the same person in the *actio in personam* means that the liability to action, in this case, once fixed whether by that person's incurring contractual or delictal obligation, cannot shift to any one else, as it can, in the case of the *actio in rem*, by shifting possession of the *res*. The individuality of the defendant, in the latter case, or, as Savigny puts it, the *real* obligation, is not fixed until a *litis contestatio* or issue joined by some individual with the plaintiff on the question of ownership[18]. Meanwhile what the plaintiff declares or claims is simply that the specified item of property *is his*, without any mention of a defendant at all. It is this silence, as to defendant, in the claim or contention (*intentio*), that most probably led to the application of the phrase *in rem* to actions loosely so called, which had nothing to do with the recovery of property (below, p. 707), rather than the vague "generality" which Austin's Glossators or Commentators found to be "universally imported" by that phrase[19].

Actio in rem. I do not think there can be any doubt that the object and meaning of the original *actio in rem* was the being restored or secured in the enjoyment of a definite material Thing, or some interest in a material Thing, which had been interfered with or menaced. *Res* is not used here in the particular sense in which it is opposed to *poena* (see § 22, p. 675), nor in that of an Obligatory Right as an article of property (§ 16, p. 552), although, as we shall see hereafter (p. 703), the question may be raised whether an Obligatory Right might not on occasion be also the subject of an *actio in rem*.

The meaning of the preposition *in*, in the phrase *actio in rem*, may be fairly explained by an obvious, though slightly loose, analogy from its use in the antithetical phrase, as there *against* a person, so here *against* a thing. It may possibly, however, have descended independently from the use of the

---

[18] See System, v. § 206, pp. 16, 17.   [19] See ll. cc. note 16.

preposition in the old *vindicatio,* to indicate the *bearing* of what is literally a *declaration of one's power* (or *desire*) *as to* or *over* the thing claimed[20].

In this explanation, then, of the phrase *in rem,* under its original and proper use with *actio, res* is understood, as against Austin (above § 20, p. 636), to indicate the *subject* of the action, not its *compass* or field of operation. It is, *in this Roman use,* confined to items of property, and is generally a material thing or a right or interest in a material thing. Perhaps it might be, in the present point of view, more correctly regarded as any right which has so much of an independent existence as to be capable of dispossession and restitution, whether literal and physical or not. Possessory Interdicts, for instance, are obviously a procedure *in rem*: but there are more difficult cases, noted below, pp. 704—706.

Anyhow, the remedial proceedings are brought directly against the *res*; whereas in the *actio in personam* they are brought against a person, without whose operation the subject or object, whichever we like to call it, of the proceedings, i.e. the payment or performance required, has no existence[21]. The gist, therefore, of *actio* being *in personam* is that it is against *a* person as distinguished from being against *a* thing:

[20] See Gellius, 20. 1. 45. Ni...quis endo (=in) eom (the insolvent debtor) vindicit. *Eom* is the reading adopted by Hertz (in the Teubner Ed.). See, however, Schöll Rell. 92, 122. For meaning of *vindicit* ib. and Corssen, ii. 272. For *in* with acc. in this sense, Roby's Latin Grammar, ii. p. 402.

[21] This attempt to distinguish the *subjects* of *actio in rem* from those of *actio in personam* must obviously be distinguished from the empirical test suggested elsewhere (§ 16, pp. 549, 550) of a man's Property generally as distinguished from his strictly Personal Rights. As a *sub-division* of Property (the English department of Realty being omitted) the present distinction is broadly represented by Hale and Blackstone's Choses in Possession or in Action (see Hale, § 23, p. 45 ; Blackstone, ii. 25, p. 396). Sohm[2], p. 325, n. 1, describes Real Rights, in Austin's sense, of *jura in rem*, simply as Absolute. (His explanation of Absolute in this sense is not very satisfactory; see, however, § 21, pp. 649, 650.) His own Real Rights are Absolute Rights *over material things* ; see below, pp. 718, 719, n. 82.

and that phrase is *not* really an abridged expression for *in personam certam sive determinatam*, although the individuality of the defendant *is* necessarily fixed in the manner stated by Ulpian (above, pp. 698, 699).

Austin's **in rem** *and* **in personam.**   In proceeding to discuss the theory of Austin more specially on this subject I must remark that the words quoted and criticised are actually taken from his statements as to the use of the phrases *in rem* and *in personam* not with *actio* but with *jus*, to which use most of his reasoning directly refers : this however being really a later, and in Roman Law a much rarer, application of the antithesis in question.   But most of his objections to *res* being regarded as the *subject* of the *rights* said to be *in rem* may be equally well noticed and met, with regard to the *actions*.

His objections to a natural meaning of res.   Take for instance the allegation that many of the rights which are *jura in rem* are either rights to or over *persons* or have *no* subject, person or thing[22].

Now surely the difficulty of the *res* in these phrases being a *persona*, if it can be said to exist at all in the view of ancient Law[23], is in fact answered by Austin himself. "Whoever is the subject of a right which resides in another person, and which avails or obtains against a third person or persons, is placed in a position analogous to that of a thing, and might be styled in respect of that analogy a thing[24]." On this right, however, and the actions connected with it I shall have to speak more particularly below.

Again, as an illustration of rights *in rem* which have *no determinate* subject (person or thing), Austin cites the case of the Roman *heres* with regard to the *hereditas* of a

---

[22] Austin[5], 14. 369.   St. 177.

[23] See Ga. 1. 9 ; 2. 13.   Also above, § 11, p. 457.

[24] Austin[5], 15. 386.   St. 188 ; T. and N. ii. 3.   Cf. pp. 939, 940.

deceased ancestor, which is as we know the subject of a
definite Roman *actio in rem*, the *petitio hereditatis*, and is no
doubt correctly "admitted or assumed by every Civilian to
be a *real* right[25]." Here I cannot but think that Austin
is more or less misled by the occasional ambiguity in the
Roman juristic language between *hereditas* meaning the
juridical aggregate of things conferred and incorporeal,
descending from the deceased, and *hereditas* meaning the
right of succession to that aggregate. It is undoubtedly in
the former sense that a plaintiff is said *petere hereditatem*;
and the complex called a *hereditas* is so obviously an article of
Property, which can be wrongfully possessed by an intruder[26],
that Austin's description of the *heres'* case as a *condition*,
true or not, is irrelevant[27].

The *hereditas* is so definite and independent an entity,
as an article of Property, that there is, as we have seen (§ 16,
p. 548), not much difficulty in considering its disadvantages
or liabilities as to be taken together with its advantages
and claims. As a subject, however, of *actio in rem*, a somewhat subtle question might arise how far an inheritance
could constitute such a subject, which consisted *entirely* of
rights *in personam* : or to put the case in a general form,
how far any obligatory right may be the subject of proceedings *in rem* (above, p. 699). The immediate object of such
proceedings is not, of course, the direct enforcement of the
obligatio upon the *obligatus* but the removal of, or satisfaction for, interference, *by a third person*, with the performance of such *obligatio*. This is a perfectly conceivable case
both in ancient and in modern Law, but depending in the
former, as we shall see, rather upon questions of *Status* or
Relative Personal Conditions, in the latter upon particular

---

[25] Austin[5], 15. 383.
[26] See above, p. 700.   Also Ga. 2. 57.
[27] Austin[5], 15. 390.

Contract[28]. Such cases, therefore, belong mostly, in recent times, to Property Law; whereas, in a few surviving Relations among ourselves, and mainly in Roman Law, they will fall more within the Personal branch, or, as Austin puts it, the Law of *Status*[29].

To return to the subject of *jus in rem*, when the *res* is a *persona*. The slave, and originally, as I believe, the free person "in power," at Rome, was treated as a *res*, and recoverable bodily by an *actio in rem* from any one interfering with the control of the *paterfamilias*[30]. For minor interference with the services or duties of the person in power, the nearest provision that I can find is the *actio de servo* or *de filio filiave familias corruptis*[31], which are, of course, actions on delict against any offender. So too with regard to the modern Relative Rights belonging to the Household or Family, which are rights in or over Persons (see § 13, pp. 506, 507), the Services or Duties corresponding, while directly due to the Person entitled, are protected from outside interference by action (on Tort or Delict) against *any* disturber or seducer. This point, however, *does* bear rather upon the *compass* than the subject of *jus in rem* (see also below, p. 707).

---

[28] In a note at the end of Austin[5], Lect. 15, p. 391, we read that any prevention of the completion of an Obligation by a third party would be no violation of a Right in the Obligee ; or if it would, would be a violation of a distinct Right. I do not understand the last few words; but the whole passage seems not in accordance at least with English Law, as more recently developed. There is a class of English cases, of which Lumley v. Gye, 2. E. and B. 216, is the leading instance, to the contrary. In that case a *stranger* was held liable *in tort* for maliciously procuring the breach of a contract. The principle is extended by Quinn v. Leathem, L. R. 1901, App. Ca. 495, though somewhat narrowed by the Trades Disputes Act, 1906. See Anson on Contract[13], 265—267 ; Underhill on Torts[9], pp. 153, 154.

[29] Austin[5], 47. 787; St. 382.

[30] *Contra* Austin[5], 15. 388. But see the very passage which he, or his authority, quotes (Dig. 6. 1. 1. 2), in which Ulpian goes on to agree with Pomponius, that a father *can* bring a *vindicatio* for his son, *adjecta causa*.

[31] Dig. 11. 3. 1. 1 ; 14. 1.

In all these cases, although an action cannot perhaps be brought for the restitution *en bloc* of the duties or services of the person who is the *subject*[32] of the *jus in rem*, I cannot see that there is any real difficulty in regarding and calling those duties or services a *thing* to which the person invested with that right is entitled.

A man's right in his *own* person, or body, is so entirely different a matter from the right *in rem* over another person that it is difficult to see why it should be dragged in *à propos* by Austin except for the purpose of having a fling at Blackstone and his Absolute Rights, of which this is naturally one[33]. Being normal or universal, as belonging to every member of a State, it will come under Austin's Law General or Law of Things (above, p. 694). In the division of a Corpus Juris here preferred it is *par excellence* personal, and belongs therefore to Personal Law.

There is another class of rights which are *in rem sensu Austiniano*, i.e. good against "the world," or any disturber, but which according to him are not rights to or over a *thing* because they have *no subject*, person or thing. The cases alleged are a man's right in his good name, in a monopoly or franchise, and generally in any *status* or condition not purely burdensome like that of the slave[34]. This view of monopoly or franchise will obviously apply to the very important modern instance of *Copyright*.

[32] This use of the word *subject* by Austin in 14. 368, St. 175, differs, as he himself elsewhere (42. 713) explains, from the use of the word by foreign jurists to indicate the person in whom the right resides (see § 12, p. 482). The difference need only, however, be noted in order to secure uniformity of expression. The distinction between a master's right against a servant for his services, and against the rest of the world, not to meddle with the servant or his services, is clearly enough drawn.

[33] Austin[5], 47, 788. As to Blackstone's Absolute Rights see above, § 13, p. 504.

[34] Cf. Austin[5], 14. 369 and 15. 389, 390. St. 177. 190.

In the three last-mentioned cases, although the *res* may not be "specific or determinate," like an ascertained sum of money or a house, it is absurd to say that the profit arising from an exclusive right to sell, or ply a business, is not, as much as they are, a definite article of property, which may be bequeathed by a man's will or sequestrated for the benefit of his creditors (see § 16, p. 547, 549).   His patent or copyright cannot well be taken *bodily* into, or recovered from, unlawful possession: but he can get damages for past infringements of them and be secured against future by injunction[35]. See below (§ 24) as to the simpler case of servitudes and particular estates in, or rights over, a material thing being the subjects of *actio in rem*.

The right in a man's *good name* or his *status* generally is perhaps the most difficult case put by Austin as an objection to the natural and literal meaning of *res* in the ordinary *actio in rem*.   One might, rather quaintly, speak of a man's *body* as his *property* (see p. 704).   One might call the contingent enjoyments derived from general approbation and sympathy, or the special rights and capacities of *status*[36],

---

[35] These are a somewhat modern developement as recognised objects of legal property (see Cod. 4. 59).   The very special Interdict *De loco publico fruendo* (by a lessee), Dig. 43. 9, can scarcely be considered a satisfactory instance (Girard[5], 277. 4).   In modern English Law, 11 Simon 53 and the long Report (11 R. P. C.) of the Magnolia etc. Company *v.* Atlas Metal Company *and others* may be consulted as good instances of protection in the enjoyment of Copyright or a Trade Name.   It may be remarked that, in spite of the general terms of the Edict, an Interdict was possibly only conclusive as to a party in the case, see below (n. 52).   This is obvious in the English Injunction, for the *personal direction* of which see Maitland, Equity, 254.   It only applies to restrain the *individual defendants* from future infringement of patent, trade-mark or copyright.   Though such an order may be said vaguely " to give a monopoly" to the applicant, fresh parties have to be added, where a renewed application is meant to be extended to them.   See p. 400 in the Magnolia Case Report.

[36] Austin[5], T. and N. ii. 3. C[c]., pp. 953, 954; 15. 390.

things which we can recover or lose[37]. But the natural view of such *things* would rather be as strictly *personal* rights, for the violation of which action *ex delicto* is the only proper remedy, and which are distinctly the subjects of Personal as distinguished from Property Law.

Austin does however speak of them as *real* rights, subjects of *actio in rem*; and of *status*, at any rate, in Roman Law, as the subject of *vindicatio*[38].

Is **status** *a subject of* **vindicatio**? Now, in so wide a field as the Digest and Codex, it is dangerous to assert a negative. It *may* be somewhere directly stated that a *status* is claimed *eo nomine* by an *actio in rem*. But I cannot at present lay my hand on such a statement; Austin, as often, gives no reference to original authorities, and I believe the true account of this matter to be rather the following, for which the title *De causa liberali* (Dig. 40. 12) is my principal source.

The question of the slavery or freedom of an individual was originally settled by a distinct *vindicatio* of the man himself into servitude or freedom, intermediate possession being given to the *vindicator* into freedom[39]. This was an undoubted *actio in rem*, the *res* being the *homo* in question. But this procedure was apparently superseded towards, or after, the close of the "classical" period[40] by a *praejudicium* or judicial enquiry *an aliquis liber sit,* being the term

[37] Cf. Iago's speech on good name. Othello, Act 3, Sc. 3.

[38] Ll. cc. The passage quoted in a note on 15. 390, as Bentham's Principles, &c. "payment," p. 246, if it is the note on p. 248, has nothing to do with Roman Law. Hugo Jur. Enc., p. 335, I have not been able to consult.

[39] Twelve Tables, vi. 6. Schöll Rel. 135; Muirhead[2], 438, &c.

[40] Lenel, Edictum[2], §178, p. 367. Moyle[4], 548, on Just. 4. 6. 13, seems to *identify* the obvious *vindicatio* in the story of Virginia (Dig. 1. 2. 2. 24) with the *praejudicium*. But by the side of such later phrases as *proclamare ad libertatem* &c., we still find such as *se adserere*, &c. recalling the old idea of the person being claimed as a *res*. See Ulp. Dig. 40. 13. 1. pr. ; Saturninus, 40. 14. 2. 1.

originally and properly applied to this case only, in which the *praejudicium* was considered to belong to, or arise from, the old civil law, other *praejudicia* owing their existence to the Praetor's jurisdiction[41]. The class of procedure was no doubt so called as being matter of previous enquiry, to establish facts which would be material in subsequent litigation, whether questions of *status* or not.

Praejudicialis actio. It is to the above passage, or its original, and perhaps to another from Gaius, that we may possibly trace the source of that vague generality which Austin finds in the phrase *in rem*, as applied by the Roman Lawyers, and more widely by the Glossators[42]. I need not apologise for entering on a somewhat difficult subject, because the passages in question are often very inadequately explained.

In Justinian 4. 6. 13 his compilers, referring probably to an opinion of Pomponius, which is quoted with some hesitation by Ulpian[43], tells us that *praejudiciales actiones videntur esse in rem.* Now *videntur* here cannot surely be taken in the sense in which Savigny prefers to take it[44], as practically equivalent to *sunt.* In the mouth of one of the Classical Jurists we should usually translate it "are considered or held"; but, taking into account the passages cited in n. 43, I rather incline to give it, with Moyle, the looser meaning "would seem to be," i.e. belong rather to the class of *actiones in rem* than to the other.

This view may, no doubt, be accounted for by the descent

---

[41] Just. 4. 6. 13, 14.   See particularly Moyle's note.

[42] Austin[5], T. and N. ii. 3. C[d]., p. 958.   Perhaps I ought rather to say a transition in the meaning of *res* from *thing* to *fact*.   See below, p. 708.

[43] Ulpian, Dig. 44. 7. 37. pr. Actionis verbo continetur in rem, in personam, directa, utilis : *praejudicium sicut ait Pomponius*, &c.   Ulpian elsewhere distinguishes *praejudicium* from *actio*, Dig. 3. 3. 35. 2.   Non solum si actio postuletur...sed et si praejudicium, &c.   See above, § 18, p. 601.

[44] System, v. § 207, p. 19.

of the first, or *civil*, *praejudicium* from an *actio in rem* strictly and properly so called (above, pp. 706, 707): but there are other explanations which cannot be passed over.

Savigny, in the sections following the passage above quoted (§§ 208, 209), appears to take the view that *actio in rem* is a general *residuary* term. Under the *legis actiones*, the remedies corresponding to actions *in rem* and *in personam* were, he says, proceedings *with* or without *manus consertio* (see Ga. 4. 16). Under the formulary system, *all* were at first *personal*, questions of *ownership* being put in issue, except in centumviral cases, by a *sponsio* or legal wager. Subsequently there was introduced into the *ordo judiciorum* the direct *petitoria formula*, often called by the old name *vindicatio*, for ownership only. This dispensation with the *sponsio* was next extended to other questions, and thus *actio in rem* became a generic expression including all but the *actiones in personam*.

Without discussing the truth or the relevancy of all the statements in the above passage, I would suggest that a simpler and less technical explanation, of a certain shifting of the meaning of *res* from *thing owned* to *independent fact*, may be indicated in Gaius' own description of the *actio in rem per sponsionem* as distinguished from that called *petitoria* (above, p. 697). In the former, he says, the amount wagered is not exacted—it is *praejudicial* not penal, the object of the wager being merely to get a decision *de re*[45]. This may of course be translated "on the question of *property or ownership*" (Poste and Muirhead): but it has also been rendered (Abdy and Walker) "on the main question." It should be "on a matter of fact[46]." In the *formula praejudicialis* of which we read in the same book, there is no mention of

---

[45] Ga. 4. 94.

[46] See the translations cited; also Eisele, Abhandl. 82—86, and Karlowa, C. P. 99, 100.

either property or ownership, the proceeding being employed
merely to settle some other fact such as the freeborn or
freedman condition of a party, or the amount of a *dos*,
which it is necessary to ascertain for the purposes of a subsequent *judicium*, but which is not the direct subject of that
judicium[47].

A developement of the use of the word *res* in the phrase
actio in rem, so as to include the *actio praejudicialis*, may
also be indicated in the curious addition made by the compilers of Justinian's Institutes to the comparatively simple
distinction of actions *in personam* and *in rem* cited above
(pp. 696, 697), from Gaius and Ulpian.   The plaintiff we are
now told, in the latter case, proceeds against a person who is
not previously bound to him by any legal tie, but he (the
plaintiff) starts a controversy against some one *about some
thing*[48].   In the extremely unsatisfactory vagueness of these
last words, the non-existence of the previous tie and the
entirely fresh start of legal relations, by the *actio*, seem to
be the main point insisted on; while the *aliqua res* might
mean either some material article of Property or quite
generally some matter or other.

I must admit that the remainder of the section is distinctly in favour of the former and stricter interpretation,

[47] Compare Ga. 4. 44 with Just. 4. 6. 13.   In his note on the latter
passage, Moyle, commenting on the former, makes the fact of the praejudicial
formula having no *condemnatio* (in fact, no defendant) a reason why these
proceedings are sometimes said to be *judicia* but not *actiones* (above, n. 43).
For explanation of the term *in rem* applied to them, he also refers to Just. 4. 6. 1.

[48] The whole of this section of Justinian is, I think justly, supposed by
Savigny, from the mention, *inter alia*, of *judices arbitrosve* to come from
some old Jurist, though not from Gaius.   The clause *movet tamen* has often
been misunderstood.   Ortolan, indeed (Exp. § 2068), saw that the plaintiff is
the subject of *movet*, or *alicui* is meaningless.   His translation, however
(*mais contre qui nous soulevons*, &c.), in which he is followed by Sandars, is
not very clear.   The meaning is well given in that of Abdy and Walker and
of Moyle.

in this particular explanation of *actio in rem*. But, so far as that phrase goes, I think there is evidence, both in Gaius and in the unknown author cited by Justinian, of an original connexion with the natural meaning of *res* as an article of property, which is occasionally extended, through *sponsio*, from the fact of *ownership* irrespective of defendant, to an ascertainment of other facts of a similar general, or universally regarding, character. It is obvious that this extension was considered by the classical Jurists themselves as a somewhat strained and improper use of words: still I do not see that the missing links, to use Austin's metaphor, are so very difficult to restore, or that it is necessary to assume any mysterious and inexplicable import of the words *in rem* [49].

Object and effect of the **Actio in rem.** On these points I find that a few final remarks, before I pass to *Jus in rem*, are necessitated, rather by a note of Austin's editor than by anything in the original. Under the formulary system, the point at issue, in the *actio in personam*, is that the defendant is under obligation to convey, do or make good (*dare, facere, praestare*) something to the plaintiff, the last word being generally supposed to refer more particularly to satisfaction in an action *ex delicto* [50]. But the point at issue in the *actio in rem* (proper) is that the subject, the *res*, is the property of the plaintiff. The actual sentence is, in both cases, if given against the defendant, an order condemning him to a money payment; with the alternative in the *actio in rem* (under what was called *clausula arbitraria*) of restitution *in specie*: this being practically enforced by the money

---

[49] Austin[5], T. and N. 958; St. 185; see, too, Goudsmit, Pandects, 247, n. 2.

[50] See the passages quoted above (pp. 696, 697) from Gaius and Ulpian. *Convey* or *assure* would perhaps be the full translation, in English law language, of *dare*, which means to make the subject the property of the recipient. The main point is to avoid the misleading narrowness of *give*.

payment being a heavy penal estimate, on the plaintiff's part, as to the amount in which he declares himself damnified[51].

I may add here a very important remark, which comes somewhat incidentally in a note by the editor of Austin, upon *actiones in rem* generally, viz. that, in spite of what I myself believe to be the original meaning of the phrase (above, p. 699), they are ultimately only *conclusive* as to the parties to the action on which judgement is pronounced, and persons *in privity* with them[52].

This remark is more immediately suggested by Austin's statement as to the recovery of *status* in Roman Law by an *actio in rem* (see above, p. 707), as compared with Declaratory Actions in England: but may be extended to *actiones in rem* generally. It comes to this—that a *sentence*, in this action, though based upon the finding that the *res* is the property of the plaintiff, is (*semble*) only good until some better title is shewn by some other plaintiff bringing a new *actio in rem*, as to the same thing, with success. This is apparently true, in English as well as in Roman Law[53]: the only *judgement* which can be called good against all the world *in futuro*, is as to some point of *fact* which has been a definite independent issue, as in the *actio praejudicialis* (see also below, p. 727 as to English Judgements *in rem*).

Jus in rem *and* **Jus in re** *in* **Roman Law.** The former of these expressions is very little used by the Roman Jurists,

[51] See Ga. 4. 48 and notes pp. 496, 499 of Poste[2], on the *jus jurandum in litem*. Also Moyle, Just.[4] Exc. x. p. 649. Into the question whether, and how, direct restitution in *specie* was actually effected, as I believe, in much earlier times, according to the plain words of Gaius l. c., I cannot enter here. See Poste, ib., p. 498 for the general opinion to the contrary.

[52] St. 191 at the end of Lect. 15. *In privity with* may here be taken roughly = claiming under. On this subject see Savigny, System vi. § 301, pp. 466, 467 and the general question of *exceptio rei judicatae* which appears under the somewhat unintelligible title *Einrede der Rechtskraft*.

[53] See Maitland's remarks, P. and M. ii. 77, 78, as to the "relativity of ownership."

but, in the few passages in which it occurs, *res* clearly means the thing itself as distinguished e.g. from its value[54]. *Jus in re*, on the other hand, is not infrequent with them, as indicating some right less than ownership in or over another person's property. It is thus opposed to *dominium* or complete ownership, its title in full being *jus in re aliena*[55]. In this sense, although it may be objected that very different sorts of right—life interests, servitudes proper, licence—are classed under one and the same expression, the general meaning, as given above, is perfectly clear. The misfortune is that *jus in re* has been used by modern civilians, in that sense of *jus in rem* in which it means right to a determinate thing, as an antithesis to *jus ad rem*, a perplexing and unnecessary modern expression, which will be considered hereafter, p. 715.

Approximations to Austin's interpretation of in rem. In all the uses of the phrase *in rem* or *in re* hitherto cited from the Roman Jurists, with the exception of those which refer to the *actio praejudicialis* and the vague *de aliqua re* of Just. 4. 6. 1, *res* distinctly means an article or item of *property*. There remain to be taken into account a certain number of other cases, mostly from the latest writers in the Digest, where the words *in rem* do approximate to the meaning given by Austin to that phrase generally. The *pactum*, for instance, *de non petendo* is held to be *in rem* if worded thus *ne petam*, or, strictly, *ne petatur*; *in personam* if worded *ne ego petam* or *ne a te petatur*[56]. The oath of exoneration, if made by a *fidejussor*, that there is no obligation

---

[54] See Ulpian, Dig. 32. 20.   Nullum quidem jus in ipsam rem habere, sed actionem de pretio. Cf. Goudsmit, 247 n.

[55] Austin[5], 50. 822 and T. and N. ii. Note 4. A, pp. 959, 960.   In opposition to *dominium corporis*, Ulp. Dig. 39. 2. 13. 1.   In Ga. Dig. 9. 4. 30 persons are opposed to *domini* as having aliquid in re jus qualis est creditor et fructuarius.

[56] Cf. Ulp. Dig. 2. 14. 7. 8 with Florentinus 57. 1 and Gaius, 28. 2.

on him (*de suâ personâ*) will *not* be good as an *exceptio* for his principal : if made *in rem*, it will[57]. *Constitutum*, too, if the same expression is used, must be paid *absolutely*[58]. In a conditional legacy, sureties for the payment "of the legacies" are liable as soon as the condition is fulfilled, although the inheritance on which the legacy is charged be not yet taken up, because their engagement was *in rem concepta*[59].

The *exceptio metus causa*, which runs *si in ea re nihil metus causa factum est*, appears to be always *in rem*, it being immaterial *who* causes the fear. The *exceptio doli* on the other hand must name the person, whose fraud is complained of, although the *stipulatio dolum malum abesse* will guard against fraud by *any one*, and so is said to be *in rem*[60].

The *operis novi nuntiatio* (notice of danger from projected alterations), which is stated to be made *in rem*, may be given to *any* sane person of age on the premises, and presumably in the employment of an owner who may be for the time incapacitated to receive such notice[61].

Finally, in the case of *missio in possessionem* of a debtor's goods, a grant of such *missio* to one creditor is said to be good *omnibus...et in rem*[62].

In all the passages last quoted here, the phrase *in rem* may well be translated *absolutely, generally,* or *without regard to any particular person*. In some, no doubt, Austin's "good against the world" may be forced into the service : but I think they are mostly capable of deduction, through steps traced above, from a natural meaning of the word *res*.

---

[57] Ulp. Dig. 44. 5. 1. 3.

[58] Ulp. Dig. 13. 5. 5. 2.

[59] Pomponius, Dig. 36. 3. 10.

[60] See Ulp. Dig. 44. 4. 4. 33 and 4. 2. 14. 3; 9. 1.　As to *dolus* cf. the passage first cited with Ulp. Dig. 7. 9. 5. pr. and see Markby[6], § 165, p. 99.

[61] Ulp. Dig. 39. 1. 10 and Paulus, ib. 11.　*In rem* does *not*, of course, mean *on* or *on to the premises*.

[62] Ulp. Dig. 42. 5. 12. pr.

The alleged employment of the distinction of *jura in rem*
and *jura in personam* (under the style of *dominia* and *obligationes*) as an actual or working main division of Law, by
the Roman Jurists, ought, on its own account, to come here :
but, being naturally connected with a suggested similar
division in modern systems, it may be better taken in a
separate section (24).

Jus in rem, in re, *and* **ad rem.** Hitherto I have
endeavoured, as much as possible, to confine my enquiry to
the uses of the antithesis *in rem* and *in personam* by the
Roman Jurists.   I must now enter to some extent into uses
of the same antithesis by *modern civilians,* possibly following
earlier canonists.   Austin's statement of these civilians'
distinction is that a *jus* or right is *in personam* or *in rem*
accordingly as it is *facultas homini competens in certam
personam* or *sine respectu ad certam personam.* This is
simple, intelligible, and agrees fairly well with some of the
later approximations, in Roman Juristic language, to Austin's
interpretation of *in rem* (above, pp. 712, 713). But in
Austin's modern authorities there appears to be involved
another distinction, or rather assumption, which is worth
consideration, not so much from its record by Austin, as from
the practical effect which it has probably had upon very
recent facts in Codification and arrangement of legal subjects.

Austin[63] refers the pair of definitions above quoted to
Grotius, but Huber quotes Grotius as authority for defining
jus in re as *facultas homini in rem competens sine respectu ad
certam personam* and *jus ad rem* as *facultas competens personae in personam* ut nobis aliquid det vel faciat[64].   On the

---

[63] I cannot find the original passage in Grotius.   In De jure, &c. 1. 1. 5
he recognises a distinction between *dominium* and *creditum* ; *jus in personas*
(2. 5. 1) means, with him, power or control *over* persons as over things.

[64] Huber quoted in Heineccius' Elementa, § 332, as Praelect. ad Inst. h. t.
(De acquirendo rerum dominio) § 12.   See also Goudsmit, § 18, p. 40 and the
passages quoted in Holland[10], p. 139.

confusion of *jus in re*, in its proper Roman signification, with the general right of ownership I have spoken above (p. 712). What we have to note here is its opposition in the latter sense, by modern civilians, to their conception of *jus* ad *rem*.

Erroneous assumptions of modern civilians. The last quoted phrase is explained by Austin[65] to mean *jus in personam ad jus in rem acquirendum*; this particular class of *jus in personam* being not a right entitling its owner simply to *any* act or forbearance on the part of the *persona obligatus*, but to the particular act of transferring to him some subject of ownership. It is unnecessary to enquire whether Heineccius and Huber did or did not really mean to include, under *jus ad rem*, some rights *in personam, ad aliquid faciendum*, as well as *ad aliquid dandum*: or, to recur to Austin's objections, whether there were not present to their minds some subjects of ownership (and so of rights *in rem*) which could not exactly be called things.

The particular point, about which we are at present concerned, is that, *à propos* of this unlucky phrase *jus ad rem*, he credits "modern civilians" with two false assumptions: one, that the acquisition of a *jus in rem* is *always* preceded by a *jus ad rem* and a corresponding *obligation*; two, that the acquisition of a *jus in rem* is *always* the scope or object of *jus ad rem*, which, if *jus ad rem* be considered, as they seem to have considered it, synonymous with *jus in personam*, means that every obligation or *jus in personam* is merely preparatory to a *modus acquisitionis*[66].

It were merely waste of time to discuss these alleged assumptions as compared with Roman Law[67]: nor is this the place to analyse the acquisition of *dominium* into *modus acquirendi* and *titulus ad acquirendum* (see below, § 25). I

[65] Compare Austin[5], 14. 376, 377 with T. and N. ii. 4. B, pp. 960, 961.

[66] Austin[5], T. and N. ii. 4. C[a]., pp. 962, 963. Much of this matter is inserted in St. (pp. 183, 184) as a Note to Lect. 14.

[67] Austin[5], ib. 965, 966.

shall therefore leave this gratuitously troublesome conception of *jus ad rem* with the remark that it is probably the cause not only of the confusions between contract and conveyance to be noticed presently, but of the strange position of the Law of Obligations generally, in the German Civil Code. It is only in view of some theory, of rights of ownership following *always* as the result or product of personal covenants, that I can see the meaning of reversing the Roman Order and making the *Schuldrecht* follow directly after the Preliminary Matter which takes the place of the *Jus Personarum*[68]. I must return to this subject at the end of the section.

Confusion of contract and conveyance. It is not, however, so much the *placing* of the subject of Obligations in modern French and German Codification, which arouses the fury of Austin[69], as the confusion of an agreement to transfer property with the transfer itself—things which, no doubt, are kept clearly apart in Roman Law, but are occasionally confused in modern, whether from ignorance of the former, or from intention, or from the erroneous assumptions of civilians mentioned above.

In the French Code Civil, differing from the older law of the country, which followed, in this respect, the Roman model, property in goods (*biens*) may be acquired and transmitted as the result of simple obligations. This is particularly developed in the case of *sale*: but the principle is laid down generally by recent commentators that where there is any obligation to *give* (i.e. transfer the " property " in the subject-matter) it is, in modern French Law, " reputed as executed," as soon as formed. "Goods" (*biens*) it should be remembered are not here confined to *moveables*, the principle being more universally applicable to *immoveables*, whereas, in the case of

[68] See, however, Austin[5], 39. 674.   The Digest of English Civil Law is, of course, bound *ex proposito* to follow the same order.

[69] Austin[5], 39. 673, 674 ; 46. 773, 774; St. 335, 336.   As to Germany, his strictures, of course, apply only to the old Prussian Code.

the former, delivery may still remain necessary to effect transfer of "property[70]."

In the German Civil Code, what corresponds to a Conveyance (*Auflassung*, strictly = Release) is required for transfer of ownership in Real Property. In Moveables such transfer may take place by mere arrangement of the parties, but does not seem so much to result from an *obligation*, as to be effected by a *constructive* delivery[71]. I should add that the *order*, in this respect, of the Civil Code follows that of the old Prussian Law, for which Savigny gives the reason alleged above[72].

It seems to me, I must confess, quite reasonably competent to a Legislature to enact that a Contract for the transfer of property (ownership) in certain forms, and, I think *we* should add, for certain considerations, should operate as an actual transfer. Something very similar to this was surely done, as between the person standing seized of lands *to a use*, and the person *having* such use, by the famous Statute of Henry VIII. (27, c. 10), but the same, no doubt, has *not* been done with regard to a so-called *equitable estate*, which Maitland rightly denies to be a true *jus in rem*[73]. And it certainly seems *à priori* desirable, for clearness, that Contract and Conveyance should be kept distinct from one another, although it is quite established in English Law, that a contract for sale of *goods*

---

[70] See Austin[5], 14. 377 and, more fully, T. and N. ii. 4. C^c., pp. 969, 970, on Code Civil, §§ 211, 1138, 1140, 1141 and 1583 as annotated by M. Rogron. Of modern commentators, Sirey is not very illuminating, but Planiol (Droit Civil, i. pp. 824—830 and ii. 480) is clear not only as to the gradual growth of the new rule, but as to its careful discussion, in view of the Roman Law, by its ultimate enactors. I may remark that the Code Espagnol pointedly adds to the clause corresponding with the end of the French, § 211, "moyennant tradition," Levé, p. 119.

[71] BGB. §§ 929, 930. On *traditio brevi manu* and *constitutum possessorium* see Scherer, iii. p. 118 and Dernburg[3], iii. p. 302.

[72] System, i. § 56, p. 375, n. *h*.

[73] Equity, ch. ix. p. 111, &c. His contemptuous treatment, however, of Austin[3], 14. 388, is scarcely just.

may, under the proper conditions, operate *as* a conveyance[74].

Before considering the practical applicability of Austin's division of Rights generally into those *in rem* or *in personam*, under his sense of the words, on its independent merits, as a main division of the Corpus Juris, I must first dispose of one or two ambiguous expressions by other authorities, which like *jus ad rem* need to be explained or cleared out of the way.

Jura realia *and* **personalia** are expressions occasionally used by modern civilians as adjectival forms for *jura in rem* and *in personam*, but only as confined to Property Law[75]. This at least seems to be the meaning given by Savigny to *jura realia*, if represented by the corresponding German *dingliche Rechte*[76].

Jura realia are however spoken of by Grotius[77] and, it may be, by others, in the entirely different sense of rights which belong to a person only as owner of a particular *res*. The case principally intended is that of the Rights (generally denoted in Latin by the correlative term *servitutes*), which are said to *belong to landed estates*[78]. These are, as Austin shews, Real Rights in his sense of *jura in rem* : but so too are the *personal* servitudes, so called, of *usufructus* and *usus*, which are, as we say, *in gross*, not *appurtenant*[79].

---

[74] Anson, Law of Contract[13], p. 21, n. 1, &c.

[75] E.g. the translator of Mackeldey, Pr. ii. § 15. Austin (T. and N. ii. 5, pp. 977, 978 ; St. Note on Lect. 14, p. 184) identifies the pairs without the above qualification.

[76] System, 1, § 56, p. 369. Alle mögliche Rechte *an Sachen*...fassen wir unter dem gemeinsamen Namen der dinglichen Rechte zusammen.

[77] De jure, &c. 1. 1. 4. Non alii competunt quam qui *certam rem* habeat.

[78] Ga. 2. 14; Dig. 1. 8. 1. 1.

[79] See Austin[5], T. and N. ii. 5. 4, pp. 979, 980 ; St. 184. But this would not be the case with vendor's covenants, which, though they would " run with the land " and belong to an assignee of the estate, would only be good against the vendor and his representatives. The *composition real*, mentioned in the preceding page, is nearer to an Austinian Real Right.

There is, of course, a standing source of confusion in
English Law, from the connexion of the adjective Real with
land (§ 16, p. 556). We may note, too, the special limitation of a *personal right of action* to those which *nec heredibus
nec in heredes competunt*[80].

In addition to these ambiguities, which are to be recognised and avoided, I fully endorse Austin's objection[81] to the
expression *jus realiter personale* and several others in which
persönlich is used to indicate Rights *over* persons.

Rights absolute and relative. There is much more to
be said for the employment of *these* terms, as they are
employed by certain German Jurists, to indicate what Austin
distinguishes as *jura in rem* and *jura in personam*[82]. He
himself scouts this use of the terms as flatly absurd, on
the ground that *all* Rights are really, as has been shewn
above (§ 20, p. 630), relative, that is, depend on correlating
Duties; which are, in the one case, incumbent upon the
world at large, or as I should rather say, upon all other
members of the given Social Community, and, in the other
case, are limited to determinate individuals[83].

The former class of Duties, however, which correlate with
what may be roughly called, in Hale's words, a man's interest
in himself, his goods, and estate (above, § 13, p. 503), are so
purely negative and ancillary, amounting to nothing more
than non-interference, that they are in general tacitly assumed, and the Rights of Security, Liberty and Reputation

---

[80] T. and N. ii. **5. 3**, p. 979.

[81] ib. ii. **3. C**[b]., p. 941. I may add an ambiguity which has occurred to
myself in the German Code. *Reallasten* undoubtedly means burdens *on*
estates, but it is by no means clear that the first half of the compound does
not indicate rather the *positive* character of the services incumbent than
that they belong to people *as owners of* estates (see § 24, p. 756, n. 65).

[82] E.g. by Mackeldey, Einl. § 15, and, in later times, by Sohm (see above,
p. 700, n. 21).

[83] Austin[5], T. and N. ii. Note 3. C. d. 5, p. 956 ; St. 184.

in Personal Law, as of Ownership in Property Law, regarded as Normal[84].

This taking of the corresponding Duties as a matter of course, or in fact leaving them out of the question, is what may be intended in calling the *jura in rem* Absolute, as opposed to the Relative Rights, so styled *par excellence*, which require either Action or Forbearance—the latter, as conscious abstention, amounting to Action—from some definite person. But I do not think this is what is meant by Hale and Blackstone, under Absolute, and I must in logic admit Austin's objection to the term[85].

Obligatio *and* (?) **officium.** The different amount of recognition which is, as a matter of fact, afforded to the different classes of Duty just referred to, is illustrated by Austin, as I think somewhat incorrectly, from the phraseology of the Roman Jurists. In the case of *jura in personam* they have a name primarily and properly significant of the corresponding Duty—*obligatio*, the Bond. Only, as the Duty and the Right are here obviously the same thing viewed from different sides, i.e. in the *onerous* or the *beneficial* aspect (see above, § 21, p. 650), the same word serves for both, and indeed, in the enumeration of items of Property, appears prominently under the latter (see § 16, p. 552).

But in the case of *jus in rem*, whether such an expression was ever used in Austin's sense by the Roman Jurists or not (see above, § 23, p. 711), no name is to be found in their works for the corresponding Duty. Austin is obliged to suggest *necessitas* or *officium* as words which they " would have used," or words which did actually "supply the defect[86]."

---

[84] See above, § 19, p. 615. I leave out of question here the Socialist doctrine referred to above, § 17, p. 586.

[85] See § 13, p. 504.

[86] Austin[5], 14. 370, somewhat modified by T. and N. i. Note 6, pp. 924, 926.

He gives no authority, however, for such use. *Necessitas* comes in Justinian's definition of *obligatio* with the sense of legal constraint generally[87]. *Officium*, which Austin himself prefers, is open to the objection that it is otherwise employed to designate *moral* Duties, not armed with any legal sanction[88].

Absolute = Normal Rights and Duties.   If the view taken above (§ 20, p. 630) be correct as to the fundamentally *social* character of every Right, there is, no doubt, in logic, an objection to the use of Absolute and Relative to describe Austin's *jura in rem* and *jura in personam*. That Rights are Absolute which belong to men "merely as individuals or single persons," if it does not exactly assume Blackstone's State of Nature (see § 20, p. 630), certainly ignores what I believe to be the true origin of both Morality and Law (above, § 3, p. 99).

Apart from these objections, Absolute as opposed to Relative *would* form in my view an intelligible, if not strictly logical, designation for the Normal Rights of every member of a Social Community, including that of Private Property. Nor can I see any great difficulty in classing the Duties corresponding to these Rights together with Duties to the Community as a whole, and placing both as a first chapter in Personal Law[89].

Jura in rem **and** *in personam* **as a main division of Law.**   With the Roman Jurists themselves, the Austinian division of *Rights* is, as has been indicated above, rather a matter of modern inference than of any direct statement. It is, however, alleged by Austin to be "as assumed by the Roman Institutional writers" the main groundwork of this

---

[87] See above, § 21, p. 656.

[88] ib. 642. Also Austin[5], T. and N. ii. Note 3, C[d]., p. 959; St. 186. The above is not true of certain *officia* due from freedmen ; but *officium* generally bears the moral meaning given it by Cicero in his well-known work.

[89] See § 21, pp. 642, 647 and § 15, p. 531.

arrangement[90], and more definitely, according to him, by later German civilians, as constituting a division of the *Jus Rerum* into *Dominia*, in the largest sense of that term, and *Obligationes*[91]. Now there is much to be said for recognising the virtual or resulting reality of some such division as that of *dominia* and *obligationes*, according to the more prominent component elements of either part, in the *Jus Rerum*; but it is better discussed separately from the one under our present consideration (see § 24).

As to the distinction of *jura in rem* and *jura in personam* in the more general Austinian sense, I am quite ready to agree with Savigny that this is an *all pervading*, or I would rather say, a *continually recurring* distinction in Roman Law, as in most others: but I maintain that it is not possible as a *principal* division either of that or of any other Corpus Juris, and I do not quite see that it is represented as such in the very obscure quotation by Austin from Savigny's Vom Beruf[92]. A fair test, however, of its practicability may be found in a well-known modern work.

Hunter's Roman Law is a very able attempt to recast the Law of the Institutes and Digest in the order of a Code, based largely upon the principles of Austin, of which the distinction of Rights as being *in rem* or *in personam* figures very conspicuously in the whole scheme.

[90] Austin[5], 14. 369; St. 176. See, too, Goudsmit, § 18.

[91] id. 46. 773; 47. 784; St. 380.

[92] " wie wichtig und *überalleingreifend* (everywhere interposing itself) im Römischen Rechte die höchst bestimmte Begriffe von dinglichen Rechten und Obligationen sind. Dasselbe gilt von Begriff des Status. Hier nun liegt die Unterscheidung von Personenrechten und Sachenrechten zum Grunde." In the later " System," *status* is Savigny's Family Law of the *Jus Personarum*, in which there are, no doubt, Austinian *jura in rem* as well as *jura in personam*. This appears to be what is meant by the same holding good of the conception of Status. The last sentence seems to me merely a statement of the Austinian distinction in other words. See, however, Austin's interpretation, or paraphrase, in 41. 696.

The part of that scheme with which I am at present chiefly concerned is that which covers the ground of the *Jus Personarum* and *Jus Rerum* of the Romans, principally as regards the latter. I have not therefore to deal here with such questions as the position of Civil Procedure or the separation, from the rest of the system, of Criminal Law. The former, as a matter of fact, is placed at the end of Hunter's scheme, while the small amount in which the latter comes within the Roman Institutes and Digest is relegated to an Appendix.

In the *Jus Rerum* Hunter is obliged, rather conspicuously, to diverge from his main principle of classification by making the subject of Inheritance, as it is in practice now generally made, into a department to itself, from its complication of the two classes of Rights. The remainder of Roman Private Law (other than Procedure) he does indeed purport to arrange under Austin's two heads, but only at the cost of very inconvenient repetitions and severances, some of which are stated below[93]. So far as the first two Books are concerned, his application of Austin's grand division does not seem likely to supersede the old Institutional one.

Other modern Jurists, who adopt, like Markby and Holland, Austin's definitions of Right *in rem* and *in personam*, do not seem to make any attempt to employ them as a practical division of the Corpus Juris.

Modern instances may be multiplied, *ad libitum*, of complication of the two classes of Rights, in the same case, and the consequent impossibility of classing the case under one head or the other. In Family Law, as we have seen above, Rights existing *over* or *to* persons are (at least in the modern point of view, which can no longer regard servant,

---

[93] E.g. the duplication of Family Law under Rights *in rem*, as *Potestas*, *Manus*, *Mancipium*, and under Rights *in personam*, as *Status*; the division of Pignus, partly coming under Dependent Rights *in rem*, partly under Equitable Contracts, &c.

wife, or child, purely as a *chattel*) both *in rem* and *in personam*[94]. In Property Law, we may have the very obvious instance of a *Universitas juris*, an Aggregate of Rights of both kinds, passing *en bloc*, notably in the case of Inheritance, which, looked at as a Right, is perhaps to be considered in its entirety, as one *in rem*[95]. But the same complication is equally inconvenient for Austin in many individual cases of Right and Duty, which it is clearly desirable to treat in one place, as an undivided whole. Austin instances Mortgage, both in English and Roman Law, and also Sale or Contract of Sale[96]. With the last subject and in particular the confusion of Contract and Conveyance I have dealt already. Nor do I propose to enter here into a somewhat speculative view of Ancient Law which, *e converso*, suggests *uncompleted conveyance* as the possible origin of at least one sort of Roman contract[97].

Conclusion. Austin's original proposal, then, to subdivide all Primary Rights (§ 19, p. 618) as being either *in rem* or *in personam* comes, under his own admissions, to require the addition of a third class, consisting of combinations of the two : and, as a matter of fact, the major part of the collections of Rights and Duties, which practice binds together, will belong to this third class[98]. In Roman Property Law, to which alone I believe any such distinction of Rights to have originally belonged, a rough division of this kind can, I think, be recognised in a general way, and has been to a considerable extent adopted in the same part of modern systems. In Personal Law, in the Law of Wrongs generally,

[94] Austin, T. and N. ii. Note 3, C[b]., pp. 938, 939 and above, p. 703. See Innes' Law of Torts, Pt 2, ch. 3.

[95] See, however, Austin[5], 47. 784 compared with 54. 871 and with Hunter Intro. xiii.

[96] Austin, T. and N. ii. Note 4, C[c]. 971—973 and above, pp. 716, 717.

[97] Maine's Ancient Law, ch. 9, pp. 319, 320. I am unable, now, to accept this view of *nexum*.

[98] Austin[5], 46. 784 ; St. 379. Above, p. 694.

and of Public Wrongs in particular, the distinction where it can be made out (see Hunter, Introd. ix.) is much better put in other ways and expressed in other terms; in the Law of Public Conditions it is meaningless.

In **Early English Law,** any adoption of the distinction *in rem* and *in personam* has been rather nominal and ornamental than real. As with the Roman Jurists, the distinction is properly and originally one of Procedure, and it is in some classification of Actions and Writs that we have to look for any distinction of Rights as *in rem* or *in personam*.

There is not, as far as I can find, anything of the sort in **Glanvill. Bracton** nominally recognises the Roman distinction of Actions, and bases the determination of the defendant, in the one case, upon contract with or delict against the plaintiff, in the other upon possession of the thing (above, p. 697). But, if the thing be a *moveable*, whether it be still in existence or not, the defendant has, from the beginning, an alternative of restoring its *value*, which must be stated by the plaintiff in bringing his action[99]. It is, as we have seen, from this distinction of *remedies* that our division of Property into Real and Personal most probably comes[100].

There are other cases following in which the action is said to be mixed, but certainly not on account of a combination of claims *in rem* or *in personam* in the proper Roman sense, and from these and many other passages in Bracton it is clear that no definite classification of the English Actions under the two Roman heads was found possible or, in any detail, attempted by him[101].

---

[99] Bracton, L. 3, de Actionibus, c. 3, §§ 2—4. Fol. 102ᵇ. This action therefore, we are told, in spite of its seeming real, is only personal.

[100] See above, § 16, p. 557.

[101] l. c. § 5. See, too, P. and M. ii. 567, 568 and ch. 9, § 1, generally.

Fleta repeats much of what Bracton had said about *mixed* actions, bringing in, *for that occasion*, the designation of an action as being *in rem* or *in personam*; but does not add any clear distinction of the two on Roman lines[102].

In **Britton** I have not found any notice of the distinction at all.

Littleton, as we have seen (§ 16, n. 33), based the difference of actions upon recovery of the actual thing or damages, but the actual thing is apparently confined to *land*. Coke's note merely repeats scraps of Bracton[103].

To **Hale and Blackstone** any classification of Rights as *in rem* or *in personam* is unknown. On their "things personal in action" I must refer to what has been said above (§ 16, pp. 562, 572). Of their Real and Personal Actions the former are such as concern *Real property only*, the latter those by which a man claims a debt, or personal duty, damages in lieu of the latter, or for some injury done to his person or property[104].

The replacement of the old Real actions by the *personal* ones of *ejectment* or *trespass* is too detailed a matter of procedure to be entered upon here[105]. I would only refer to a concluding remark of Blackstone upon the subject, which once more brings us into conflict with the idea of a *Right* good against all the world.

In the principal of the above-mentioned Actions—the Writ of Right—the party who shews the better title retains

---

[102] L. 5, ch. 9, §§ 1—4.

[103] Co. Litt. § 492, pp. 284[b], 285[a]. The reference to Fleta (i. c. 16) is not in point.

[104] Blackstone, iii. 117, 118.

[105] Blackstone, iii. chaps. XI. and XII. Stephen, vol. iii. p. 412. See Halsbury, i. 46, for modern legislation on the subject, ending in the Judicature Act of 1875. This put an end to the old forms of action, by enacting that in the writ of summons (a procedure, of course, *in personam*), with which civil actions now begin, it should not be necessary to state the *precise* ground of complaint or the precise relief claimed.

or recovers the land, but only as against *the other and his heirs,* for ever. That is, this action, like (*semble*) the Roman *actio in rem* (above, p. 711), does *not* really confer a *jus in rem* (*sensu Austiniano*) good against the world. *That* can only be obtained in our case (subject to the exceptions which will be noted directly) by the effect of certain Statutes of Limitation which enure to bar all claims[106]. In **modern English Law** the expression *in rem* does not occur much as applied to Rights, either when confined to those of Owner-ship or when used in the wider Austinian sense above (§ 20, p. 639). An Action, however, *in rem* may still be brought in the Admiralty Division of the English High Court for certain specified cases: in which judgement is said to "operate directly on the *status* of the property" so as to transfer or vest an *absolute* title, at least in the case of a purchaser under the sale directed by the Court[107].

And, more generally, certain judgements are recognised by English Law as being *in rem,* where these words bear the adverbial or adjectival sense of what is decreed *absolutely* or *without regard to any particular person,* noted above (p. 713), among Roman approximations to Austin's interpretation of the phrase. A judgement is said to be *in rem,* when it is adducible against persons other than those who are parties to the case decided or who claim under such parties[108]: in other words, when it is one by which all persons, whether party to the proceedings or not, are *estopped* from averring that the *status* of persons or things, or the right or title to

[106] This subject is briefly introduced in Blackstone iii. p. 195. Compare P. and M. ii. 62 and see, for fuller treatment of Limitation, Stephen, Book 5 (of Civil Injuries) ch. 13, noting the difference between Statutes which extinguish the hostile (outsider's) Right, and those which only bar the Remedy.

[107] Halsbury i. pp. 47, 48.

[108] Austin[5], T. and N. ii. Note 3, C[d]., pp. 957, 958.

property, is other than the Court has, by such a judgement, declared it to be[109].

Continental Law. A few remarks upon the order of arrangement in some Continental systems of Law may be added here, because one of the most prominent features in the latest Codification is possibly based on what has been treated above as a misconception of modern civilians (pp. 715, 716). In the codified Civil Law (*Bürgerliches Gesetzbuch*) of Germany, while our own cleavage of Real and Personal Property still occurs (in the form of Land and Moveables) as a subdivision, the main divisions, sometimes also called Real and Personal, correspond rather with those attributed to the Roman Institutional writers by modern inference, viz. *Dominia* and *Obligationes* (§ 16, p. 552). On the reverse order of treatment, and its possible origin, I have spoken in the early part of this section. The introduction of this order into a modern body of Law is apparently attributed by Savigny to the authors of the French Code, whose arrangement he regards as giving a virtual priority to Obligations over Ownership, indeed over the rest of Private Law generally[110]. Whether the original error was not that of the Jurists who compiled the old Prussian *Landrecht*, as seems rather to be the case[111], we need not stop to enquire. It is, as has been said, to that error that we may most probably trace the position of the *Schuldverhältnisse*, or Law of Obligations, *before* the *Sachenrecht*, or Law of Things, in the recent German Civil Code; an order of treatment, as it appears to me, not only *à priori* unreasonable, but as a

[109] Halsbury xiii. on Estoppel, p. 460 as to the subjects of these judgements, p. 472 as to their effects.

[110] System i. § 56, p. 374 n. *h.* Query, however, whether the ultimate arrangement of the *Code Civil* quite justifies this view. See the headings and contents of Livv. ii. and iii.

[111] Savigny ib. and Austin 39. 674.

mode of facilitating study and education, at least in English Law, very inconvenient.   It is scarcely time, however, yet to pass judgement on the results of imposing the German arrangement upon our Corpus Juris, as shown in the **Digest of English Civil Law**, which follows the plan of the *Bürgerliches Gesetzbuch*.

On the first Book of the German Code I have spoken elsewhere (§ 15, pp. 533, 535).   The second (*Schuldverhältnisse*) is represented correctly, as to order and name, in the English Digest by "Obligations."   To the contents of this Division, and their internal arrangement, I have little or no exception to take.   The elements of Contract generally are first of all well treated.   Particular contracts follow.   There is only some question whether, under the head of *Employment*, everything can now be considered as matter of Contract, or some social relations may still be treated as depending on *Status*, and so fall under Personal Law[112].

Quasi-Contract is taken, as it has naturally always, I think, been taken, directly after Contract.

Tort (see § 22, p. 670), which comes next, in both the German and French systems, to Quasi-Contract, ought certainly *not*, as a matter of intelligent study, to be very far removed from Criminal Law, which it continually overlaps, although the subjects must be separated on the whole, as they are in Blackstone and all modern systems.   On the other hand, Tort has been almost invariably connected, in our modern English teaching, or in the modern Codes, with Contract.   Its place, accordingly, in an educational course, seems to fall decidedly under Obligations, whether we make it a separate final division under the head of "Private Wrongs" or not.   The intrinsic propriety or desirability of such a separation from the *primary* Obligations of Contract

---

[112] See § 15, p. 536.   Also Mr Jenks' Preface to Bk ii. Pt i. of the Digest of English Civil Law.

and Quasi-Contract has been discussed above (§ 18, p. 604 and § 19, pp. 617, 621): the fact of the same (Civil) Procedure being applicable to breaches of Contract and to Tort would not weigh against such a separation, if Procedure be treated generally, in view of Educational purposes, as matter of Appendix (see § 18, p. 607).

The intrusion, on the other hand, of any mass of Law so as to break the natural sequence of the above-mentioned subjects (Contract, Quasi-Contract, Tort, Crime) is much to be deprecated.

Of Family Law and Succession which come in the English Digest, following the German arrangement, at the end of the "Civil Law," the former certainly belongs best to Personal, the latter to Property Law. Succession, under its Roman name of Inheritance, whether regarded as a mode of acquisition or not, fits perfectly well as a detached and homogeneous subject into the Roman Institutional system just before Obligations, dividing them distinctly from the rest of Roman Property Law (see § 16, p. 555).

This division is as we have seen (§ 16, p. 571) not at all clearly marked in our English Institutional works even of the present day. The original Book ii. of Blackstone is, in fact, taken up (except in a small part of one Chapter) with the Property Law strictly so called which is usually treated in the two well-known books of Joshua Williams, coinciding almost exactly with the *Sachenrecht* of the B.G.B.

As to *priority* of treatment, I can merely re-state the opinion, which I hold very strongly, that whether we make Succession into an independent section or not, there seems neither reason nor convenience in changing the old general order according to which Rights of Ownership, or Proprietary Rights strictly so called, *precede* those dependent on Obligation. That arrangement appears to be maintained in Stephen, Book ii. on "Rights of Property" (as distinguished from "Rights in Private Relations, Book iii.), subject to the necessary retention, as yet, of the English distinction into Realty and Personalty, and the peculiar difficulties arising therefrom in reference to the treatment of Succession (see § 16, p. 571). The collection of this last-mentioned matter into an entire and distinct subject will be, to my mind, a vast improvement on its treatment by Blackstone, when scientifically carried out, as may be expected from the hands to which it is entrusted under the plan of the new English Digest of Civil Law. At present it appears merely as a name, occupying the place which it was bound to occupy in a scheme professedly based on the German Code.

I have endeavoured to shew the very partial extent to which Austin's second leading division of Rights appears to be practically applicable in modern systems of Law and the superiority, on general grounds, of Blackstone's main scheme. The remaining part of Austin's Jurisprudence (Lectures 47—57) consists of a more detailed carrying out of his own theoretical arrangement, so far as it was ever completed. These Lectures, though not, to my mind, of equal importance with the preceding ones, contain, nevertheless, much that is interesting and suggestive, by the side of much to which I have several times had to refer as unsuited for a beginner or first year student.

§ 24. SUBDIVISIONS OF RIGHTS OF OWNER-SHIP

Conclusion of Austin's extant work. The present section deals with the latter part of Austin's fourth division of Lectures (47—57). A few words will suffice to shew where and how this part of the work comes into his general scheme.

In Austin's first great division of Law into General and Special, the former, which he calls the "Law of Things," was to be taken into consideration first, and, of its two subdivisions, those Rights and Duties which are Primary, i.e. which do not result from Injuries. The Absolute Duties (*sensu Austiniano*), being Primary, should naturally come in this first subdivision, but are postponed, for convenience, to the later one of Secondary or Sanctioning Rights and Duties[1]. I have elsewhere suggested reasons for giving a somewhat more extended meaning, than that of Austin, to Absolute Duties, and for placing a brief statement of them in what is here preferred as a first division of the Corpus Juris, that of Personal Law[2].

To return to Austin's scheme; there should come next Relative Primary Rights, with their corresponding Duties. Of these Rights, the difference between those *in rem* and *in personam* being first described, and established as a principal division, four subdivisions are recognised by Austin, viz. Rights *in rem per se*, Rights *in personam per se*, less complex combinations of the two, and the more complex combinations which are styled *universitates* of Rights and Duties, such for instance as arise by universal Succession[3]. On the second of these divisions Austin has left a few fragmentary notes, on the third and fourth nothing.

I need not repeat what has been said above (§ 23, pp. 722—724) about the difficulty of taking the distinction of all Rights into those *in rem* and *in personam* for a main substantive division of a Corpus Juris; but may remark, as a practical illustration, the obvious acquiescence of Austin in a general *consensus* of moderns, to make Inheritance a distinct block of subject-matter including both kinds of Rights, as it is in fact treated in the Roman Institutes[4].

---

[1] Austin[5], Outline 66, Lecture 47, pp. 783, 784.

[2] See § 15, p. 531 : § 19, p. 617: § 21, p. 648.

[3] Austin[5], 46. 773: 47. 784: St. 379; also id., Outline, p. 46.

[4] See above, § 16, pp. 504, 566. As to a somewhat different matter, viz. the separate treatment of the *universitas*, in this case, carrying with it that of Succession to a particular Thing or Right, Austin[5] 54. 871.

With regard to a further subdivision by Austin[5], of his Rights *in rem per se*, by their "subjects," what has been said above (§ 23, pp. 703—705) may suffice for Rights " of which the subjects are persons," or " which have no specific subject." The only Rights of which Austin directly treats, in this last batch of Lectures, are Rights *in rem* over Things in the strict acceptation of the term, i.e. as permanent external objects which are not persons. Accordingly Ownership and Rights less than complete Ownership over material objects form the subject of Lectures 47—53, while Modes of acquisition and alienation with regard to the same objects are treated, under the head of Titles, in Lectures 54—57.

This subject must unavoidably descend to some extent into detail of the individual legal systems cited for example, which is obviously unfitted for an elementary treatise. It seemed therefore to myself very questionable whether it should come into an introductory Jurisprudence at all. The definitions, however, of the various estates or interests to be considered in the following pages, have, I think, some general value, from their applicability not being absolutely confined to material objects; as well as from the distinctions relied on being mainly *natural*, or, to speak more exactly, matter of obviously necessary occurrence and continuance. They do not, that is, depend altogether on special modern history, the results of which are tending to disappear with ourselves and possibly with other nations also.

In dealing with the subject in question, I propose in general to take the Roman types, and Austin's comments, which are on the whole more particularly made with reference to the Roman types, for text, and only bring into comparison briefly and incidentally such general conclusions as can be drawn from modern Codifications or Educational

[5] Austin[5], 47. 787, 789: St. 381, 382.

arrangements. It must however be premised to the reasoning on Roman Law that from that Law itself we have
seldom anything approaching formal definition: the place
of which is taken sometimes by mere derivational fancies,
like *dominus* from *domus* (below n. 13), sometimes by a bare
statement of the particular points wanted for the case in
hand, and sometimes by what do appear to be fundamental
principles, though perhaps very casually noted, as matter
of course. We are therefore often obliged to begin with
Austin, and have to avoid his occasional anticipations of
modern Law as best we may.

Austin's last Lectures, then, which attained any degree
of completion, consisted in an application of his principle
of division among Primary Rights to part of the subject-
matter which I have preferred to regard as Property Law.
Dealing with " Rights *in rem* over Things proper," it is an
attempt to reduce to general terms of scientific description
the various Rights of Ownership (§ 16, p. 552) which may
be enjoyed in material objects, apart from the modes of
creation, acquisition and alienation with which they are
much complicated in the Roman Institutes, though the
two subjects are, or are intended to be, treated apart from
one another in the English Institutes and, though not
quite so distinctly, in Modern Codes (see § 16, p. 570, and
§ 25, p. 786). The latter subject, of Titles (a term to be
explained hereafter), which occupies Austin's last four fragmentary Lectures contains, besides a considerable amount
of what seems to me useless disquisition, several suggestions
which are of value as bearing on the best arrangement, for
Educational purposes, of a Corpus Juris.

The seven preceding Lectures, though nominally beginning with a minor subdivision (*Dominium* and *Servitus*),
assume the existence of a prior or fundamental one, corresponding, within the Roman *Jus Rerum*, to Austin's main

division, within his Law General, of *Jura in rem* and *Jura in personam*. This division, into *Dominia* and *Obligationes*, has been referred to above (§ 16, p. 552) as one between Proprietary and Obligatory Rights, but deserves rather more consideration here, as the terms, at least those of its first member, require some explanation, before we come to the Lectures in question themselves. *They* deal with subdivisions of what I may anticipate so far as to call "*Dominia* in the wider sense"; generally beginning with estates and interests belonging to the Roman Institutes and Digest but passing frequently into considerations which involve a somewhat detailed study of English Law.

I have already mentioned the difficulty which this anticipation of a later study entails upon the writer of an elementary or first year book. I may also now remark the *omission* of a subject, which is often prefixed to Rights of Ownership by writers on Jurisprudence, viz. Possession. In this omission I shall follow the example of Austin in postponing the treatment of that "anomalous and perplexed subject," which is only very partially sketched out in his Outline of the Lectures that never were completed[6].

The subject of Title, into which Possession undoubtedly enters, may be, and is here, treated *generally*, as a matter of classification and arrangement, not *particularly*, so as to enter into an analysis of its individual elements.

Dominia and **Obligationes.** This division has been several times referred to above, as imputed by various modern Jurists (including Austin) to the Roman authors of the Institutional *Jus Rerum*; if not *eo nomine*, at any rate in their practical arrangement. Of the two terms of the division the second is not here in question; nor, at present, the fact, or the convenience, of the arrangement. As to the first term, *dominium*, it must be admitted that

---

[6] Austin[5], Outline 51—53. See also below, **p. 742.**

the Roman use of the word, singular or plural, does *not* appear quite to justify its modern use in the antithesis referred to.

Dominium and **proprietas.** *Dominium*, with the writers of the Institutes and Digest, is mainly, though not perhaps exclusively, applied to the case of *material* objects[7]. It is a mere etymological fancy however (Austin l.c.) that the term was originally used in relation to the *slave* only, and afterwards extended by analogy to Things "strictly so called," though some support might be given to the idea by the derivation of *dominus* which is perhaps most generally received (see note 13). As to the "caprice" imputed to the Jurists, in *not* applying the same word to the case of a "son in power," I must refer to what has been said in § 23, pp. 701, 703, n. 30.

Dominium again, except in occasional expressions, which may be accounted for by some particular antithesis, is scarcely ever said of any proprietary rights *in rem* short of *complete* ownership (see below p. 740). In the divided, or rather, apparently duplicated, *dominium* of Gaius' time, to which reference has been made in a previous section (§ 16, p. 546), the person who has the bare Quiritarian ownership is indeed *dominus* at law, but he has no practical right as compared with the person who has the property *in bonis*, i.e. in beneficial ownership[8].

---

[7] See Austin[5], 47. 790: St. 384. A *heres* may conceivably have been called *dominus* of the *hereditas* as an aggregate, though I have no instance immediately to hand. This is of course a different use from that of the *hereditas* itself being *pro domino* habita (see Hermogenianus, Dig. 41. 1. 61).

[8] The two *dominia* of Gaius 2. 40 and 1. 54 are in so many words identified by Austin (48[5]. 800: St. 389: see however 14. 377: St. 182) with English *legal* and *equitable* property. That there is *no analogy* to our "equitable ownership" in Roman Law, as Markby[6] (§ 336, p. 172) maintains, seems to me put too strongly: but it would be out of place to enter here upon a chapter of particular English Jurisprudence, in which, to begin with, the propriety of talking about equitable *ownership* at all may be questioned. See Maitland's Equity, the opening pages of Lectures 9 and 10.

The owner, on the other hand, who has granted away the Usufruct (generally regarded as a life interest in the grantee) of a slave or other property, although what he retains may be called *nuda proprietas*, remains *dominus*, and has, as *dominus proprietatis*, substantial rights attaching to his ownership[9]. The ordinary ownership not subject to Usufruct outstanding is said to be *plena*[10].

Proprietas is thus, as we see, opposed to *Ususfructus*. Of its opposition to *servitus* in the proper sense (*real* or *praedial*, see below p. 752), as alleged by Austin, I do not find an instance. Between the words *dominium* and *proprietas*, moreover, which he treats as synonymous[11], a distinction may generally be observed in the Roman juristic writings. *Dominium* is properly predicated of the owner, *proprietas* of the thing owned: the ideas are correlative rather than identical. Identification of the one with the other does, however, occasionally occur : sometimes the *dominus* is said to *have* the *proprietas* : sometimes the *proprietas* is spoken of as, to all intents and purposes, equivalent to the *res ipsa*[12]. Some derivational evidence as to the meaning of these and cognate words is given below[13].

[9] Ga. 2. 30, 91.   See Roby R. P. L. i. 435.

[10] Papinian, Dig. 7. 4. 2. pr.

[11] Austin[5], 47. 790 : St. 384.

[12] See Neratius, Dig. 41. 1. 13. pr. Dominium id est proprietas : Ulpian, Dig. 29. 5. 1. 1, Domini appellatione continetur qui habet proprietatem. For *proprietas = res ipsa* see Ulpian, Dig. 47. 2. 46. 6 : Javolenus ib. 75. and Ulpian, Dig. 47. 1. 13—14 : 15. 1.

[13] *Dominium* is ownership : *proprietas* (to coin a word) *own-ness. Dominus*, from which the former comes, is more generally taken to be (in reference I suppose to the wild creature or the slave δμώς) the tamer or subduer (see Fick[3], iv. 124 ; Curtius, § 260, p. 232 ; Brugmann ii. 142). Jhering (ii. 162) accepts this derivation, which seems, on the whole, preferable to the tempting suggestion of Lange (quoted by Curtius l. c.) that *dominus* is the Giver— he who gives his household their meat in due season. *That* is probably the true meaning of *pater* and its cognates, and might be compared with Lord,

Dominia in the present antithesis. Hitherto we have
been dealing with what Austin calls the narrower of the
two senses of *dominium* which he attributes to the Roman
Institutionalists, i.e. the strict sense of *complete ownership*,
which I will for the present assume to be a fairly simple
and generally intelligible idea[14]. In a second or larger and
vaguer sense the term is used, according to him, by the
same authors, to indicate a division of the Law of Things
into *Dominia* and *Obligationes*, or *jura in rem* and *jura in
personam*[15].

It is not very clear, owing to Austin's use of the phrase
" Law of Things " in his own peculiar sense (=Law general),
whether he means that the Roman Institutionalists opposed
jura in personam (*obligationes*) to *jura in rem* within the
Roman *Jus Rerum* only, or to *jura in rem* generally (in
his own sense), as *Dominia*. I shall assume the former to
be the case, and that what he understands to be included
under his wide sense of *Dominia* are merely *jura in rem*
relating to Property.

Hlafweard; the latter however being rather *loaf-keeper* than *loaf-distributor*.
Corssen (Beit. 249) takes *dominus* to be the *house-man*, cf. our Husband. The
same idea was doubtless present to Ulpian when he described the *paterfamilias*
as *qui in domo dominium habet* (Dig. 50. 16. 195. 2).

Proprietas is literally *own-ness* from *proprius = own*, generally connected
with *prope, near*, as said of one's immediate surroundings. Jhering's *pro
privo* (Geist. 1. 210), after Pott, is out of the question as a derivation. The
German *Eigenthum* is an almost exact rendering of *proprietas*, though the
meaning of *eigen* itself (Anglicé *own*) is not that which is *near*, but that
which is *owed =* had or possessed, as one's own. See the new English
Dictionary s. v. *own* and Kluge Etym. Germ. Dict. s. v. *eigen*, Stratmann's
Dictionary of the Old English Language, s. v. *âgen*, and any A. S. Dictionary
s. v. *âgan* or *âgen*.

[14] The modern definitions attempted, for instance, in the French and
German Codes (Code Civil, § 554, and B.G.B. § 903), do depend upon comparatively simple and general ideas. That of Austin on the contrary is unintelligible without reference to the feudal system and its particular results in
English Law. See Austin, Lecture 51 and below p. 747.

[15] Compare Austin[5] 47. 784. 790: St. 46. 380, 384.

Now as to the conscious intention of opposing *Dominia*, meaning Property Rights *in rem*, to *Obligationes*, it is true that the scheme of the Roman Institutes does rather pointedly mark off the latter from other rights of Property Law, but any express recognition of such an opposition, in these terms, is modern. The passage to the subject is not made with any strong term of separation[16] and *Obligatio* is spoken of, in the enumeration of items of Property, as simply one in the list of Incorporeal Things, a list including undoubted Rights *in rem*, such as *Ususfructus*[17]. There is not a word on the part of Gaius or Justinian as to subdividing the second member of their triple division[18] or substituting a quadruple one.

To return, for a moment, to individual uses of the word *dominium*: we never find it used by the Roman Jurists as to the enjoyment of a Servitude (proper); rarely, and merely for some special purpose or argument, as to that of *ususfructus*[19]; only I think in one special and difficult enactment by Theodosius and Valentinian do we have the possessors of an interest so nearly approaching complete ownership as *emphyteusis* called by anticipation *fundorum domini*[20].

For the virtual existence of such a division in the *Jus Rerum* as a matter of practical fact there is much to be said. Obligations do no doubt come conspicuously at the end of Gaius' 3rd Book, separated from the rest of Property Law

[16] "Nunc transeamus ad obligationes," in the middle of a Book. Ga. 3. 88: Just. 3. 13. pr.

[17] Ga. 2. 14. Cf. 4. 3.

[18] As Austin says the compiler of Justinian's Institutes virtually does, Austin[5], 43. 740, n. 4. The separation of Obligations ex delicto from those ex contractu § 18, p. 604, has, of course, nothing to do with making Obligations *en bloc* into a separate head.

[19] See Roby, De Usufructu, pp. 41, 42 on Dig. 7. 1. 4. A special application to the *usufructuarius* in Dig. 42. 5. 8 is apparently to make his estate *assets* in Bankruptcy. See above, § 16, p. 549.

[20] Cod. 11. 61. 12.

by the isolated block of Inheritance—a separation in which Savigny[21] particularly notes the difference between the clear view of the Roman arrangement and the erroneous assumption of moderns referred to above (§ 23, p. 715) with its consequences—and they are distinguished as requiring a special mode of transfer; that which is owed to us by some one being only transferable to a third person through that some one being *released* from us and *bound* to him[22].

We may therefore, I think, recognise a broad division of the *Jus Rerum* into *Dominia* (taken in Austin's wider sense) and *Obligationes* as a real and practical one, according to the more prominent elements in the two classes of Interests, and one which will apply in a general way to bodies of modern Property Law as well.   As to the conception of *jura in rem* as distinguished from *jura in personam* in general, I must continue to accept the view (so far as I understand it) of Savigny (above § 23, p. 722) with (as a corollary or rather modification) the unfavourable result of Hunter's application of the principle in practice, to this effect: that the distinction is no doubt one continually interfering or interposing itself, and continually to be taken into account, in legal transactions and ideas, but that it is not suited for a main division of a Corpus Juris.

Subdivisions of Proprietary and other Rights. The original draft of this part of my work proceeded to examine, somewhat in detail, the different interests which come under *Dominia* in the wide sense, and which are treated by Austin under such heads as *servitus, ususfructus, jura in re alienâ,* Rights *vested and contingent,* &c.   But it was found that the Lectures in question not only involved considerable supplementation as to difficult questions in Roman Law, but so much advanced reading in English, that they should either be omitted altogether from an introductory treatise for first

---

[21] System i. § 56, p. 374, n. *h*. [22] Ga. 2. 38.

year students, or very much abbreviated and compressed. I have adopted the latter course, I fear with only partial success.

Any detailed subdivision of *other* branches of Law—Personal, Contractual, Quasi-Contractual, Public or Private Wrong—farther than has been indicated in the preceding Sections, or may be in the final one on Titles, does not enter into the present scheme.

Apart from the probability that such subdivisions are for the most part too much matter of individual or particular National Law for a work on General Jurisprudence, there is the fact that Austin's great power of analysis and regrouping never reached application to these matters, or the results have only reached us in a very fragmentary and confusing condition. As to the subjects with which he did to some extent deal, a very brief sketch of his final Lectures will suffice to shew that they may form the groundwork of an advanced study in comparative Jurisprudence, but are, *in extenso*, unfit and even prejudicial for beginners.

In **Austin's last partially completed Lectures** full ownership and rights less than full ownership over material objects form the subject of Lectures 47—53, while modes of acquisition and alienation with regard to the same objects are treated, under the head of Titles, in Lectures 54—57.

Possession which, on the whole, belongs to the subject of Rights of Ownership in the wide sense, fails us in Austin, being postponed to a part of his course which was never completed. The "anomalous right" as he calls it, which comes under this name, may be regarded principally either as an element in acquisition, or as an independent interest, with its own rights, obligations, and remedies. The former is apparently the view of the French Code[23], where Possession

---

[23] Code Civil, Liv. 3, Tit. 20, Ch. 2.

appears late, as an element of *prescription*, and it is in this
bearing that Austin evidently meant to treat the Right of
Possession. The subject is dealt with in a more substantive
manner, it would appear, in the German Code, where it comes
prominently at the head of the *Sachenrecht*[24], in close connexion, it is true, with Rights over Land, but preceding the
general subject of Ownership, which covers both Landed and
Moveable Property[25]. The *indirect* Possession of an Owner
where the Thing in question is (physically) in usufruct,
pledge, lease or deposit with another, is described in the
first section : prescription and acquisition of Ownership in
the detail of the third[26].

In English Law Possession plays an important part towards acquiring Ownership though perhaps not so great
a one, proportionally, as it does in the Roman system and
the foreign ones more considerably founded on it. In Land,
a dispossessor of the true owner does acquire what is called
a "parliamentary title," by virtue of the Statute of Limitations, from his "adverse possession." But it is not so
much with its constitution of a "root of title" as with its
obligations and remedies as an independent Right, that our
Common Law mainly deals with Possession. Most indeed
of the cases on the subject would seem to come more
naturally under the Law of Tort or Delict than anywhere
else[27], which was possibly the general view taken of the
subject by Savigny[28]. I am of opinion that it is better
taken, as a whole, in the early part of any full study of

[24] In which *Besitz* occupies the first division, §§ 854—872.

[25] Compare Absch. ii. and iii. ; in the latter Titt. 1 and 3.

[26] Compare §§ 854, 862, 868 with §§ 927 and 937—945.

[27] "Possession and trespass in relation to the Law of Theft " is a subject
occupying more than half of our principal text-book (Pollock and Wright).

[28] Who would class it according to Holland, under Delict. The passages
referred to, however, only appear to cover the subject of possessory Interdicts.
See Holland 10 p. 197 and Vom Besitz (Perry's translation) pp. 23, 27.

Property Law. It certainly requires a monograph, or at least a very considerable chapter, including not only some résumé of the Roman Law on the subject, as treated by Savigny and Jhering, but a further illustration of the matter by modern theory and practice, as appearing notably in the more recent commentaries on the German Code. But for the present this subject, which is one of much difficulty, will be postponed to those actually treated by Austin.

The largest Right of Ownership. The subjects, of which the completed part of Austin's last Lectures does treat, are rights of ownership entire or fractional[29], of greater or less duration, in actual possession or expectancy, vested or contingent, but all alike matter for *actio in rem*. Most of the degrees or qualifications here enumerated meet us in the English Institutes with special reference to Land, though they have been also made applicable to other property, where the nature of the case will allow, in the case of Wills, or through the medium of Trusts[30].

In considering the limitation of the Right of Private Property by the principle *sic utere tuo ut non laedas alienum* (§ 17, p. 587), we left out of the question the possible interests of more specific individuals than one, in the same subject-matter, the idea being merely that of non-interference with the rights of outsiders generally. Such fractional or concurrent interests, however, *here* form the greater part of our subject, and have, at least if we follow Austin's mode of definition, to be taken into account from the first, as will

---

[29] Austin quotes this term from Bentham, Traités i. 151. I find it in the Vue Générale, ch. 14 (Traités iii. pp. 288, 292). Austin seems to confine it to Servitudes proper. Bentham's use of the word is quite vague.

[30] I think this general proposition may be admitted as fairly true, in spite of Maitland's undoubtedly justifiable caution as to Equitable Estates and Interests, in "Equity," pp. 122, 134 and generally Lecture 10. See Chitty's long supplementary note on Blackstone, ii. 25. 398 and Stephen[14], ii. pp. 9, 11.

be seen when we look into his definition of the most complete form of individual Ownership.

Dominium stricto sensu is described by Austin as a right indefinite in point of user, unrestricted in point of alienation, and unlimited in point of duration, over a determinate thing[31].

With this may be compared the simpler definitions accepted in the two main Continental Codes of modern times. According to the French Code Civil Property is the absolute right of using or dealing with a thing as we will, provided that we do not use it in a manner which is prohibited by laws or *réglemens*[32]. The above translation, due to Austin (48. 799, 800), does not quite give the full force of the French *disposer*, which implicitly includes an idea more clearly expressed in a definition of *dominium* attributed by Laveleye to "the Roman Law," though I have been unable to trace it to any Roman Jurist. *Dominium est jus utendi et abutendi re sua quatenus juris ratio patitur*[33]. The latter part of both these definitions, although not exactly amounting to a mere truism, does not, as Austin shews[34], add much to our comprehension of the subject : but I would call attention to the fact that *disposer* probably, and *abuti* certainly, indicate the power to *use up* and so *do away with* the *res*.

The nearest to a definition in the German Code is the section allowing the Owner, "so far as the Law and the

[31] Austin[5], 47. 790; 48. 795: St. 384, 386. This definition is adopted *faute de mieux* by Holland[10], p. 200. Salmond[2], ch. 12, gives no specific definition, but in § 86 contrasts Ownership with Possession and Encumbrance and in subsequent Sections treats of the different kinds of Ownership, e.g. Corporeal and Incorporeal, Trust and Beneficial, Vested and Contingent.

[32] C. C. § 544. Text given above (§ 17, p. 588 n. 39). Sirey (Code Civil, i. p. 484) gives a number of such restrictions resulting from special legislation, alleging, however, beyond all these, a general obligation not to injure the property of another.

[33] Laveleye. Primitive Property (1878) p. 338.

[34] See generally the last page or two of Lecture 48.

rights of third parties do not stand in the way, to deal with the Thing as he chooses and to exclude others from any interference with it[35]."

The right of enjoying and disposing of, or dealing with, the subject-matter as one will evidently includes that of alienation and of consumption or destruction where that is physically possible: it does not literally *express* that of excluding others, but that principle must be assumed as lying at the foundation of Private or individual Ownership altogether[36]. All this is as true of a *res incorporalis*, which is part of a man's Property—even of a *jus in personam* (see § 23, pp. 702, 703)—as of a material object. It is, however, with the latter that we are at present mainly concerned.

Beyond the above statement of right, little seems to be gained by attempts to define Complete Ownership or Absolute Property in a material object: but we are compelled to dwell a little upon Austin's more exhaustive account of the right which he styles *Dominium* in its strict sense, if only to shew how much of that account is based on matter peculiar to England, to Land in England, and part of a system which is practically passing away.

Unlimited in point of duration. That the Absolute Owner's right must be "unrestricted in point of alienation and unlimited in point of duration" is a complex statement, the connexion between the points of which is not very clear at first sight. It is made a little more intelligible by the

[35] Der Eigenthümer einer Sache kann, soweit nicht das Gesetz oder Rechte Dritter entgegenstehen, nach Belieben verfahren und Andere von jeder Einwirkung ausschliessen, B.G.B. § 903. See however § 905, which somewhat limits the old maxim *Cujus est solum ejus est usque ad caelum.* Der Eigenthümer kann Einwirkungen *nicht* verbieten die in solcher Höhe oder Tiefe vorgenommen werden dass er in die Ausschliessung kein Interesse hat. Who is to be the judge?

[36] Austin[5], 48. 797, 798: 49. 810, 811 includes the power of *exclusion* under that of indefinite user.

words substituted in St. "not restricted by regard to the
rights of others whose enjoyment is postponed[37]." So far,
however, it merely expresses the general principle stated
below (pp. 750, 759), which may be briefly instanced here in
the fact that a Fructuary was confined to treatment of the
subject-matter *salvâ substantiâ*, in the interest of the *dominus
proprietatis* or Reversioner[38]. But the fact that the power of
alienation has to be backed by or connected with a right of
"unlimited duration" belongs exclusively to considerations
of feudal tenure in English land Law. It postulates a series
of successors who are definitely contemplated by the laws of
the particular country, but from all of whom the present owner
can alienate the subject-matter, as also from any right expectant on the determination of such a series[39].

The doctrine of the Sovereign succeeding as *ultimus heres*,
on the natural determination of a series of such expectant
rights also, has been spoken of above[40]. But the whole subject,
either of such an original or expectant series, is too complicated
to be treated merely as ancillary to the right of alienation,
and too peculiarly national to enter into the province of
general Jurisprudence. The whole idea of such a series
marked out by relation to the present owner, from whom the
latter only gradually acquired the power of alienating *res* of
which he was apparently *dominus* (below, p. 748), would seem
to be alien from any Roman conception of Property. Austin,
indeed, professes to illustrate the case of the English Tenant
in Tail, before the introduction of Fines and Recoveries, by
a supposed joint ownership of the *sui heredes* with the *paterfamilias, viro quoque parente*[41]. But the supposed case is not

---

[37] Compare Austin[5], 47. 790 with St. 384 (1).
[38] Above, p. 738. See Paulus, Dig. 7. 1. 1 and Ulp. Dig. 7. 1. 9. 2.
[39] Austin[5], 51. 831, 836. On his comparison of the case of a *mesne lord*
with *emphyteusis* see below, p. 755.
[40] Austin, ib. and 52. 845. See above, § 17, p. 591.
[41] See Paulus, Dig. 28. 2. 11 and Girard[5], 844. Ga. 2. 157 is as capable, it

exactly parallel, and this explanation of the term *suus*, though supported by Roman Jurists as well as moderns, of high authority, is open to question. There is no proof that such presumptive ownership carried with it any check upon the *paterfamilias'* power of alienation.

So much, therefore, of Austin's definition of complete ownership as depends upon, or assumes, our old English Law as to an estate in *fee* or *fee tail* may be left out of consideration for general Jurisprudence, though a short digression may be permitted here upon the results of that Law, according to orthodox English theory, and a few words may be added hereafter as to its possible origin in late Roman Law. The more simple definitions of Property or Ownership above quoted from the French and German Codes are, on the whole, much to be preferred for our present purpose.

No absolute property in English Land. In a previous section (17, pp. 590, 591) reference was briefly made to the orthodox English doctrine of no absolute private ownership in Land, and we therefore, in our Law, according to Austin (47. 790), only talk of *property* in a moveable thing. Some qualification of the above positions may, however, be gathered from the passage of Maitland also referred to (p. 591, n. 46) and from his important later Chapter on Ownership and Possession. He there maintains, with much success, the view that, in comparison with the above conventional principle as to Land, still less did our Medieval Law apparently recognise an absolute Ownership in Chattels. His argument is based upon the remedial procedure, or rather lack of remedial procedure, for the restitution *in specie* of moveables

seems to me, of the translation "*own* heirs" (i.e. of the testator or ancestor) as of the one generally received "heirs of themselves" or "in their own right." See however Austin[5], 51. 833. His αὐτοκληρονόμοι is no doubt in favour of the popular view. But I do not know to whom this rendering is to be attributed. It does not appear in Theophilus' translation of Just. 2. 19. 2.

(see § 23, p. 725). I mention this passage (Moveable Goods
P. and M. ii. 153—181) mainly because of some misconception which might perhaps arise from it as to Roman
Law. When we read there of a *dominium* which may rise
above *dominium* (p. 180 l.c.) we must remember that this is
not the Roman *dominium* of Gaius and Justinian. It is
Lordship, only relating to Land, and of which there may be
several distinct degrees, each with its protective remedy:
theirs is Ownership pure and simple, with its one *actio in rem*,
brought against the literal possessor for the time being, and
so practically "good against the thing." Nor, as to the old-
time inferior position of Chattels, must we forget that the
middle-age doctrine *mobilia non habent sequelam* has no place
in Roman Law. The *actio in rem* might seem, in fact, to
have dealt *primarily* with moveables, Land being subsequently
brought into Court by an actual fragment, not merely a
symbolic representative[42], and restitution *in specie* being
probably, in the older procedure, directly carried out by the
Court (see § 23, pp. 710, 711), though only enforced in that
of the Classical Jurists, by a heavy alternative valuation[43].

Here, however, I must leave the feudal Law as to the
Estates in English Land which approach nearest to complete
ownership. Nor have I found it possible to follow Austin's
treatment of Rights of Ownership limited in duration
(Lecture 51) under a separate head, except implicitly, or
conversely, as above (pp. 746, 747). The whole of this subject
is necessarily much complicated with peculiar English Law.
The estates or interests described now exist mainly in their
employment for the purpose of "tieing up" property by way

[42] See Ga. 4. 16, 17.

[43] I may also venture to say with reference to Maitland's note on pp. 151,
152 l.c. that I cannot see any great force in the later formation of the
substantive *owner*, if the adjective or rather participle *own*, and the verb
from which it comes, existed and were applied long before. See above,
p. 739, n. 13.

of Settlement, a subject which will be briefly referred to hereafter (pp. 768, 769), though mainly with reference to the simpler methods employed by Roman and Continental Law for attaining some of the objects of English Settlement than to the complicated procedure of the latter[44]. I return, at present, to the remaining part of Austin's definition and its bearing upon the question what may be considered more properly parts of Ownership and what mere *jura in re alienâ.*

Austin's Indefinite power of User, which was the part of his account of Absolute Ownership left over (above, p. 746), requires a little explanation. It does not appear so much to mean that the person, of whom it is predicated, is free from care to be taken of the property generally, in view of some future indefeasible owner[45], as that he is free from any present rights of enjoyment over his property belonging to any other person. The converse obligation in the former case, where there *is* some indefeasible future owner, is obvious. The latter freedom from present external rights is predicated of the property itself in Roman Law by the expression that a dwelling-house for instance (*aedes*) is in the "richest and fullest" condition[46]. And the indefinite user, of which Austin speaks, is meant by him to apply particularly to the owners of those limited interests in Roman Law which are inaccurately termed Personal Servitudes, e.g. the Usufructuary, the Usuary and the legatee of a *habitatio.* For these, although of course debarred from such use of the subject-matter as would destroy or prejudice the interest of the *dominus proprietatis* (above, p. 747), had nevertheless an enjoyment of that subject-matter *indefinite* or general *as compared with* the limited and specified rights enjoyed over an estate by

---

[44] See particularly Austin[5], 51. 834 and the notes to Lecture 53, p. 869.
[45] See Austin, 51. 832, 834.
[46] Optimae maximaeque, Ulp. Dig. 50. 16. 90.

the owner of a Servitude "properly so called." Austin's "Indefinite User" must therefore be understood to be frequently considered by him in a somewhat qualified sense, as limited by the particular opposition of the above-mentioned interests to Servitudes proper (see below). Both are in Austin's sense *jura in rem*: both therefore, as items of Property, will come under the wide meaning of *Dominia* as opposed to *Obligationes*: but to the former only can the term *dominium* or *property* be "properly and strictly" applied[47]. I doubt whether the actual word *dominium* is said by the Roman Jurists of either the limited Ownership or the Servitude.

Salmond, it must be remarked, takes the main point of difference, between these modes of Property or Ownership and Servitudes proper, to be that the latter do not involve *Possession* of the subject-matter concerned, which the other Rights referred to do[48]. This is, at first sight, an obvious improvement on Austin's "indefinite user," though, if the word be taken in its direct physical sense, as conferring present enjoyment, it comes to much the same thing. The introduction of Possession in any technical or legal sense would involve difficulties which can scarcely have been contemplated by the learned author of this distinction. Austin's appears to me preferable, although somewhat subtle.

Servitudes Real and Personal. The distinction of Servitudes properly and improperly so called has been hitherto looked at from Austin's point of view, with regard to the definite or indefinite amount of user enjoyed by their respective owners. The corresponding styles given above depend on another principle. From its original meaning of *burden* the word *servitus* is continually transferred in meaning, like *obligatio* (above § 21, p. 651), to the correlative advantage

[47] Austin[5], 49. 807—813: 50. 823—826: St. 391, 399.

[48] Salmond[2], p. 406: Campbell, Note on Austin, 50, p. 229 speaks of "*some* present enjoyment."

or accommodation[49], which latter idea is expressed in the English word Easement, and it is in this beneficial sense that Servitudes are said to *belong to* res (i.e. house and lands, *praedia*) or to persons[50]. Neither of the adjectives Real or Praedial occurs, to my knowledge, in Roman Juristic writing: and it is perhaps as well to remember that Real, in this use of the word, does *not* mean either "strictly or properly so called," or that the rights spoken of are *over* Things, or that they are Rights *in rem*, however true these facts may otherwise be[51]. There is a great deal in Austin's 49th and 50th Lectures on these Servitudes proper, as to whether they are *affirmative* or *negative*, how the latter can be *jura in rem*, what is the difference between an *easement* and a *particular licence*, between *appurtenant* and *in gross*, &c.; but all this is too much matter of detail, and frequently of peculiar English Law, to be treated in the present work. Like Possession (above, p. 744) this is a subject, so far as Roman Law alone is concerned, for distinct independent treatment; and, in a more advanced study of Jurisprudence, for a full comparison not only with the English Law (which is to some extent attempted by Austin) but also with the corresponding part of modern Codes, and their national commentators. I can only touch upon the subdivision generally laid down by Austin, of his *Dominia*, in the wider sense, into *Dominia* in the narrower sense, and *Servitutes*. The subject was already debated in Roman Law under the following particular question.

Is Ususfructus dominium or servitus? The prevailing opinion, on the whole, among the Classical Jurists, appears

[49] Austin[5], 49. 814.

[50] See Marcianus Dig. 8. 1. 1 and Gaius 2. 14: Dig. 1. 8. 1. 1. The genitives in these passages are *possessive* not *objective* (Roby Grammar, ii. p. 128), and should be translated so as to shew this.

[51] See Austin[5], 50. 817, 818 where what he says is, I think, mostly true but involves the matter in some degree of haze.

to be rather that the holder of a Usufruct—the largest of the Personal Servitudes—was, equally with the person only entitled to a Servitude proper, a simple encumbrancer having merely a *jus in re alienâ*[52], not a "limited or temporary owner," to use Maitland's words with regard to the English Life Estate in Land[53].

The reversioner, as we should call him in English Law, was the only true *dominus* in Roman, and much stress is laid on this fact, and the peculiarity of our English separation into present Estates existing side by side, by Hunter, Markby and Maine (ll.cc.).

Jura in re alienâ. The question put on the last page may be stated more broadly in this form—what interests, in what is primarily or principally another man's property, are or are not to be regarded *merely* as *jura in re alienâ*. The distinction relied on by Austin of Indefinite User will certainly serve as between *Ususfructus* and *Servitus*. It is not quite so satisfactory as between *Servitus* and Lease. Salmond's test, too, of physical Possession (above, p. 751) would seem to place this interest among Modes of Property, whereas it is regarded by himself as *jus in re alienâ*. Apparently however he would extend the latter expression so as to include the Roman Ususfructus and (*semble*) the English Life Estate[54].

So too Austin's Editor Mr Campbell would place Servitudes both "properly" and "improperly" so called under the common head of *jura in re alienâ*. The main obstacle to this, as a general rule of Codal or Educational arrangement, lies in the Life Estates known to English Law. He accord-

---

[52] Hunter p. 224: Markby[6], § 330, p. 166: Maine, Early Law and Custom, c. 10, p. 344. For the other view, to some extent maintained in Classical Roman Law, Gaius, Dig. 46. 1. 70. 2: Paulus, Dig. 7. 1. 4; 50. 16. 25. pr. On the whole question Roby, de Usufructu, p. 42.

[53] P. and M. ii. 10. On the curious developement of the modern meaning of *Estate* see i. p. 391.

[54] Compare Salmond[2], pp. 213 n. 3, and 406.

ingly rather labours the points of difference between these and the Roman *Ususfructus*[55]. Whether these points of difference are or are not likely to disappear in course of time, I certainly, as a matter of convenient arrangement, should prefer to ignore Austin's subdivision, and to take all his *Dominia*, in the wider sense, together, simply observing an order of greater or less importance.

Superficies and Emphyteusis. There are, however, certain *jura in re alienâ*, about which special difficulty arises, as they are brought before our notice rather prominently by Austin.

The somewhat anomalous rights or interests, in later Roman Law, called *Superficies* and *Emphyteusis*, are generally classed by modern expositors of Roman Law (under the head of *Servitus* proper) together with the *jus in rem* which is taken by a creditor under pledge or mortgage, as *jura in re alienâ*. On the two former interests there arises, in Austin, an awkward cross-division which is some argument for the general classification *together* of *all* Proprietary Rights less than complete ownership suggested above (p. 753). As conferring Indefinite User, *Emphyteusis* and *Superficies* ought to be classed with *Ususfructus* as modes of Ownership: but since they have an indefeasible Reversion expectant on them, they are *jura in re alienâ*. The same is true of *Ususfructus* itself if limited to the life of the "owner" (? holder or grantor)[56].

This idea of an indefeasible reversion, at least if extended beyond the life of the grantor, brings in once more the feudal principles (see above, p. 747) which it has been thought well to leave out of the question, for *general* Jurisprudence, as, now at least, peculiar to the English system. In the

[55] Austin[5], 50. 827—829 (Note). Also 52. 847 and n. 74. See, however, St. 400, 401 (Notes).

[56] Austin[5], 32. 847—851.

particular tenure, however, of *Emphyteusis* some writers, including Mr Campbell, find the true origin of middle-age feudal tenure in general[57], of which traces are no doubt still to be found in Continental systems also, where the German rather than the French or Roman element has maintained some influence.   This may to some extent account for the different arrangements or classifications of the interests above mentioned which will be briefly referred to hereafter.

Strictly *Emphyteusis* and *Superficies* are exceptional forms of Lease, which, in its ordinary or generic sense is classed by Salmond, together with Servitudes, Securities and Trusts, under his general head of *jura in re alienâ*[58].   I do not propose here to go into particulars on these two difficult subjects. The fact of the former being *in perpetuum*, and the latter being either the same or at least for a very considerable period (*non ad modicum tempus*), made these interests approach near to ownership.   Their conditions, however, evidently reserved a certain amount of control and the possibility of forfeiture or reversion to the original *dominus* or his representatives on persistent failure to pay the *pensio* or *solarium*.   In this important respect they differ materially from the English *ground rent* (see below, p. 770).   The parallel drawn by Roby of the English *building lease* to *superficies* does not seem to me so good a one as that of the obsolete *vesture* adduced by Austin[59].

Continental Codes.   In the French system of the present day I cannot find anything corresponding to these anomalous Roman interests.   *Usufruct, Usage, Habitation* are defined as rights in another person's property, but, in point of position and treatment, are apparently regarded, somewhat like our Life Estates in Land, as independent interests approximating

---

[57] Austin[5], 52. 855 (Note).
[58] Salmond[2], § 158, p. 404.
[59] Roby, R. P. L. ii. p. 176: Austin[5], 52. 851.   See Co. Litt. 4[b] and 122[a] on *vesture* as the subject of a *freehold* separate from that of the soil.

more to Ownership than the Servitudes[60]. The latter are distinctly described as Praedial (*Services fonciers*), concluding the subject of Property *per se*, as distinguished from the modes of acquiring it.

In the *Sachenrecht* of the new German Code the subjects of Ownership, Claims arising out of Ownership, and Joint Ownership[61], are immediately followed by the subject bearing the untranslatable title *Erbbaurecht,* which is identified by the Commentators with *Superfizies*[62]. It is a Personal right, alienable and hereditable, to "have a building on or under the ground property of another." It is regarded as a part-ownership, or at least nearer to ownership than are the Servitudes. Next follow the latter, covering not only those which belong to or affect Landed Property, but Usufruct and the more limited Personal Servitudes of the Romans[63]. Then, after a brief notice of Rights of Pre-emption, come Burdens on Property[64] which differ from Servitudes in that these require *positive* services, whereas *servitus in faciendo consistere non potest*[65].

Money charged on Land, whether as a capital debt or by way of rent charge (*Grundschuld, Rentenschuld*) follows. I wish specially to call attention to the statutory power of *redemption* reserved to the owner of the land by § 1201. These subjects are combined with *Hypothek* (Mortgage) in one principal section; Pledge (of Moveables) or Lien coming last[66].

[60] See Code Civil, L. 2, Titt. 2, 3, 4.

[61] BGB. 2, Absch. 3, Titt. 1—3, 4, 5.

[62] Literally Inheritable Right in Buildings, BGB. ii. Absch. 4, §§ 1012—1017. For its approximation to Ownership see Scherer iii. p. 173.

[63] BGB. ii. Absch. 5, §§ 1018—1093 (*Dienstbarkeiten*).

[64] Ib. Absch. 6, §§ 1094—1104 (*Vorkaufsrecht*); Absch. 7, §§ 1105—1112 (*Reallasten*).

[65] Scherer iii. p. 435.   See Austin[5], 49. 811: St. 394.

[66] Ib. Absch. 8, *Hypothek, Grundschuld, Rentenschuld*; Absch. 9, *Pfandrecht.*

In this apparent gradation of *jura in re alienâ* there may possibly be inferred a tendency to regard *charges* on property (mostly referring to Land) as matter of personal and temporary imposition, thus making against inalienability, or legal difficulty generally in dealing with the subject-matter. But, as my small knowledge of German Law is derived merely from books, I cannot venture to go beyond calling attention to the facts of its Codal arrangement.

Other jura in re alienâ.   Lease, Securities, Trust. To return to Salmond's list (p. 755).

Lease, except in the particular Roman instance noted on p. 755 and the somewhat similar case of ground-rents, &c. in English and German Law, would certainly seem to belong more properly to the Law of Contract than of Ownership; the estate or interest of the Lessee being accordingly treated not, as by Salmond, in the light of an Encumbrance on Property[67], but in that of an accessory to an Obligation.

Securities. In the case of Mortgage Pledge or Lien[68] the same appears to me more decidedly the case. The *jura in re alienâ*, however they may vary in different legal systems, or in different times of the same[69], are here so distinctly ancillary to the main purpose of the contract that they ought to go with it, on principle, apart from the inconvenience and repetition which have resulted from the awkward separation of the *jura in rem*, in this business, and the *jura in personam*[70].

This separation is, however, maintained, and the substantive object of the transaction subordinated to the ancillary, not merely in English juristic treatment, where Mortgage appears rather among creations of an Estate in Real Property

---

[67] Salmond[2], pp. 207 and 404, n. 3.
[68] On the general use of this word see Salmond[2], p. 408, n. 3.
[69] Austin[5], 52. 851, 852.
[70] See § 23, p. 723, n. 93.

than as a means of securing a loan, but in the German Codal arrangements[71].

Trust. This subject is treated by Salmond, principally as a kind of *Encumbrance*, under which the Ownership of property is limited by an equitable obligation to deal with it for the benefit of some one else. The owner of the encumbered property is the Trustee, the owner of the encumbrance, the Beneficiary[72]. As I consider that the whole subject of Trust ought to be looked at from the Personal point of view, I will confine myself to referring to what has been said above (§ 15, pp. 538, 539) on Trustees.

I must now however pass from the intrinsic amount or character of the different Rights of Ownership comprised under *Dominia*, in the wide sense, to consider the same Rights a little more particularly as limited in duration, future in enjoyment and vested or contingent.

Rights of ownership limited in duration. In considering the Lectures and Notes of Austin on these subjects, the caution given above (pp. 749, 752) and elsewhere must be continually borne in mind. As in the largest Right of Ownership, so too in others of less duration such as an estate for life, or for a less "quantity of interest," to use Blackstone's phrase, Austin seems in general to have almost exclusively before his eyes the peculiar English Law, particularly as developed in the case of Real Property. Now, to take the first instance above mentioned, an English life interest, in spite of occasional early identification with the Roman

---

[71] See Blackstone, ii. 157—160 on Mortgage, and 451 on Bailment, where practically the only treatment of Pledge is in Chitty's note. Compare, too, Stephen[14], Index (Vol. IV.), Artt. Mortgage, Pawn, and Pledge.

For similar treatment in the BGB. see above p. 756. In the French Code both *Gage* and *Hypothèque* are regarded as subsidiary to Contract (Code Civil, §§ 2071, 2114, 2124). The confusion, however, between Contract and Conveyance in this legislation must be borne in mind. See § 23, p. 716.

[72] Salmond[2], 217, 230—232.

Ususfructus[73], was certainly much modified by, if it did not originate in, the feudal conditions of Land, and indeed only became applicable, through the indulgence shewn to Wills, or through the intervention of Trusts, to other branches of Property also[74].

Consequently, to *begin* with the English particular estates in Land, or limited interest in Personality, for matter of General Jurisprudence, is out of the question. And even a comparison with Rights of Ownership of limited duration, &c., in other systems, cannot be relied upon to establish any great amount of general principle. Such Rights appear to myself to be approximating rather to the more prevalent Roman idea of *jura in re alienâ* than to the other conception (above, pp. 752, 754, 757): but I shall confine myself at present to one fairly safe generalisation, which applies to Rights both of limited duration and future enjoyment. Wherever a certain, or possible, future interest in Property is recognised by Law, which is *indefeasible* by the owner of a previous limited one, the State must necessarily prevent any intermediate treatment inconsistent with the coming into existence of such future interest, or at any rate furnish remedies, to secure compensation for detrimental treatment, to its holders, when it does, if ever, come into actual enjoyment[75].

Rights of future enjoyment, vested or contingent. With regard to interests being *Vested* or *Contingent* there is still more reason for hesitation in adopting any of Austin's

[73] See P. and M. ii. 8.

[74] Compare the brief notice in Blackstone, ii. 25. 398, as to time of enjoyment &c. in Personal Property with Chitty's long supplementary note. See also Stephen cited above, n. 30.

[75] In this very brief statement of the general principle of Waste, I have endeavoured to combine the matter of Austin's last paragraph in Lecture 51 (p. 838) with the first part of Mr Campbell's note. That the restrictions on the "limited owner" may *vary* according to the rights expressly allowed him, or reserved to others (Austin[5] 48. 798, 799: St. 386, 387), seems obvious.

conclusions as matter of general Jurisprudence, particularly for a first course. It has been found by me very difficult, if not impossible, to consider this question, as Austin rightly attempts to do[76], "abstracted from all the peculiarities of the English Law." I do not merely refer to such an obvious digression as his criticism of Fearne's test for distinguishing a contingent from a vested remainder[77], which most ordinary students would probably omit as a matter of course. Nor do I suppose that much difficulty will be caused to a reader, who is accustomed to attach meanings to words, by the expression "*vested Rights*" as used in popular, or antipopular, oratory[78]. It may, however, be desirable to enter a caution against identifying *vesting* with *possession*, which would be fairly correct for our older legal history[79], but misleading as to our modern use of the phrase. Nor should it be forgotten that English Law has a different signification of *vested*, when applied to different subjects, e.g. a Remainder in Real Estate and a Legacy[80].

The expression "Rights of future enjoyment" was adopted by Austin so as to obviate these difficulties or misapprehensions, and also a less important one which is started early in his Lecture 53. Since "a present and certain right to *possession* (or enjoyment) is *not* necessarily of the essence of a present and certain Right," therefore, in *every* case of a Right of future enjoyment, the chance of such enjoyment

---

[76] Austin[5], 53. 867.

[77] Ib. 864 and notes 91, 92 (replaced in St. 423—425 by a statement of Mr Campbell's own, based on Hawkins). It may be added that this peculiar distinguishing feature of the old Contingent Remainder has now ceased to exist. See below, n. 87.

[78] Austin[5], 53. 856, 857: St. 427 primly omits the suggestion (obviously a joke) of Cornewall Lewis about rights being so styled from money having been *invested* on them.

[79] Austin, St. 424. See P. and M. ii. 32, n. 4. Also Spelman's Glossarium s. v. Investitura.

[80] Austin l. c. Lecture 53 is much re-written by Mr Campbell.

ever being actual or present is uncertain, from the mere uncertainty of life.   With this *contingency*, however, we have here nothing to do: it does not prevent the right itself from being present and certain, if it satisfies the conditions, the absence of which are to be considered below[81].

The general upshot of the discussion in Austin's 53rd Lecture, and his editor's considerably altered revision in the Student's Austin, is to substitute, for the distinction of Rights as *vested* and *contingent*, that of Rights as *complete* and *inchoate*, or even of Rights and Chances or possibilities of Rights[82].   The old style is retained by Salmond[83], but he clearly uses the words in the sense expressed by Austin under *complete* and *inchoate*, which is probably the one they would generally bear if abstracted, as Austin puts it, from the peculiarities of English Law.

The opposition, by Austin, of Rights (properly so called) of future enjoyment, to what he styles Chances or Possibilities of Right (rather than Contingent Rights), is inevitably bound up with some of these peculiarities; but there is one point in it capable of general application.   To the existence of a Right *at all* two points are, according to him, essential—one, that the fact to which the law annexes that right must be *at present* complete ; the other, that there must be a *present determinate person* in whom the Right resides[84].   This idea of the necessity of a determinate person in whom *any* Right, strictly taken, is to reside has been questioned above (§ 21, pp. 643, 648) with reference to the conceivability of Rights residing in the Community.

---

[81] Austin[5], 53. 858: St. 420 and note * (much less clear, I must say, than the original text). See also the distinction drawn by Austin on p. 866 between the *right* and the *time of enjoyment*.

[82] Austin[5], 53. 866, 867: St. 422, 423.

[83] See generally Salmond's excellent § 92. "Vested and contingent ownership."

[84] Austin[5], 53. 856, 857.

The present question is different: it is whether we can properly conceive of a Right, as belonging or to belong to a person individually specified but who does not now and may never exist (e.g. the eldest son of *A*, *A* now having no son). In *our* practice, at any rate, such interests are undoubtedly recognised as conceivable and are regularly known as Contingent Rights[85]. Very different is the *mere* chance or *spes acquisitionis* of becoming the owner of property with which one has, at present, no legal connexion whatever[86].

Austin's Conditions of a Contingent Right. Disregarding, then, these somewhat gratuitous difficulties, we may proceed to regard a Contingent Right as existing in the two alternative cases put by Austin (l.c.), which however may obviously coexist. (1) If the person in whom it is to reside or vest be not at present in existence, and may never be: (2) if the title or mode by which the right is to vest in that person be not at present complete, and may never be. This is put as a general proposition, but it is obviously worded in view of a well-known English Law, as it is undoubtedly illustrated by English instances[87]. This is also conspicuously the case when Austin proceeds to put another form of his first element of contingency: i.e. when the person contemplated in the creation of the Right may be *in esse*, but is not yet definitely ascertained. The instances cited for this case, which appears to me to belong, as stated by Austin, rather to his *second* alternative, are the *spes successionis* residing in the English *presumptive* or *apparent* heir[88]. *Spes* suc-

---

[85] See Austin[5], 53. 859, 860.   [86] Ib. 866 and Salmond[2], p. 235.

[87] Austin[5], 53. 859. Compare Blackstone's description of "contingent or executory remainders" limited to take effect "either to a dubious and uncertain person, or upon a dubious and uncertain event." For the instances see Austin l. c. For the modern amendment of the old Law, Stephen[14], i. 192, citing, in particular, the Contingent Remainders Act 1877.

[88] Ib. 861, 862 and St. 420 note †, where the difference between these two cases is more clearly put than in Austin. See Stephen[14], i. p. 226.

cessionis is a fairly correct description of this Right(?), which differs very slightly from the mere chance or possibility referred to above (p. 762). It is the case afterwards put, apparently as a second thought, by Austin himself, where the *existence* of the party (the heir presumptive) at the time appointed (the death of the ancestor) is *part of the contingency*, on which the Right is to vest; and, if he dies before that time, the Contingent Right can never vest, and there is no possibility transmissible to his representatives. This so-called Right is therefore, as it seems to me, somewhat loosely spoken of by Austin as *inchoate*, i.e. commenced though not complete[89]. That description is more true of the legal position of the Roman *heres* who, after the death of the ancestor intestate, has still *adire hereditatem*; as also of the English instances cited by Austin[90]. In fact the *second* Condition of Contingency according to Austin (above, p. 762) has a positive as well as a negative side. The negative, that some fact has *not* happened which is necessary to the complete vesting of the Right in question. The positive, that the Contingent Right must be something *inchoate* or begun : the Title, or the string of facts which is to complete its vesting, must have partly taken place. It is obvious, of course, that a mere general capacity or chance of acquiring cannot constitute such a beginning, or every Right of Ownership in the world would be a Contingent Right of everybody but its present possessor : a Contingent Right in legal contemplation must be marked out by some specific incipient fact or qualification[91].

It is obviously this *inchoate* character which gives to

[89] Compare Austin[5], 53. 865 with 862. See, however, p. 867.

[90] The heir, under old English Law, before *seisin*, and the parties entitled to *administer*, before taking out letters of administration. Austin, ib. Halsbury (xxiv. p. 238, § 434) is quite clear as against any transmissible interest in a *spes successionis*. But see iv. 376, § 797.

[91] See Salmond[2], p. 235: Austin[5], 53, pp. 866, 867.

a Contingent Right the very important property possessed by it in many legal systems, of *transmissibility to representatives*. The object, indeed, or utility of investigating the difference between a Vested and a Contingent Right, as a matter of general Jurisprudence, lies mainly in the fact briefly touched on by Austin towards the end of his Lecture 53. A *Vested* interest becomes, in all reasonable systems of Law, at once part of a man's Property, generally alienable and, unless determined, i.e. terminated, by his death, transmissible to his representatives. This may or may not be the case with a *Contingent* interest, so that we cannot take non-transmissibility as an exact test of Contingency[92]; but when we distinctly recognise a Right as contingent, we are put on our enquiry as to what sort of Contingent interests are generally, or in the particular Law, alienable or transmissible and why?

It will be observed, in reading Salmond's article above referred to (n. 83), that he disregards the non-existence, or conversely assumes the existence, of a person in whom the interest in question is to reside (see p. 762), and only deals with the perfect or imperfect character of his title. In fact Austin's first condition of Contingency, to any one not specially familiar with English Law, would seem rather to suggest the natural enquiry, to begin with, for what persons, if any, *not in existence*, the Law of the particular State could possibly allow an indefeasible Right of future enjoyment to be created.

Settlement. Such an enquiry opens up the wider question how far a State will recognise or permit the remoter effects of the settling or *tieing* up of a man's Property for some definite or indefinite period after his decease. This is properly matter of State Policy, and falls rather within the province of the Science or Principles of Legislation (see

---

[92] Compare Austin[5], 53. 865 with St. p. 426.

§ 1, pp. 10, 11) than that of Jurisprudence; which, finding such interests as those mentioned on p. 762 in actual use, attends merely to the manner in which they are created or secured.

The Editor, however, of Austin, in his mainly re-written Lecture 53, while insisting literally on Austin's doctrine of Rights as the direct creation of the State, has thought it desirable to enter into a somewhat laboured account of the *purpose* or *object* of the State in *conceding* these particular Contingent Rights, among other *limited* Modes of Property, involving of course special Duties incumbent upon other persons, towards the owners of these Rights[93].   In this account, however, I find very little beyond a statement of the *immediate operation* of such limitations, in English Law: for a wider treatment of the subject we must look to more general or ultimate purposes apparent in the usage of other States besides England, which have attained or endeavoured to attain similar objects by different means. This subject will be briefly considered at the end of the present section (pp. 771, 772).

Contingency applicable also to jura in personam. Before, however, quitting the difficult and somewhat unsatisfactory Lecture 53, we have a few final remarks of Austin, of which we must briefly take note.

His reasoning, as to rights Vested and Contingent, applies, more directly, to *jura in rem* only. That it may be extended to *jura in personam*, where the performance of the obligation is dependent on a condition, is no doubt true, but the case comes more naturally under the proper heading of Obligations, as also does that where the right to performance is fixed (and may properly be called *vested*), but the time for performance has not yet arrived[94].

---

[93] See St. 406, 409—421.

[94] Austin[5], 53. 868. As to the last mentioned case (where *dies cedit* but *dies non venit*, see Moyle[4], 297 on Just. 2. 20. 20.

Rights subject to a resolutive condition. A right completely vested may be made to *determine* upon a subsequent Contingency, i.e. upon the happening of some specified event, before lapse of the time for which the right would otherwise endure. The term *resolutive condition*, used by Austin, is, to my mind, more expressive and intelligible than that of *condition subsequent* used by Salmond, as opposed to conditions *precedent*, on which the *vesting* of a contingent right depends[95]. That the same *determination* may equally apply to a contingent right *after becoming vested*, if it ever does so, is shewn by Austin (l.c.). He adds a caution, perhaps scarcely necessary, against a common popular *restriction* of the word *condition* (as applied to contingency) to the act or performance of the person who is by way of acquiring a right.

The determinable rights here spoken of have a good example in the *executory interest*, or rather in the prior interest to which the executory interest puts an end[96]. This, however, is matter of special English detail. The more particular and most important point of view in which the whole subject of interests contingent or executory comes into the subject of general Jurisprudence appears to me to be that indicated above (p. 764), viz. How long can an owner of property exercise control over it, and so prevent its free alienation, in the future?   And this question is connected, by a common private object or public inconvenience, with a slightly different practice—that of restrictions on alienation in the present. I shall treat the whole matter very briefly and rather with reference to the simpler methods employed in other Law than to the devices of feudal precedent in English.

---

[95] Austin[5], 53. 868: Salmond[2], p. 236.
[96] Joshua Williams R. P.[21], p. 376.

Ancient and Modern Settlements. In Roman Law there are many Contingent Rights connected with Succession, and not so exclusively dependent on Praetorian introduction as is suggested by the words of Austin[97], except in the case of *fidei commissa* or Trusts. The necessity for acceptance, or entrance on, an inheritance, in the case of all *heredes* except *necessarii*, and originally *sui*[98], renders their interest, as we have seen (above, p. 763), a contingent one. An expressly conditional institution might perhaps seem a better instance, particularly if the condition were *not* one the fulfilment of which was entirely under the intended *heres'* own control (see above, p. 766). The condition in this case is in effect only *suspensive,* and the conditional *heres* came to be treated almost as if his interest were a *vested* one, subject to a resolutive condition[99].

The *substitutiones,* on the other hand, which appear to have depended rather on the Interpretation of Civil or old Roman Law than upon Praetorian intervention, partake more distinctly of the character of our Contingent Remainder.

Substitutio vulgaris is the institution of a *specified* person (*Maevius*) as *heres* to a Testator in case the *heres* originally instituted fails to accept the inheritance within a certain time, or generally fails to become *heres.*

Substitutio pupillaris is the similar substitution of a specified person in case the original *heres,* being in power and under the age of puberty, dies before attaining that age, and is consequently unable to make a will.

Substitutio exemplaris is a substitution framed on the

---

[97] Austin[5], 53. 869 and notes.

[98] Gaius 2. 153, 157, 158. On the question whether some *legacies,* though left unconditionally, were before acceptance or *acknowledgement* on the part of the legatee, in the same condition as the inheritance before aditio, see Ga. 2. 195, 200 and Girard[5], 926. 2.

[99] Just. 2. 14. 9 and Moyle's note thereon.

pattern (*exemplum*) of the last, where the original *heres*, being insane, dies without ever recovering sanity[100].

It does not appear that in any of the Cases of Roman *Substitutio* was the vesting of the Contingent interest post-poned beyond the termination of a life in being at the testator's death; nor, indeed, in the second above-mentioned, beyond fourteen years from such death. In the first it must vest within a comparatively very short period[101]. In all these cases, moreover, it is obvious that the element of Contingency first mentioned by Austin—Blackstone's " dubious and uncertain person " (above, p. 762, n. 87)—finds no place.

Substitutio, in an extended application, was largely used in old French Law for the creation of what corresponded to our Entails, though gradually limited towards the close of the Monarchy[102]: but it was abolished by the Revolution and finally prohibited by the Civil Code, except so far as tieing up property for the benefit of grandchildren or, failing children, of nephews and nieces[103].

In the German Code, on the contrary, the Roman *sub-stitutio vulgaris* is retained and the others replaced by a *fidei commissary* substitution, which is in some respects more extended but appears to be narrowed within the space of 30 years from the Testator's death or other demise of a life then in being[104]. Under the scheme of that Code the whole subject comes, not under the general Law of Things or Property specially so called, but under the distinct heading of Inheritance.

In the old English Land Law we had a feudal system, developed originally, as I believe, out of the late Roman

[100] These limitations are only stated generally from Gaius 2. 174, 179 and Just. 2. 15. pr. and 16. pr. 1.

[101] Ga. 2. 174. See, too, 170. [102] Brissaud, § 513.

[103] Code Civil, §§ 896, 898, 1048.

[104] BGB. §§ 2096—2109 (Scherer, v. pp. 204—216).

Emphyteusis (see above, pp. 754, 755), by which the landed property concerned was confined to a special course of devolution and consequently restricted to a limited amount of alienation [105].

By practice, judicial decisions, and legislation the indefeasibility of future estates created by Settlements under this Law has been gradually avoided : so that, at the present day, the person for the time beneficially entitled to possession (broadly = receipt of rents and profits) has, as far as the property itself is concerned, power of disposition little short of that enjoyed by an absolute owner. Reinvestment of course remains as an obligation; but, so far as the original land is concerned, settlement does not now operate as any substantial restraint upon alienation [106].

There are, however, some devices of our Law which appear to keep alive and some which actually do keep alive an indefinitely postponed control over Land, and therefore require a few words of explanation.

Rent charges. A case closely resembling *Emphyteusis* is that of a perpetual rent charge payable out of Land granted in fee simple, mostly, in practice, for building purposes. The important point of difference, however, is that while *Emphyteusis* is still in Justinian's latest enactments regarded as *jus in re alienâ* and the tenant is accordingly liable to *ejectment* on continued failure to pay his *pensio* [107], no such power, of permanently recovering the

---

[105] I do not at present propose to go into the imposition of similar restrictions upon non-landed property by means of Trusts (see Joshua Williams' Personal Property [16], p. 359).

[106] See the Settled Estates Acts from 1882 to 1890 (Maclaurin's Title to Realty, p. 235). Subsequent legislation on the same subject generally refers only to application of the purchase money, except the Land Transfer Act of 1897 which does not, however, affect the above power (60 and 61 Vic. ch. 65, § 2 (1)).

[107] Cod. 4. 66. 2.

Land, is enjoyed by the owner of the English ground rent, who can in a similar case *re-enter* but can only hold or let the land so far as is necessary for satisfaction of arrears due[108].

Redemption of perpetual charges.   The act just referred to contains in its next section an important provision for the *compulsory* redemption, at the instance of the tenant, of perpetual charges on land.   A provision to the same effect in the German Code has been noted above (p. 756).   There can be little doubt that the application of this principle will be generally established in the future if it is not so already.   In our own case the compulsory enfranchisement of Copyholds was an important early step in this direction[109].

Long terms of years, technically so called, scarcely require notice, as they do not affect to be *in perpetuum*.   These are, according to their statutory definition, such as were originally created for a period of not less than 300 years, and have a rent *of no value* incident to the reversion.   They may now be " enlarged " into an estate of fee simple under the Conveyancing Acts[110].

Building leases, on the other hand, which are sometimes of 99 or even 999 years, do involve what may be a very long postponed control exercised by the landlord over the land.   Apart from the regularly inserted provisions for intermediate forfeiture (by re-entry and determination of the term) the land reverts, as of course, with all the erections on it, to the lessor at the end of the lease.

There may be no obstacle in the way of the alienation of their interest, for what it is worth, by the tenant or his assignees: but there is always impending a fixed date,

---

[108] Conveyancing Act (1881) § 44.

[109] See the Copyhold Acts of 1852 and 1858.

[110] 44 and 45 Vic. ch. 41, § 65: 45 and 46 Vic. ch. 39, § 11.

however long deferred, at which that interest will entirely
cease to exist. This no doubt may and should be calculated
on by the holders of such leases: but in general I imagine
that a feeling of real grievance and hardship is sure to arise
in their minds towards the end of the term. Whether it
might be wise to impose some statutory restriction upon
these leases for the future is a matter of Politics, not of
Jurisprudence. As to the injustice and impolicy of enabling
the *compulsory* purchase of the reversion by *existing* tenants
(except on a decidedly favourable valuation of the landlords'
interest) there can be no question.

Restraints on alienation generally. Remarks, originally
meant to be confined to a consideration of the different fragments of ownership or *jura in re alienâ*, have imperceptibly
drifted into the employment of such interests for the general
purpose of Settlement, and particularly for the English
variety. This, though originating in a much fettered Land
Law, can, as we have seen, be scarcely regarded, in the light
of our recent legislation, as constituting much practical
restraint upon free dealing with the original subject-matter.
But, as the *proceeds* of the sale or otherwise of settled Land,
and non-landed property generally, may be subjected, through
the medium of Trusts, to limitations in a great measure
resembling those originally framed for Land, the questions
asked above (pp. 764, 766) still exist for us in the wider
form, How long can property generally be kept out of the
course of free dealing and circulation: or, in other words,
how long can indefeasible future interests be created—why,
and for whom? I cannot speak with any degree of exact
knowledge as to the actual working result, or the motive, of
legislation on this subject in France and Germany. The
enactments themselves (above, p. 768) appear to allow
decidedly less extent of "tieing up" property than our Law,
to which I shall confine these last few words.

The subject of restraints on alienation, and the limits within which it is allowed by English Law, involves a combination of certain principles more especially peculiar to that Law with other and more generally applicable considerations. It is to the latter that my remarks will be addressed. They arise mainly in connexion with Wills. The question is—How long shall a Testator's wish, speaking vaguely, to "keep his property in his family" be allowed to withdraw that property from the general dealings of the Society in which he has lived?

The desire to provide for ascertained existing objects of the Testator's affection or esteem, during their lives, will be almost universally admitted by legislatures as proper and laudable : and the further *protection*, in certain cases, of such life interests, by some such means as hereinafter mentioned, will be naturally recognised as allowable. The extension of his power, so as to limit the ultimate devolution of his property to descendants in the next generation, appears to be the governing principle of the further directions generally permitted, with the natural corollary that the interest of the intended beneficiaries should be kept substantially intact during their *non-age* according to the particular law of their country[111]. The last restriction may obviously be still further extended by authority of the legislator, though not by the mere will of the Testator. I must leave the matter in these very general terms, for the subject of the Perpetuity, which our Law professes to discourage, and the consequent Rule against it, are far too wide and difficult to be broached here.

Certain *protected* life interests which, so far as they extend, operate in restraint of alienation, may be briefly

---

[111] The time allowed for "suspension of vesting" is briefly stated as a life or lives in being and 21 years and a possible period for gestation after, in Halsbury, xxii. pp. 300, 301. On the further restriction of accumulation, by the Accumulations Act of 1892, see ib. pp. 370—384.

mentioned. *Ususfructus* may, in its origin, have been intended as some such provision, in Roman Law, for a connexion or relative of doubtful business capacity, but it evidently soon became capable of practical anticipation[112]. It is just possible that *precarium*, or *locatio* "*quamdiu volam*," may have been adopted, with greater efficiency, for the same purpose[113]. Our "restraint on anticipation," employed in the case of a married woman during coverture[114], will occur at once to the English reader: also the more questionable measure of limiting property to any one "*until some act of bankruptcy, &c.*," on his part[115].

But I fear that I have already been betrayed, by Roman parallels or otherwise, into far too much detail on the modern subdivisions of Proprietary Right.

[112] Roby, De Usufructu, on Dig. 7. 1. 12. 2.
[113] See Dig. 19. 2. 4.   [114] Halsbury, xvi. pp. 359—376.
[115] ib. xxii. § 839, p. 412.

§ 25. TITLES

Use of the word by Austin and Bentham, &c. This
term is adopted, on the ground of convenience, as short for
the more correct, or at least the more expressive, heading
with which Austin introduces his last three completed Lectures, 54—56, and the fragmentary 57, viz. "Titles, modes
of Acquisition, or Investitive and Divestitive Facts." The
subject is there treated by him with special regard, in the
main, to the particular class of Rights which has been broadly
described, in the present work, as Rights of Ownership[1]. To
this special use of the term I shall return towards the latter
part of this section; at present I propose to consider the

---

[1] See above, § 16, p. 552. In Austin's language they belong to that de-
partment of the Law of Things which deals with Primary Rights *in rem* over
Things, as existing *per se*, i.e. not in combination with Rights *in personam*.
He therefore leaves out of his present consideration succession *ab intestato*
and *ex testamento*, as well as, of course, Rights *in personam* and *Status*.
Austin[5], 47. 783, 784; 54. 870, 871. I cannot give definite references to the
Student's Austin, in which these Lectures are much re-arranged.

subject as Bentham[2], and occasionally Austin himself does, in a more broad and general way.

We have seen how the plan of the second division of the Roman Institutes finally adopted was to class the Res or items of Property under their Modes of Acquisition and Alienation, the description of the Rights which constituted these Res being, with some variations of order between the two, taken together with such Modes.   Also, how the English Institutionalists improved in some respects upon the plan of the Romans, taking the Modes of Acquisition, &c. separate from the description of the Rights, and treating them in independent Chapters under the style adopted by Blackstone of Titles[3].

This style is open, as we shall see, to considerable objections, and must, at any rate for students of Roman Law, be clearly distinguished from the use of the word by the Roman Jurists. With them, it generally means either a style of *honour*, or a title in the modern sense of *heading*, particularly heading to a Chapter in the Edict or Digest, whence it has in practice been transferred to the contents of the chapter itself[4].   The use of *titulus* as " part of a complex mode of acquisition," though stated by Austin to occur occasionally in Roman Law[5], is, I believe, really due to post-Roman Civilians, who divided acquisition of ownership into a *titulus* conferring only *jus ad rem* and a *modus acquirendi* conferring *jus in re*[6].   Whether this division was actually applied to all acquisitions of

---

[2] As in extending his événements collatifs investitifs, etc. to the case of contrats and états, chs. 16 and 17 of the Vue Générale (Traités, iii. pp. 320, 329).

[3] See § 16, pp. 566—571.

[4] So that it becomes necessary to distinguish the actual heading as the Rubric.

[5] Austin[5], 55. 883, 884, 886: St. 435, 438.   I can find no clear authority in the Roman authors.

[6] Above, § 23, pp. 715, 716.   See, too, the passages quoted in Holland[10], p. 152, n. 1.

ownership or only to some[7] is not very material. The distinction is in much less favour with more modern authorities[8]: but it is not entirely devoid of interest and meaning, nor, as may be shewn hereafter (p. 789), of some practical application in framing an Educational scheme for a Corpus Juris.

The French word *Titre*, on which Austin appears to me to express himself rather too positively, has no very definite technical meaning[9].

Blackstone replaces **Hale's** intelligible talk of the *manner* in which Rights in Things may be acquired or transferred (above, § 16, p. 570) by the term Title used in a sense which appears to be a somewhat confused application of the Civilians' *titulus* and *modus acquirendi*. In Things Real it is clearly the Right to the Estates which may be had in such Things and we read of the manner of acquiring and losing *it* (the Title not the Estates). In Things Personal it is the Right to the Property " to which they are liable " and again we read how *it* (the Title) may be lost and acquired: while elsewhere it is directly the *means* of acquiring and losing such Property as may be had therein. Stephen's version of Blackstone adopts the last and most reasonable view, practically coinciding with the meaning attached to Title by Bentham[10].

[7] Omne enim dominium etc., Heineccius as quoted by Austin T. and N. ii. 4 c. p. 964 with the same authors Elementa §§ 339—380, where the *natural* acquisitions appear to be only *modi*.

[8] E.g. it is " *grundfalsch* " according to Mackeldey, § 244 e.

[9] " *Titre* in the French Law is always understood in the same sense," Austin[5], 55. 884: St. 436. I find, amongst other usages in the Code Civil, those of heading (§ 1370) legal ground (§ 1745) and document of title, in a very special sense (du titre authentique) as a proof of Obligation (§§ 1317—21). The German *Titel* is generally like the *titulus* of the Roman Jurists, the heading or contents of a Chapter.

[10] Blackstone, ii. 2, p. 16; 24, p. 388; and 26, p. 400. Stephen describes Title as the manner of acquiring and losing estates in Land or the various means of acquiring and losing property in Things Personal.

These are among the passages on which Austin bases his statement that Blackstone often uses Title to designate a fact which *ends* a Right as well as one which begins it.   He himself does not therefore consider that there will be much shock to established usage in applying the word to "every fact whatever through which the Law confers or extinguishes a Right or imposes or exonerates from a Duty[11]."   The name of Title, however, is too generally appropriated, both in legal and popular usage, to cases falling under the first only of Austin's four heads (confined, too, to the acquisition of Rights of Ownership) to be used, without explanation, for the other three.

It is certainly a convenient heading, if translated, as Bentham phrases the matter, out of the language of fiction into that of reality—which rather means, out of the language of ordinary life into that of Jurists.   If used as a general term, it should be definitely explained as equivalent to the double phrase originally employed by Bentham himself, of Investitive and Divestitive Facts[12].   These terms themselves are intelligible enough, as used by Hunter in his Roman Law, nor does there seem so much difficulty as he anticipated in speaking of a man's being *invested* with a Duty.   There is a convenience also in his third term Transvestitive, though it does not seem to be absolutely necessary[13].   We shall find, that, in order to secure the wider view and scope above referred to (p. 774), we may have, on occasion, to add to the three descriptions of Investitive, Divestitive and Transvestitive

[11] Austin[5], 55. 883: St. 435.

[12] Vue générale, ch. xv. (Traités iii. 313—316).   He himself uses the word *événement* which no doubt is wider than *fait*.   So too, however, is the English word *fact*, which certainly suits better for our purpose than *event*.

[13] See Hunter's Roman Law, Table of Contents and Introduction, p. xvi. The same phraseology is accepted by Holland[10], p. 151 (cf. 318 etc.) and Salmond[2], pp. 363, 364.   For further remarks on Terminology in this matter see Austin's Note at the end of Lecture 55, pp. 885, 886.

the more general one of Generative Facts (Generative, that is, of Rights or Duties).

We must now pass, however, from the nomenclature of the Facts included under the style *title*, to the more important subject of the place of Titles generally in the Educational Course of a Corpus Juris—the object, of course, being to avoid repetition so far as is consistent with clearness and continuity.

Application of Titles in the wide sense. In this very wide and general sense the style Titles may of course be pressed into the service with reference both to Rights *in personam*, to *Status*, and to Rights *in rem* other than those specified above. Austin, indeed, in his actual treatment of the subject, is evidently thinking only or mainly of Titles with reference to Rights of Ownership over Things " in the proper acceptation of the term ": their other applications he omits or postpones[14]. A slight notice however of such other application, which has been to some extent carried out by Austin's followers, may be admitted here as matter of Educational system.

In **Hunter's** re-arrangement of Roman Law the definitely independent consideration of Investitive and Divestitive Facts runs through the whole of the Civil Part (see § 23, p. 723) of the book. Besides the Proprietary Rights of the Roman Institutes (Gaius' Book 2 and the early part of Book 3), each *status* of Book 1 has, in Hunter, its Investitive or Divestitive Facts regularly assigned to it, requiring not infrequently to be collected from sources outside the Institutes or even the Digest. To these earlier Institutional departments I shall return presently.

To proceed with Hunter's plan. The same principle of arrangement is also carried out, though rather intermittently, by him in his Second Book, as to Rights *in personam*, involving,

---

[14] Austin[5], 54. 871, 872.

as it seems to me, a good deal of that *morcellement* which Austin somewhere deprecates, quite apart from the amount of *repetition* that necessarily follows from the nonconformity of the main Austinian division with the Institutional, of Personal and Property Law (see § 14, pp. 511—513).   With the latter subject, however, we are not now concerned, and need only consider, of Hunter's Rights *in personam*, the Obligations recognised by Gaius in his third Book, with regard to the separate treatment or generally the position of their "Titles."

Delict.   To take the simpler cases first.   That of Delict scarcely requires more than a moment's consideration.   The wrongful Act is so obviously the only Generative Fact that it must precede, directly and continuously, the Rights and Obligations to which it gives rise[15].

The same remark applies to the cases of Private Wrong arising from professional incapacity, negligence or carelessness, which Justinian groups together under the head of **Quasi-Delict**[16]: as also to the still plainer case of Public Wrong or **Crime**, where the more serious consequences have generally necessitated some approach to a legal definition.

The mental condition of the offender as affecting his liability enters, to some extent, into all the cases enumerated in the last two paragraphs, but most conspicuously in the more serious cases of Crime.   It is therefore in that department that we shall find the best place for consideration of anything abnormal bearing on the above subject (see § 1, p. 31), outside the general conditions of legal Capacity which are to be taken under Personal Law (§ 15, p. 532).   The particular Duties required from *professional men* have been referred to above (ib., pp. 538, 539) as coming within the same principal division: but a rather wider view of that class

---

[15] Holland[10], p. 316.

[16] Just. 4. 5: Gaius, Dig. 44. 7. 5. 4—6.   In Austin's Fragment, p. 912, he does not appear to me to state the Roman Law quite correctly.   See his further note 7 to Tab. I. (p. 927).

would seem to justify the insertion of an Article on *professional negligence*, in the special chapter or chapters there suggested, it being remembered that this sort of liability will in many cases belong more to Delict than Crime[17].

Into the **classification of Delicts** I do not propose to enter. It is a subject which has been inconveniently and illogically complicated, both in our own system and in others, by arrangement rather with regard to the *remedies*, which have been from time to time provided or applied, than to the lesion of the right or interest affected[18]. The former should of course be regularly referred to, but will find their own place best under the separate heading or Appendix of Procedure (see above, § 18, pp. 607, 608). The latter should undoubtedly be the basis of classification, which does not appear to be a matter of extreme difficulty.

Infringements of Personal Rights would naturally come first, including, of course, among the Absolute ones (§ 12, 478; 13, 504) Reputation, and among the Relative ones those generally of Private Relation connected with the Family or Household: infringement of Rights over or connected with Property will follow[19]. A general or residuary third head has been found necessary by English Writers on this subject, to cover other violations of Public or general Right arising from Deceit or Fraud, general Negligence (dis. *professional*), or positive Acts of Nuisance[20]. The Classification of Crimes would broadly follow similar lines, and the opening remark under the commencement of the paragraph Delict on p. 779,

---

[17] See a remark on the treatment of Negligence in the note, p. 154, to the Digest of English Civil Law Book, ii. Pt III. (continued).

[18] See the remarks of the Editor of the Digest of English Civil Law in his Preface to the Part above cited, p. xiv.

[19] See Stephen[4], iii. pp. 343, 405, 407: Kenny, Cases on Tort, Contents, pp. viii., ix.

[20] Kenny, ib. and p. 435: Stephen, ib. p. 451.

as to the position of the Generative Fact, holds good for all the cases of Delict, Quasi-Delict and Crime[21].

Quasi-Contract. Beyond the fact that they are all sources or causes of obligation, the only thing common to the cases where a man is said to be bound *quasi ex contractu* is that the obligation does *not* arise from Wrong nor from any Contract expressed or understood[22]. It is therefore possible, and necessary, to point out some individual event, in each case, from which the obligation arises, though it seems sometimes rather an abuse of words to speak of *investitive facts*.

Negotiorum gestio, the volunteer transaction of another person's business in his absence, is a case where this expression may be quite correctly used, as is also *solutio indebiti* the payment of money not due[23]. The obligation to restore this

[21] As to classification in detail, Bentham in the 19th chap. of his Vue Générale (Traités iii. p. 332), when proceeding to settle the *Titres* of his Code Civil, lays it down that *all* the body of the latter ought to be included (*enclavé*), at least by reference, in his Penal Code. The propriety of this last named division and style has been considered elsewhere (§ 22, p. 683). As to the present point, I do not see that his arrangement is based upon any very definite plan of Private Rights.

Chapter 2 of the French Engagements sans Convention (Code Civil, Liv. iii. Tit. 4), comprising Délits and quasi Délits, has but one section 1382 strictly belonging to the former, or directly causing *dommage à autrui*, which has been, however, most voluminously annotated. The rest of the chapter is on the class of responsibility corresponding generally to the Quasi-Delicts of Justinian treated in 4. 5. 1—3. The corresponding *Unerlaubte Handlungen* of the BGB., §§ 823—853 (Scherer, ii. pp. 1239—1379), are generally described, at the outset, as illegal injury to the life or limb, health, freedom or property of another. They include both Delict and Quasi-Delict (see §§ 836—838). To all these the remark on p. 779 applies.

[22] Austin, T. and N. ii. 6. Cᵃ,ᵇ, pp. 983, 984 citing Gaius, Dig. 44. 7. 1. pr. The more important passage in the same title 5. pr.—3 is the main source of Just. iii. 27.

[23] Ga. l.c. pr. and 3: Just. l.c. § 6. The exception in the following section (7) is better explained I consider by Girard[5], 619. 4 than by Moyle[4], 393, on Just. 3. 14. 1 or Poste[4], 267, on Ga. 2. 283, see Paul. Sentt. 1. 19. 2. On the other hand Buckland, Elementary Principles of Roman Private Law, 304.

money (enforced by *condictio*) has been somewhat question-
ably extended to *any* case of unjust or undue enrichment of
one party at the expense of another, where there is not always
any very definite Investitive Fact assignable for its imposition[24]. This ground of Obligation is vaguely referred to by
Austin but appears to be expressly included in the German
Civil Code[25]. In the cases of *communitas sine societate* and
cohereditas[26] an Investitive Fact can be definitely pointed
out. But the relations between Tutor and Pupil, or *Heres*
and *Legatarius*, are simply questions of Right or Duty
belonging to the particular *Status*, and falling properly under
Personal Law, or that part of Property Law where the whole
subject of *Hereditas* is, for convenience, taken together[27].

In **Contract** proper, general Capacity to contract is of
course assumed; the actual Agreement, with its particular
object or gist, and the Formalities required by the particular
system of Law, are all equally essential: but the whole affair
is one, and to single out any particular part as specially
Investitive Fact seems to me arbitrary and useless.

In *Status*, on the other hand, here understood as the
Private part of Personal Law (§ 10, pp. 443, 444), the Investitive Facts, if not always the Divestitive, are distinctly
assignable and treated as of principal importance. This has
been shewn in my review of the first Book of Gaius, where
I have endeavoured to explain some no doubt remarkable
exceptions[28]. The large proportion of space occupied by
marriage as the basis of the important Family Relations has
been pointed out[29], and may be compared with the long

---

[24] See Girard[5], 610 and 623 on Condictiones sine causa.

[25] Austin, l.c. p. 911: see the extremely general terms of BGB., § 812.

[26] Just. l.c. §§ 3, 4.

[27] ib. §§ 2, 5. Observe the odd connexion, in Hunter (p. 475), of Quasi-
Contract and *Status*. See also above, § 15, pp. 536, 539.

[28] See § 12, pp. 466, 468, 472.

[29] ib. 467.

account in Blackstone's Chapter 15[30], the space given to Marriage, Divorce &c. in the Code Civil[31] and the still larger amount of preliminary or introductory matter in the German *Familienrecht*[32].

But, as has been indicated above, p. 778, our main consideration of Titles will be in reference to that part of Property Law which deals with Rights of Ownership over Things: this being the part principally dealt with by Austin in his Lectures on Titles, although some of his remarks are scarcely intelligible without explanation by some such sketch, as the foregoing, of the more general application of the idea.

Rights and Duties arising ex lege immediaté.   It will, I think, appear, from a mere cursory view of Hunter's Roman Law, that the principle of assigning and marking off certain events as Investitive or Divestitive Facts, cannot with any special advantage be extended throughout the *whole* of a Corpus Juris.   But before leaving the question of this wider application, I must devote a few words to some of Austin's distinctions and refinements which seem to belong to it but have, in my opinion, very little bearing either on the intelligent study of Law or the satisfactory arrangement of an Educational legal system.

The subject heading the present paragraph is one of these.   The origination of Rights and Duties *ex lege immediaté, ipso jure,* or by *mere* operation of law[33], which is a

---

[30] How marriages may be made or dissolved, i. pp. 434—442.

[31] L. 1. Titt. 5, 6.

[32] Before we come to the Effects of Marriage there are 55 sections on its Preliminaries, Contraction, and its Nullity or Contested Validity, with special provision for the case of Second Marriage or alleged death of one of the parties to the First.

[33] The expression "act *of* the law" is once used by Salmond (p. 306) in opposition to "act of the party" but only, I think, in Austin's large and loose sense (see next page).   Acts *in* law, otherwise juristic acts, acts by parties, but having a legal significance or effect (*Rechtsgeschäfte*), are quite a different matter.

good deal laboured by Austin, is, as he shews, if the words are taken strictly, confined to the special case of Rights and Duties (mainly the former) conferred or imposed upon *specifically determined individuals*[34]. This is surely so exceptional a case as scarcely to require mention in the view of general Jurisprudence. I would merely therefore refer to what has been said above (§ 2, pp. 55, 56) on *privilegium*, with the caution that what Austin says on that subject must be taken with some reserve, as a statement of Roman Law.

The words, however, in question, if used at all, are generally used in a wide or "improper" sense to signify that though there are facts distinguishable from the law, to which it annexes the Right and Duty as consequence or effect, none of such facts is the act of the party concerned or the result of his option[35]. This is intelligible, but I do not believe that such expressions as *ex lege immediaté* will be used, by any careful writer, of cases where the Rights and Duties do obviously arise from intermediate facts, or series of facts, but the latter merely do not happen to have acquired concise names, such as *tradition, occupancy, prescription*, &c.[36] Into Austin's further refinements on this subject I do not mean to enter, but shall pass to more practical questions, which do bear obviously on the best arrangement *pro tanto* of certain branches of Law for purposes of Educational Study if not of cognoscibility by the laity (see § 1, p. 12 ; § 9, p. 416, &c.).

Is Right or Title the better basis of arrangement ? It is not so much with regard to the wider meaning and application of Title generally, but to the narrower scope

[34] Austin[5], 55. 876—878: St. 431, 432.

[35] Austin[5], 56. 894—896: St. 439, 440. The last words seem to cover the case of Austin's "third improper application of the above expressions," which I therefore omit.

[36] As Austin alleges on p. 896: St. 440. He compares the Roman use of the phrase Quasi-Contracts. A better parallel would be those Roman Obligations called by moderns Innominate Contracts, as opposed to those *quae nomen suum habent*, if *they* had ever been said to arise *ex lege immediaté*.

within which we ordinarily use the word (see above, p. 783), that Austin practically asks this question at the end of Lecture 54.   He prefers to take the kinds of Rights as the basis and the Titles as incidental or ancillary.   This is the way, he says, in which they are commonly treated, referring, I imagine, principally to the arrangements of Hale and Blackstone with regard to English Property Law (see § 16, p. 570).   He also, however, quotes in support of the same principle the "Roman lawyers" for the somewhat inadequate reason that they treat first of *dominium* and then of *jura in re alienâ*[37].

It will be remembered that, according to the view here taken of the Roman *Jus Rerum*, it would seem as if a classification begun by reference to the Rights and Duties themselves had to be replaced or, at any rate, supplemented by another based on Titles (see above, § 16, pp. 553, 566). The latter principle, in fact, it is, which accounts for the separation of Inheritance *en bloc* (together, it is true, with other acquisitions *per universitatem*) from other Rights of Ownership, which is so much emphasized in other modern systems than our own: though rather perhaps on grounds of general convenience than of deference to Roman precedent.

It must be admitted of course that, throughout the Roman Institutes, the interests themselves are frequently intermingled with their modes of acquisition in anything but a clear and definite order, particularly by Justinian (see § 16, 568, 569).   But it should not be forgotten, on the other hand, that the ancillary treatment of the Title, which Austin prefers, is distinctly reversed in Book 1, in which the prominent position of the Investitive Facts has been followed both by English Institutes and Foreign Codes (above, pp. 782, 783), and appears to be generally regarded as the natural order.

[37] Austin[5], 54. 873, 874.

Even if, however, we confine the question at the head of this paragraph, as I think Austin practically does, to Rights of Ownership, it is not solved, by those who adopt Austin's views, in so unanimous a manner as to render the decision easy. In Blackstone's Rights to Things Real and Rights to Things Personal, their respective Titles follow after each division of Rights, as a whole—subdivided of course into such heads as Forfeiture, Alienation (with further subdivision under Deed), and Devise, for Real; and a similar arrangement *mutatis mutandis* for Personal Property. This plan is followed, on the whole, in Stephen, subject to important omissions and additions resulting from the Settled Lands and Conveyancing Acts, which have been so often cited above, from the introduction of new Death Duties, &c. Some differences, too, in the treatment of Contract will be noted below (p. 789).

In the two modern Codes to the divisions of which I have mainly referred, the Titles are also treated as ancillary or secondary to the Rights, but in different ways. In the French Code Civil a comparatively short "Titre" (above, p. 776, n. 9), *De la propriété*, is followed by the huge one, *Des différentes Manières dont on acquiert la propriété*, which takes up the remainder of this Code, including *inter alia* Succession and Contract[38].

In the German BGB, on the other hand, the subject of Acquisition and Loss (*Erwerb* und *Verlust*) is similarly treated as ancillary, but is much more distributed over, and directly connected with, the several particular interests, reference also being freely made to other portions of the Code, such as Succession, &c.

The latter certainly seems the most convenient method

---

[38] Being at present simply concerned with the relative position of Right and Title, I need only refer to the confusion of Contract and Conveyance noted above (§ 23, pp. 717, 718).

of the three above described, and it appears to be the plan
mainly preferred in the treatment of our Law of Property
by the New English Digest, so far as the German system
can be followed into the divisions, at present fundamental,
of our English one[39].

A certain amount of Repetition, however, could be
avoided by the use, where possible, of a common Appendix
framed on the principle recommended above (§ 18, pp. 607,
608) in the case of Procedure, the application of which will
be considered shortly. Some remaining points of Austin
require a little previous notice.

Titles simple or **complex: Matter essential** or
accidental. A general division of Title as simple or complex, suggested by Bentham, is rightly treated as useless
by Austin, all Titles being, he says, practically complex, and
their greater or less complication a mere question of degree[40].
But the division of the Facts, which make up a complex
Title into principal and accessory, or essential and accidental,
also due to Bentham, is shewn to be more important. For
here comes in a consideration of what Austin terms the
function of a Title, i.e. the reasons for which Rights and
Duties are commonly conferred or imposed (according to the
Austinian theory), through Titles, and for which Facts of
some kinds are selected to serve as such in preference to
Facts of other kinds[41].

Of Austin's disquisition on the *functions* of Titles I
can find little beyond the stock reference to Utility: the

---

[39] In the subjects of Land, Chattels Corporeal and Choses in action, the
initial chapters on the interests, rights, and liabilities etc. in the first, possession and ownership in the second, and the nature generally of the third,
are *severally* followed by their respective modes of acquisition and alienation.
See Book iii. pp. ix., xii.

[40] Bentham, Vue Générale (Traités, iii. p. 308): Austin[5], 56, pp. 887, 888:
St. 436.

[41] Austin[5], 55. 880, 881.

main *result* of their consideration seems to be this:—that Facts, which are not naturally and intrinsically essential to the purposes (expressed or assumed) of the legislature in conferring the Right or imposing the Duty, may become essential to the Title if *indispensably* required by the particular national Law. He instances the case where the evidence of a writing is indispensable to the Title, and the writing is not admissible unless stamped *when* the alleged Title arose; as distinguished from that when the writing *may* be admitted although the stamp has been affixed, on payment of a penalty, afterwards[42].

Most of this reasoning appears to me very barren of result, where it is not distinctly circular. The essential elements of Title are a pure matter of fact settled by the Law of the particular country: those which may be waived or deferred will certainly require some statement special for the individual case; and it is only in patent ambiguities that the *purpose* of the legislature is to be safely taken into account. On the whole these distinctions of simple or complex, essential or accidental are either mere trifling or furnish no line that can be laid down as a general principle of Jurisprudence.

Titulus and **Modus acquirendi.** This old civilians' distinction, on the other hand, is capable of a practical application, in the arrangement of a Corpus Juris, to the place as a whole, of an important department of Property Law.

I do not propose to revert now to the erroneous double assumption that a *jus in rem* is always preceded by a *jus in personam* and a *jus in personam* always followed by a *jus in rem*[43]. The former of course fails in the case of the

---

[42] Austin, ib. and 889—892. For the *presumptiones juris et de jure* here referred to see his Lecture 26, p. 492.

[43] Above § 23, pp. 714, 715 and ll. cc. To which add T. and N. ii. 4. C^{b,c}., pp. 964—968.

Roman *occupatio*: the latter where the *jus in personam*
is a Right corresponding to the obligation *ad aliquid
faciendum*.

But in those cases where the preceding *jus in personam*
has for its object the acquisition of *dominium*, or Ownership,
over a Thing, the entire acquisition is clearly divisible into
a *titulus ad acquirendum* and a *modus acquirendi* corresponding very nearly to Contract and Conveyance, which
were kept fairly well apart in Roman Law[44] though confused
in some modern.

The confusion is notable in French Law, where it is
stigmatised in much detail by Austin[45]. Nor is our own
Law entirely free from reproach in this respect. Although
the truer view may be considered, by good authorities, to
be established as to the so-called Equitable Estate in Land[46],
and the old language of our Jurists as to Title by Contract
in the case of Goods is now much modified[47], the trans-
ference of Property in certain cases of Sale of Personalty
still continues, though under special conditions[48].

In the German Code, whatever may have been the faults
of its predecessor[49], there does not now appear to be this
confusion. The Code, if not statutorily recognising *titulus*
and *modus* in terms, is certainly regarded, by some of its
commentators, as practically treating them in the light of

[44] Digest 18. 1 and 19. 1, for instance, are on the whole confined to Contract of Sale and Remedies for breach of the Contract. Conveyance, as
remaining in Justinian's time, comes far apart under the general head of
acquiring Ownership, in 41. 1.

[45] See particularly Code Civil, § 1138: Austin[5], p. 970 (T. and N. ii. 4.
Cᶜ): and generally above, § 23, p. 716.

[46] See § 23, p. 717.

[47] Compare the words of Blackstone on Title by Contract (ii. 13, p. 440),
about vesting a property in action, with Stephen at the beginning of his chapter on the same subject, ii. p. 55.

[48] Compare Blackstone, ib. 448 with Stephen, ib. 106, 107.

[49] See above, n. 69 on p. 716.

two separate essentials[50], at least in cases of acquisition by alienation. The *titulus* is the Agreement (*Einigung*) of the parties: the *modus* is the Registration of landed, or the Delivery of non-landed property.

Conclusion. To return, however, to the consideration of Title, in the wide sense, generally. We have seen that while the separate treatment of Investitive and Divestitive Facts is shewn to be possible and desirable, by actual previous use, in *Status* or Personal Law (see above, p. 782), in the Property Law of Contractual Obligation it is useless, and, in Delict and Crime, so obvious as not to require any such distinctive phraseology (above, pp. 779, 780, 782).

The case of Rights and Duties arising *ex lege immediaté*, on which Austin spends so much time, seems to me too isolated and unusual to require more than mention. But, in the strictly *proprietary* part of Property Law, to which the whole of his remarks more particularly apply, the distinctions and the principles of arrangement discussed by him require more serious consideration.

A thoroughly satisfactory basis of arrangement, for this part of Property Law, has not, to my mind, been attained, though I prefer the principle of the German Code (above, p. 787). Such a basis might seem to be facilitated by the splitting up of Titles into their essential and accidental elements: but I doubt if any general principle can be laid down on this subject, and I rather deprecate arguments from the "purpose or object" of the legislature. In fact I feel inclined to fall back upon the old distinction of *titulus* and *modus* for the main practical suggestion which may be drawn from the whole consideration of the subject of this Section.

Place of Conveyancing in a Corpus Juris. In the following words I am looking merely at our English system and

[50] See Scherer, iii. pp. 2, 35 on § 873, and p. 337 on § 1206.

confining myself to the cases of our Property Law where we can fairly divide a Title into a *Titulus and Modus acquirendi.* Whether regarded as Principal and Accessory or not, I think both are generally, in practice, *essential* : but there is the difference that the *modus* which comes, as a matter of fact, last, may be common to many different preliminaries in the Title.   This is certainly the case with us, in whose Law many Titles, though not all, will culminate in some Document of a comparatively uniform and stereotyped character.   There appears to be here a strong argument similar to that urged in the case of Procedure (§ 18, pp. 607, 608) for final and separate treatment.   The reason alleged by the authors of the new Digest of English Civil Law for placing Conveyancing, together with Procedure, outside of their subject is the complicated and technical character which unsuits it for the general student of Law, and still more so in his more elementary course. I think this certainly holds good for Conveyancing as a whole, and somewhat isolated, subject.   But I believe that an Appendix of simple Precedents of such Documents as above referred to would be of service, even to the learner, in calling his attention to the essential points of Titles, as they will be generally indicated in the Documents in question.

À propos of Conveyancing, I may add, to the meanings of Title given above, the technical signification of a historical record of Investitive Facts which is, in English legal practice, as also no doubt elsewhere, furnished by the Vendor to the intending Purchaser of the Estate or Interest to which they refer.

Overleaf is a suggested course of Reading for Law Honours at Cambridge, slightly modified from that at present in existence, to be followed by alternatives of Post-Graduate Study at some Centre of Legal Practice, or at the University.

SUGGESTED COURSE FOR LAW HONOURS
AT CAMBRIDGE.

Explanatory references to pages of preceding work.	
	1st Part.
	Roman Law.
14, 15, 34–8	Elementary and general Jurisprudence.
	International Law, General Principles of Public.
447, 523	English Constitutional Law in wide sense.

2nd Part.

	English Law of Rights. 1. Personal Law.
528, 721	Absolute Rights and Duties.
	Relative Rights and Duties.
537, 538	Trades, Professions, Corporations, Trustees.
622, 623	With the last, general principles of Equity.
	English Law of Rights. 2. Property Law.
	Preliminary. Land, Goods, Sea, Rivers, Air.
552, 587, 588	Rights and Duties of Ownership.
571	Inheritance Testate and Intestate.
	Rights and Duties of Obligation. Contract and Quasi-contract.
791	Appendix of Common *Modi acquisitionis.*
	English Law of Wrongs. 1. Private.
606–9	Breach of Contract &c., and Delict, with brief references to proper Civil Procedure.
779, 780	2. Public, with special consideration of mental responsibility for Crime, and references to proper Criminal Procedure.
609, 692	Appendix of Civil Procedure, Criminal Procedure and Evidence.

LONDON OR OTHER LEGAL CENTRE, FOR FURTHER STUDY
OF ABOVE APPENDICES, AND PRACTICE GENERALLY,
IN LAW CLASSES, CHAMBERS, OR COURT.

Alternative Post-Graduate Studies at University.

Special Roman, with direct survival in modern systems.

Advanced and Comparative Jurisprudence as preparatory for Politics and Legislation.

Advanced International, including Conflict of Laws.

INDEX

Absolute may be said of Rights and Duties, in the sense of Normal 528, 529, 719, 726, 733

Absolute Duties, of Austin 529-531, 626, 642-648; of Blackstone 613, 630; alleged implicit treatment of, by Roman Lawyers 603; proper place of, in a Corpus Juris 529-532; proximate and ultimate end of 643, 644

Absolute Rights, as Normal see above; of Personal Security, Liberty and Private Property 478, 504; in what sense *bona* 479

Abuti re suâ 745

Acquisition *per universitatem* 547, 733

Actio, various meanings of 600-602

Action *in personam* 636, 696, 697; *certam sive determinatam* 697-699

Action *in rem*, Austin's explanation 636; natural meaning of 700, 701; Austin's objections discussed 701-706; its true object and effect 710, 711; English *actio in rem* early and modern 725-727; *actio in rem*, as a rule, not penal 675-677

Actiones coordinated with Personae and Res 599

ἄγραφοι νόμοι 313, 314

Administration, vague meaning of word 170, 171; of justice essential to the idea of a State 168, 169

Aelius Sex. his *Tripertita* 362, 363

Aequitas in general Roman sense 106, 107; according to Austin and Maine 107, 108; derivational meaning of and early moral idea 109, 110; in Cicero and the Jurists 110-112; *aequitas legislatoria* and *judicialis* 113

Agere, see *actio*

Agnatio, how brought into *Jus Personarum* 468, 469

Air and aërial transit 566, 579, 746 n. 35

Alienation and acquisition, modes of 566-569, 775; restraints on alienation generally 771, 772; during life of particular beneficiary 567, 772, 773

America (United States), President of 183, 187; Supreme Court of 197, 251

Analysis of Pervading Notions by Austin, why divided here 29-31

Anglo-Norman administration 385-387

Anglo-Saxon Law and its names 384, 385

Aristocracy in Austin's *generic* sense 201; truer conception of an A. 202

Arrêts de règlement 401

Athenian Ecclesia 227

Attainder 591

Austin, his general scheme 16-35; his digression in Lectures 2, 3, 4 explained 66; his Law properly and improperly so called 59-64; positive and strictly so called 65, 67; of Persons and Things based on a suggestion of Bentham 511, 512; equivalent to Special and General 512, 513; considered as an independent arrangement 513, 519

Australian Commonwealth, Senate and Electorate 221; Referendum in 269, 270